MONSTROUS IMAGINARIES

MONSTROUS IMAGINARIES

The Legacy of Romanticism in Comics

MAAHEEN AHMED

University Press of Mississippi / Jackson

The University Press of Mississippi is the scholarly publishing agency of the Mississippi Institutions of Higher Learning: Alcorn State University, Delta State University, Jackson State University, Mississippi State University, Mississippi University for Women, Mississippi Valley State University, University of Mississippi, and University of Southern Mississippi.

www.upress.state.ms.us

The University Press of Mississippi is a member of the Association of University Presses.

Copyright © 2020 by University Press of Mississippi
All rights reserved

First printing 2020
∞

Library of Congress Cataloging-in-Publication Data available

LCCN 2019021693
ISBN 9781496825261 (hardcover)
ISBN 9781496825278 (paperback)
ISBN 9781496825285 (epub single)
ISBN 9781496825292 (epub institutional)
ISBN 9781496825308 (pdf single)
ISBN 9781496825315 (pdf institutional)

British Library Cataloging-in-Publication Data available

CONTENTS

ACKNOWLEDGMENTS VII

INTRODUCTION
Charting Monstrous Territory   3

CHAPTER ONE
Romantic Monsters: A Brief History   21

CHAPTER TWO
Swamp Thing: Patchworks and Panoramas in Monster Comics   54

CHAPTER THREE
Monstre: Monstrous Fluidity   85

CHAPTER FOUR
Hellboy: Nostalgia and the Doomed Quest   112

CHAPTER FIVE
The Crow: Spectacularity and Emotionality   141

CONCLUSION
Comics Monsters: *Per Monstra ad Astra*   166

NOTES   183

BIBLIOGRAPHY   216

INDEX   228

ACKNOWLEDGMENTS

Most of this book was written during a two-year postdoctoral fellowship cofunded by Marie Skłodowska-Curie Actions and the Académie Louvain. It was polished during a four-year postdoctoral fellowship funded by the Research Foundation Flanders. I am grateful to these foundations as well as the hosting institutions and their personnel, the University of Louvain and Ghent University, for all their financial, administrative, and infrastructural support.

I am especially grateful to the many kind colleagues and friends I have made at both universities for their intellectual stimulation and camaraderie. A very special thanks goes to all the wonderful people at the University of Louvain's Groupe de Recherche sur l'Image et le Texte and Ghent University's English section. I would also like to thank comics studies scholars for being so enthusiastic, fun, inspiring, and encouraging. The comics research groups ACME (University of Liège) and La Brèche deserve special mention. Most of all, I would like to thank Julia Round for cheerfully agreeing to review yet another manuscript of mine (twice!) and for offering kind encouragement and thorough, extremely useful, practical advice. I was lucky to have Brian Cremins as my second peer reviewer, who also had the patience to carefully go over the manuscript twice. I remain indebted to his corrections and creative suggestions. All persisting faults are my own.

I would also like to thank Norman Ware for his meticulous copy-editing and Shannon Li for her detailed index. A very special thank you is due to Cedric Van Dijck for his cheerful, enthusiastic proofreading. A heartfelt thank you is due to the helpful, patient, professional, and friendly staff at the University Press of Mississippi, especially Vijay Shah, Lisa McMurtray, Valerie Jones, the production team, and the marketing department.

I am very grateful to DC Comics's Mandy Barr, Casterman's Christel Masson, Katii O'Brien, and Dennis Kitchen for walking me through the permissions process. I am also grateful to the publishers and artists—Enki Bilal,

Mike Mignola, and James O'Barr—for granting me permissions to reproduce the images included here.

The cover image has been used with kind permission from Brecht Evens. Titled *Warhammer*, this image aptly visualizes the wonder and marvelous ambiguity evoked by the monstrous. It captures the main concerns of animation, spectacularity, and monstrosity that run through the book.

MONSTROUS IMAGINARIES

INTRODUCTION

CHARTING MONSTROUS TERRITORY

All romance, literary and human, is founded upon enchantment.
—HAROLD BLOOM[1]

The Uses of Monsters

Monsters are inevitably linked to humans and not always as mere opposites.[2] This mutating, binary-confounding relationship between humans and monsters becomes even more complex due to the diversity of possible monsters. In a treatise from 1573, Ambroise Paré came up with more than thirty categories for monsters, coupled with what he and contemporaries like Pierre Boaistuau called "wonders."[3] Such a juxtaposition of monsters and wonders is crucial to the good comics monsters that this book focuses on: this troubling ambiguity serves as the tightrope connecting monsters to humanity. As deviations—as too much or too little of something, as evident in Paré's dexterous if nowadays seemingly random categorization—monsters signal the shunning of norms and give form to the impossible. Both monsters and wonders fascinate and even awe their beholders. In accordance with their Latin root, *monstrare*, they point toward something:[4] the Other, abnormal fantasies, or ordinary desires,[5] since desire itself is the ultimate other that one strives in vain to absorb in oneself.[6] Yet, *monstrare* also implies teaching and is thus related to the monster's other etymological root, *monere*, which means to warn.[7] Here, good comics monsters teach us about the romantic inclinations forming and driving their characterization and the medium of comics itself.

This book draws out the persistence of romantic tropes, similarities with monsters from (dark) romantic literature, and romantic art in heroic comics monsters to highlight the remnants of romanticism in popular culture. This introductory chapter provides an overview of the ways of interpreting

3

monstrosity that are relevant for this study on good comics monsters. These interpretations center on the othered, abnormal body; animation; and emotionality, which in turn lead to themes of ambiguity, rebelliousness, and immersive entertainment (including immersive visualizations and relatable, human attributes). Romantic monsters and their related themes are then introduced in the last section. The second chapter elaborates on the history of romantic monsters and their connections to comics monsters as well as the medium of comics. In addition to the specific characters and works of art discussed in the first chapter, the close readings in chapters 2 through 5 show how three monsters with strong romantic inclinations—Frankenstein's monster, Baudelairian ennui, and the trickster (included for his playful ambiguity and love of spectacle)—share attributes with comics monsters while personifying the different potentialities of the medium.

To my knowledge, the relationship between comics, especially comics monsters, and romanticism[8] has rarely been explored in detail. While monsters have received some, mostly recent, attention in comics studies,[9] the four comics brought together in this book have attracted limited scholarly attention. The romantic imaginary has likewise not been mapped in comics. Although *Swamp Thing* and *Hellboy* have already attracted some scholarly attention, most notably in Julia Round's *Gothic in Comics and Graphic Novels* and Scott Bukatman's *Hellboy's World*, this attention is much more limited in the case of *Monstre* and *The Crow*.[10] Hailing from the two dominant Western comics milieus, France and America, each comic exemplifies how distinctive characteristics making up the romantic imaginary have been incorporated and modified by ambiguous monsters.

Theorizing Monsters: Pinning Down Monstrous Imaginaries

The body of scholarship on monsters is immensely rich and interdisciplinary. Having grown rapidly in recent years, this scholarship ranges from analyzing the cultural representations of monsters to their philosophical statements and sociohistorical significance.[11] Gender, queer, and race studies have also turned to monsters as figurations of social identity constructions and mechanisms of othering.[12] This vast scope implies that the cultural work done by monsters, while rich, remains unwieldy and difficult to sum up. As Asa Mittman puts it, "[m]onsters do a great deal of cultural work but they do not do it *nicely*."[13] Jack Halberstam makes a similar observation regarding monstrosity, locating the "interpretive mayhem" that gothic novels create to produce fear "in the body of the monster."[14]

Jeffrey Jerome Cohen offers seven theses on monsters as "a method of reading cultures from the monsters they engender."[15] As Cohen and later Edward J. Ingebretsen show, monsters have an unprecedentedly strong presence in contemporary life, with fictional and real monsters (usually humans engaging in monstrous acts such as serial killing and cannibalism) being prominent in the media, permeating public discourse as well as culture.[16] Ingebretsen also quotes Paul Oppenheimer's observation regarding the decline of religion, "but not of its images and metaphors, which continue to serve as a shorthand for contemporary emotional states."[17] Annie Le Brun makes a similar claim regarding the recession of faith and sees it as leading to vaguer,[18] more uncertain identity constructions for humans. This is where the relevance of ambiguous monsters comes in, as illustrated by Cohen's seven theses on monsters:

The monster is a cultural body;
the monster always escapes;
the monster is the harbinger of category crisis;
the monster dwells at the gates of difference [by embodying racial and gender prejudices but also blurring some of the distinctions separating individual and national bodies];
the monster polices the borders of the possible;
fear of the monster is really a kind of desire;
the monster stands at the threshold of . . . becoming by [questioning perceptions and misrepresentations].[19]

Cohen's theses resonate with those of Allen S. Weiss, who writes: "Monsters symbolize alterity and difference in extremis. They manifest the plasticity of the imagination and the catastrophes of the flesh. [...] Monsters exist in the margins. They are thus avatars of chance, impurity, heterodoxy; abomination, mutation, metamorphosis; prodigy, mystery, marvel. Monsters are indicators of epistemic shifts."[20] Weiss' words reappear in Scott Bukatman's introduction to his book on *Hellboy*.[21] This underscores the centrality of elements such as ambiguity and emotionality but also imagination and marginality for comics monsters.

Referring to René Girard, Cohen states that "[m]onsters are never created *ex nihilo*, but through a process of fragmentation and recombination," incorporating features from different sources including—and here Cohen cites Edward Said—those stemming from the fringes of society.[22] Girard's and Said's seminal works—*Deceit, Desire, and the Novel* and *Orientalism*—provide two different but equally important aspects of otherness that also play a role in monstrous constructions. While Girard's mimetic desire unfolds on an individual level with the other being the object of mimesis or emulation, Said positions the relationship in a more conflictual sociopolitical context with the other being fashioned according to the postcolonial agenda of polarizing and thereby taming, controlling, and profiting from the other.

The sociopolitical implications of monsters are thus not to be doubted. But what if monsters were also able to reflect their media contexts and the imaginaries giving them tangible form? This is precisely what this book tries to answer by exploring the connections between comics monsters and romanticism, including late or dark romanticism. Examining the monstrous figures popular in the dark romantic period, Hartmut Böhne writes: "[O]n a affaire ici à une forme culturelle extrême de la rencontre avec soi. L'homme demeure à ses propres yeux un étranger. Le monstre: *ecce homo*" (We are dealing with an extreme cultural form of facing the self here. Man remains a stranger in his own eyes. The monster: *ecce homo*).[23] This is comparable to Cohen's declaration that "[m]onsters [...] still serve as the ultimate incorporation of our anxieties—about history, about identity, about our very humanity. As they always will."[24] The monster not only defines but also questions notions of the human and humanity. It consequently offers insight into practices and effects of othering.

Susan Stryker has movingly shown how the monster works at and against the interface of othering, of defying bodily and sexual norms.[25] Her essay "My Words to Victor Frankenstein above the Village of Chamounix" also exemplifies how Frankenstein's monster can fulfill an identification function for marginalized people and communities. In the same volume as Stryker, *The Transgender Studies Reader*, Nikki Sullivan builds on the wonder attached to the figure of the monster and introduces the trope of transmogrification in order to collapse the binary of normal and strange or other in favor of a more relational understanding between such dichotomies.[26] The concept of transmogrification suggests that all "bodies are entwined in (un)becoming" rather than just being.[27] Sullivan adds that "bodies of knowledge" and "bodies of flesh" as well as the relationships between them also transmogrify. Frankenstein's monster, with his imperfectly sewn-up body, is the ideal reminder of the centrality of the body in discussions of monstrosity; the body is where the monster's troubled and often violent relationship with the world unfolds. From the monsters introduced in this book, Baudelairian ennui, fluid and eternally troubled, seems to personify transmogrification itself.

Like, to a certain extent, Jack Halberstam in *Skin Shows*, where he draws out the connections between nineteenth-century gothic monstrosity and its postmodern variations in horror films; and like Julia Round in *Gothic in Comics and Graphic Novels*, where she argues for the strong connections between the gothic and comics on the levels of both form and content, I seek to trace the continuities of a much older movement or consciousness by examining the stories and inclinations of heroic comics monsters. Although romanticism may seem a less obvious contender than the gothic for tracing such continuities,[28] it can shed new light on our understanding of monsters, which are often too easily conflated with the gothic. It also encourages a rethinking of the cultural hierarchies associated with monsters as well as comics. This is already apparent in Catherine Spooner's introduction to *Contemporary Gothic*, in which she points out that artists such as Goya or Munch or Cézanne would rarely be described as gothic on their own, especially "by any self-respecting art historian."[29] Indeed, respect and gothic rarely go together, much in contrast to romantic writing and arts, which have a comfortable place in the canons of the high arts. Yet the gothic and romantic are closely intertwined; and although it might not be particularly fruitful—or even possible—to clearly distinguish between the two, especially when monsters are involved, it is worthwhile, in light of the contemporary interest in the gothic, to consider whether, and which, vestiges of romanticism are discernible through and alongside the gothic.

Fred Botting sees the convergence of romance and gothic in popular culture as a distinctly postmodern phenomenon. Since the boundaries between gothic and romantic are hazy (fascination with spectacle, excess of emotion, rebellion against the values of the Enlightenment, reaction against modernity), this book considers its monsters as incarnating the node at which the gothic and the romantic meet, as exemplified by Frankenstein's prototypical monster, who unrelentingly haunts the comics analyzed here.[30] His human characteristics call for alternative interpretations of comics and monstrosity, particularly through their predilection for romantic themes.

Conduits of Monstrous Lives: Imaginary, Remediation, Presence

Having always been a part of the human imagination,[31] the monster's increasing prominence and anthropomorphization echoes the technological progress that made it possible to manipulate not only images but bodies themselves (as concretized by Donna Haraway's notion of the cyborg and its eventual replacement by the posthuman, which indicates a structural transformation of the human).[32] The possibility of adding extensions to the body reduced the differences between mechanized and human limbs. Already, Heinrich von Kleist's famous essay on puppet theater, "Über das Marionettentheater" (1810), ascribes anthropomorphic qualities, particularly grace, to inanimate puppets, going so far as to declare them more graceful than humans. Animation was also a romantic obsession, reflecting both contemporary uncertainties and scientific advancements. Writing about the early nineteenth century, science and technology historian John Tresch draws connections between the interest in fantastic literature (a term coined by Jean-Jacques Ampère in the 1820s), advances in illusion-generating machines providing an unprecedented range of sensory experiences, and the conversion of science itself into a "production of effects":[33] "[T]he imagery that recurred throughout the fantastic arts—reanimated objects, living machines, and dynamic, protean fluids—captured this period's ambivalent admiration for world changing machines, as well as its metaphysical and political uncertainties. The fantastic in both form and content, dramatized the power of technology to remake nature or destroy it, to liberate humanity or enslave it."[34] Affirming their links with cyborgs and posthumans, anthropomorphic monsters share certain similarities with humans relying on prostheses (which can be both mechanical and biological); monsters, however, assimilate the consumption of not only technologies but also desires, myths, and imaginaries.

Animation is a recurrent theme in the comics examined here. Playing on the ambiguity between life and death, it reflects both the fear of other and the creation and dissimulation of life. It is also a place where the battle between control and freedom plays out, an inconclusive battle that all comics monsters in this book have to face. Frankenstein's monster, ennui, and the trickster incorporate these anxieties in different ways: Frankenstein's monster through his patchworked, unacceptable appearance; ennui through its disconsolate fluidity; and the trickster through his spectacles and ambiguous playfulness. All three incarnate the hyperbole of the culture of the senses, especially visuality,[35] cultivated by romanticism.

Although monsters change with time, they always remain bodies where the imagination and its visual repertoire, the imaginary, find embodiment, usually molded by sociocultural and media-specific elements. In spite of their corporeal essence, these bodies have varying degrees of plasticity due to a paradox ensconced in monsters: "[T]he monster's body is both corporal and incorporeal; its threat is its propensity to shift."[36] Monstrous phenomena encompass "not only the objects (desires, behaviors, and, above all, their agents) . . . but also the affective structure of ordinary humans in response to these objects."[37] This is where the emotionality of monsters comes in.

For philosopher Brian Massumi, affect is difficult to pin down, in contrast to emotions, which distill affect into more comprehensible and interpretable forms.[38] The pioneer of affect theory, Silvan Tomkins, introduced affect as a complex "primary motivator" that precedes emotions, having physical manifestations while being likewise affected by physical sensations and being "more urgent than drive depravation and pleasure and even more urgent than physical pain."[39] Affect and the privileging of excessive emotions, combined with other phenomena manifested through the comics monsters discussed here, such as anthropomorphism, solitude, and rebelliousness against a rationalized, normative mindset, all played a formative role in romantic ideology.[40] Ambiguity, a staple of art, takes center stage in many key works of romanticism through its destabilization of established polarities, above all the binary of good and bad. Such tempering of polarities is exemplified by the protoromantic Satan in John Milton's *Paradise Lost* (1667) and continues through Mary Shelley's late-romantic Frankenstein's monster. Inspired by Milton's Satan, Shelley's monster also identified with Adam.

Correspondingly, the monsters used here have been chosen because of their refusal to adhere to the traditional paradigm whereby they become synonymous with evil. Instead, they flesh out the strains of humanity already evident in the creature Frankenstein stitched together, to become almost as—and sometimes even more—human than those surrounding them. Julia Round, citing literary scholar Peter Otto, points out that Frankenstein's monster incarnates gothic intertextuality, which is also a modus operandi for comics through their combination of diverse elements.[41] Emma McEvoy similarly suggests considering *Frankenstein* "as a text in dialogic debate with other variants of Romantic outsiders, as well as with overtly Gothic texts."[42] While "romantic outsiders" are in many ways the focus of this book, since monsters are per se pariahs, they often interact with and reconfigure gothic tropes, already in *Swamp Thing* (chapter 2) but also in *The Crow* (chapter 5). Both *The Crow* and *Monstre* (chapter 3) activate central themes such as spectacularity and the mutability and ambiguity of the trickster figure. The spectacle is also a key trope in *Hellboy* (chapter 4). Baudelairian ennui contributes toward a better understanding of monstrosity in *Monstre*. It captures the fluidity and the existential instability of monsters, which persist to a less blatant extent in all comics monsters encountered here.

The comics monsters discussed here are understood as constructions reflecting on the nature and even tastes of the media and their times.[43] Part of the contemporary imaginary—the shared set of images and the nexus of personal and collective imagination—these monsters carry remnants of the romantic imaginary. This tendency toward continuities, toward reviving an older cultural movement, is in itself monstrous; comics monsters are self-reflexive to the extent that they incarnate the medium's nature. The rebelliousness and hybrid ambiguity of the comics monsters examined here thus articulate the desires of the comics medium itself, desires that in themselves share similarities with the gothic, as shown by Round, but also with romanticism, as I show here by focusing on the romantic tropes mentioned above, which converge in the shared traits of ambiguity and rebelliousness.[44] Since comics monsters today are inheritors of a past in which horror comics were decried as having detrimental effects on their readers—a past that resonates most strongly in the revival of horror in Alan Moore's run of *Swamp Thing*, in which such prejudices are also dethroned—their rebelliousness resonates beyond their storyworlds to question the labels that have been placed on comics and relegate them to a marginal status.

Each comic combines several aspects of romantic, monstrous imaginaries that travel across media, particularly literature and the visual arts. They thus point toward broader inclinations in contemporary popular culture to remediate the romantic imaginary. Three theoretical concepts underpin the study of monsters in the chapters that follow: the imaginary, remediation, and presence. I will now briefly elaborate on each one of them.

Imaginary

The word "imaginary" is perhaps best known through sociologist Cornelius Castoriadis's use of the term to describe a network of ideas, rationales, and conventions that influence individual behavior while underpinning social structures. The imaginary, although rooted in the image and thus being a shared repertoire of images as suggested by Gilbert Durand, has deeper implications,[45] as Castoriadis explains: the imaginary "is the unceasing and essentially *undetermined* (social-historical and psychical) creation of figures/forms/images, on the basis of which alone there can ever be a question *of* 'something.' What we call 'reality' and 'rationality' are its works."[46] In the contemporary age of overflowing images, transitional bodies, and spaces, the imaginary has become part of a social practice, to take up Arjun Appadurai's oft-quoted paragraph:

> The image, the imagined, the imaginary—these are all terms that direct us to something critical and new in global cultural processes: the imagination as a social practice. No longer mere fantasy (opium for the masses whose real work is elsewhere), no longer simple escape (from a world defined principally by more concrete purposes and structures),

no longer elite pastime (thus not relevant to the lives of ordinary people), and no longer mere contemplation (irrelevant for new forms of desire and subjectivity), the imagination has become an organized field of social practices, a form of work (in the sense of both labor and culturally organized practice), and a form of negotiation between sites of agency (individuals) and globally defined fields of possibility. This unleashing of the imagination links the play of pastiche (in some settings) to the terror and coercion of states and their competitors. The imagination is now central to all forms of agency, is itself a social fact, and is the key component of the new global order.[47]

Wolfgang Iser has famously emphasized the anthropological significance of the interplay involved between the fictive and the imaginary through texts, which interact in a more or less random, playful manner, with personal and collective imaginaries.[48] In the case of comics, this playfulness can be tongue in cheek and double edged, like the playfulness of the trickster, piecemeal and fragmented, like the body of Frankenstein's monster, or elusive and eternally troubled, like Baudelairian ennui.

These monsters reflect on the medium of comics, which is monstrous through its penchant for visual garishness as well as through the intensity of the hybrid, symbiotic—but also tussling—word-image relationships often involved in comics.[49] Monsters in comics are of particular interest because, by virtue of being a popular medium, comics reflect the inclinations of the times.[50] Anthropomorphic comics monsters are used here to point toward the infiltration of the romantic imaginary in contemporary comics. They also help trace the remediation of ambiguous monsters from literature and the visual arts to comics.

Remediation

For Jay Bolter and Richard Grusin, remediation is "the representation of one medium in another."[51] Karin Kukkonen explains it as "the historical interaction of older and newer media in a culture's representational practices."[52] These media scholars, like Hans Belting, also emphasize the effect of media on the way self and the world are perceived.[53] However, in contrast to Belting, who traces the evolution of images of the body through death masks and emblems, Bolter and Grusin focus on new media such as television and the internet. It is worthwhile recalling that before Bolter and Grusin's book was published, the term "remediation" was primarily used to describe an environmental sanitation process.[54] Transposed to the terrain of media, the term preserves the sense of recuperation, which persists through nostalgia for the older media influencing them. This nostalgia coexists with competitiveness, a power play, among media.

Bolter and Grusin propose two strategies of remediation: hypermediacy, similar to self-reflexivity, whereby the role of the media is evident, and immediacy, whereby the role of the media is hidden. In a later essay, Grusin points out how this "double logic of remediation," the attempt to simultaneously conceal and reveal media, exemplified by the traditional tactics of television and the internet, respectively, becomes evident with the coverage of 9/11, particularly "by simultaneously multiplying mediation in the now-familiar collage-like look pioneered by CNN [...] and erasing the evidence of mediation in presenting the immediacy of the extreme close-up of the Twin Towers in flame."[55] For Grusin, the shock of 9/11 generated a shift from the notion of remediation to premediation, according to which "the future has always been *pre-mediated*" by the incorporation of futuristic technologies that eventually become realities.[56] This will be taken up during the analysis of comics with more futuristic settings, such as Enki Bilal's works.

Bolter and Grusin use the science fiction film *Strange Days* (1995) to exemplify the logics of both premediation and remediation. One of the central devices in the film is a gadget that records the experiences and memories of its wearer, saving it on a disk and thus allowing others to relive that experience. This recording and sharing of personal experiences premediates one of the main goals of current technologies (starting with film and moving on to virtual reality, for instance). Remediation unfolds in the process of capturing the immediacy of experience and camouflaging the role of the media involved in doing so.

The relevance of remediation for this book lies in its concern with "the formal relations within and beyond media as well as [...] relations of cultural power and prestige."[57] Analyzing remediation entails considering the differing degrees of the presence of media within each medium and their effect on the information being communicated. The romantic themes and inclinations discussed in this book are remediated through both the indigenous tendencies of the hybrid medium of comics and the monsters inhabiting it. Moreover, the comics monsters also function self-reflexively—and therefore remediate comics, often with funny mirror-like exaggerations—by reflecting the rebelliousness and the spectacularity of the medium itself, both of which in turn are also romantic features.

Referring to the portrayal of beggars and other social outcasts in genre paintings, the baroque artist Salvator Rosa famously ended his satire on painting from the middle of the seventeenth century, *Pittura*, with the words

"Quel che aboriscon vivo, aman dipinto" (What they abhor, they love to see in pictures).[58] This observation draws attention to the mediated essence of the image, its distance, and the voyeuristic fascination it arouses and indulges in. Monsters can be seen as an outcome of the desire for voyeuristic entertainment in "a society that has created and commodified 'ambient fear'" and relishes spectacles.[59]

Presence

The desire for immediacy propelling remediation is closely related to the desire for presence, the kind of presence generated via media that mediate the real to such an extent that they often serve as substitutes for reality, as in news videos but also, to varying extents, in fiction. Presence and immediacy in turn cater to the reader's (or viewer's) desire for intensive, even immersive, engagement with a work. Hans Ulrich Gumbrecht's concept of presence is useful for understanding the power exercised by comics through their intense, affective visuality, since the effects of images reverberate beyond meaning.[60]

By rejecting reason and contradicting meaning or even dissolving it through an overload of connotations, monsters consolidate an existence based on presence in lieu of uniformly decodable meaning. Such presence is further consolidated through the visual essence of comics. Intensely visual works like comics can often involve readers beyond semantic dimensions. Because "[t]he demand of the picture is personal and unmediated,"[61] it can have an immediate and even lasting effect. This power is also transmitted to the visualized monster, who is immediately accorded an almost tangible, material body. In the case of comics, which usually rely on seriality (within and beyond a specific issue's covers), the body is usually involved in both movement and mutation and is consequently in a never-ending flux. Such a constant state of transition creates the perfect habitat for mutating monsters to thrive in. Transition in turn can also make it difficult to fix connotations and meaning, thus lending more, potentially transitory, importance to presence.

Describing presence as being something almost elusive by unfolding both in tandem with and beyond meaning, Gumbrecht mentions philosopher Jean-Luc Nancy's more mystical concept of presence as well as literary scholar George Steiner's emphasis on "the relationship (or should we rather say mutual interpenetration?) of layers of meaning and layers of substantive presence in a work of art."[62] In his tracing of the historical background for moving beyond meaning, Gumbrecht mentions "the long-term effects of the nineteenth century's epistemological crisis" triggering a set of so-called progressive intellectual reactions as well as reactions "characterized by a feeling of loss and by a nostalgia" essentially for the "(belief in) a world-reference."[63] Tendencies toward meaning and presence effects can be associated with the trajectories of these reactions.

For Gumbrecht, aesthetic experience unfolds in "specific distributions between the meaning-component and the presence-component—which depend on the materiality (i.e., on the mediatic modality) of each object of aesthetic experience," with one component being less when the other is more. Although images may not have the same intensity of presence as music, they do have the ability to confound referentiality.[64] The desire for presence is proposed as "a reaction to an overly Cartesian, historically specific everyday world that we at least sometimes wish to overcome."[65] The analysis of such desires inevitably combines the longing for both meaning and presence.[66] Monsters, in their intense corporeality, exaggeration, and confounding of meaning also incorporate the desire for presence triumphing over rational meaning-content. Moreover, comics monsters can be seen as revealing and reveling in the presence effects of the medium, with presence itself being a factor contributing toward the success of both comics and monsters. Something proximal to this claim is already present in Thierry Groensteen's assertion that "l'image dessinée n'a pas le même pouvoir illusionniste que l'image filmique. Incomplète, stylisée, immobile, elle ne saurait être confondue avec une présence réelle. Il appartient au lecteur de convertir le visible en présence, d'animer et de compléter l'effigie en se projetant dans la fiction" (The drawn image does not have the same illusionistic power as the cinematic image. Incomplete, stylized, motionless, it cannot be confused with a real presence. It is up to the reader to convert the visible into presence, to animate and complete the effigy by projecting oneself in fiction).[67]

It is through the comparison with film that the distinctive presence effects of comics are brought out. On the other hand, as many image theorists are careful to emphasize, the image is a complex entity, tied to the medium carrying it and making it visible;[68] Belting highlights the difficulty of separating "the mental and physical images of any given age" due to their interaction.[69] Thus "public images have always controlled personal imagination; and the personal imagination, in turn, either cooperates with them or resists them."[70] Comics, especially those with good monsters, reflect a struggle against the limits of binaries (of good and evil, human and monster, self and other) but also, through their intense action and mutation, test the limits of sequential representation. Through the spectacularity[71] of their rich visual imagery, they also thrive on the tension between the sequential flow of reading and contemplation of individual panels.

Building on this theoretical background of the (romantic) imaginary, (comics) remediation, and presence, the book's five chapters:

(a) work out the relationship between positively rendered comics monsters and the key themes of romanticism, which in turn reflects the influence of romanticism in contemporary popular culture; and
(b) highlight comics' remediation of romantic tropes and inclinations in comics, the significance of which is traced to the dominance of images and their ability to communicate on aesthetic and emotional registers, while playing with concepts of the human and the mechanics of othering through their anthropomorphic monsters.

The Monsters of Romanticism in Comics

As with monsters, and more recently human monsters, the influence of romanticism on popular culture has not been ignored by scholars. In his study of popular music, Christoph Reinfandt has delineated the persistence of romanticism in contemporary culture.[72] Similarly, Jerome McGann has questioned the notion of romanticism not only with reference to its construction and its exemplifications but also with reference to its temporal limits.[73]

Here, certain recurrent tenets of romanticism help trace the movement's legacy, beginning with the reclamation of imagination, to which monsters, and their unusual worlds that are precariously linked to reality, bear testament. To cite Cohen once again, "[t]he monster *haunts*; it does not simply bring past and present together, but destroys the boundary that demands their twinned foreclosure."[74] In the case of the comics monsters analyzed here, their haunting is intertwined with the legacy of romanticism. Of particular relevance are the later manifestations of romanticism in Britain and France in the nineteenth century, which Mario Praz theorized as exemplifications of dark romanticism.[75] Although this tendency, by courting the horrific and the fantastic, overlaps with the gothic, it avoids the latter's excess. While excess is discernible in the comics discussed here, the monsters themselves are not evil; they court an ambiguity between good and evil that is closer to the darker currents of romanticism. Romanticism's broader spectrum, its concern with the individual and his environment, its penchant for the fragment, is suitable for examining the vast range of concerns manifested, or at least alluded to, by ambiguous monsters in comics, especially in their tendency toward rebelliousness.

Ambiguous and rebellious inclinations are highlighted throughout the book and distilled in the conclusion. Chapters 2 through 5 examine the manifestations of key romantic themes such as the romanticization of the sordid, the role of solitude, and pantheism, nostalgia, spectacularization, and emotional excess in specific comics. While these are characteristics that recur in all of the comics examined here, and indeed others with similar "good monsters" for protagonists, the focus on specific characteristics in each work enables building and reconfiguring an entire network of interconnected romantic themes that are discernible across a broad spectrum of comics, ranging from mainstream publications to graphic novels with more literary and artistic ambitions. Good monsters themselves abound in comics, since the medium has often reveled in a fondness for othered beings, with the most famous example being the American superhero and his or her revamped versions, which we will encounter in this book. Awkward, troubled, or alienated protagonists and antiheroes, who are recurrent in comics and graphic novels, incorporate many of the romantic features highlighted here, particularly those of solitude and rebelliousness.

This book seeks to trace the continuations of romanticism in contemporary comics. In focusing on comic books that were published from the 1980s onward, the book considers works that are in many ways on the fringes of the deepening split between popular, mainstream comic books and graphic novels with literary and artistic ambitions. These works also offer a positively connoted version of monstrosity. While this in itself is not new, as exemplified by the monsters of romanticism, it is part of a recent trend in popular culture that shows a strong preference for ambiguous protagonists and the testing of the good-evil binary. These works are also representative of a context that is in itself monstrous through its in-betweenness, hovering between mainstream and alternative streams of comics publishing. The selected comics feature protagonists incarnating different shades of monstrosity, but who are essentially good or at least ambiguous (instead of being typically villainous, evil monsters). The first volume of Enki Bilal's *Monstre* tetralogy, for instance, was originally published by the artists' collective Humanoïdes Associés (also known for the adult comics magazine *Métal Hurlant*) in 1998, even though the tetralogy was eventually republished by the successful mainstream publisher Casterman. This in-betweenness is further enhanced by Bilal's use of "direct color," or a combination of painting and mixed media to replace the traditional comics techniques of drawing and inking. Similarly, Alan Moore's revival of *Swamp Thing* (originally with artists Steve Bissette and John Totleben), which started in 1984 and is thus the oldest series examined in this book, foreshadowed the kind of adult, alternative comics published by DC Comics' Vertigo imprint. Published by the young independent press Dark Horse Comics, which was founded in 1986, Mike Mignola's *Hellboy* series creates a universe that remains indebted to the superhero tradition and indeed, like *Swamp Thing*, builds on the inherent monstrosity of the superhero while merging it with the stuff of myths, legends, and fairy tales. First published in 1989 by independent publisher Caliber Press (1989–2000) and subsequently published by other publishers such as the creator-owned Image Comics, James O'Barr's *The Crow* examines the overlap between the gothic and the romantic as well as the limits of monstrosity itself, which persist in the comic through the presence of excess (of emotions) as well as spectacularity (with spectacularity, as we will see in chapter 5, being a more appropriate term than theatricality, owing to the latter's close links with the spectacle and the spectacular as well as the specter or ghost).

From the perspective of comics history, these comics exemplify the different publication contexts in which comics were on their way toward being legitimized as graphic novels: Moore's *Swamp Thing* already challenged mainstream publication practices by openly refusing to adhere to the Comics Code and unabashedly targeting an adult readership. *The Crow* transposes the stuff of superhero comics into a gothic idiom that is simultaneously a reworking of a personal trauma. Such autobiographical elements have become a recurrent feature of graphic novels. *Hellboy* caters to both a fan readership and a "new" readership of graphic novels by responding to relatively recent exigencies of visual aesthetics and narrative complexity. Finally, *Monstre* with its direct color aesthetics and nonseriality also reflects the increased flexibility and experimentation in comics publishing, which has moved away from mainstream formats while remaining accessible to a large audience. That all of these comics were reprinted in collectable editions, as graphic novel–like volumes (sometimes, as in the case of *Swamp Thing* and *Monstre*, by major mainstream publishers like DC and Casterman), reflects the marked shift in the kinds of material publishers are willing to republish.

Starting with *Swamp Thing* (chapter 2) and ending with *The Crow* (chapter 5), this book examines attributes channeling the romantic imaginary into the contemporary one. These include:

- Solitude, the quest for comprehending the self and its place in the world, pantheism, and environmentalism exemplified through Alan Moore's *Swamp Thing* run (in collaboration with several artists and letterers). It is also here that we encounter Frankenstein's monster, refigured as the Patchwork Man. This Patchwork Man embodies a personal trauma of the man the Swamp Thing thought he was. As we will see, he can also be read as an embodiment of both the medium of comics and its tense history of censorship.

- The romanticization of the sordid and ruins in Enki Bilal's *Tétralogie du monstre*. Having already referenced Charles Baudelaire's *Les Fleurs du mal* in *La Trilogie Nikopol*, Bilal maintains a similar atmosphere in *Monstre*, thus highlighting the congruence between the Baudelairian world and science-fictional dystopias. In *Monstre*, it is Baudelaire's "delicate monster," ennui, who, like Frankenstein's monster, captures the connections between romanticism and comics. Its fluidity also reflects the essential ambivalence of good monsters and their ability to rupture categories.
- The nostalgia for older, premodern worlds brought out through the resurrection and intertwining of myths, legends, fairy tales, and other stories in Mike Mignola's *Hellboy* series. The brokenness of Frankenstein's monster and the fluidity of time symbolized by ennui are figured here through the main character and the worlds he is thrust into.
- The prominence of the spectacle and emotional excess in James O'Barr's *The Crow*, which also juxtaposes Arthur Rimbaud's poetry with the lyrics of the postpunk gothic rock band Joy Division. The Crow incorporates the trickster's playfulness and ambiguity.
- The role of ambiguity and rebellion discernible in the comics is distilled in the concluding chapter, which also draws out connections with the medium's predilections. Ambiguity, as already suggested, unfolds primarily through the paradox of the good monster but remains an outcome of the monster's inherent rebelliousness. Both traits are complemented by the medium of comics itself.

This list does not imply that romanticism can be reduced to these aspects alone, since the movement, like most movements, was complex and full of contradictions.[76] The intention here is not to work with a fixed definition of romanticism; instead the focus is on the remediation of certain features that are recurrent in romanticism and are filtered through monsters, both romantic and contemporary. The attributes serving as the focuses of each chapter take up a prominent part of romanticism's manifestations across the arts. They echo the changes entailed by the "new kind of sensibility" resulting in different mythic structures (glaringly evident in William Blake's works), which prevailed over the arts in the West from the end of the eighteenth century onward, propelled by the revolutionary fervor of the era and a correspondingly changing manner of understanding the world.[77] In highlighting the romantic inclinations of anthropomorphic monsters through the remediation of the above attributes, the book shows how romantic ideas prevail over popular culture often, and quite deceptively, through the guise of good monsters. While the influence of romantic consciousness on our contemporary era has been acknowledged by scholars of romanticism such as Isaiah Berlin and Northrop Frye, its influence on popular culture is less apparent and, as I show here, often camouflaged by the monstrous body. Frye, for instance, claims that the "residual anarchism at the heart of the Romantic movement is still with us." This can be extended to the persistence of rebellion in comics, especially through their good monsters as suggested throughout this book.[78]

The above selection of concepts was guided, first, by the peculiar aesthetic popularized by Baudelaire, a major poet of dark romanticism who emphasized the volatility, mutability, and even paradoxicality of the beautiful.[79] This and the other themes that are addressed in the following chapters can also be found in Isaiah Berlin's "In Search of a Definition" lecture on romanticism.[80] Although Berlin himself is careful to highlight the resistance of romanticism to definition, he does include the concepts structuring this book as romantic features, particularly recalcitrance and rebellion[81] but also solitude, which he traces to the concept of *Waldeinsamkeit* or "solitude in the woods of a half delightful and half terrifying sort."[82] Such solitude is often accompanied by pantheism and self-searching, as in *Swamp Thing*. Nostalgia, along with paranoia, is one of the "interesting and obsessive phenomena which are then very present both in nineteenth- and in twentieth-century thought and feeling."[83] This "famous infinite *Sehnsucht* of the Romantics," what Novalis considered "the search for the blue flower," was also a reaction to the Enlightenment conception of "a closed, perfect pattern of life." It found its expression through "the exotic, the strange, the foreign, the odd, all these attempts to emerge from the empirical framework of daily life, the writing of fantastic stories with transformation and transmogrifications of a most peculiar kind [...] all attempts to go back home."[84] Nostalgia, in other words, is uncurable. It drives romantic protagonists to indulge in fantasies, much like the Swamp Thing and Hellboy, as we will see in chapter 2 and in particular detail in chapter 4. Finally, one of the hallmarks of romantic consciousness was the "great turning towards emotionalism," tied to the yearning described above as well as to the "interest in the primitive and the remote [...] outbreak of craving for the infinite."[85] Although preceding romanticism and continuing long after it, emotionality or sensibility as it was then called remains a key element of romanticism, as can be seen from literary critic M. H. Abrams's claim that the romantic poet's mind was—in contrast to the Enlightenment philosopher John Locke's notion of the mind as a mirror—"bathed in an emotional light he himself projected."[86]

Most of the above attributes are found in Northrop Frye's *A Study of English Romanticism*, in which, after describing the romantic myth, Frye examines the "romantic macabre" by focusing on *Death's Jest-Book* by the often overlooked romantic poet and playwright (and physician) Thomas Lovell Beddoes. Frye claims that "Beddoes is a portent of a change in sensibility, also marked by the absorption of Poe into Baudelaire, which regards the grotesque as exuberant rather than 'morbid.'"[87] Beddoes's creation of the "tragicomic grotesque" and the absurdity accompanying it have, as we will see in chapter 5, many similarities with *The Crow*. In the same book, Frye examines the role of pantheism and the imagination through John Keats, and the "romantic revolutionary" through Percy Bysshe Shelley.[88]

Before proceeding to thematic analyses of the comics, in the next chapter I elaborate on romantic artists' experimentation with increasingly flexible print-making techniques and the creation of imaginative, vivid monsters, as exemplified by the works of Goya and Blake.[89] The chapter also takes up key romantic monsters in literature—Frankenstein's creature, the Hunchback of Notre Dame, and Gwynplaine—to bring out the characteristics shared by the comics monsters analyzed here, focusing in particular on their outsider status and the human element that renders them ambiguous, and sets them apart from the villainous monsters populating the earlier literary imagination. After elaborating on the romantic features listed above to highlight the similarities between specific romantic and contemporary monsters, the chapter concludes with a historical, visual perspective on the romantic connections of comics monsters.

CHAPTER 1

ROMANTIC MONSTERS
A Brief History

> Aux objets répugnants nous trouvons des appas [. . .]
> (By repugnant objects we are lured . . .)
> —CHARLES BAUDELAIRE[1]

Monsters and Entertainment

Through the centuries, the monster has established itself as an essential entity of popular culture. Exploring the eighteenth-century case of Mary Toft, who allegedly gave birth to rabbits, Dennis Todd points out that monsters were a guaranteed way of making money because of the English public's fascination with them.[2] He also cites Trinculo's first encounter with Caliban from Shakespeare's *The Tempest* to underscore the link between monsters and the money-making spectacle they automatically engendered:

> A strange fish! Were I in England now (as once I was) and had but this fish painted, not a holiday fool there but would give a piece of silver. There would this monster make a man; any strange beast there makes a man. (act 2, scene 2)[3]

The monster eventually became the center of the popular spectacle, epitomized by the freak shows that reached their zenith in the nineteenth century.[4] By staging natural oddities, freak shows unsettled the boundaries between real life and fantasy. In addition, evolution theory raised the specter of the missing link, which encouraged the creation of anthropomorphic monsters that visualized the transition from apes to humans.[5]

Remnants of the characteristics informing the success of freak shows—combining the spectacle with the spectral—remain discernible in the many movies with monsters, which reflect the same aura of fascination that the freak shows sought to foster. This in turn could have played a role in showing monsters in a positive light, since the threat was tamed and contained within a spectacle that "captured the *hearts* of audiences," as Stephen Asma puts it when describing the popularity of freak shows.[6] The spectrality of monsters stems from their suggestiveness and shying away from absolute truths. By being so different, encapsulating wonder, much like faraway cultures were once a source of wonder and speculation, they also represent alternative ways of living. Tied to the body and yet striving to go beyond the assumptions that accompany its abnormal form, the heroic monster blends horror and fascination. Its spectrality is therefore also an outcome of the many fears regarding the human body's imperfection, as mocked in the conclusion of Alexander Pope's "The First Epistle of the First Book of Horace," in which the reasoning man (Pope himself), "that reas'ning, high, immortal Thing, / Just less than Jove, and much above a King" finds himself "half in Heav'n—except (what's mighty odd) / A Fit of Vapours clouds this Demi-god."[7] Here Pope, unsurprisingly, suggests that the body, while housing the mind, also anchors it; that both mind and body are linked and uncomfortably fluid. As we will see in chapter 3, ennui captures such fluidity of categories and the anxieties associated with it and modern existence at large.

According to Michel Foucault, "the monster provides an account, as though in caricature, of the genesis of differences."[8] It is, in other words, a necessary corollary of modern thought, of the conceptualization of evolution and progression, the schema of which is mirrored by the sequential form of comics. Foucault's observation also highlights the role played by the visual aspect of monsters and the wild forms they adopt, which in turn is corroborated by Cartesian logic, according to which imagining is linked to succumbing to corporeal, material desires since "a mind abandoned to the imagination is a mind abandoned to the body."[9] In such cases, ideas are "reduced" to corporeal, visible forms and are often propelled by the baser power of desire (as opposed to the higher powers of intellect and reasoning)—aspects that also play a role in comics, through the predominance of action and slapstick humor, for instance, and have contributed toward its status as a popular, low art. The monster likewise embodies this notion of the imagination allowed to mutate beyond control and consequently inherits the disparagement and distrust attached to the imagination.[10]

However, as scholars working on the imaginary, especially Gilbert Durand, have suggested, the imagination comprises elementary structures and motifs that mold human thought.[11] The recurrence of monsters in romantic art and literature is therefore not an insignificant case of letting the imagination run wild. It exemplifies the ways in which monsters—and by extension the possible subversion of norms—were conceptualized. Notably, some of the most famous romantic monsters—the monstrous humans populating Goya's prints and *Black Paintings* or Victor Hugo's Quasimodo, to name a few—are usually more anthropomorphic than bestial in appearance. This aspect acquires a certain piquancy when one notes that the notion of the abnormal itself was engendered and solidified in the nineteenth century, in the drive toward modernization and its penchant for classifications.[12] Concurrently, however, an aesthetics of the "Horrid and the Terrible" was developed, most notably in Edgar Allan Poe's writings, the darkness of which Baudelaire admired and emulated.[13]

In his treatise *An Historical Sketch on the Art of Caricaturing* (1813), the engraver James Peller Malcolm saw caricature as existing naturally in humans and beasts, in the sense that any form that simultaneously alluded to and distorted the norm became a caricature. Malcolm also saw caricature as an outcome of unskilled attempts to imitate nature, for "[he] that draws the human face divine for the first time is a caricaturist *per* force: he views the lines of the original, and, attempting to imitate them, produces a monster; and it is only by patience and perseverance he conquers his propensity to distortion."[14] Grotesques and caricatures were thus attributed to so-called primitive minds: the savage "seems to lose all recollection that he had ever viewed the human species, and creates monsters from his own disordered imagination."[15] Although for Malcolm the grotesque creatures of the Saxons exemplified lack of good taste,[16] Malcolm's contemporaries Goya (1746–1828), Blake (1757–1827), and Henry Fuseli (1741–1825) gave their imagination free rein, in protest, at least in part, against the repercussions of civilization and the deceptive notion of rationality. Of the three, it was Goya who fully embraced the sociopolitical horrors of his context in order to allow "the overwhelming to overwhelm."[17] As opposed to the smoother, clearer lines of his contemporaries, Goya's lines "scratch forms into existence and [...] splinter them [...] to create the distorting visual detritus that shudders around the edges of things seen in agonized haste or in semi-conscious distraction, in fear or self-disgust."[18] Art historian and comics scholar Scott Bukatman emphasizes the close link between Goya's art and comics cemented through the artist's imaginative expressionism: "The Romantic sensibility of Francisco Goya bubbles up within the mass medium of the comics, a medium that, as we've seen, exceeds the rationalism of linear, phonetic language and allows the imagination access to other worlds, to other modes of reading and of reading the world."[19] Hillary Chute points out that Goya's monstrous visualizations of history have had a deep impact on famous underground artists such as Robert Crumb and Art Spiegelman.[20] The influence of Goya, however, goes far beyond underground comics, not the least perhaps because Goya himself alternated between painting and etching, and his influences ranged from Blake to William Hogarth and also included contemporary caricaturists such as James Gillray and Thomas Rowlandson:[21] jagged lines and overflowing outlines are also characteristic of Enki Bilal. Although Bilal does not shy away from the sordid, he does adopt a more aesthetic style for his *Monstre* comics. The harshness of Goya's lines and chiaroscuro effects also persist in Jim O'Barr's drawing style for *The Crow*. Heavy dramatization and a penchant for the grotesque and the horrific permeate the worlds of both *Hellboy* and *Swamp Thing*. The art in *Swamp Thing* is closer to the art of horror comics, especially those drawn by Bernie Wrightson, who visualized the first Swamp Thing and, years later, in 1983, also published an illustrated version of Mary Shelley's *Frankenstein*. The art in *Hellboy*, on the other hand, wears a distinctive nostalgic veil that pays homage to horror and the grotesque. Mike Mignola's art for the series stands out through an aesthetic based on flattened, contrast-rich forms.

Referring to the emergence of prints in the fifteenth century, Anne Hollander asserts that "the black-and-white media have had a special power to move the world ever since. By harnessing the elements of light and shade, and by making pictures not only repeatable but movable and adaptable, they have shown what is essential for getting images to do their deepest emotional work."[22] From the comics discussed in this book, the theatricality of black-and-white images is most evident in *The Crow*. However, chiaroscuro is also regularly employed in the other comics, especially in *Swamp Thing* and *Hellboy* through their incorporation of relatively traditional, "flatter" coloring techniques in contrast to the use of direct color in *Monstre*. For Bukatman, the distinctive flatness and abstraction of Mignola's art for *Hellboy* acquires sculptural dimensions and thus enhances layers of both meaning and presence.[23]

David Kunzle attributes the emergence of caricature to the freer technique of etching—in contrast to the more stringent line of engraving—which was developed around the sixteenth century, popularized through the invention of printing and then fine tuned by artists like Jacques Callot (1592–1635).[24] Hollander (in turn resorting to Kunzle) links the further development of caricature to popular picture-stories in the mid-eighteenth century and their increased concentration on psychological aspects through the influence of contemporaneous physiognomic studies.[25]

In tracing the history of caricature, Malcolm highlights the close, interlinked relationship between monsters and caricature as well as the monstrosity of caricature and uses illuminated manuscripts from the British Museum to illustrate "natural and intended caricature."[26] Natural caricature, as exemplified by religious manuscripts such as the *Liber Psalmorum sec. tradit. S. Hieronimi*, illustrates "the near relationship between caricatures and the drawings of genius."[27] This is not only because of the monstrous creatures present in the manuscript but also because of the disproportionate renditions and awkward postures attributed to Christ. These plates, like those of many older illuminated manuscripts, create a space that is relatively flat, almost merging with the figures. As elaborated below, a similar style imbues Blake's work.

Besides medieval manuscripts, Malcolm also examines the post-Renaissance caricatures merging man and beast of Agostino Carracci (1557–1602) and Callot, both of whom used such hybrid forms for portraying outsider figures, including freaks and carnival characters. Carracci became known for perpetuating the comic effect of exaggeration by *caricatura*, or loading a portrait.[28] Later satirical prints, in particular the engravings from 1643 that were attributed to John Vickars, used the biblical iconography of monsters to mock the pope.[29] The moral caricature of William Hogarth (1697–1764), in which exaggerated forms are hidden from the cursory glance, remained more successful.[30] For Hollander, Hogarth was "moving [...] toward demonstrating the excruciating pleasures of strong feeling," which contributed to his success.[31] Such "excruciating pleasures of strong feeling" recur in the romantic monsters discussed below and persist in the comics monsters examined in the coming chapters. The forms that remained discrete in Hogarth's prints take over many a comics world and before that, the world of nineteenth-century visual arts.

Romantic Visualizations of Monsters

According to the philosopher Gilles Barroux, the eighteenth century was a period of transition for hard sciences such as medicine that were still more in the process of searching for and questioning knowledge than affirming it.[32] In this period of change, the monster often symbolized the ill body for scientists. Instead of being a subject that simultaneously evoked fascination and repulsion, the monster attained the status of the unviable or greatly suffering human.[33] This notion is reflected in the romantic monsters discussed below: Quasimodo, Gwynplaine, and Frankenstein. It is also present in the artworks of artists such as Blake, Goya, and Fuseli, albeit usually from an inverted perspective: their monsters are products of the artists' troubled imaginations. They point toward and protest against the prejudices of the contexts in which they are engendered, by giving, in stark opposition to the rationality favored by the Enlightenment, free reign to their imagination and full expression to their emotions.

For a long time, even after the Enlightenment, monstrous imaginings were considered strong enough to materialize as newborns when imagined by a pregnant woman ("Let the pregnant women beware!" is one of the cries heard when Quasimodo is chosen as the Pope of Fools).[34] With the secularization established by the Enlightenment, it was the power of the human imagination that was seen as the source of abnormalities and aberrations instead of the increasingly less credible God or devil.[35] The imagination was conceived as an image-making faculty, which also acted as a realm of fantasy, representing the liminal region beyond the knowable,[36] a mediator between the mind and the body.[37] It also led to a turn from seeing monsters as an inevitable part of nature toward relegating them to the realm of fantasy.

Visually, however, monsters have largely been based on the imagination rather than reality, even when their existence was believed to be real, as with the renditions of the inhabitants of faraway regions inspired by writings such as Pliny the Elder's *Natural History* (from the first century AD). Supernatural demons, which were subjects of frequent, eagerly vivid portrayals, also contributed greatly to the visual repertoire of monsters. Being imaginative constructions, monsters combine a jumble of organic elements, and this awkward assemblage is their essence.[38] The mixed essence of monsters is also described in Genesis, according to which all monsters are the offspring of Cain and are thus both hybrid and evil.[39] Although usually composed of disparate components, several parts of the monster are indeed normal, while others may be exaggerations of those normal features. Physical deformities also played an important role in monstrous imaginaries. Comparable to the attraction wielded by freak shows, which showcased real-life deformities, monstrous images—be they visual or literary in essence—induced a fascination mixed with uneasiness. This uneasiness is in part linked to what Dennis Todd describes, in the context of the Mary Toft hoax, as the "levelling tendency of the imagination," which transposes everything, including aspects such as sense perceptions that are not originally visual, into images.[40]

Hence, despite their inherent unreality, images of monsters are very real and have a powerful, significant presence. They incorporate certain fears, which can be generalized as the fear of the impossible and the unknown. That the unknown had a certain tantalizing pull that was felt more strongly than before is evident in the changes distinguishing the romantic age, many of which are concretized by Edmund Burke's philosophy. Burke described a sublime based upon the sensation of pain, "productive of the strongest emotion the mind is capable of feeling," and opposed it to the pleasure of beauty.[41] Yet, like the "positive pain" of solitude,[42] the pain of the sublime was life affirming. Such emphasis on the positive aspects of conditions usually perceived as negative persists in the ambiguous monsters as well as the good ones discussed in the coming chapters, including Warhole (an example of the former), the Swamp Thing, and Hellboy (examples of the latter). In Goya's works, however, there is little that is redeeming in the ambiguity between people and monsters.

Goya's Narratives of the Body

Both Goya and Blake adopted print making as their preferred means of expression in lieu of traditional painting. Being easily transportable and reproducible, and hence cheap, prints shunned the grandeur of the higher arts and their elite viewers. Materially accessible to a larger set of viewers than works of fine art, prints had the potential to establish more intimate contact with viewers as well as a more significant presence in the collective imagination.[43] Communication was consequently an important constituent of these prints, ranging from the politically charged messages of Goya's series *Los Desastres de la guerra*[44] (The disasters of war, 1810–1820) and the more whimsical but still bitterly critical *Los Caprichos* (Caprices, 1799) and *Los Disparates* (Follies, but *disparates* can also be translated as "proverbs" or "dreams," 1816–1823), to Blake's complex cosmology, which unfolded across the expanse of his oeuvre.

These two artists, both of whom revolutionized print-making techniques to make them more pliable and thus more individualistic, reveal certain distinct if often interconnected tendencies in the visualization of anthropomorphic monsters: Goya's monsters are frequently caricatures of humans or human-beast hybrids, whereas Blake's are more organically and holistically constructed, obscuring the origin of their individual components. This corresponds to the different themes in the two artists' works: while Goya's monsters were often figurative representations of men, Blake's monsters were mythical, primordial creatures, maintaining a degree of dignity that is stripped from many of the beings inhabiting Goya's satirical works. This contributes toward what Hollander describes as Goya's "romantic-realism," "calling attention to the extraordinary in the ordinary," which continues today in certain films.[45] Anthropomorphic monsters and monstrous humans embody such a confluence. Furthermore, in the *Hellboy* comics, where the boundaries between the real and the paranormal are highly permeable and where a demon destined to lead the army of the apocalypse ends up consecrating himself to doing good, Goya's first set of prints, *Los Caprichos*, figures prominently in one of his adventures.[46]

As suggested by the title, *Los Caprichos*, the caprice or play with form and historical events is accorded a central role in these prints. Comprising eighty aquatints, the series, like the three following it, conveys social critique portraying inequality, the exploitation of the poor by the rich, and the unjustness of the clerics. The monsters are thus often men who have a certain social position and power, who revel in cruelty and look like monsters. Clergymen are often rendered as dwarves or even more openly demonic beings, as in *Duendecitos* (Little goblins; plate 49). Although dwarves recur in Spanish painting, most famously in Diego Velázquez's paintings (including *Las Meninas* and other portraits of court dwarves) or in Jusepe de Ribera's *El Pie varo* (The clubfoot, 1642), Goya's dwarves in *Duendecitos* are darker, more physically distorted creatures caricaturing the disreputable members of the Spanish clergy. Clergymen reappear in larger, bestial, and more distorted forms in *Nadie nos ha visto* (No one has seen us; *Los Caprichos*, plate 79).

In a similar vein of horrific deformations, the wealthy men who have frequented brothels retain only their heads, as the rest of their bodies are swapped with those of chickens, in *Todos caeràn* (Everyone will fall; *Los Caprichos*, plate 19) and *Ya van desplumandos* (There they go plucked; *Los Caprichos*, plate 20). Goya's monsters often fly, usually with the aid of bat-like wings, as in the *Disparates* plates *Modo de volar* (A way of flying, plate 13) and *Disparate volante* (Flying folly, plate 5). Indicative of Goya's continuous experimentation with monstrous creatures as hybrids of men and beasts, bat wings replace the ears of the official in *Contra el bien general* (Against the common good; *Los Desastres de la guerra*, plate 71). Other officials are shown with wings, deformed limbs, and claw-like nails in *Se repulen* (They spruce themselves up; *Los Desastres de la guerra*, plate 51). Winged creatures also appear carrying away horrified monstrous passengers in *Soplones* (Talebearers; *Los Caprichos*, plate 48) and *Buen viaje* (Bon voyage; *Los Caprichos*, plate 64). The winged monster maneuvering through the sky, which remained unconquered by man at that time, represented a greater danger and unpredictability than the monsters roaming on land.

Correspondingly, winged monsters also populate the most famous *Capricho* plate, *El Sueño de la razón produce monstruos* (The sleep of reason produces monsters, plate 43). While the preparatory drawing leaves the monsters vague, the print's clearly delineated monsters flying over the tortured, slumbering man resemble nocturnal creatures. In contrast, the monster in ¡Quien lo creyara! (Who would have thought of it!; *Los Caprichos*, plate 62) is confined to the shadows at the lower edge. Yet even the monsters in *El Sueño de la razón* retain their ambiguity to the extent that the creatures allude to, without fully resembling, nocturnal animals. In a manner comparable to Victor Hugo's drawings, *¡Quien lo creyara!* creates ambiguity through the obscurity of the renditions, generating uncertainty and subsequently increasing fear.

In keeping with the romantic zeitgeist, Burke hailed obscurity as a means of exciting and captivating the imagination, emphasizing: "It is one thing to make an idea clear, and another to make it *affecting* to the imagination."[47] The preference for ambiguity and obscurity is therefore closely linked to the importance of feeling in romantic works. To this effect, the valorization of shadows, of possibilities half shown, half hidden, played an important role, especially in Goya's and Fuseli's works (including Fuseli's illustrations of dramatic scenes from Shakespeare's and Milton's works but also his iconic *The Nightmare* from 1781). Such dramatization through chiaroscuro and theatrical lighting is retained in comics and is especially prominent in *The Crow* with its use of black-and-white contrasts. It also raises another concept that played a key role in romantic works: the spectacle, the staging of a performance, and the power of that performance to captivate the audience. Moreover, the Satan of Milton's *Paradise Lost*, who incarnated the most perfect type of masculine beauty for Baudelaire, illustrates the more ambiguous conceptions of beauty and the sublime discussed by Burke as well as the related blurring of boundaries between good and evil, which obscured the clarity valued by the Enlightenment.[48] The obscurity and mutation in Goya's prints exemplifies the freedom of imagination and drawing, whereby anything can take visual form even while entire events are still only suggested. To this end, he improved and mixed his techniques manipulating aquatint etching with drypoint, silverpoint, and burin, thus making it a more malleable vehicle for capturing the monsters of his imagination. This resulted in highly realistic, and horrific, images.

If comparisons are to be made with the images in the comics examined here, Goya's prints are closest to the images found in *Swamp Thing*. Both bodies of work feature grotesque, unabashed realism. Although a cursory glance would reveal more differences than similarities—*Swamp Thing*'s panels are in color and, being part of a sequence, are usually less static—both involve dense images that relish in detailing the horror of the scene and the atrocities suffered, and committed, by the body. And while all monstrous comics are naturally obsessed with the body, it is *Swamp Thing* that visually captures the horrific, violent possibilities of the body (including violence perpetuated by and on the body) in a way that is comparable to Goya's *Los Caprichos*. Unsurprisingly, Goya's monstrous depictions have had a strong impact on underground comics.[49] Their haunting persistence in *Swamp Thing* exemplifies how unconventional tropes—such as sociopolitically loaded monstrosity—is reabsorbed into the mainstream, or at least the fringes of the mainstream.

Figurative mutation, exemplified by the clawed official with bat wings for ears in *Contra el bien general*, persists in *Los Caprichos*. *Los Chinchillas* (plate 50) illustrates the uselessness of the members of the Spanish aristocracy, with the blinded and deafened figures embodying blind obedience and loyalty to anyone able to provide for them. Frankenstein's monster in James Whale's *Frankenstein* film (1931) was modeled on their bodies, which Felix Krämer considers indicative of the continuing fascination with dark romanticism.[50] Both Frankenstein and the blinded, deafened officials are trapped in their bodies. However, in addition to their blocked senses, the *chinchillas*' movement is also constrained. Their monstrosity lies both in their form and in their willful, immoral subjugation.

Hollander discerns another link between Goya's works and film by considering Goya's art as prefiguring the motion picture. She distinguishes between cinematic and noncinematic images, whereby the former are moving images in the sense of not only containing motion and dynamism but also provoking emotional responses. For her, it is the subjectivity of Goya's prints, the artist's involvement, that makes the works cinematic.[51] This is reinforced by the graphic or "unbearably immediate" quality of the images as well as by his positioning of the viewer before scenes that are usually fragments of the entire event.[52] Regarding the aquatints of *Desastres de la guerra* as "an arrow into the future," Hollander writes, "Goya, in working with and never against fashion, linked himself with the romantic temper as well as the modern one, and with modern film as well as modern art."[53]

Yo lo vi (I saw it; *Los Desastres de la guerra*, plate 44) emphasizes the aspect of witnessing as well as the reality of the horrifically fantastic images alluding to the French invasion of Spain in 1808.[54] An imagined reality, it was nonetheless a nightmare that was very real. In this series, more than all others, monstrosity manifests itself through deformities, the rendition of excessive and varied mutilation in which the perpetuators act monstrously and the victims are rendered monstrous through the violence inflicted on them. According to Gilbert Durand: "Des *Caprices* aux *Désastres de la guerre*, le peintre espagnol a fait une insurpassable analyse iconographique de la bestialité, symbole éternel de Kronos comme de Thanatos" (From the *Caprices* to the *Disasters of War*, the Spanish painter has conducted an unmatchable iconographic analysis of bestiality, the eternal symbol of Chronos [the personification of time], as well as Thanatos [the personification of death]).[55] In interlinking time with death, bringing in elements of inevitability and mortality, Goya incremented the sensationalism of the grotesque images and their emotional hold on the viewer.

Romanticism was witness to a surge of sensationalist imagery. For Ian Haywood and John Halliwell: "A crucial development [of the increasingly popular and diverse visual culture of romanticism] was the cultural authority of theories of sensibility and the sublime, both of which placed an intensified emphasis on the visual representation of suffering."[56] Much in contrast with today's views, such representations were regarded as having moral, redeeming effects on viewers. Goya's *Desastres de la guerra* series remains one of the most intense depictions of the ravages of war. Mutilations populate the series, as in *Estragos de la guerra* (Ravages of war, plate 30), which shows a haphazard pile of mutilated bodies, and ¡*Grande hazaña! ¡Con muerto!* (A heroic feat! With dead men!, plate 39), in which men with amputations hang from a barren tree. ¡*Que locura!* (What madness!, plate 68) highlights the similarities between mutilated parts and the masks and puppets surrounding the uneasy, hooded central figure. Mutation and the spectacle are intertwined in *Farándula de charlatans* (Charlatan's show, plate 75), in which the foregrounded figure in clerical robes has the head of a bird. Surrounded by an almost indistinguishable, pleading mass, it remains unclear whether the figure is really human, for he has claws instead of hands. Goya's spectators in such scenes show a variety of emotions, as can be seen in the mix of horror, incredulity, and fascination on the faces in the crowd surrounding the conjoined twins in *Disparate de desordenado* (Matrimonial folly; *Los Disparates*, plate 10). Notably, the conjoined twins are not the only monsters in the picture, although they form the spectacle. Many features of the spectators themselves are so heavily caricaturized that they also appear deformed. Furthermore, like the conjoined twins, the members of the audience form an inseparable mass, with often only their heads being distinguishable as they merge and fade into the background.

For Hollander, Goya's works, distinguished through their dynamism of composition and space, stand apart from Blake's and Fuseli's fantasies by fully embracing the sordid and wanting "the overwhelming to overwhelm."[57] The fantastic in Goya's works is not only more tortured but also blatantly physical. However, not all of Goya's monsters are the creations of an apparently tortured mind. They are often just playful mockeries of stereotypes, as appears to be the case with the twenty-two prints making up the *Los Disparates* series of aquatints. *Los Disparates* merges the fantasy and the horror of the previous two series by tempering the latter, as can be seen in the comparison between the aforementioned *Modo de volar* and *Disparate volante*. In the former, men wearing headpieces resembling birds fly with self-made bat wings. In the latter, a monster, a hybrid of several possible animals, does the flying but is, uncharacteristically for the prints discussed here, not repulsive. The partially contemporaneous mural paintings *Pinturas Negras* (Black Paintings, 1820–1823), like *Los Disparates*, contain monsters that are grotesque or organic hybrids, combining bestiality with anthropomorphic features. Fluidity of bodies and spaces is present not only in Goya's works through the inclusion of hybrids and shadows that obscure forms but also in Blake's works, albeit in a different way, namely by reducing the distinction between bodies and spaces.

Blake's Archetypal, Organic Monsters

In contrast to Goya's intaglio print-making technique, Blake used relief etching, which employs a thicker support, usually wood, instead of a copper plate. While acid is used to create textures and forms in intaglio prints, in relief etching the image is carved directly into the surface. The line is consequently less sharp and the image less detailed. In Blake's case, this resulted in, on one hand, a monumentality that echoed the god-like status of his figures and, on the other, a kind of "primitivity" or naïveté and frankness to his drawings that echoed his aim of conveying, as directly as possible, his spiritual illuminations. As we will see in chapter 4, a certain monumentality or sculptural quality in the *Hellboy* comics enhances the protagonist's timelessness and transcendence of different storyworlds.[58] A more direct relationship between comics and Blake's art can be drawn through the frank nature of the drawings, in which realism is not as important as the affective communication of a concept.

Many of Blake's pictures were used to illustrate his poems, and the words were also etched in the same way as the images. His illustrations helped "to bring the metaphorical structure of the poem clearly into view."[59] Most of his poems delineate a complex cosmology comprising god-like, archetypal beings. As with the binary between God and man, Blake controversially avoided the distinction between mind and body.[60] According to Northrop Frye's interpretation, Blake's world itself "has the form of a giant man's body" with Urizen as the head (city) and Orc as the loins (soil).[61]

According to literary scholar Martin Price, Orc "embodies the rebellious principle of renewed and independent life."[62] In contrast to the rational demiurge, Urizen, Orc is young, rebellious, and emotional, "the human protest of energy and desire, the impulse to freedom and to sexual love."[63] He is the fallen or satanic form of Luvah, who, like Urizen, is one of the four beings created out of the first man, Albion. Blake's primordial beings capture the conflicting mix of the divine and the human, reversing the story of Prometheus by being fallible gods. "Thou art the image of God who dwells in darkness of Africa," says the unnamed daughter of Urizen to Orc in *America a Prophecy*.[64] Correspondingly, Blake's frontispiece to *America* is described by Harold Bloom "as an epitome . . . of the torments of self-consciousness in relation to the contraries of nature and emergent imagination, and of the conflict between revolutionary energy and the organic context from which it emerges."[65] More than half of the frontispiece shows a crouching and chained Orc. His useless wings tower over him and his face is bent, covered by hair. It is this hairiness that is underscored at the opening of *America*, indicating Orc's animal-like nature. Orc's attributes of rebelliousness and passion, in turn inherited from John Milton's Satan, are discernible in all of the protagonists in the comics discussed here—Nike, Warhole, the Swamp Thing, Hellboy, and the Crow—affecting the turn of events both positively and negatively. Moreover, the image of Orc finds a visual continuation in the pyrokinetic (having an ability to generate and control fire) Liz Sherman in the *Hellboy* comics. And the "red Orc" mentioned in the first line of *America* quoted above persists in Hellboy's being, hinting at the possibility that Hellboy, the son of a lord from hell and a witch, can easily transform into the bestial creature that is represented by his form. Another observation by Frye regarding Blake's view of cosmology is also relevant to the solitude as well as the germs of rebellion that were so central to the romantic world view and that accompany all monsters, but perhaps none more than Hellboy: "For Blake, the God who created the natural order is a projected God, an idol constructed out of the sky and reflecting its mindless mechanism. Such a God is a figment of man's alienation, for the tyranny of an absurd and meaningless nature suggests and guarantees the tyranny of exploiting ruling classes."[66]

Blake's bold, vibrant style, which is most obvious in his sketches and prints, reflects his belief that "[t]he certainty of line is given only to those who are Copiers of Imagination."[67] Consequently a more illusionistic and realistic style—"possession by 'Venetian and Flemish demons'"[68]—and palette were rejected in favor of flatter depictions with clear outlines using fresco pigments or watercolors, much in the vein of earlier, especially medieval, art. Moreover, the following marginalia by Blake on Joshua Reynolds's comment in *Seven Discourses on Art* against works resembling Gothic and Dutch art, which "attends to the minute accidental discriminations of particular and individual objects," underscores the importance of symbolism for Blake: "Minute Discrimination is Not Accidental. All Sublimity is founded on Minute Discrimination."[69] In other words, it is through the intervention of the imagination that the sublime is generated. The unreal is therefore not only rich in symbolism but also very powerful. Faithfulness to the imagination is one of the aspects that led Frye to describe Blake as "the first English poet to work out the revolutionary structure of imagery that continues through romantic poetry and thought to our own time."[70] This revolutionary drive manifests itself in the artist's blatant disregard of illusionistic image-making and revival of older techniques and styles that were mostly used for religious paintings seeking to instruct but also to encourage meditation, which tied in well with the spiritual inclinations of Blake's art.

The aspiration toward spirituality in painting is exemplified by *The Ghost of a Flea* (1819–1820), which, with its mahogany support, was made using the outdated technique of tempera used frequently in early religious paintings. That Blake was playing on this religious legacy is also evident by his incorporation of gold in the painting. In religious art, especially Orthodox icons, gold represents a mystical space providing access to the divine through its contemplation. Based on one of Blake's visions, the monster in *The Ghost of a Flea* is the soul of a greedy man who, like all greedy or bloodthirsty men, has been reincarnated as a flea. The creature's wild eyes, reptilian skin, and tongue along with his gigantesque stature overpower his anthropomorphic shape and make him monstrous. Furthermore, even the very space he inhabits is otherworldly, with the trees sharing some of the ghost's bestial qualities, such as their scaly texture and organic form, which in turn reflect the organic quality of Blake's work. Such organic forms take over a print made between 1805 and 1810 showing Behemoth and Leviathan:[71] exemplifying Blake's symbolism, the monsters' inwardly curved forms suggest that they not only engulf worlds but are in fact worlds in themselves—the worlds of war and destruction on land and on sea.

Blake's interweaving of words and images and their framing can also be described as organic. The words and images are interlinked, thriving on the "high tension" generated through their juxtaposition and interdependence.[72] This is evident in the title page of *Songs of Innocence and Experience* (1789), on which the forms of the elaborately curved words sprout vegetation and echo the shape of the tree on the bottom half of the page. Vines are used in the introduction to frame the page, which is comparable to the decorative use of vines in several panels and splashes in *Swamp Thing*, hinting, in both cases, toward the dominance of nature and its powerful organic force. Reminiscent of the drolleries at the edges of illuminated manuscripts—an area where the artist's imagination was unbridled and which thus became an important birthplace of original, playful monsters—Blake's images often create different kinds of frames around the words, ranging from the more curvilinear framing of the entire text as a block in "Sick Rose" and "Infant Joy" to the snake slithering through the title of *Europe: A Prophecy* (1794) and segregating its individual parts.

Blake's art also exemplifies the aspect of naïveté complementing, according to Charles Baudelaire, romanticism: "[S]i l'on veut entendre par romantisme l'expression la plus récente et la plus moderne de la beauté,—le grand artiste sera donc [...] celui qui unira à [...] la naïveté,—le plus de romantisme possible" (If one wants to interpret romanticism as the most recent and most modern expression of beauty—the great artist would then be [...] he who merges [...] naïveté with—as much romanticism as possible).[73] This quotation also highlights the overlap between modernism and romanticism, which is mirrored by Baudelaire's own writing. As shown in the third chapter on Enki Bilal's *Monstre*, the confluence of romantic and modern sensibilities persists through the combination of individualism and strong emotions in a disintegrating world. Before turning to a broader discussion of the romantic connections of monsters in comics, I would like to briefly turn to the different versions and reincarnations of Henry Fuseli's immensely popular painting, *The Nightmare* (*Le Cauchemar*, 1781–1782).

In contrast to the relative flatness and symbolist rendering of Blake's *The Ghost of a Flea*, Fuseli's *The Nightmare* uses a more literary style. Apart from *The Nightmare*, the artist is best known for his illustrations of scenes from Shakespeare as well as Greek and Nordic mythologies. In contrast to Blake's anthropomorphized monster, Fuseli's monster is smaller and more bestial. It sits on a fainted woman whose beauty, fragility, and vulnerability reflect all that the monster is not. Due to its popularity, Fuseli ended up painting several versions of *The Nightmare*, with the version from 1790–1791 trading the landscape orientation for a portrait orientation, placing the monster on the divan instead of on the fainted woman, and giving it a more angular face and pointed ears. Moreover, the more recent monster grins and looks at the overwhelmed woman instead of at the viewer. Even though *The Ghost of a Flea* resembles Fuseli's beast by having a similar coloring and head, the ghost has a more human form rather than a bestial one. *The Nightmare*'s popularity also led to its being widely caricaturized. Although Thomas Rowland's caricature of the painting, *The Convent Garden Night Mare* (1784), replaces the woman with a Whig politician, the monster retains its original appearance, and its almost human facial features are even accentuated, thus playing on the unsettling nature of monsters who bear resemblances to humans.

Made a hundred years later, the sculptor Eugène Thivier's *Cauchemar* (1894) retains the notion of a nightmare; its monster—a hybrid of several animals, including bats and dogs with the torso of a woman—seems to provoke a reaction that hovers between fear and sexual ecstasy. In this way, Thivier's monster captures the ambiguity of the monster's form as well as the reactions it triggers. Literary scholar Henri Baudin describes this effect as rooted in "une horreur de fascination,"[74] which in turn reflects the Baudelairian coexistence of opposites, namely the attraction of the repulsive.[75] Exemplifying the self-reflexive hints that are often discernible in comics, one of Fuseli's 1781 versions of *Cauchemar* appears in *Swamp Thing*, where the protagonist looks—and sometimes, particularly in the volume in which the painting is referenced, acts—like a nightmare.[76] Although only a vague shadow of the painting is discernible, hanging in the bedroom of the Swamp Thing's lover, it is his description of a leering incubus sitting on a sleeping woman that makes the reference indubitable. Tracing back the "lineages of drawing" enables us to "connect the work of the hand across differently marked spaces."[77]

While the artists discussed in this section show a preference for certain types of monsters—which are often anthropomorphized in Goya's and Blake's works—their monsters reveal one major common characteristic: they give the imagination free rein to unearth even the most horrific, often unacceptable, but simultaneously powerful and rebellious images.

Monsters from Romantic Literature

Quasimodo

Victor Hugo's *Notre-Dame de Paris* or *The Hunchback of Notre Dame* (1831) builds its story around the hunchbacked, deaf, and almost mute bell ringer of Notre Dame Cathedral. An ugly, large, and deformed man lacking the words to defend himself, Quasimodo is a social abnormality and an outcast. Like most outcasts, he is a source of fear and is therefore caught up in the vicious cycle that also plagues Frankenstein's monster: in keeping with the notion, which persists today, that ugliness is an indicator of bad character, monsters are automatically deemed harmful and never given a chance to pledge their innocence, which in turn makes them resort to wrongful deeds. Although Quasimodo is never redeemed from the burden of his appearance, his name, ironically enough, refers to the first Sunday after Easter, the liturgy of which celebrates the purity of children, the redemption of sinners.

Quasimodo is repeatedly described as incomplete, lacking, an almost-human.[78] Nonetheless, he shares a crucial similarity with the beautiful, exoticized Esmeralda, who, like him, was abandoned at an early age and forced to become a pariah. Moreover, both of them create spectacles. While Esmeralda uses her dancing and her goat to make a living, Quasimodo is roped into public scenes against his will by being elected as the Pope of Fools in the beginning and later being put in the pillory; eventually, he carries Esmeralda into the cathedral, the only time in the novel when he is described as beautiful.

Romantic monsters and comics monsters share many similarities. For instance, relationships between the misfit or outsider and the exotic foreigner also appear, to different extents, in *Hellboy* and *Swamp Thing*: the Swamp Thing's love interest is the eccentric white-haired Abigail Holland, née Arcane, who was brought up in the Balkans, whereas Hellboy eventually falls for the red-haired Irishwoman Alice Monaghan, whom he had rescued as a baby from the fairies but who remains a part of their world. Another similarity lies in the monsters' attachments to certain places. Quasimodo's attachment to the incomplete cathedral's architecture, its style, and its grotesque sculptures, which he longs to resemble,[79] is comparable to the Swamp Thing's abode in the swamps, which mark his body. *Monstre*'s Optus Warhole similarly reflects the unfathomable, almost unattainable other dimension of his origin, as concretized by his mysterious entry point to earth, the Site de l'Aigle. The monsters in most of these comics have far greater luck than Quasimodo, who is never loved and only gets to hold Esmeralda after her hanging, forming the novel's final, resounding image of two skeletons, one embracing the other amid a pile of hanged criminals.[80] A similar couple appears in *Swamp Thing*, when the illusions the Swamp Thing created for himself start crumbling: the couple is Alec Holland—the person whose consciousness the Swamp Thing swallowed—and his wife, Linda, who partake in a lifeless embrace,[81] capturing "a hideous sexuality" animated by desperate fantasy while also evoking the embrace concluding Hugo's *Notre-Dame de Paris*.[82]

As literary scholar Arnaud Laster describes in his introduction to the novel, Quasimodo is reduced to subhuman status and denied humanity because of his deformities and "incompleteness."[83] Quasimodo's incarnating the soul of the cathedral is an apocalyptic reversal of inside and outside, also testifying to the monster's subversive potential.[84] The subversion of these romantic monsters lies in their similarities with humans. Laster goes on to liken the author to the monstrosity of the protagonist and his writing to the mimicry of the cripple.[85] Similar to Laster's linking of the writer to his creations, the philosopher José Ortega y Gasset drew a parallel between Goya and the monsters he made: "Goya es un monstruo, precisamente el monstruo de los monstruos, y el más decidido monstruo de sus propios monstruos" (Goya is a monster, more precisely the monster of monsters and the most determined monster of his own monsters).[86] A similar transfer of monstrosity from creator to creation can be seen in *Frankenstein*, in which the protagonist's desire to create life echoes the subversion of Prometheus's creation of man in the image of the gods.

Frankenstein's Monster

The monster in Mary Shelley's novel *Frankenstein; or, The Modern Prometheus* (1818) is manmade. Created by Victor Frankenstein to not merely mime man but to surpass him, the monster's appearance shatters Frankenstein's hopes. Shunned by all who lay eyes on him, he eventually becomes the horrific being suggested by his appearance. Echoing Laster's interpretation of Quasimodo, philosopher Stephen Asma sees Frankenstein as the "tragic archetype of the misunderstood outcast."[87] Sociologist Brigitte Munier regards *Frankenstein* as a means of questioning the myth of human genesis, much in the vein of Milton's Satan, whose words are the epigraph of the novel's first edition: "Did I request thee, Maker, from my clay / To mould me man? Did I solicit thee / From darkness to promote me?"[88] Shelley acknowledges the inspiration provided by Milton as well as Shakespearean and Greek tragedies. These influences are also discernible in the emotional intensity of the characters and atmosphere. Indeed, the romantic features in Milton's and Shakespeare's works are accentuated with dark romantic fervor manifest in the passionate natures of the main characters as well as the persisting unpredictability and sublimity of nature, which is concretized by the weather and the mountains that mirror and accentuate the changing moods and course of the story. Notably, nature is a source of comfort for both Frankenstein and his monster and is, like their emotionality, another commonality between the normal and the abnormal.

Moreover, both the monster and Dr. Frankenstein himself embody the interpretation of monsters "as symbols of prideful insurgency" that dominated medieval thought.[89] Hubris is likewise indulged in most blatantly by the Swamp Thing and one of Optus Warhole's clones, the artist Holeraw. Nonetheless, the two comics characters undergo very different fates: while the former is made to rue his episode of pride and forced into humbleness, the latter is never really taught a lesson. Frankenstein's monster himself appears in the final volume of *Swamp Thing*, first in the recollection of Abigail's childhood fascination with Mary Shelley's story. Later, after a disappearance of fifteen years, it is her father, Gregori Arcane, who returns in the monster's form, the patchwork essence of which also echoes his brother Anton Arcane's creation of Un-Men by stitching up injured World War I soldiers from the first run of *Swamp Thing*. Notably, such a patchwork or collage is also reflected in the medium of comics itself, which, to use Thierry Groensteen's terminology,[90] braids multiple references.[91] The remediation of Frankenstein's monster is discussed in further detail in chapter 2, and all of the chapters examine patchwork or collage aesthetics to different degrees. For now it is useful to concentrate on the additional characteristics of the romantic monster brought out through Frankenstein's monster.

The monster, self-reflexively enough, admires *Paradise Lost* and *The Sorrows of Young Werther*. He identifies with Milton's Adam and Satan but also Goethe's Werther, whose "despondence and gloom" the monster inherits.[92] Likening himself to Milton's Satan, the monster adds that, unlike that devil, "I am quite alone"[93] and thus voices the solitude that all the monsters discussed here are inevitably confronted with.

The inspiration behind Frankenstein's monster was a nightmare Shelley had of "a hideous phantasm of a man" brought to life through galvanization, who awakens to reveal "yellow, watery but speculative eyes."[94] Frankenstein's monster retains the attributes suggested by these eyes: he embodies the dialectic of monstrosity and humanity, dangerously juxtaposing the abnormality and horror of the yellow eyes, with speculative distance and thoughtfulness as well as emotional vulnerability. Like many heroes of comics (including the ones discussed here as well as those belonging to the superhero genre), he is lost and struggling to carve an identity for himself. For Munier, Frankenstein's monster—who was supposed to be beautiful but is in fact hideous in appearance and eventually in behavior as well—is a modern descendant of the golem, the intelligent, rebellious robot condemned because he lacks a soul and is not human.[95] Yet, as Munier points out, man himself is described as a golem in the Psalms—an "unformed substance" according to the English Standard Version—brought to life by God: "Your eyes saw my unformed substance; in your book were written, every one of them, the days that were formed for me, when as yet there was none of them" (139:16).[96]

The frontispiece for the first edition of *Frankenstein* shows two horrified figures: Frankenstein looking at his monster and the monster looking at himself, maladroitly bunched up in the foreground like a broken figure and with transparent skin revealing his insides. This highlights the extent to which the monster abhors himself and ultimately seeks to make others, especially Frankenstein, get a taste of his own solitude and despair.[97] Like

Frankenstein, and other romantic protagonists, the monster feels too much, and the steady rejection at the hands of others pushes him toward taking revenge by making others suffer. Frankenstein's monster, by virtue of being a giant, is a symbol of excess, which in his case is an excess of emotions that makes him act ruthlessly, thus increasing his misery and regret and eventually driving him to suicide.[98]

The horrific nature of the tale stems in part from Shelley's ability to arouse compassion for the monster, despite his actions. This compassion is based on the monster's humanity, his human condition (which also applies to the golem).[99] Like Quasimodo and Gwynplaine, Frankenstein's monster is brought into a hostile world. His persistence and current popularity can be attributed to what Max Weber called *Entzauberung* or the eventual loss of belief that life has a sense of purpose.[100] That the monster's life is "wantonly bestowed," thrusting him into a world that does not want him, heightens the injustice of his situation.[101] This sense of injustice is augmented by Frankenstein's initial unwillingness to listen to his monster, before the creature gives in to bitterness and resentment.[102] That the monster's sense of being lost—not knowing why he was made or what he is meant to do in a world that does not want him—leads to despair is a reaction that is, paradoxically, only too human.

In contrast to Quasimodo and Gwynplaine, Frankenstein's monster is always relegated to the peripheral, unfrequented audience seats rather than the center stage: he is forced to watch the spectacle of life, the serene life of Frankenstein's family and the more difficult one of the cottagers, instead of becoming a spectacle himself. His appearance is so horrific that it terrifies all who see him, driving out any possible sense of compassion. In addition to being misunderstood, monsters like the Swamp Thing and Frankenstein's creation are a source of horror, which results in their exclusion from human society and their consequent solitude. However, the solitude of Frankenstein's monster is more complete than that of the other romantic monsters, since even his creator, his only human contact, despises him. Frye points out the ironic implications of the contradictions captured by Frankenstein's monster:

> The whole point about the monster is that he is not a machine, but an ordinary human being isolated from mankind by extreme ugliness, Blake's "different face." The number of allusions to *Paradise Lost* in the narrative indicate that the story is a retelling of the account of the origin of evil, in a world where the only creators that we can locate are human ones. Frankenstein hunts down his monster in the same way that moral good attempts to destroy the moral evil it has itself created.[103]

For Pierre Ancet, Frankenstein's monster already embodies the concept of the posthuman by reflecting "l'humanité machinée et le corps technologiquement refondé" (the mechanized humanity and the technologically reconstructed body).[104] Indeed, Shelley's tale was inspired not only by German folktales but also by speculation about Darwin's discoveries and the possibility of creating life through galvanization.[105] More specifically, the unnamed monster is born out of Frankenstein's curiosity for "the principle of life" and "the cause and progress of decay."[106] This discovery is kept secret, ensuring that Frankenstein's monster will remain a unique, lonely being.

However, all monsters, manmade or not, exemplify the eternal recurrence of the Other, the inevitable presence of deviations from norms, which usually only attract mistrust and horror. Superficially, *Frankenstein* seems to replace magic with science (which also holds for *Monstre*, whereas the tussle between the two persists in *Swamp Thing* and *Hellboy*). Yet Frankenstein's experiments are described as being little different from those used for magic, because they involve dead bodies and various animals that might also be found in a witch's cauldron. Like Frankenstein's creature, all of the four monsters discussed in this book are also manmade or brought into being by man's actions. Hence, it is through willful actions that the monsters are created, often to replace the human, but sometimes to hide the human, as is the case with the Crow, who recalls Hugo's *The Man Who Laughs* (1869).[107]

Gwynplaine

According to Beate Ochsner, it is through his deformed protagonist Gwynplaine that Victor Hugo subverted the classical model with the romantic one.[108] "J'incarne tout. [...] L'homme est un mutilé" (I incarnate everything. [...] Man is a mutilated being), Gwynplaine famously declares in his speech to the House of Lords, who only scoff at it. This mutilation—a smile carved into his mouth—makes Gwynplaine a source of entertainment. And it was through the performance involving uncovering the deformed part of his face that he and his adopted family of outcasts can live. With his deformed face, Gwynplaine oscillates between being an object of mockery and a successful actor. In either role, he remains an outcast in search of effacing his deformity, of becoming normal. His relationship with Dea, the blind orphan girl, whom he finds before seeking refuge with Ursus, is doomed. Ursus, who adopts the two children, is an itinerant, knowledgeable, and philosophizing entertainer and seller of potions who travels across England with his hut and his wolf, called, ironically, Homo.

An awareness of the spectacle—its attraction, fragility, and temporality—persists through most of *The Man Who Laughs*. The spectacle is not only limited to the makeshift stages set up by Ursus but also dominates, even more completely, the life of the baroque English court, where the aristocracy play out an elaborate masquerade.

Ursus, Homo, Dea, and Gwynplaine's successful show *Chaos vaincu* (*Chaos Vanquished*) is made up of dramatic summaries of their lives, which are abstracted to bring out their universal significance.[109] The first scene involves a battle between a man and two beasts, with Homo playing the dog and Ursus the bear (thus juggling the roles suggested by their names), and Gwynplaine, covered by a sheet, playing the man. It is only upon hearing Dea's song offstage that he manages to defeat the beasts once and for all. This recalls the young Gwynplaine's long battle with the elements at the novel's beginning, when he found himself abandoned on the coast. A little later, he picked up the infant Dea from the arms of her dead mother, and it was in part because of the infant that he pushed himself to survive the harsh night. Growing up with Gwynplaine, the blind Dea falls in love with him—a love that Gwynplaine often doubts because of his scarred face. Similar to Esmeralda's striking physical difference from Quasimodo, Dea is the complete opposite of Gwynplaine. The Duchess is in turn the opposite of both Dea and Gwynplaine by embodying the destructive beauty of the femme fatale. And fatal she is to both Dea and Gwynplaine, because after Gwynplaine leaves to go live with the Duchess, Dea's health starts deteriorating to the extent that when Gwynplaine finally does return, it is only to witness her final moments and carry her corpse into the water, into which he also disappears.

In contrast to the novel, *Chaos Vanquished* ends with a powerful anticlimax: as Gwynplaine kneels before Dea in the darkness, a sharp light is thrown on his face, which makes the audience burst out into laughter. This recalls the reason behind Gwynplaine's disfigurement. The *comprachicos* who bought and sold children had established a monster-making industry. However, instead of scaring people, these monsters were made to make people laugh, to entertain them, much like the freaks that were part of traveling shows such as P. T. Barnum's traveling American Museum. By mimicking biographical events, *Chaos Vanquished* blurs the lines between the real and the unreal. A similar inability to separate the real from the unreal occurs when the character is overcome with emotion, as for instance when Gwynplaine receives the Duchess's declaration of love and summons to meet her.[110] Indulgence in emotions as well as the imagination is a romantic trait discernible not only in the monsters here but in protagonists like Goethe's Werther. Correspondingly,

Baudelaire once described romanticism as lying in the "manière de sentir" (way of feeling).[111]

Like the other monsters before him, and like many other romantic protagonists, Gwynplaine is also solitary, from the very beginning of the novel, when he finds himself in the deserted landscape.[112] That the landscape comes to life—a tree appears to be a man, for instance—exemplifies the anthropomorphism characterizing romanticism but also persisting in contemporary popular culture, especially in comics such as *Swamp Thing* and *Hellboy*, in which inanimate objects take human forms. Gwynplaine's solitariness is also evoked as being part of his job as an actor.[113] While Ursus and Homo are additional personifications of unending solitude, Dea shares Gwynplaine's solitude by virtue of being different and damaged. One of the extended implications of such solitude is that the solitary character often has a distinct, unconventional perspective. The solitariness also ties in with the rebelliousness of romantic characters as well as their drive to fulfill their quests, all of which will be elaborated below after summarizing the human attributes of these monsters, the kinds of spaces they inhabit, and their inevitable participation in spectacles.

Characteristics of Anthropomorphic Romantic Monsters

Imperfect Humanity and Ambiguity

The most glaring similarity between the above three monsters is the humanity and ambiguity they instill in the concept of monstrosity. This in itself reflects the change in the course of the nineteenth century as a result of which "by the end of the century, monstrosity was no longer necessarily being viewed as an aberration of nature visited upon the very few, but as something residing within apparently normal, respectable, and respected individuals."[114] All three of the romantic monsters above imbricate conceptions of monstrosity and humanity. While Gwynplaine is human, a man behind the permanent mask of deformity forced on him, Frankenstein's monster, deemed at his inception as a failed attempt at being not only superhuman but also human, is never accorded the status of a human. Although human, Quasimodo, who is only rarely feared and mostly mocked, is relegated to a bestial status due to his deformity. Asma's observation regarding Frankenstein's monster is also applicable to Quasimodo and Gwynplaine, for all three, because of their human aspects, indicate the "shift in the way we think about monsters. [. . .] [W]e think of them as churned out by abstract alienating systems, social and ideological machines that cannot feel the beating hearts inside them," creating a contrast between the label of monster thrust on them and their human characteristics.[115] These humanized monsters are thus indicative of the romantic desire to generate empathy with the figure of the outcast. Comics, on the other hand, have been bringing the outsider closer to readers for some time, since comics protagonists are often quirky (the mock heroes of Rodolphe Töpffer's *histoires en estampes*) and hail from the fringes of society (the Yellow Kid, the X-Men). Otherness is even a prerequisite for the extraordinary powers of superheroes, which in turn alienates them from the very people they protect.

Inhabitants of Spaces of Exile

In keeping with the romantic inclination of resurrecting material from a past that is often too quickly forgotten, the worlds of all three monsters are in some way or another steeped in older worlds. This is most obvious in the setting of the yet to be completed Notre Dame Cathedral. However, even Frankenstein, the modern Prometheus, had been fed on medieval philosophy at a young age. Gwynplaine himself is the product of a disappearing "art" or industry of child disfiguration.[116] The simple, itinerant life he lives with Ursus, Dea, and Homo is likewise the remnant of a much older lifestyle unfolding outside the regulations of modern society. All three, in addition, haunt places of exile with which they develop a close sense of affiliation: Quasimodo is relegated to the bell tower of Notre Dame; Gwynplaine remains, for most of the story, in Ursus's moving hut; and Frankenstein's monster is driven to places that are only irregularly frequented by humans, such as the forest, which is also sought out by other romantic protagonists.

The tragic endings of most of these dark romantic novels usually have more ambivalent if not outright positive counterparts (*Swamp Thing*) in the comics discussed here. Even the endings of the novels themselves are not completely tragic, since a better solution is proposed in the afterworld. The persistence of such ambiguous or negative endings asserts one of the most recurrent features of monsters: their unviability for reality. In contrast, as Gwynplaine's story shows, monsters thrive in the make-believe world of the stage and guarantee a successful spectacle.

Making Spectacles and Generating Emotions

In its tendency to remove all mediation and encourage direct involvement, romanticism was even iconoclastic.[117] Instead of images, poetry and art were seen as a means toward a more intense imaginative or conscious experience. The romantic era can thus be seen as a time when presence in the form of an "extra-sensory link between the percipient and the representations" was sought.[118] This in turn led to the popularity of entertainment relying on visuals to create an all-encompassing experience, as in the case of the phantasmagorias.

Emerging in the late eighteenth century, these phantasmagorias, in which horror stories were projected in darkened rooms with the aid of magic lanterns, aimed to affect the spectator, producing a frisson by eliminating all manner of critical distance and environmental disturbance. As film scholar Tom Gunning has shown, remnants of this intention persist in the convention of submerging cinema and theater audiences in darkness, which, originally, was necessitated by the projections.[119] Showcasing monsters in, for instance, freak shows had the same aim of inducing frissons through their difference from humans, as well as their possible similarities, which, by verging closer into the realm of the possible, had stronger effects on their watchers.[120] A comparable interchange of identities is suggested by Dennis Todd, who illustrates the question of identity and identifying raised by monsters by recalling Gulliver's fluid identities, which changed according to each new situation and required embracing difference and becoming a monster to entertain others.[121]

William Hogarth grew up in Smithfield in London, which was known for its heady activity, especially its summer spectacles, including parodies, pantomimes, and acrobats.[122] Like Hogarth's prints, the space in comics continues to mirror the experience of popular spectacles, reflecting the vivacity and intensity of such events through vibrant colors and energetic compositions that encourage readers to submerge themselves in the worlds offered to them.[123] The spectacularity of comics heroes, which is exaggerated in superheroes, reinforces the centrality of the spectacle in comics stories.[124] Media scholar Sarah Sepulchre adds that it is the differences of monsters—and superheroes—that make them objects of curiosity and spectacle.[125]

For Ian Haywood and John Halliwell, "the idea of 'spectacle' implies the emergence of conspicuous new types of visual effects in British culture of the late eighteenth century."[126] The reverberations of this developing, increasingly popular visual culture also have an impact on the portrayal of characters and the construction of stories, manifested most prominently in the emphasis on the characters' emotionality and the abundance of drastic events, aspects that are discernible in all of the comics analyzed here as well as in a considerable proportion of popular literature in general, in which the romance elements of romanticism continue to have a strong influence.[127] Moreover, like the monsters of romantic literature, the monsters in comics stories inevitably create spectacles and are often, albeit not always, at the center of them: orchestrating all of the spectacles or drastic events in *Monstre*, Optus Warhole does not always take center stage as, alternately, protagonist or antagonist; the Crow's revenge is planned out as a spectacle with himself at its core; and both the Swamp Thing and Hellboy create spectacles through their very presence. Besides emotionality and the emerging strategies of spectacle making, another inclination that is remediated to comics from the romantic arts, especially literature, is that of the quest.

The Quest and Solitude

Harold Bloom emphasizes romanticism's close ties with medieval chivalric romance by showing how the quest, which played a central role in medieval tales, is internalized by the protagonists of romantic poetry.[128] He describes Milton's Satan—a "heroically defeated Promethean quester" whose Prometheanism or desire to acquire god-like powers was internalized—as an archetype of the romantic quester.[129] The change in attitudes in the romantic era are highlighted by Milton's demonization of the very quality that lies at the core of many romantic protagonists: the internalization of the quest as a result of which "the Promethean hero stands finally, quite alone, upon a tower that is only himself."[130] Hence the quest or search within the self for attaining a higher consciousness provokes the withdrawal from, and shunning by, society.

Notably, both stages of romanticism initially differentiated by literary scholar Morse Peckham—namely, negative romanticism and positive romanticism—result in solitude: in negative romanticism, "the individual was isolated by the loss of a meaningful relationship with the universe," and while a meaningful relationship with the universe was also present in positive romanticism, "the individual [...] was still alienated from his society, which continued to live on Enlightenment and pre-Enlightenment principles."[131] Although solitude is often willfully sought by romantic protagonists instead of being thrust upon them as in the case of the comics monsters discussed here, the Swamp Thing, Hellboy, and the Crow also seek solitude, which provides them with opportunities for contemplation and self-reflection.

Quests are, to different extents, integral to the monsters in all four works: Optus Warhole's seemingly incongruous and incomprehensible actions culminate in uniting the protagonists forming the trio from Sarajevo; having met Abby, the Swamp Thing struggles to remain with her while also striving to understand who and what he is; the Crow aims at avenging his and his lover's brutal deaths; and Hellboy pursues the almost impossible quest of reversing his destiny as harbinger of the end of the world.

Since all of these protagonists withdraw into solitude but are also involved in conflicts against established structures, the nature of their quests is comparable to the two stages of the romantic quest described by Bloom, with the latter taking precedence over the former:

> Generally, Prometheus is the poet-as-hero in the first stage of his quest, marked by a deep involvement in political, social, and literary revolution, and a direct, even satirical attack on the institutional orthodoxies of European and English society. [...] The Real Man, the Imagination, emerges after terrible crises in the major stage of the romantic quest, which is typified by a relative disengagement from revolutionary activism, and a standing aside from polemic and satire, so as to bring the search within the self and its ambiguities.[132]

As a result, "[t]he final enemy to be overcome is the recalcitrance of the self."[133] Rebelliousness consequently takes two forms. The first form is the external rebelliousness against society, whereas the second and more untamable one is the rebelliousness of the conditioned self and its refusal to give in to the demands of convention. This conflict takes on different shades in protagonists such as the Swamp Thing and Hellboy, who are partially conditioned by human society while still remaining othered by it.

Rebelliousness

"Each of the Romantic heroes rejects established laws, norms and conventions (and as Werther admits, 'Ich kehre in mich selbst zurück, und finde eine Welt'), is forced to make the self the center of existence."[134] Romantic monsters, however, are pushed to the margins from the very first day of their existence, prior to any expression of rebellion. In other words, the rebel in the monsters is only awoken after being rejected by society. Gwynplaine's rebellious nature prompts him to look at the Duchess when kissing Dea during the play. Enticing the Duchess, this bold action eventually leads to Gwynplaine's becoming her lover, discovering his inheritance and title, and even entering the House of Lords. As already pointed out, Frankenstein's monster also becomes increasingly rebellious; and Quasimodo, when trying to protect

Esmeralda toward the end of *Notre-Dame de Paris*, loses his fear of Frollo (the archdeacon of Notre Dame who had adopted him) and other people.

The monster's rebelliousness often has political connotations, since it highlights the inefficacy or even injustice of political and religious systems that are unable to offer monsters any refuge. This, to a certain extent, echoes the writers' anti-authoritarian predilections. Hugo's disparagement of and irreverence for the authorities, for instance, underlies his monsters and eventually surfaces in Gwynplaine's confrontations with the English aristocracy and Quasimodo's defiance of Frollo. I will now turn to monsters in comics to highlight the deep links to romanticism that can be seen in both the history of the medium and its techniques.

Rebellious Visualities: Monsters in Comics and Their Romantic Connections

In this section, I will first briefly outline the strains of rebelliousness in comics drawing. I will then elaborate on the burgeoning visual culture of the nineteenth century and its effect on the monstrous, romantic visualizations in the comics this book focuses on.

Anne Hollander regards film as perpetuating the same "illustrative impulse" governing painting and other graphic arts.[135] She calls such practices romantic, since "[t]he desire to make pictures in this way, using certain optical effects to appeal to unconscious feelings rather than to the conscious intelligence, is essentially romantic in the deepest sense, committed to the personal in its very form."[136] Although the transposition of observations on cinema to comics entails some qualification, Hollander's emphasis on the links between the graphic arts and cinema, particularly the fascination with movement, is also applicable to comics. This description of film, for instance, also holds for comics, even if they are composed of still images: "The world is presented in a fluid medium that depends on incompleteness, quick change, and often on ambiguity. Cinematic art therefore engages our anxiety and empathy first, and allows beauty to arise from the very quality of contingency that informs the images."[137] In comics, the kind of involvement described by Hollander, which is in itself romantic due to its ambiguity and emotionality, is structured by different aspects such as the drawing style, the gutters, and different reading speeds, which vary with each reader and context. Singular instances of romantic influence on comics are also occasionally pointed out as suggested in the previous chapter, through Grant Morrison's and Charles Hatfield's interpretations of Jack Kirby's work.[138]

There is, however, another significant romantic inclination that persists in the very technique of comics making, as elaborated by Thierry Smolderen. Blake's drawings retained a certain naïveté and primitivism in rejecting the conventions of illusionistic drawing. As Smolderen points out, a different kind of primitivism or stylized, simplistic drawing is exemplified by the graffiti on the wall in George Cruikshank's illustrations to William Harrison Ainsworth's *Jack Sheppard* (1839), which in turn echoes graffiti in the process of being made in the first print in William Hogarth's *The Four Stages of Cruelty* (1751).[139] Exemplifying the referencing and interactions between different media, the persistence of these drawings highlights the reliance on schematization and stylistic drawing that forms the basis of preparatory sketches common to comics and all other arts. By offering a space of confrontation between the higher (history painting) and lower arts (graphic satires, signs, graffiti), prints such as those by Hogarth and later Cruikshank contributed to the evolution of an ironic, humorous polygraphic language that persists in comics.[140] Smolderen is careful to specify the relationship and interaction with other modes of expression as being a playful one, and thus per se humorous, indirect, and unsystematic.[141] Such a relationship is in itself monstrous, for it mocks while remaining playful, distorted, and incomprehensible. Hence the polygraphic language of comics is in many ways the language of the trickster.

The difference between Hogarth and Töpffer, who is frequently hailed as the father of the modern comic strip, is considerable, even though they are situated within the same field of popular image making.[142] Töpffer's happy disregard of classical drawing, in contrast to Hogarth's meticulousness, is an outcome of the romantic era's preference for the so-called primitive modes of expression such as graffiti, caricature, grotesques, and drawings by children.[143] Such art protested against the rigidity and artificiality of academic drawing. Reveling in its freedom, it also had a certain claim to authenticity. This is evident in Töpffer's preface to his *roman en estampes*, *Le Docteur Festus* (1840): "Il y a aux confins de la région du sérieux et du raisonnable, un espace vague, immense, peuplé de fantômes extravagans, de visions récréatives, de folles figures touchant quelquefois à la ligne du vrai, mais n'y séjournant pas" (At the borders of the region of the serious and the reasonable, there is a vast, vague space, peopled by extravagant phantoms, entertaining visions, mad figures that sometimes touch the line of the real, but never stay there).[144] These words, marking out the space for excess and madness, phantoms and entertainers, in one of the earliest graphic novels in Europe, also implicitly designate it as an ideal, fertile ground for harboring monsters. The quotation hints toward the rebelliousness of comics' characters as well as their creators.

Scott Bukatman emphasizes the presence of such rebelliousness in comics and animation: "Comics and cartoons [...] are the archetypes—media that, nearly from their inception, set about overturning established orders and hierarchies, frequently pausing to meditate on their own possibilities."[145] Apart from the medium's rebellious traits, the perpetuation of monsters in comics has been encouraged by the close relationship between comics and pulp fiction owing to the latter's thriving on unbridled excess. Certain aspects of the form of comics also encourage the development and proliferation of monsters. The sequential arrangement of panels, for instance, lends itself to transformations and metamorphoses, echoing the nineteenth-century diagrams visualizing the evolution of different species, such as the transition from ape to man. It was this sequentiality that was instrumentalized by Töpffer for mocking the modernized world, its linear idea of progress, and the accompanying predilection for compartmentalization and categorization.[146] However, as literary scholar Philippe Willems discusses in detail, Töpffer's *histoires en estampes* also "playfully deconstructed" certain tenets of romanticism (solipsism, escapism, liberalism).[147] Comparable, somewhat ambiguous mockery is retained in contemporary comics, most prominently through the persistence of caricature. In this book, such ambiguity and ambivalence is personified through the figure of the trickster.

Michel Foucault saw monsters as a necessary outcome of thinking in continuities. Monsters function as "the background noise [...] the endless murmur of nature."[148] They rebel against predictability and question it. Comics monsters continue such questioning, and the mocking element is further strengthened by their close ties to caricatures and satirical drawing. By being so malleable, drawing has a certain lively quality, which, according to Töpffer, is most prominent in stylized, simple drawings: a stick figure, despite being reductive, is livelier, more individual and open to variety, than a realistic portrait.[149] However, it is not only monsters in prints, such as the grotesques from medieval manuscripts, that are remediated into comics but also monsters from other media, including literature and architecture. Unlike medieval drolleries, which are relegated to the margins of a page, or the grotesque sculptures hiding in the nooks and crannies of Gothic buildings, monsters in comics, whenever present, end up taking center stage, be it as villains or as heroes.

Comics monsters are inheritors of a vibrantly transformed visual culture rooted in print media but branching beyond it from the eighteenth century onward, which witnessed the creation of the earliest automatons, Jacques de Vaucanson's *Le joueur de flûte traversière* in 1737. Monsters proliferated in James Gillray's (1757–1816) caricatures, complementing the elements of horror and repulsion with the elements of satire and mockery. Under Edmund Burke's table in *Cincinnatus in Retirement* (1782), monsters reappear in the form of birds with the heads of men in Gillray's *A Great Stream from a Petty Fountain* (1806). *The Gout* (1799) focuses on one miniscule but ferocious monster biting into a swollen foot with his pointed teeth. He breathes fire, and his tail swings as his claws dig deeper into the foot, displaying a violent intensity that is absent in the prints mentioned above. In recalling the more bestial form often attributed to the devil, this monster also resembles Hellboy and shows how deeply rooted, and interconnected, the basic forms of monsters and devils are.

Ian Haywood and John Halliwell situate Gillray's and Blake's art in the context of the burgeoning romantic visual culture:

Though they are poles apart in many ways, Gillray and Blake were both concerned to visualize sublime power and hyperbolic experience. However their work must also be placed in a much broader and diverse economy of visual spectacle and display which embraced both polite and popular culture: [...] the rise of institutions of polite leisure and "socioscopic" recreation [...] such as urban pleasure gardens, the masquerade, landscaped country estates, and public art galleries; [...] popular urban "shows" of all kinds, many of which exhibited new and innovative visual technologies such as the eidophusikon, panorama, diorama and phantasmagoria.[150]

Giving free rein to the imagination in a manner comparable to the artists discussed above while maintaining a strong allusive link to reality, surreality is the foremost aspect of imagery from the romantic visual arts that persists in the comics analyzed here. Besides the monsters already discussed, the surreal colors and forms of the vegetation in many of Samuel Palmer's (1805–1881) earlier, less naturalistic landscapes, such as *The Garden in Shoreham* (1830) and *Early Morning* (1825), are echoed in comics, particularly in *Swamp Thing*.

Another shared aspect is violence, which comics inevitably indulge in and which owes a great deal to the development of popular visual culture and the notion that the sublime, even the horrific sublime, can serve a moral purpose. As Haywood and Halliwell point out: "The idea that sensational violent imagery could have a redemptive moral effect on the suitably refined reader or spectator had a profound impact on eighteenth-century literary and artistic culture. In response to the cataclysmic events which became the historical bedrock of Romanticism—revolution, global warfare, imperial expansion, the slave trade—an expanding romantic print culture invested heavily in set-piece dramas of hyperbolic distress."[151] Monsters, the natural stars of sensationalist situations, were already part of the visual culture during the Enlightenment.[152] The only difference in romanticism was their grudging acceptance beyond the popular classes. Jonathan Swift, for instance, regarded such entertainment as an indication of the "forces of Dulness" that make fascination push away critical thinking.[153] And yet Swift himself was an avid watcher of monsters, as eager in his enjoyment of them as he was in his criticism of their display and reception.

An important aspect of the developing visual culture was the imitation of the real, facilitated by the devices already mentioned, including photography but also magic lanterns, which made absent objects present. As explained in detail by John Tresch, a change in the concept of the imagination occurred in the first half of the nineteenth century, with the help of illusion-generating machines concretizing the imagination and providing an unprecedented range of sensory experiences. Robert Baker's invention of the rotunda, which provided panoramic views of paintings that surrounded the viewer, "spawned a mania for painting on a large scale, including sublime views of the beginning and ends of worlds."[154] Phantasmagorias "participated in the romantic secularization of the supernatural, an 'uncanny' process in which spectrality was displaced from religion to the psyche."[155] Usually catering to a younger audience, phenakistiscopes were often populated by grotesque and fantastic figures, which acquired a new vivacity across media in this age.[156] In the same era, Jean-Jacques Ampère coined the term "fantastic literature" in admiration of the "natural" or organic marvels populating E. T. A. Hoffmann's recently translated stories.[157] Hence, owing to innovations in the burgeoning realm of visual entertainment and the change in literary inclinations, the supernatural, rather than remaining on the spiritual plane, began to infiltrate the realm of the real and the everyday, even though it remained confined to specific theaters.

Some of the physical features of the monsters analyzed in the coming chapters reflect general traits associated with monsters while also capturing their romantic inclinations. The figures of Frankenstein's monster, ennui, and the trickster are also present to varying degrees. Through their ability to change forms, Optus Warhole and the Swamp Thing incorporate the fluidity of the monster, its ability to mutate and overflow across outlines. In doing so, they also act as the nodes where the material and the immaterial or supernatural merge, a union that is often problematic. Such uncomfortable merging of the heavenly with the earthly, the immaterial and the material, hovers ominously over the *Hellboy* series, tormenting its main character, who is demonic in appearance and human in actions and thoughts. In contrast to the first three comics stories, which deal with different kinds of mutants (extraterrestrial, vegetal, bestial), the protagonist of the last comic analyzed here, the Crow, is essentially human. Victim of a brutal murder, he is resurrected as an indestructible being with the aim of vengeance. In this state of a revenant, the Crow paints his face to resemble a clown (or the Joker), with grotesquely exaggerated eyes and smiling lips; in this guise, which is monstrous in its exaggerations, he methodically executes his revenge with considerable theatricality. Spectrally hovering between the realms of the living and the dead, the Crow's monstrosity consciously creates and even revels in spectacle. It is accompanied by his permanent smile, which contrasts with how his tormented being feels. Besides the differences in appearance and attitudes already discernible in these brief descriptions, all of these monsters incorporate several traits raised by the romantic monsters, as suggested in the preceding sections.

The Swamp Thing, the first monster to which I will turn, well captures the dynamics between the medium of comics, comics history, monstrosity, and romanticism. His story is closely intertwined with that of the Patchwork Man and Frankenstein's monster and thus also enables drawing out connections between the patchworked nature of the ambiguous monster created by Shelley and the medium of comics and its monsters.

CHAPTER 2

SWAMP THING

Patchworks and Panoramas in Monster Comics

> Nature is a temple, where the living
> Columns sometimes breathe confusing speech;
> Man walks within these groves of symbols, each
> Of which regards him as a kindred thing.
> [. . .]
> Having dimensions infinitely vast,
> Frankincense, musk, ambergris, benjamin,
> Singing the senses' rapture, and the soul's.
> —*CHARLES BAUDELAIRE*[1]

Swamp Thing is a comics series created by writer Len Wein, known for his work on *X-Men*, and artist Bernie Wrightson, known for his horror comics, in which variations of Frankenstein's monster continued to reappear, as evinced by the Muck Monster in *Eerie* no. 68 (1977). *Swamp Thing* remains their best-known collaboration. Loosely based on a creature introduced in Wein and Wrightson's short story in *The House of Secrets* no. 92 (1971), the first issue of *Swamp Thing* was published a year later in August 1972. Although this first run was short lived, it was made into a film by Wes Craven in 1982, which was accompanied by another attempt at the comic series, this time renamed *The Saga of the Swamp Thing*, written for the most part by Martin Pasko and drawn by Tom Keates for the first nineteen issues. After Pasko's departure, Wein contacted the British writer Alan Moore, an upcoming name in comics at that time, now renowned for his poetic and revisionist writing for comics. Running from January 1984 to September 1987, Moore's run of *Swamp Thing* was drawn by John Totleben and Stephen Bissette, with Bissette later being replaced by Rick Veitch. This run was republished in six volumes as *Saga of the Swamp Thing* by DC Comics' Vertigo imprint between 2009 and 2011. Wein and Wrightson's original *Swamp Thing* stories were also collected, initially as *Swamp Thing: Dark Genesis* in 1991 and later, in 2011, as *Roots of the Swamp Thing*.

Wrightson's Muck Monster is an intermediary between Frankenstein's monster and the Swamp Thing. Told from the perspective of a mouthless anthropomorphic monster brought to life by a disappointed scientist, the story recounts the suffering of the creature as he is killed by his maker moments after being born or animated. The very first panel of the story is a typically dark romantic setting of a cemetery, as the creature announces: "I am! Only of *that* am I *completely certain!*"[2] When his creator dissolves his body in acid and pours the liquid down a drain, the red liquid streams down a rugged terrain that recalls the wild, desolate landscape cherished by many romantic artists, writers, and philosophers. A Burkean aesthetics, combining the horrific and the beautiful, permeates this entire page visualizing the remains of the monster flowing down to the realm of the dead.[3] Miraculously regenerated, the creature returns to try and comfort his maker, only to realize that he had turned mad after confronting his creation's monstrous face. Destined to be solitary forever, the creature seeks comfort and finds a home in the mountains. In this brief story, we find many romantic attributes that we will continue to encounter in the other comics examined here. These include a sympathetic, misunderstood, solitary monster who suffers from his otherness and can often only find comfort in solitude. All of these monsters embark on a quest, motivated by positive sentiments but rarely coming to a happy end.

Horrific Beginnings: Alan Moore, Stephen Bissette, and John Totleben's *Swamp Thing*

Echoes of Wrightson's expressive art and his empathy for monsters reverberate through later versions of *Swamp Thing*. Most of Moore's run was drawn by Stephen Bissette and John Totleben, with covers and colors by Tatjana Wood. All three artists share strong affinities with the horror comics tradition. Moreover, Wood had previously worked on comics by Entertaining Comics (EC Comics) and continued to color DC/Vertigo horror series such as *House of Mysteries*. Moore transforms the human who mutated into a monster in the original *Swamp Thing* stories into a plant elemental, a vegetal consciousness who assumes he was once human.[4] Not only is Moore's Swamp Thing more powerfully connected to all plant life but he is also more directly anchored in the swamps of Louisiana and comments on "the social and cultural histories of racial oppression."[5] In her reading of *Swamp Thing*'s commentary on the history of the US South, Qiana Whitted uses the concept of rememory introduced by Toni Morrison in *Beloved* for "framing an experiential understanding of the present as being physically and psychologically inscribed with traces of the past."[6] It conveys "the lasting materiality of thoughts and emotional resonances": places are imbued with "thought pictures," the affective quality of which is transmitted to others.[7] In *Swamp Thing*, such places can be extended to the more fluid spaces of consciousness through which the protagonist eventually learns to travel. These places also extend to the layers of comics history on which the series is palpably propped, since its very imagery is indebted to Bernie Wrightson's expressive and organic horror comics artwork and the history of horror comics themselves. This particular rememory is loaded in that the monstrosity it depicts and celebrates is mirrored by the monstrosity associated with horror comics during the anticomics movement of the 1950s, which claimed that such works perverted the minds of their readers and which triggered the formation of a regulatory body, the Comics Code Authority (CCA).

Moore's *Swamp Thing* made a point of rejecting the conventions of the CCA and almost completely stopped bearing its seal of approval after its thirtieth issue. The thirty-first issue from December 1984 bears the recurring title of "Sophisticated Suspense."[8] As Jean-Paul Gabilliet points out, the CCA's control had started weakening in the early 1970s with the development of a direct sales network and a reliance on comic book shops replacing the traditional dependence on newsstand distribution.[9] Two years after the thirty-first issue, however, in the wake of renewed protests against explicit, "sick comics," DC introduced a new system of rating comics as "universal," "mature," or "adult."[10] Seen as impeding creative freedom, many of the artists and writers working for DC, including stars such as Moore and Frank Miller, petitioned against this system and its accompanying guidelines.[11] Unaffected by the protests, issues of *Swamp Thing* bore the rating "For Mature Readers" from the fifty-ninth issue (April 1987) onward. This label was later reworded "Suggested for Mature Readers." It was swiftly accompanied by a "brand new format" (from the sixtieth issue onward) and a higher price (one dollar instead of seventy-five cents starting with the sixty-first issue). These changes—a more book-like format, higher price tag, and the eventual shift from newsstands to comic book specialty stores—also mark key steps toward the transformation of comic books into graphic novels.

According to Gabilliet, Moore "transformed *Saga of the Swamp Thing* into a rite-of-passage story grounded in a gothic atmosphere and a scathing rereading of the secondary characters of the DC universe."[12] These characters include Cain, who hosted *House of Mystery*, and Abel from *House of Secrets*, both of which were horror comics series that had run intermittently since the 1950s. Although both series carried the CCA's seal of approval, they did, within limits, continue with the tradition of sensationalist, gory horror comics, such as those produced by EC Comics, which the CCA had effectively censored out of existence. Moore's *Swamp Thing*[13] also introduced new antiheroic characters who went on to star in series of their own. Most notable among these is John Constantine, who combines magical skills with the persona of a detective and pushes the Swamp Thing toward the quest of understanding himself and the extent of his powers.

Mentioning "the shifting boundaries between monstrosity and humanity and how the monster can represent aspirations, even heroic ones," monster studies scholar John Block Friedman brings up the Heap, a precursor to the Swamp Thing who incarnates an "archetypal mantra" of struggle, death, and regeneration.[14] Created by Harry Stein and Mort Leav, the Heap was a German pilot transformed into a monster after a plane crash. In many ways a revamped, more nuanced version of the Heap, the Swamp Thing not only enacts an archetypal mantra but also manifests characteristics and emotions, such as loneliness and love, that are profoundly human, even though his quest is to ultimately transcend the human. While Moore's run of *Swamp Thing* has often been described in gothic terms, reviving styles and tropes of older horror comics, it also has a profound connection to romantic tropes, which already begins with the character's essence as a "plant elemental."[15]

The original Swamp Thing was Alec Holland, a scientist who, with his wife Linda, had invented a biorestorative formula, originally as an anti-aging potion encouraging organic growth in hostile circumstances. The impact of a bomb explosion in his lab threw him into the Louisiana swamps outside, and he woke up as a giant conglomeration of vegetation maintaining the shape of a man: the Swamp Thing. Moore's *Swamp Thing* nuanced the protagonist's identity by making him a vegetal consciousness that thought it was human because it had absorbed Holland's body and mind. It was "a plant that was trying its level best to be Holland."[16] This adds a fluid, nonhuman feature to the Swamp Thing, who nonetheless proves to be more human than many of the other characters by demonstrating an emotionality coupled with a sense of solitude that is essentially human.[17] Coming to terms with his emotions and his essence as a consciousness makes up his quest. In his striving to test and extend the limits of his consciousness, the Swamp Thing also enacts a quintessentially romantic quest.[18]

Resurrected Monstrosity

Notably, the violent acts against the Swamp Thing are often also acts of violence against the environment. This exemplifies the destructive potential of humans, which is embodied by mutant creatures such Woodrue and Nukeface, who are outcomes of a combination of technological hazards and social issues, particularly the tendency to ostracize freaks (which increases Woodrue's resentment against humans) and those confined to the lower ranks of society (having lost his job, Nukeface was a tramp who eventually got addicted to the nuclear waste that turned him into a mutant). On a mythical note, the Swamp Thing alludes to the age-old but elusive figure of the Green Man, a parallel that is evoked by the cover of *Swamp Thing*'s fourth volume, on which the Swamp Thing's face blends in with the vegetation. Comics scholar Colin Beineke sees the "Swamp Thing as a modern day incarnation of the Green Man," embodying Moore's "analysis of the way modern America views the relationship between 'nature' and 'civilization.'"[19] Moreover, the very monstrosity of the creature lies, at least in part, in its embodiment of the gap between humankind and the untamable, vegetal world. Besides his human characteristics, the Swamp Thing's romanticism also lies in his incarnation of the pantheistic ideal, his oneness with the natural world.

The saga begins with the death of the Swamp Thing's archenemy, Anton Arcane. Born into an aristocratic family in the Balkans at the beginning of the twentieth century, Arcane learned to combine magical and medicinal skills to bring to life dead or fatally injured soldiers by stitching them up. The First World War provided him with ample opportunities for experimenting on injured German soldiers. Not completely human, these beings, called "Un-Men," blindly follow Arcane's instructions. It was during the same war that Arcane met an injured pilot who was half man and half plant, another Swamp Thing. Wanting to acquire the Swamp Thing's powers, Arcane tried to lure the pilot into agreeing to a spell transferring those powers, but the pilot eventually saw through his ruse and refused to give in. As a result, Arcane vowed to seek revenge against all Swamp Things. The Louisiana Swamp Thing's attachment to Abigail Arcane, a niece whom Arcane had been abusing since her childhood, only increased Arcane's thirst for vengeance.

Despite his relationship with Abby, which starts and develops over the course of Moore's saga, the series' first issue, "Loose Ends," establishes the Swamp Thing as a lonely figure, having only the remains of his enemy Arcane for company. Continuing his monologue with Arcane as he walks away from his lifeless body, the Swamp Thing remarks: "We're things of the shadow, you and I . . . and there isn't as much shadow . . . as there used to be."[20] These opening panels of the new series establish the Swamp Thing as a monster who is intimately connected to his environment, since he mirrors it through his body. His form is anthropomorphic but his eyes are an inhuman red, signifying not only anger and violence but also energy, in the creative sense of the word. He is also a creature who longs for the past, expressing a romantic nostalgia for a preindustrialized world where nature was dominant and there was room for monsters and shadows, which have now been chased away by "shopping malls and striplights and software."[21]

A little later he loses his life to flamethrowers operated by the Sunderland Corporation's employees working with snipers from the US Defense Department Intelligence (DDI). Like most monsters, the Swamp Thing is thus both alone and persecuted. This persecution is visualized on the page recounting his death in three consecutive, page-wide panels in which he is shown running and getting closer to his persecutors, or being increasingly magnified by them through a reflector sight (fig. 1).[22] The vertical panel covering the rest of this page depicts multiple bullets piercing his flesh, as his arms are raised in despair and his darkened, crumbling shadow becoming all that remains. Punctuating the horizontal panels is the hand of General Sunderland (CEO of Sunderland Corporation), who pushes several pendulums into chaotic movement. Sunderland's persecution and the consequent death of the Swamp Thing plunge the monster into a state of chaotic nonbeing from which he will emerge all the stronger and more grounded in the primal energies and consciousness of the world (and, ultimately, the universe).

Both Arcane and the Swamp Thing are resurrected, and the main narrative thread running through the six books of *Saga of the Swamp Thing* follows Arcane's persecution of the Swamp Thing and Abby, with Sunderland and the DDI being additional enemies. Causing much destruction and havoc by allowing demons from hell to come to earth and creating "a shockwave of nightmare,"[23] Arcane is sent back to hell and condemned to ceaseless torture by demons in the course of the series,[24] leaving open the possibility that he will return as a demon himself in another run of *Swamp Thing*. This is also suggested by the concluding, open-ended quotation from Shelley's *Frankenstein* that closes the issue: "He was soon borne away by the waves and lost in the darkness and distance."[25] He is a threat, then, that can never be completely eliminated and is reborn, unlike Sunderland and the DDI, who eventually meet their end in "Loose Ends (Reprise)" in the saga's final volume. The possibility of reappearance suggested by the quotation is realized by Frankenstein's monster, who appears in "Reunion" in the last volume of the saga. Exemplifying the kind of intertextuality described by Peter Otto, which combines elements from diverse sources and tailors them to fit the comics world, Frankenstein's monster undergoes a cruel remediation as the confused Patchwork Man, who was once Gregori, Arcane's brother, and Abigail's father, brought to life by Arcane in his typical inhuman fashion, animating the body while distorting it and leaving its sutures for all to see. Although his body crumbles to pieces in the swamps, his head remains lost (fig. 2),[26] thus maintaining the possibility of a return as well as the continuation of the "mortal immortal" figure who recurs in both gothic and romantic stories including vampire stories as well as Goethe's *Faust*.[27] Frankenstein's monster is omnipresent in the story. The environmentalist Chester Williams, on seeing the Swamp Thing for the first time, likens him to Frankenstein's monster.[28] Such continuous returns of characters and motifs in comics involve remediation from other media. In *Swamp Thing*, the original connotations of Frankenstein's monster have been merged with other features that increment the ambiguity regarding the inherent evil of monsters. In the case of Gregori Arcane's new form, the horror provoked by the mere sight of Frankenstein's monster is combined with an incremented fragility as a patchwork man who proves to be mortal. The patchworked essence of Frankenstein's monster also reflects the medium of comics.

Swamp Thing retains, alongside allusions to Eugène Thivier's *Cauchemar* sculpture,[29] more overt connections with romantic art, in particular Goya's work: an entire issue is named after Goya's *The Sleep of Reason Produces Monsters* and takes up its theme of embodying nightmares by populating them with deformed bodies and inscribing them into popular print.[30] This indicates a move toward a more bodily and not merely imaginative involvement with the image, to recall Hans Belting's interdependent triad of image, medium, and body. In addition, the manner in which the romantic images have been resurrected and in the process remediated confirms the impact of not only gothic tendencies but also monstrosity itself, which imbues worlds, such as those of *Swamp Thing*, with horror and the even more destabilizing sense of uncertainty.

Also relevant for tracing the effects of romanticism are the implications of ceaseless returning and reanimation in comics as a disavowal of both logic and rationality. Remediation itself is a form of reanimation, resuscitating the material and features of one medium in another. Although essentially driven by commercial concerns, such a practice gives emotions and horrors (the eternal recurrence of one's worst nightmare) precedence, imbuing the story with dark romantic and gothic elements. *Swamp Thing* exemplifies the kind of horror fiction that indulges in "pushing back the barriers, of risking the absurd in order to reach the sublime, just as Jason Woodrue does by eating a tuber of Swamp Thing's" (which leads to Woodrue's euphoric delusions of being at one with the vegetal world).[31] Tied with this is the series' strong emotional element through being not only a tale of horror and adventure but also one of relationships and the difficult road toward acceptance—themes that in themselves are quite common, with the interest in subjective passions and perversions being particularly developed in romanticism,[32] but that are rare for stories with monstrous protagonists.

At the saga's opening, the Swamp Thing describes Arcane as his opposite, a means of defining himself. Both belong to the same world that was full of shadows and open to monsters, which is now fading away. The dialectic between monstrosity and humanity is made explicit early in the saga when the Swamp Thing tells the dead Arcane: "*I had my humanity . . . taken away from me. I've been trying to claw it back*"[33] and points out that Arcane, in contrast, deliberately got rid of his humanity. Later, however, the Swamp Thing's humanity is also seen as a hurdle that he must overcome in order to become invincible.[34] In the nightmare preceding his first regeneration, he desperately holds onto the skeleton of Alec Holland as *his* humanity as other demons try to snatch it away from him.[35] Such constant switching between humanity and monstrosity persists throughout the series. Consequently, the word *monster* is used both for and by the Swamp Thing for himself and for humans as well as for the creatures he has to fight.

That the Swamp Thing will extend beyond his body and fight his internal and external battles on a plane that is out of reach for humans is already evident in "Loose Ends," in which he appears larger than life from behind the panels on two pages showing the director of the DDI, Dwight Wickers, and Sunderland plotting to kill the Swamp Thing as well as the other employees affiliated with the project that led to Alec and Linda Holland's deaths and the rise of the Swamp Thing.[36] These employees include two couples who were close friends of the Hollands, Matthew Cable, an agent of the DDI, and his wife, the white-haired Abigail Arcane, as well as Dennis Barclay, a doctor employed by Sunderland, and his girlfriend, Lizbeth Tremayne, a journalist.

I will now highlight the romantic aspects of the places where most of *Swamp Thing* is situated. This is closely tied to the technique of providing overwhelming, panoramic visualizations, which are examined later on. The kinds of horrors portrayed and their distortion of reality are then discussed. This is followed by a discussion of the many visualizations of psychological states and how they trace the protagonist's quest. Continuing to examine the romantic fascination with the power of the imagination and the questioning of self-identity and its boundaries, the final section traces the intersection of notions of monstrosity, humanity, and artificially animated matter or automatons. It consequently also examines the theme of control and freedom introduced by the presence of automation and animation. The tenuous relationship between humanity and monstrosity, which is embodied by Frankenstein's physically and psychologically broken creature, plays a central role in these readings.

Monstrous, Damaged Environment

The swamps with their abandon to pure nature and solitude are a romantic setting, recalling the mutating forms and intertwined vegetation populating William Blake's plates. They also share similarities with Samuel Palmer's (1805–1881) less realistic renditions of nature, such as *Oak Trees, Lullingstone Park* (1828), the rhythmic forms and intense colors of which are comparable to the forms and palette used in several panels of *Swamp Thing*, among other comics. However, in contrast to the serenity of Palmer's works, *Swamp Thing* indulges in horror after horror involving demons, angry spirits, and ruthless humans. In "The Sleep of Reason" issue, in which the Monkey King, the demon who makes nightmares real (and who, ironically enough, closely resembles a stuffed monkey), is summoned, Goya's aforementioned print is both directly referenced and then echoed by grotesque forms and graphic violence, an echo that resounds throughout the series.[37] The sharp, slanting edges of the panel and the contrasting red tones of "The Sleep of Reason" reproduction suggest, visually, that Goya's print is actually an underlying reference and inspiration of the story about nightmares coming to life and even conquering known reality.

"I think ... they finally ran out of room ... for monsters," muses the Swamp Thing a short time before his first death.[38] Indeed, the Swamp Thing's world "is a red and angry world ... Red things happen there. The world eats your wife ... Eats your friends ... Eats all of the things ... That make you human ... And you become a monster."[39] After making these observations, the Swamp Thing leaves his body and enters a new world, "somewhere quiet ... somewhere *green* and *timeless*."[40] This "green," as opposed to the red of the violent human world, is a place that the Swamp Thing explores with his mind by connecting with other vegetal matter. The Swamp Thing's first experience of this world is disturbed by the infiltration of an old, even forgotten, DC Comics villain, Jason Woodrue, who first appeared as the Plant Master in the *Atom* comics series (from 1962 onward) and turned into the Floronic Man in *Swamp Thing*.[41] Woodrue's infiltration is visualized as an amorphous cancerous body, "painting everything with the sticky darkness of old blood," shooting out tendrils to control vegetation.[42]

Ramsey Campbell describes Woodrue as "Swamp Thing's darker self" who is "more articulate than monsters usually are."[43] Labeled by Sunderland and later a doctor at Arkham Asylum as a freak,[44] Woodrue is an evil, talented botanist who can adopt the vegetal form but is, unlike the Swamp Thing, unable to merge completely with it. In an effort to become like the Swamp Thing, he eats the tubers the Swamp Thing produces in his dormant state. These hallucinogenic roots, functioning like "cosmic litmus paper," provoke different reactions throughout the series,[45] varying according to the proclivities of the person eating them. The Floronic Man ends up taking *Swamp Thing*'s environmental concern to an extreme by proclaiming war on all humans and animals, claiming that he incorporates "the *regret* and *anger* of the *forests*" against all "meat."[46] Paradoxically, he only succeeds in reflecting the inadvertent destruction wreaked by humans on the environment. However, as the Swamp Thing and later Abby tell the delusional Woodrue, plants cannot survive without humans, and the defeated Woodrue, recognizing his mistake, runs away screaming in agony and ends up in Arkham's asylum.[47] Hinting at the series' mutation of the superhero genre on a monstrous, psychological scale, the superheroes or "over-people" of DC Comics' Justice League, who watch over earth from space, are unable to fight Woodrue. Instead, it is the Swamp Thing who succeeds in making Woodrue realize that his destruction epitomizes "the way . . . of *man*," poisoning the vegetal world with personal desires and selfishness.[48]

In "The Nukeface Papers," Nukeface personifies the evil outcomes of nuclear technology and its lingering potential for damage.[49] Revealingly, Nukeface himself does not seem to realize the damage caused. Although the Swamp Thing is undefeatable, his nemeses are also nemeses of the plant world. These include the flamethrowers that were used to kill him, and nuclear energy, which also burns his body and is the cause of his second death. The Swamp Thing therefore corporealizes and anthropomorphizes the presence of the living world of plants, lending it an anthropomorphic animation and mobility that it does not possess. This metamorphosis also gives plants a new kind of presence that captures their connections to other living beings. His humanity consequently involves a humanization of the monster and the vegetal world itself. This in turn highlights the threat and extent of environmental damage and its dire repercussions for humans.

Pointing out that vegetal monsters are somewhat rare, Henri Baudin discerns a tendency of vegetal monsters to combine deadly, animalistic qualities with the potential of vegetation to procreate and spread on very little, which is exaggerated to nightmarish proportions.[50] Describing the eighth chapter of Joris-Karl Huysmans's *À rebours*, literary scholar Aude Campmas mentions how exotic plants are constantly likened to monsters.⁵¹ This exemplifies the ease with which anything unusual and unfamiliar becomes monstrous even if it is only vegetal matter. Huysmans's monsters incorporated, much like Enki Bilal's *Monstre* for the postmodern era as discussed in chapter 3, the decadent fin de siècle mentality: "Les plantes représentèrent le crime ou la dépravation morale, la part monstrueuse du monde" (The plants represent crime and moral depravity, the monstrous side of the world).⁵²

The Swamp Thing's monstrosity combines the vegetal, starting with the fluid vegetation of the swamps, and the human. The coexistence of these two identities is monstrous, since the Swamp Thing is neither one thing nor the other and thus confounds categorical definitions. His human side is repeatedly underscored, as for instance in the issue ". . . a time of running . . ."⁵³ After his battle alongside Jack Kirby's eloquent demon Etrigan against the Monkey King, the Swamp Thing tells a young boy that he, too, was scared upon seeing the Monkey King and facing his worst fear, fire, which was the cause of Alec Holland's death and his own two deaths at the hands of the DDI.⁵⁴ Indeed, the trauma of Holland's death works in two ways, for it is in part his own death and a haunting of what he thought he was, as is evident in the opening pages of *Swamp Thing*'s second volume, when he is visited by Holland's ghost.⁵⁵ This once again underscores how, despite his vegetal essence, he remains human, damaged and haunted by memories, much like Warhole and the other protagonists of *Monstre*.⁵⁶ Coming to terms with his elemental, nonhuman essence defines the Swamp Thing's quest, as elaborated below.

As Woodrue explains to Sunderland, who hired him for his skills as a botanist to study the Swamp Thing's corpse, the creature is a combination of the consciousness of Holland and the vegetation of the swamp.⁵⁷ This highlights the strong link between the monster and his habitat. Like the creature it has engendered, the swamp is also a liminal but secluded place, with its distinctive ecosystem hovering between water and earth. Located in Houma, Louisiana, this swamp is a far cry from the urban environments that prevail in most superhero comics. Hence, while establishing connections with the characters of the multiple worlds of DC Comics, it is evident over the course of the series that the mainstay of superheroes is of only marginal use against the evils faced by the Swamp Thing. As one of the "over-people" or superheroes watching over earth exclaims when Woodrue starts his war against humankind, "We were watching for New York, for Metropolis, for Atlantis . . . but who was watching out for *Lacroix, Louisiana?*"⁵⁸ Later on, Batman is unable to save his city from the onslaught of vegetation caused by the Swamp Thing in an attempt to force the authorities to release Abby.⁵⁹ Batman is also unable to grasp the magnitude of the impending apocalypse as the increasing manifestations of nightmares—vampires, ghosts, and demons becoming more vicious and present in the human world—move toward the awakening of a primordial darkness.[60] Only the Swamp Thing can effectively tackle the psychological facet of the apocalypse.[61] One of the related implications of the shift to a wilder, more unfamiliar terrain is that the enemies, based less on feats of technology and more on nightmares, are different from the villains usually fought by superheroes.

Given the interpenetration of horror and reality in the comic, the swamp is described as Abby and the Swamp Thing's "damp cosmos," secluded from the madness of the real world, able to exist independently; and it is here that the two settle down at the end of the saga.[62] When, in "The Brimstone Ballet," Arcane claims to have taken over the swamps as part of the apocalypse he is ushering in, the balance of power is reversed and Arcane is defeated when he confronts the Swamp Thing in the swamp, affirming the close connection between the creature and his environment.[63] It is also here that the Swamp Thing affirms the elemental force within him instead of being the creature who thought he was Alec Holland.[64] The swamps, the original habitat of the Swamp Thing, therefore also play a crucial role in the creature's understanding of himself. This is comparable to the liberating effects that a natural setting, unmarred by the effects of industrialization, has on romantic artists and thinkers.

That the Swamp Thing is the only plant elemental to still survive in the world underscores both his uniqueness and the solitude that accompanies such a difference.[65] This solitude is reinforced when he encounters other beings who were once like him but now form the Parliament of Trees. Located in the depths of a Brazilian forest, this Parliament of Trees is formed by elementals who have "grown too *wise* for the distractions of the world."[66] The place they inhabit is tinged with "an unbearable *nostalgia* . . . a haunting sense . . . of *familiarity* . . . and *déjà vu*" for the Swamp Thing, since the memories preserved in the forest contributed to the formation of his consciousness.[67] Consequently, this is the one place beyond the swamps that he is tempted to call home. Yet there is a circularity in the nature of the stories as well as his own emergence, for, as the elemental tells the Swamp Thing, "[t]he stories . . . of all . . . that are rooted here . . . have their similarities," adding that he, like the other elementals, is made from a "consciousness . . . borrowed . . . from a dead *man*."[68] Hence the World War I plane that seemed familiar to the Swamp Thing is the relic of his predecessor, a German pilot, who went through the same pattern of a traumatic death and regeneration: "A man . . . dies in *flames* . . . a monster . . . rises from the *mire* . . . sacrifice . . . and resurrection . . . that is *always* . . . our beginning."[69] This mire, which is the birthplace of the monster, has a distinctive consistency that is neither solid nor liquid, and is thus a negation of space, much like the place Baudelairian ennui has been situated in.[70] "Stories shape the world . . . The glaciers have their legends. The ocean bed entertains its own romances," says the Swamp Thing.[71] In a similar manner, the swamp shapes its creature and the boundary transgressing stories about it.

In a world with retreating shadows, Abby sees Gotham as a dark city, full of shadows.[72] The modernized, capitalistic city with its "heart, pumping green blood to the gray giant," its high rates of poverty and crime, is not unlike the dismal city we encounter in Blake's poem "London."[73] When the Swamp Thing, exploiting his god-like powers, declares war on Gotham in order to get Abby back, the entire city turns into a wilderness, with modern life strangled by vegetation: the green takes over, "sidewalks begin to bleed *emerald*," moss appears on skyscrapers, drains are choked, and city life halted.[74] This transformation of the cityscape also brings about a change in its inhabitants, who return to a "primal," lawless state. This once again confirms the effects of space on the beings within it, the interdependence of animate and inanimate, which was emphasized in romantic ideology through its embrace of the natural.

The organic connection between bodies and spaces is also concretized by the blue planet on which the Swamp Thing finds himself during his exile from earth triggered by his third death. Surrounded by a void and replete with rare gases like helium,[75] everything on the planet is blue. Blue is the color "of loneliness . . . of melancholy," and correspondingly the Swamp Thing is the planet's sole inhabitant.[76] Something of the sublime can be gleaned from the opening page, the panels of which gradually progress toward a magnification of the surroundings and the diminution and abstraction of the protagonist, albeit not to the same extent as in the *Hellboy* panels examined later on (see fig. 13): here the sublime is enhanced by the rich, fantastic detail of the images, which evoke, without really being in themselves, iconic collages such as those used by Jack Kirby in *Fantastic Four* by incorporating space photographs.[77] In this issue—produced by Moore's central artistic core for *Swamp Thing*, namely Bissette, Totleben, and Wood as colorists, collaborating with inker Alfredo Alcala and penciller Rick Veitch (who also took up writing *Swamp Thing* stories after Moore)—strong links are maintained with the imagery of the previous issues, particularly its combination of horror and fantastic comics iconography. The blue planet can be interpreted as a metaphorical space where the Swamp Thing learns more about himself and comes to terms with his solitude. It is also the place where he gets to experiment with his body and explore its relationship to the planet's alien atmosphere.

This, like the psychological visualizations in *Swamp Thing*, exemplify what Scott Bukatman calls the "plasmatic possibility" of comics, incorporating the impossible, which is very often accompanied by untamable, rebellious characters and spaces.[78]

Similar to the Swamp Thing's organic form as well as the mutating horrors populating his universe, the breaking down of worlds and realities is recurrent in the series. This culminates during the Swamp Thing's outer space travels when, while trying to reach the mysterious "source" of all universes in "Wavelength," he and the comics deity Metron are tricked by the protectors of the source into believing that they have entered it by bombarding them with the earth's entire history condensed in a moment.[79] Space and time also merge in an earlier volume, when the primordial darkness is woken.[80] A little later, Constantine and the Swamp Thing are teleported to a satellite where they can see the multiverses ending as a result of the impending apocalypse: in a glass globe, they watch the remaining worlds merge into each other, resulting in temporal and spatial destabilization.[81] Such dissolution of time and space is the ultimate horror, and it persists as a realm beyond hell where the original darkness resides.[82]

Secrets and mysteries themselves have served as places in the DC universe, notably as structures or houses that already appeared in the 1950s in *The House of Mystery* (1951) and *The House of Secrets* (1958).[83] Both series were increasingly constrained by the Comics Code Authority's restrictions and had to tailor their tales of horror in order to fit in with the CCA's stringent requirements. Run by the biblical Cain and Abel, these houses allude to metafictional concerns regarding comics stories and the constrained conditions of their production. Some constraints are imposed by regulating authorities. Other constraints take the form of the requirements of continuity, spatiotemporal, and generic limits. Continuity in particular was a topical issue: between April 1985 and March 1986, DC comics orchestrated the *Crisis on Infinite Earths* crossover event, written by Marv Wolfman with art by George Perez, to level out the contradictions in continuity created by parallel universes. As the Swamp Thing and his allies put together an army to battle the unconceivable, primordial darkness that has been the ultimate result of the horrific paranormal activities in the earlier issues of the saga, Cain points out the existential facet of such polarized battles between good and evil for the stories populating comics as well as his own biblical story: "On the *battlefields* beneath us, all our *stories* of *right* and *wrong* may come to their inarguable conclusion ... and what then. [...] [W]hat shall become of us *then*?"[84] Similarly, when wandering through the House of Secrets, Abel, much to Abby's annoyance, points out that all things that seem real are in fact stories insofar as they have already happened: "*everything* is made of stories."[85] Using a large ring as a symbol of the circularity of stories, he eventually reveals the secret that the Swamp Thing she knew was not the first of his kind and that his creation was not an accident but a defense mechanism of the earth, which needed "an elemental *champion*."[86] These hard times are brought about by Arcane's unending need to unleash evil.

Swamp Thing, like the other comics discussed here, hovers between reality and fantasy, with each indiscriminatingly interacting with the other, as during the shooting of a soap opera set in the colonial era, when the actors start believing that they are the characters they are playing.[87] As with most conflicts in the *Swamp Thing*, this strange behavior is provoked by demonic, supernatural forces, raising the undead while exacerbating the conflicts of the contemporary world ranging from environmental issues to racism (as in the case of the colonial-era drama). Such exacerbation enhances the links between the real and the fantastic, which are embodied by the figure of the monster himself. Moreover, as suggested by the art of Goya and Blake, representations of horrific unrealities not only give free rein to the imagination but are also imbued with symbolic significance that is often only barely removed from reality, as in the case of Goya's graphic Disasters of War. The overlap between reality and fantasy is accompanied by a dark ambivalence between good and evil. A similar ambiguity is incorporated by the monstrous protagonists in this book. This ambiguity also pervades their unsteady worlds.

In *Swamp Thing*, a romantic ambivalence between good and evil is exemplified by the anticlimactic resolution of the seemingly unstoppable primordial darkness. In the Swamp Thing's words, the primordial darkness is a monstrosity that is "too *big* ... to even fully grasp ... its *shape* ... it seems to be ... like a *mountain* ... or an *island* ... moving endlessly *forward*."[88] This brings in monstrous characteristics that were already suggested in the beginning; the comparison with the mountain indicates the creature's magnitude, which can take sublime dimensions, and the comparison with the island indicates his solitude. Most monstrous, however, is the impossibility of defining the being as well as its amorphousness: resembling a cloud, it swallows everything in its path and changes form and dimensions when attacked. Significantly, the darkness is itself in pain, and longs for knowledge and understanding.[89] This pain started when light first came into being and forced the darkness to question what it was, needing assurance of its existence through a name and consequently an identity.[90] As it tells Etrigan after swallowing him: "I have a very great *need*. Before *light*, *I* was; endless, without *name* or *need* of name. Then *light* came. Witnessing its *otherness*, I suffered my first knowledge of *self*, and all contentment *fled*."[91] When Etrigan answers that its name is evil, the dissatisfied being throws him out. Only the Swamp Thing gives the darkness a satisfactory answer: admitting that he does not know what evil is, the Swamp Thing echoes the words of the Parliament of Trees, who insisted that there was no evil, only the circle of life in which everything comes from and returns to the soil, flourishing and decaying to give way to more life and death.[92] Letting the Swamp Thing go, the darkness is contemplative and then forms a crooked hand to reach out to, and then merge with, light's perfect golden hand stretching from heaven.[93] Thus, light and darkness, heaven and hell, are mitigated through their interdependence. "In the heart of *darkness*, a *flower* blossoms, *enriching* the shadows with its promise of *hope* . . . In the fields of *light*, an *adder* coils, and the radiant tranquility is lent *savor* by its sinister *presence*" echoes the change introduced by romantic consciousness.[94] Monsters and humans embody a similar interdependence of opposites. Dreams and reality form a comparable couple, locked in a Quasimodo-Esmeralda embrace that is only possible in death.

Animated Dreams and Nightmares

While the Swamp Thing regrets that there are not enough shadows for monsters like him, shadows or horror take over the lives of most of the human characters in the story, including Dennis and Liz, both of whom become psychotic.[95] In a desperate effort to hold a crumbling relationship together, Dennis tricks Liz into believing that Sunderland is still after them and uses it as an excuse to shut her away from the world, consequently breaking, in Abby's words, "*every bone* in her soul" and making her fully dependent on him.[96] That Dennis had been in Vietnam[97] renders Abby's comment about Liz applicable to other characters in the face of monstrous impossibilities, as concretized by the patchwork body of Frankenstein's monster that Abby's father ends up in: "It doesn't take much to dismantle a human being. We come apart so easily."[98] Already the mere imagining of monsters has disastrous consequences in *Swamp Thing*, as exemplified by the Monkey King's power. As mentioned above, Goya's *The Sleep of Reason Produces Monsters* appears twice in the Monkey King story, having been bought by Jason Blood, Etrigan's human counterpart, who is heavily, but not completely, under Etrigan's control.[99] This is the first issue in which the dangers of imagining evil are raised since the Monkey King feeds on dreamers' fears and mutates to mimic their nightmares. One volume later, Etrigan tells the Swamp Thing during their journey through hell that its "halls were carved by *men* while yet they breathed."[100]

Most of the evil that unfolds in the saga is prefigured or augured by nightmares. In "Love and Death," Abby's dreams about the Swamp Thing disintegrate into nightmares involving insects on her skin when she moves to a new house with an apparently reformed Matt, who is under Arcane's control and has started doing a job at a company ominously called Blackriver Recorporations, where all of the employees turn out to be resurrected psychopaths.[101] Arcane's violence against Abby unfolds primarily on a psychological level, by making her nightmares come to life, invading her dreams, and haunting her with the smell of burning insects. These insects symbolize Arcane, who had been restricted to the form of a fly before taking over Matt's dying body in a car crash.[102] Throughout the series, Arcane retains the form of mutating insects with disintegrating human faces. As with Matt's delusions, Abby's nightmares have horrifically tangible consequences, making her feel as if she is losing her mind and eventually resulting in her death and banishment to hell due to Arcane's plotting. As the Swamp Thing carries Abby's body away from Arcane and his zombies, he realizes that his nightmares have in fact been hinting toward future events, since the Abby in his dream had seen Matt talking with the insect-mutant Arcane.[103] The Swamp Thing likewise walked through Nukeface's dream of the sunken town of Blossomville ruined by nuclear waste, which foreshadowed his battle with the vampire colony in another town, Rosewood.[104]

Matt Cable can make his dreams and delusions real, seeking solace in them and alcohol instead of tackling the issues of his relationship.[105] Not only does Matt indulge in sexual fantasies, but he makes his imagination come to life in a manner that eerily recalls Abby's disturbed childhood, when she was convinced that she was surrounded by supernatural beings but had no proof of it.[106] Hearing voices or experiencing foreboding dreams and visions made Abby suspect that she was a paranoid schizophrenic.[107] However, her nightmares and suspicions of paranormal activity often predict the near future, as was the case with Woodrue's attack on the human world through plants and the demons conjured through Matt's imagination. It is on a similar, psychic level that her sexual relationship with the Swamp Thing unfolds.

Both the Swamp Thing and Abby indulge in daydreams about their ideal life of acceptance denied to them, both as a couple and individually, for Abby is not only a foreigner but also stands out because of her striking white hair. As explored in the last section, the aspect of animation driving these illusions, which range from being carefully constructed by the characters themselves to the nightmares that they are forced to live through, introduces a tussle between the animated and the animator (be it a villain or the writer-artist team behind the comic), while simultaneously highlighting the fluctuation between reality and fantasy. Although the constructedness of Abby and the Swamp Thing's dreams is made apparent, with settings resembling film sets and people being mere fleeting specters, Gregori's illusions are even more fragile, ripped apart at random, like the mind conceiving them. While Gregori is also caught up in his memories, his narrative is more broken and full of contradictions. Unlike Abby and the Swamp Thing, he is unable to give in to his illusions even while he constructs them because he cannot, not even for a fleeing moment, go beyond the jarring differences between past and present, his crumbling mix of illusions and reality.[108]

Besides dreaming, another means of generating illusions is the hallucinogenic fruit dropped by the Swamp Thing, which merges his experience with the proclivities of the person eating it. Hence, while eating the fruit enables Abby to have a spiritual-sexual experience with the Swamp Thing,[109] it provokes megalomania in Woodrue. Similarly, the experience of the bullying drug addict Milo Flynn involves reliving Alec Holland's death by fire, as well as the combat with the mother of the vampires and the Monkey King.[110] For Milo, the world turns into a "monster city [...] a whole planet full of *torture, madness, death*," with the delusions, which are nonetheless founded on reality, forcing him to run into oncoming traffic.[111]

In this respect, it is worthwhile recalling Bukatman's observation that dream in the American context "stands not for indolence or sloth, escape or decadence, but for a creative engagement with the world, an imaginative engagement that has an effect on the world, that, it can be said, builds a world."[112] This legitimization of dream space holds for both *Swamp Thing* and *Hellboy*, whose later battles also unfold in supernatural realms rather than the real world. As already shown, *Swamp Thing*'s nightmarish world is often foreshadowed by dreams and unfolds on a psychological plane: nightmare overshadows reality due to the demons awoken by Arcane. Since the world is affected by the psychic and psychological states of its inhabitants, evil is defeated essentially by acquiring internal strength. For the Swamp Thing, this involves coming to terms with his nonhuman, vegetal essence as well as Alec's trauma.

The Swamp Thing's Quest to Become an Elemental

Owing to the Swamp Thing's essence as an "elemental" being who is not constrained to his body, visualizations of the psychological plane are inevitable. The consummation of the Swamp Thing and Abby's love, for instance, unfolds on this plane of disembodied, abstract consciousness after she has eaten one of his hallucinogenic tubers, which makes her absorb his consciousness and see the world through his eyes, revealing the interconnectedness and beauty of the world.[113] The episode evokes an idyll and a shunning of the confines of a hostile reality, provoked by an exotic fruit, much like the Victorian poet Alfred Tennyson's "The Lotos-Eaters." However, in keeping with the series' romantic inclinations, the same disassociation that is painted as laziness and delusion in Tennyson's poem is celebrated as a spiritual union and the establishment of a deeper connection with the world.

The Swamp Thing's development unfolds through out-of-body experiences. In visualizations of these experiences, the Swamp Thing retains his body, which eventually becomes fluid and merges with other plant life or, in the case of sex, with Abby.[114] Romanticism relied on symbols comparable to the visualizations of psychological realms in *Swamp Thing* for capturing reality. The Swamp Thing's psychological visualizations function as realms where the story's conflicts are resolved rather than as pathways into escapist realms.[115] These conflicts in turn are tied to the Swamp Thing's monstrosity, which provokes unrelenting persecution and solitude. Traumatic memories of Holland's death have already left their scars on the Swamp Thing. "They wouldn't let me human ... and I became ... a monster. But they wouldn't let me be a monster ... so I became a *plant*,"[116] the Swamp Thing tells Woodrue when he starts manipulating the green world. The persecution of others is consequently endless, an omnipresent threat, as manifested by Arcane's endless hate.

However, it is through the Swamp Thing's struggles against his enemies that he learns to harness his inner strength. During his conflict with Woodrue, for instance, he acquires a deeper understanding of his close ties to the vegetal consciousness. By destroying his body, Nukeface makes him realize that he does not need a body, and he gradually learns to create new forms for himself through his mind. Nukeface's attack, being the first effective attack on the Swamp Thing's body since the DDI shooting, forces him "to try ... to leave [his] body ... send ... [his] mind ... out into ... the *green*."[117] This development strengthens what can be described as the Neoplatonic facet of the Swamp Thing and his psychological journey. Neoplatonic symbols, discernible in the work of romantic artists such as Blake, emphasize the interconnectedness of all elements in the universe; the Swamp Thing gets his power from a similar, closely interconnected network. Even the apocalypses ushered in by Arcane and other dark forces, such as the Brujería wizards, thrive on the links between material and immaterial realms.[118] This interlinking is also reflected by the page layouts: as with Abby and the Swamp Thing's first sexual encounter,[119] the Swamp Thing's rebirth is based on one large image that is intersected by several panels converging toward the center of the page and capturing the progression of thoughts and experiences (fig. 3).[120] As already suggested, such single- or double-page spreads evoke the romantic panorama or all-encompassing image. Notably, the Swamp Thing's third death is not an outcome of his being burned but rather the loss of his ability to connect with the green, brought about by a forced change in his "bioelectrical" configuration.

It is only after Arcane sends Abby to hell that the Swamp Thing realizes he is not confined to his body and learns to control where he travels.[121] Once in hell, the Swamp Thing finds several superheroes who help him save Abby's soul from hell, starting with the Deadman or Boston Brand, who is followed by the Phantom Stranger and eventually the Spectre.[122] Recovering Abby involves going through, in the Spectre's words, the "borderlands of *form* and *reason*," alluding to the subversiveness inherent in the lack of form;[123] from the monsters discussed here, both *Monstre*'s Warhole and the Swamp Thing openly indulge in formlessness and mutations. Being a demon, Hellboy is also able to access realms beyond earth and human reality, although his body remains a constant instead of being a "shade" of the actual body on earth, as is the case in the Swamp Thing's otherworldly wanderings. The lack of space and time in *Swamp Thing*'s hell increments its horror, since regular magic and defense mechanisms are useless there.[124]

The Swamp Thing's birth after being burned by Nukeface therefore leads to a new realization of his capabilities, giving him more independence and changing him as he understands the extent of the possibilities open to him.[125] Death and rebirth strengthen the Swamp Thing, on both psychic and corporeal scales, and he boldly declares to John Constantine: "I ... know ... what ... I ... am!"[126] However, it is thanks to Constantine and the different situations he forces the Swamp Thing to resolve in a world where vampires and zombies are gaining power and encroaching upon reality, that the Swamp Thing grasps the extent of his regenerating powers, which remain unconstrained by space and time. While fighting Rosewood, Illinois's displaced settlement of vampires who breed underwater in a pool of nuclear waste, the Swamp Thing's initial defeat at the hands of their monster leads to his realization that his limitations stem from the fact that he remains too human in his thoughts and actions.[127] In his next encounter with the vampires and their monster, the Swamp Thing extends his force to the entire mass of land and water surrounding the dump, merging with it and channeling it in order to inundate the vampire settlement, realizing: "I can ... *regrow* myself ... I am *beyond* ... any *harm*."[128]

The Swamp Thing's trip to the Parliament of Trees visualizes his "mental immersion" into the older minds as a falling of his body through unknown terrain and in the water of their "bottomless ... *memories*."[129] This is when he realizes that he still has not fully understood the potential of his vegetal being and of "how *limited* ... how *human* ... I have been in my *thinking*."[130] He learns that he is not limited to a certain size or shape and can even animate other objects with his consciousness. That the Swamp Thing still has to mature is made evident by the "*disturbance* and uncertainty" that the Parliament of Trees senses in him, which is still an outcome of his human nature, since "[f]lesh doubts, wood *knows*."[131]

The essence of the Swamp Thing as an elemental is romantic in itself, retaining qualities comparable to what nineteenth-century philosopher and essayist Thomas Carlyle saw in Muhammad, the prophet of Islam: "a fiery mass of Life cast up from the great bosom of Nature itself,"[132] incarnating "an elemental force."[133] Constantly regenerating himself from ruins, the Swamp Thing merges with the elements and attains a deeper understanding of his essence as an elemental.[134] To fully realize the scope of this elemental power, the Swamp Thing must confront his, or more accurately Alec Holland's, trauma and memory, the rememory that persists in the swamps and in his very being. This also involves drawing the line between his identity and that of Alec, which forms a part of his internal quest. "I have his consciousness ... his *memories* ... but he is dead ... I will not ... be haunted ... by myself," thinks the Swamp Thing as Alec Holland's ghost appears behind him.[135] The ghost resembles a black-and-white, flickering hologram. Like Shakespeare's murdered king of Denmark, Holland's ghost can only suggest, not speak. The ghost leads the Swamp Thing through scenes of Alec's past: his happy life with his wife, his work on the biorestorative formula, and his murder by the Sunderland Corporation. When the Swamp Thing tries to prevent Alec from dying again, he realizes his powerlessness in the illusion, for he is unable to use physical force on the specters.[136] Uncontrollable and untiring, Holland's ghost like the ghost in *Hamlet* embodies traumatic memory.[137] In forcing the Swamp Thing to confront the wrongs of the past, the ghost also offers him a means of redemption: after waiting by the banks of the lake in which Alec had fallen while burning, the Swamp Thing witnesses himself appear, and it is his unspeaking, ghostly self who ultimately leads him to Holland's skeleton, enabling the Swamp Thing to fill the grave he had desperately dug at the beginning of the story in the hope of resolving his identity confusion with Alec.

Burying Alec's skeleton and the consequent assertion of his being is another step in the Swamp Thing's journey or quest toward becoming an elemental. Yet another step involves overcoming the fear of fire stemming from the trauma of Alec's death. He overcomes this fear in "Strange Fruit" when, instead of curing his burning body after a shot, he stokes the fire and goes into the haunted house in order to destroy the power that was manipulating the locals' minds.[138]

Regarding the romantic quest and dreams as analogues, Frye interprets the quest in terms of a dream analysis, with the quest-romance being "the search of the libido or desiring self for a fulfillment that will deliver it from the anxieties of reality but will still contain that reality."[139] The confrontation with Alec's ghost and his own appearance in "Burial" underscores the Swamp Thing's solitude and projects it on the loneliness of Alec's skeleton, which had been abandoned by both Alec's flesh and his mind.[140] It also alludes to Woodrue's description of the Swamp Thing as "just a ghost. A ghost dressed in weeds."[141] On the other hand, it is safer for the Swamp Thing to exist as a ghost or a hallucination instead of forcing people to confront an abnormal reality.[142]

The quest must be carried out alone, as the Parliament of Trees makes apparent through its laconic answers and refusal to let the Swamp Thing stay among them and learn more, much to the Swamp Thing's sadness, as he tells Constantine: "They were creatures . . . like me . . . like me . . . and they cast me *out*."[143] This reaction is human, and it is because of the Swamp Thing's humanity that the Parliament of Trees rejects him. Although he remembers their teachings, it takes him the entire course of the saga to learn how to shun all human inclinations, especially the wildfires of power and anger.[144] Constantine echoes the Parliament of Trees' advice, predicting the Swamp Thing's giving in to his anger and the exploitation of his god-like powers.[145] Indeed, a little later, blinded by fury after Abby's imprisonment as sex offender, the Swamp Thing starts acting like a vengeful god, likening himself to disastrous natural forces such as hurricanes and earthquakes.[146]

In the saga, the Swamp Thing's quest is therefore one of self-understanding, entailing the acceptance of his vegetal essence and taking responsibility for his powers. His inevitable solitude is also a fulfilled one, thanks to his connections with the green. Two kinds of solitude are hence distinguishable in the series, one being fulfilling and illuminating (like the kind eulogized by romantic art and philosophy) and the other being a void (like the one experienced by Woodrue once he realized he was delusional and had no real connections with the green,[147] or entailed by hell, where, as the Stranger tells the Swamp Thing, "[e]ach soul must enter *alone* . . . otherwise, how could it truly be *hell*?").[148] This solitude becomes complete after the Swamp Thing's third death, when the DDI agents use napalm combined with a communications scrambler that changes the Swamp Thing's bioelectrical configuration, dislocating his "electroskeleton"[149] and thus preventing him from reestablishing a relationship with the vegetal consciousness, the green. He is consequently exiled to outer space and travels to many planets before learning how to modify his wavelength in order to synchronize it with the earth's vegetation. The first of these planets is the blue planet, and his stay there becomes a quest for overcoming loneliness, coming out of the limbo of the deserted blue planet as well as the rut of his memories and desires.[150] The biggest hurdle is overcoming his tendency to lose himself in daydreams of a perfect life with Abby.[151] The Swamp Thing continues the quest by risking further contact with the void, and, after destroying the comforting illusions he had taken days to construct, he flies off "into *territories unglimpsed* and *unfathomable* . . . into the wild blue yonder."[152] On returning to earth, the Swamp Thing's spiritual growth is indicated by his changing color with the dusk. This oneness with the universe is further underscored by the portrayal of his face spreading across the space of two pages.[153] The use of double-page spreads, especially in *Swamp Thing*, evokes another romantic feature: fascination with the panorama and the subsequent popularity of large-scale landscape paintings aimed at providing an all-encompassing experience.[154]

When, a little later, he constructs a fairy-tale house in a large, exotic plant for himself and Abby, the Swamp Thing seems to have completed the second stage of the quest, as described by Bloom: he has become more distanced from revolutionary activities and, after concentrating on personal growth, has resolved the ambiguities within himself and liberated his imagination.[155] He becomes a real god, distanced from the activities of humans, understanding why the Parliament of Trees chose to remain "rooted . . . inert and omnipotent."[156]

After returning to earth, killing his killers and reuniting with Abby, the Swamp Thing starts following, like the Parliament of Trees, "the way of the wood," which entails watching as guardian of the earth rather than using its power to manipulate the flow of life.[157] This is a contrast to the earlier, intense empathy that the Swamp Thing felt, absorbing and being paralyzed by the world's pain when the apocalypse started, hearing "the *moans*, the *whimpering* that people made deep in their *souls*. He heard the *bedlam* of a mass *mind* faced with *extinction*."[158] Similarly, on being bombarded with the earth's history and memories of Abby during his exile, the Swamp Thing temporarily loses his mind.[159]

The Monster's Humanity, Monstrous Humanity

While acquiring greater significance and ambiguity during the romantic era, monstrous humans, as Dennis Todd points out, were not unknown to the literature of the Enlightenment. Francis Bacon's Richard III, for instance, is described as a monster because of his detachment from all human emotions, with his body being as deformed as his mind.[160] This assumption of the body and the mind as mirrors of each other is overthrown in romanticism, most blatantly by Hugo's protagonists. Similarly, contemporary comics worlds have not merely "run out of room ... for monsters," but the monsters themselves are "getting harder to *recognize*."[161] Just like Heinrich von Kleist's description of the marionettes' grace or the human characteristics of Frankenstein's monster, the boundaries between monsters and humans are blurred in *Swamp Thing*. While helping the Swamp Thing in the realm of the dead, the Stranger describes Etrigan as "[t]he demon that fancies himself half a man."[162] This humanity is not only incorporated by the human form of Jason Blood but also by Etrigan's demanding, soon after the Stranger's remark, a white flower that the Stranger had picked from heaven in exchange for gathering an army of elite demons to help the Swamp Thing fight against the original darkness.[163] In "Mysteries in Space," Adam Strange, a human who is randomly teleported between Earth and the planet Rann, and the first to befriend the Swamp Thing in space, muses on how he, due to subtle differences from the Rannians—body hair, an appendix—is a monster, an ape man, in their eyes.[164] In the case of the Swamp Thing, however, the fluctuation between human and monster is at its strongest.

"The big green man, he's my friend," Abby tells a child early in the saga, and she continues to emphasize the human side of the Swamp Thing by insisting on calling him Alec.[165] Yet the public reaction to Abby and the Swamp Thing's relationship suggests that monsters and humans cannot mix. This strong reaction, which leads to Abby's imprisonment as a sex offender, indicates that the very possibility of monsters and humans mixing is unacceptable, since the boundaries between the two are never blatant; monsters can act in a human manner and humans can become monstrous, as epitomized by the villains in *Swamp Thing*, primarily Arcane but also Woodrue, Nukeface, and the serial killer, the Bogeyman, whose apparent death makes the Swamp Thing wonder: "Another monster dead ... How many more? How many more ... before this country ... has been squeezed dry ... of nightmares?"[166] Here, the monster is used in its arguably most recurrent, colloquial form, designating particularly vicious, cold-blooded criminals.[167]

The Swamp Thing himself is not above playing the conventional role of the frightening, ruthless monster when facing enemies, like the Bogeyman, when his sudden, angry eruption from the ground takes over a single splash page;[168] or during his attack on Gotham, when he lets vegetation take over the city while he adopts the form of a colossal monster trampling everything in his wake.[169] Yet this monster recalls the human form by standing upright, displaying anthropomorphic feet, a rib cage (albeit inversed), and joints.

Although the Swamp Thing's appearance is monstrous, he also shares many similarities with the human body, resembling a vegetal écorché after having painfully formed his internal organs to mime those of a human. Already this anthropomorphic form that is adopted and discarded at will when he explores his powers as an elemental, personifies the Swamp Thing's simultaneous humanity and monstrous otherness. While this is an issue for all of the comics monsters discussed here, the Swamp Thing's story stands out in that it is a quest to clear the misperception of ever having been human and to understand the scope of powers that come with his otherness. As discussed above, the nature of the quest as an internal journey toward a more profound understanding as well as the unsettled categories of monstrosity and humanity are romantic. Correspondingly, apart from the few occasions during which the Swamp Things acts as a monster or is perceived as a threat, characters usually notice the Swamp Thing's humanity. "Flesh ... speaks ... wood ... *listens*," declares the Parliament of Trees, clearly demarcating the line between an elemental and a human, for the Swamp Thing insists on speaking instead of absorbing the wisdom already present in the earth.[170]

The creator of the original Swamp Thing, Len Wein, described him as "everyone's favorite muck-encrusted mockery of man."[171] Wein and Wrightson's original story was based on the familiar superhero origin story in which an accident or attack, often chemically infused, both traumatizes and transforms the protagonist. These traumatic memories, and descriptions of the Swamp Thing as, for instance, "a twisted *caricature* of humanity," were already present in the original *Swamp Thing* story;[172] the tenuous line between monstrosity and humanity has therefore been a running theme in *Swamp Thing*. However, Moore's shifting of the emphasis from the Swamp Thing's human essence to his monstrous essence radically changed the perspective on the monstrosity versus humanity debate.

As evident in the name he chooses for himself, the Swamp Thing asserts his thingness, his not being Alec.[173] This change occurs after his discovery of Woodrue's report on him. Woodrue's dissection of the Swamp Thing's corpse revealed the extent of his monstrosity: while Woodrue was hoping to find another hybrid human like himself, he found purely vegetal matter that was mimicking human insides without functioning like them.[174] Similar to Wein, Woodrue describes the Swamp Thing as a "pathetic, misshapen parody," "a plant that was trying its level best to be Holland,"[175] but was only "the moss-encrusted *echo* of a man. Not a man at all."[176] The Swamp Thing's agony on reading Woodrue's report and notes is transposed into insatiable anger at having lost the one thing that was keeping him alive: "[T]hroughout his *miserable* existence, the only thing that could have kept him *sane* was the hope that he might one day regain his *humanity*."[177] This is also the lost hope of Frankenstein's monster, who desperately struggles for acceptance and a "normal" life before giving up.

On meeting Matt and Abigail in the swamps where he had planted the Swamp Thing's body, Woodrue describes the damage to the Swamp Thing as being essentially psychological and not physical.[178] Hence, the Swamp Thing, like all of the monsters in this book, is traumatized, a condition mostly associated with humans and animals. The reader soon enters the nightmares plaguing the dormant Swamp Thing as he tries to deal with the fact that he is not who he thought he was.[179] Consequently, he goes through both Alec's loss of his wife Linda as well as his loss of Alec. As he continues to struggle through the nightmares, his humanity is reduced to a fragile skeleton, all that is left of Alec after the worms.[180] Trying to encourage the Swamp Thing with platitudes, the skeleton urges him to continue running the race that humanity is thrust into. It is only after burying the skull that the Swamp Thing attains peace and a new kind of freedom.[181]

During his coma in the swamps, the Swamp Thing dreams of Alec and Linda's wedding reception at which Linda sinks into the ground and Alec is zipped into a mud suit by the guests with the pretext of helping to get Linda back (fig. 4).[182] Eventually, however, the guests end up scooping out bits of his body like mud. "[W]here's Alec?" Abby asks Matt, looking at the remains of the body, to which Matt replies: "Alec isn't in there."[183] This nightmare from early in the saga illustrates the identity confusion haunting the Swamp Thing and also suggests that such confusion lies at the existential core of monstrosity. In his nightmare, the Swamp Thing ends up retrieving both Linda's and Alec's remains from the worms, but he is only able to carry Alec's skeleton. As he tries to fight off the zombies, who also include Arcane, from grabbing the skeleton, he exclaims: "It's my *humanity* ... it's all I've got *left*."[184] "Tell it to the *marines*, son! [...] We *all* lost our humanity. We *all* need patchin' up," retort the zombies, confirming the fluid lines between humans and monsters that persist through the saga and are often blurred through the impact of trauma, as in the case of the Swamp Thing and Matt Cable. Alec's trauma resonates through the Swamp Thing's being and identity: "I have his consciousness... his *memories*... but he is dead... I will not... be haunted... by myself."[185]

Although the burial from the Swamp Thing's grotesque dream is eventually carried out, it entails reliving Alec's last moments and his own emergence from the swamps. At first unable to bury the ghost, the Swamp Thing is also unable to control it, as it forces the Swamp Thing to experience Alec's life and violent death all over again. Even after the burial, Alec's memory and trauma of burning to death persist through the saga as a reminder of the Swamp Thing's humanity. Moreover, the Swamp Thing's "birth," the moment when he regenerates himself in Sunderland's laboratory (who assumed he had killed the Swamp Thing and Alec Holland for good) is portrayed in a manner that is similar to the development of a human fetus, even as Woodrue tries to explain to Sunderland that the Swamp Thing is in fact a plant.[186] Later, when he fights vampires, the Swamp Thing is shown in the Vitruvian Man's iconic pose.[187] Yet even this episode is not without ambivalence, since the vampires are portrayed as a persecuted community trying to grow and preserve its members much like any human community would. Speaking before a statue of the Swamp Thing at his funeral service, Gotham's police commissioner, James Gordon, concludes: "A unique and special being walked amongst us and we didn't look *after* him well enough."[188] Hearing this, Abby thinks how Gotham's law enforcers, including Batman, could not cope with the Swamp Thing's reality and were unsure of whether to side with him or against him until his death; monsters are often subjected to such uncertainty and animosity.

When the Swamp Thing returns from his exile, he goes into the depths of the earth and then comes out of it, in the process of which fossils unite with monsters. This illustrates Foucault's discussion of the paradoxical, ambiguous similarities between fossils and monsters, despite the former's role in consolidating identity and the latter's role in disrupting it:[189] "[T]he coal seam is a reef of jet, its plates precariously stacked, like dirty dishes, and, below that, monsters, monsters and their footprints before miles of stone and ultimately fire. The buried riverbed's a pebble ribbon where the fish bones hover, dreaming of their former lives."[190] With time, the fishbones and the monsters become the same. Just like fossil and monster are confounded, monsters are rendered indistinguishable from humanity. Another example of the tussle between humanity and monstrosity can be seen in the numerous acts of animating bodies and dreams that are present in *Swamp Thing*. Control, or lack of control, over bodies and minds is a running concern in *Swamp Thing*. This highlights the comic's affiliation with horror and weird fiction. Such control is exerted not only by Arcane, who takes over Matt, but also through the emphasis on how the various apocalypses thrive on fear, whereby the frightened collective consciousness sets the apparatus of the apocalypse in motion.

Automatons, Animations, and Issues of Control

According to Bukatman, comics and cartoons "tapped into an animist fascination with anthropomorphic animals and objects, as well as with plasmatic exaggerations and distortions of the body."[191] The Swamp Thing indulges in such experiments with animation when he learns the extent of his powers and the possibilities of moving his consciousness from body to body, as a result of which some of his bodies are left in the swamps, resembling him to the extent of making Abby believe they are real, but crumbling away when touched.[192] For Bukatman, the awkwardness of the animated is linked to the troubled relationship with corporeality as expressed through their changing forms.[193] Besides the Swamp Thing himself, another example of awkward animation is Arcane's transformation of Gregori into the Patchwork Man, whose body also remediates Frankenstein's monster. Abigail was fascinated by *Frankenstein* as a child, and the first panel introducing Gregori shows him reading her favorite passage: "Remember that I am thy creature; I ought to be thy Adam but I am rather the fallen angel."[194] When the young Abby asks for a different ending to the one suggested in the novella, Gregori starts narrating a different one, which continues the monster's life, merging it with Gregori's life after his death in the minefields and his resurrection at the hands of Arcane as "[a] patchwork man ... an un-raveling crazyquilt of flesh."[195]

The patchworked Gregori has difficulties concentrating, since most of him is falling apart; his thoughts are likewise crumbling and confused, although in "Reunion" he is painfully aware that "his world has gone to *pieces*," emphasizing the link between the broken body and its world (fig. 2).[196] Despite the confusion raging in his mind and his body's disintegration, Gregori's love for his daughter persists: just like he had tried to "save" her from the Swamp Thing in an earlier *Swamp Thing* run, seeing his daughter for the first time in decades in the saga, he tries to spare her the horror of watching his monstrous body falling apart.[197] That the Patchwork Man holds a rag doll with Abby's photograph taped over its face further underscores the tussle between animated and unanimated bodies in comics, which is discussed in detail by Bukatman.[198] It is thematized in the *Swamp Thing* through the role accorded to the physical and psychological manipulation of bodies and worlds. The potential for animation as well as the connection to the human is already evident in the object of the doll. Pierre Ancet, discussing the use of dolls in art, such as in Hans Bellmer's work, sees the doll as a mirror reflecting the body, acting as its double: "Toute poupée exprime la vie, s'agirait-il de cette vie reconstruit" (Each puppet expresses life, this reconstructed life).[199] Abby's father is a reminder of how resurrection can go wrong and fall apart. The Swamp Thing's attempted resurrection of Alec Holland was similarly disastrous for him.

Like Gregori, the Swamp Thing also allows himself to give into illusions of a better life. Tellingly, Gregori's narrative is broken and full of contradictions despite being based on reality; unlike the Swamp Thing, he is unable to hold onto the illusion even while he constructs it. The Swamp Thing, in contrast, while exiled on the blue planet, indulges in elaborate illusions of a happier life with Abby. Just like Abby indulged in a cruel dream of a perfect life in which she and the Swamp Thing were accepted by the locals, but in a place where the people were unnaturally colored and the buildings mere stage facades, the Swamp Thing sets up a "puppet show," beginning with the creation of a blue Abby.[200] Since this Abby is made up of his being, he starts seeing the planet through her eyes, where "[t]he world becomes a place . . . of *charmed perspective* . . . and ambiguous *depths* . . . of solid space . . . unfolded as easily . . . as an *origami flower*."[201] On the twenty-first day, he reconstructs Houma for her by molding the planet's blue vegetation through his energy, just like he had on earth.[202] "Almost, almost flawless," this facsimile of Houma is then populated by people, emerging from the ground as skeletons, gradually acquiring familiar forms and faces.[203] These figures include Alec and Linda Holland, who provoke an "aching nostalgia" in the Swamp Thing as they walk through his constructed town.[204] Constantine also appears, as the voice of blunt truth, and points out that the entire town is an illusion.[205] Indeed the Swamp Thing's illusion gradually gives in, and it starts to rain on his town. Based as the town is on alien plant life, the incessant rain provokes spontaneous bursts of vegetation, and "[t]he reflection of *Houma* becomes irritatingly *blurred* . . . at its edges . . . as do . . . its *inhabitants*."[206] Creepers take over cars and buildings (much like they once had during the Swamp Thing's attack on Gotham), but the people themselves also start revealing their vegetal essence. Linda, for instance, has a large flower sprouting from her cheek as she walks by the Swamp Thing with Alec. Before smashing the blue Abby, the Swamp Thing is once again tempted to play the "macabre *puppeteer*" and struggles against retaining the only thing that had helped to counter his solitude: "I try . . . to hold the world together in my mind . . . but it slithers. From a grasp . . . made slippery by sap . . . in despair [. . .] I let the buildings *unravel* . . . I kill the world."[207] Realizing that the illusions are his prison and could cost him his sanity, the Swamp Thing leaves the destroyed Houma, "the ruined dreams," in a desperate bid to find a way back to earth.[208] Besides being an important stage in the Swamp Thing's quest for (coming to terms with) his identity, this story also works self-reflexively to capture comics' capacity for animating worlds but also playing with them, whimsically transforming and even ending such worlds.

Literary scholar Sianne Ngai and art historian Rosalind Krauss have highlighted the paradox of automatism: it can be seen both as a form of automated animation, since it combines industrial culture's manipulation of bodies, and as the surrealist technique of creating freely, without the restraints of conscious thinking.[209] Although Bukatman goes on to distinguish the unruliness of animated characters from monstrous creatures on account of the latter being in positions of power, damaged monsters—Frankenstein's monster, the Patchwork Man, the Swamp Thing—indicate that these positions of power are not only compromised but come with their own constraints. Moreover, the powerful monster also remains trapped in the frame of otherness. Its struggle to break those frames by being the protagonist rather than the antagonist, a struggle that is literalized by the comics monster, is comparable to the romantics' quest to break away from the shackles imposed by society and rational thinking by rejecting and even overturning the ideals of the Enlightenment—the Promethean struggle, which acquired iconic status for the romantics, becomes, as foreshadowed by Percy Bysshe Shelley's lyrical drama *Prometheus Unbound*, a very human, darkly romantic struggle of the monster. While the presence of the comics' monster is based on horrific spectacularity, more solid than the images projected in phantasmagorias but confined to a page rather than an atmospherically darkened room, these monsters reflexively point toward the influence of romantic culture on their worlds. They also continue their rebellious struggle to break the mold of otherness in which they are trapped by expressing their human qualities.

According to Bukatman, the animatedness of the cartoon also applies to comics characters to the extent of their being "exaggeratedly emotional," as a result of which entire worlds can be destroyed and even the constraining elements of the medium, such as the frames, can be shattered.[210] Cultural theorist Norman Klein's related remark, "Cartoons are automata that struggle," is also to a large extent applicable to comics.[211] And although the figures may be automata and appear inhuman, their struggle or rebellion is in itself a human trait, or at least one that is very familiar to humans. Referring to the coexistence of hellish scenes and demonic battles with the sensitive portrayal of Abby and the Swamp Thing's relationship, Jamie Delano (writer of the

Hellblazer series, which continues Constantine's adventures) describes the Swamp Thing's world as being "both grotesque and deeply human—grotesquely human," thus capturing the tension, the shaky reconciliation of opposites, that lies at the core of anthropomorphic monsters.[212]

While the Swamp Thing, as a consciousness harbored by the vegetal world, embodies a fluidity that is monstrous in its transgression of boundaries, the next chapter turns to Enki Bilal's *Monstre* comics to extend the analysis of instability introduced by the fluidity and ambiguity of monsters. In addition, *Monstre* broaches issues such as political and social engagement, the fracture of the other in the self (as highlighted by the clones), decay, and nostalgia for lost times and worlds. It also incorporates a trace of idealism going beyond the divides created by conflict. Such sociopolitical engagement takes the form of environmentalism and, as is the case with all positively rendered monsters, the pledge to tolerate others in *Swamp Thing*. From the monsters discussed here, Warhole and the Swamp Thing have the most fluid forms. This is once again a characteristic that has self-reflexive relevance for comics; a tendency that, according to comics scholar David Kunzle, appeared in the late nineteenth century with the constant playing with the form of the body, and that embodies what Bukatman calls the "plasmatic energy" of comics.[213]

CHAPTER 3

MONSTRE
Monstrous Fluidity

> Le sommeil dans son cinquième stade, le rapide, le paradoxal, est un monstre insaisissable...
> (Sleep in its fifth, rapid, paradoxical stage is an elusive monster...)
> —NIKE, IN ENKI BILAL, *LE SOMMEIL DU MONSTRE*[1]

This quotation, making a monster out of the abstract state of sleep, recalls Baudelaire's ennui in "Au Lecteur" [To the Reader], which likewise awakens a monster through the abstraction of boredom.[2] Going beyond abstraction, it is the elusiveness of the monster that lies at the core of Enki Bilal's *Monstre* tetralogy, which in turn embodies the notion of incomprehensibility and, to further strengthen the Baudelairian link, the transience of life through the mutations permeating the story. Incessant mutation in turn is also captured by the medium of comics owing to its reliance on sequentiality. Although Baudelaire is not directly quoted (unlike in Bilal's earlier *Nikopol* trilogy), *Monstre* opens with its protagonist, Nike Hatzfield, thinking, "J'ai dix-huit jours et I remember" (fig. 5),[3] alluding to "*Remember! Souviens-toi!*" (italicized and bilingual in the original) from the poem "L'Horloge" (The Clock).[4] While *Monstre* also alludes to Georges Perec's autobiographical *Je me souviens* from 1978 (in turn inspired by Joe Brainard's *I Remember*), as reinforced by the inclusion of Georges Perec's portrait,[5] this chapter focuses on the Baudelairian connotations of the phrase, for the purpose of highlighting the comic's dark romantic inclinations. The opening panel is significant in two ways. This panel, a traditional establishing shot, plunges us into an abyss, which is the sky seen through a bombed-out roof of a hospital, as we eventually learn. The amorphousness of the forms alludes to the motif of the amorphous monster—closely related to Baudelaire's ennui, as this chapter will show. It also captures the elements of both painterliness and literariness (reinforced by the allusions to the contemporary history of literary memoirs). Correspondingly, the text appears in two captions (top left and bottom), resembling an experimental book combining word and image rather than a comic. Our first glimpse of the protagonist is an over-the-shoulder shot of him with a journalist in a taxi hurtling through what seems to be a blank space. "You're sure you remember? At [the age of] eighteen days?" ("Vous prétendez vous souvenir? À dix-huit jours?"), she asks.[6] Our protagonist affirms that he does and thus establishes, together with the abysmal, amorphic world of the opening panel, a reality that is founded on fluid memories.

The pain of transience and memories burdens Baudelaire as much as Nike, an orphan of the Bosnian war, trying to recover the memories of his very first days. That "Le Voyage," the closing poem of *Les Fleurs du mal*, ends with the cry to death, "Ce pays nous ennuie" (This country bores us),[7] shows how ennui is not merely confined to a body but imbues the entire epoch, much like the fluidity of monsters in *Monstre* echoes the transformation of bodies and the traveling through space made possible by technological advancements in the dystopian future painted by Bilal. This fluidity traverses corporeal bodies and forms of knowledge. The monster after whom the book is named multiplies othered forms while it remains an amorphous, abstract being who reflects the effects of othering: monsters suffer from not being seen as other than monsters.

The *Monstre* tetralogy took Bilal nine years to complete. Its first volume, *Le Sommeil du monstre*, was published in 1998, followed by *32 Décembre* (2003), *Rendez-vous à Paris* (2006), and *Quatre?* (2007). It is set in 2026, in a typically dystopian but also partially bizarre Bilalian future.[8] The story revolves around three orphans, Leyla, Amir, and Nike, born in Sarajevo during the Yugoslav wars in a hospital called Kosevo. The orphans end up in different corners of the world, with Nike in New York, Leyla in the Nefud Desert on the Arabian Peninsula, and Amir in Moscow. Nike, having a phenomenal memory, is the only one who fully remembers their early days. Having sworn to protect the younger orphans, he seeks to reunite the three of them. This is, paradoxically, accelerated by his presence during an attack by a fundamentalist terrorist group called the Obscurantis Order. Although Nike survives the attack, his wounded nose remains unhealed. Since Nike is a target for the Order, which seeks to eliminate all traces of culture and memory, he is declared dead by the Federal Bureau of International Investigation, the FBII, in keeping with its protection program. Operated on by a certain Dr. Optus Warhole, Nike suffers from a permanently damaged nose and has to face the reality of being not only manipulated by Warhole but also cloned. And it is these clones who end up contacting Leyla and Amir first. In this respect, it is worthwhile recalling that Henri Baudin describes androids as extensions of the prosthesis, because prostheses were intended to replace human limbs, ideally in an inconspicuous manner.[9] Indicating technological progress on one hand, the android, like the monster, incorporates in-betweenness, for: "[L]'androïde, c'est déjà presque l'homme, et ce n'est pas encore lui (tout comme, avec l'altérité par altération ou aliénation c'est encore presque l'homme, et ce n'est déjà pas lui)" (The android is almost already a man, but not quite a man [just like alterity, by alteration or alienation, produces an almost man, that is no longer a man]).[10] Prosthetics, the manipulation of human bodies by merging them with inanimate parts, developed considerably in the wake of the two world wars. It dissolves the boundaries between the organic and the inorganic, further humanizing the inanimate. Prosthetic body parts are the plastic pendants to the cultural constructions of monsters.

While Leyla is an astrophysicist, Amir and his girlfriend, Sacha, unknowingly enlist themselves with the Obscurantis Order. Amir, who as Nike remembers killed flies with his hand since he was only a few days old, smashes the Warholian fly used by the Order to brainwash and control its new recruits as they are sequestered, while Sacha remains under its control for a long time even after she is rescued by Pamela Fischer and the FBII lieutenant Cobbéa. Pamela, who was once Nike's girlfriend, has been replicated several times by Warhole to the extent that the real Pamela, who had worked for Warhole, never appears in the comic. Throughout the tetralogy's second book, *32 Décembre*, Amir is running after a completely transformed and volatile Sacha, while both are under treatment for the trauma they suffered at the hands of the Obscurantis Order.

Bilal's world is populated by androids and humans who are also technologically transformed, patchworked. The trope of Frankenstein's monster thus persists. It soon turns out that Warhole controls the world through his flies—the Obscurantis Order's "workers of God"—who are "electronic, organic, chemical, and even virtual."[11] They spy on and infiltrate people, enabling Warhole to manipulate them and make clones.[12] It is Warhole who is directly referred to as the monster of the tetralogy, and who from the tetralogy's second book onward adopts the persona of an artist, Holeraw. A proponent of "brutal art," Holeraw orchestrates destructive happenings. This exemplifies the bizarre, unpredictable turns of events in the series, an unpredictability and mutability that is embodied by Warhole, who, in the course of the four volumes, transitions from being a heartless inventor and manipulator, to an artist thriving on violent spectacles, to a parasitic growth on Nike's body controlling his mind and perception. Already, Warhole's first form suggests a mix of organic and inorganic parts (fig. 6):[13] the nose is clearly inorganic and grafted, and so is the top of his head and part of his chin. While the nose establishes a link with Nike, whose nose was manipulated by Warhole, the presence of inorganic parts also hints toward his monstrosity. The impending destruction (of others but also himself) is further emphasized by the bright red coloring around his throat, one of the most vulnerable parts of a living being. In finally adopting the amorphous form that had been his original appearance, Warhole turns toward doing good. He tries to compensate for his previous actions by, among other things, uniting the three orphans for the first time since their birth, freeing Sacha from the fly destroying her system, and becoming Nike's friend. Toward the end of the tetralogy, Warhole reveals that he has been on earth for seventy million years as a result of an interdimensional accident and has had to mutate constantly in order to survive.[14] He gradually evolved from taking the forms of different flies to adopting the shape of humans. Once human—"albeit elusive and indefinable"—he became an explorer of the organic, physical, and mental aspects of the human being.[15] This kind of exploration is enabled by all monsters, for they highlight and sometimes, as with the monsters populating this book, blur the distinctions between themselves and humans. Because this exploration is in part an exploration of individual identity (again, a concept that propels several romantic notions such as that of genius), the three protagonists of a broken country are also monstrous to the extent that their identity, like that of Warhole and anthropomorphic monsters in general, is rendered fluid by the war that ravaged their country.

This chapter begins by drawing out the similarities between Baudelairian romanticism, especially the Baudelairian monster, ennui, and the protagonists and aesthetics of the *Monstre* tetralogy. It goes on to highlight connections between monstrous spaces and their monstrous inhabitants. A discussion of the amorphousness of monstrosity is followed by an examination of the roles of spectacularity and rebelliousness. The chapter ends with a brief reflection on how *Monstre* and fluid monsters reflect on modern and contemporary history.

Overlaps between Baudelairian Romanticism and *Monstre*

While common tendencies are shared by many romantics, including the features guiding the readings in this book, romantic artists and writers do not limit themselves to a single set of romantic tropes. This is especially true for Baudelaire, who captures both romantic and modernist concerns;

most of his works, for instance, unfold in the city instead of the countryside. This overlapping is evident in Baudelaire's description of romanticism as a modern art, which he goes on to specify as being "intimate, spiritual, aspiring toward the infinite" or representing the unrepresentable.[16] In *Monstre*, this aspiration toward the infinite is incarnated by the final form of Warhole as Sutpo Rawhloe, taking up the unrepresentable—in Leyla's words, the "pure cosmic mash"—that Rawhloe was essentially made of (fig. 7): no feature of Rawhloe's head, apart from his eyes, is defined. His features even seem to be in a constant state of movement, as suggested by the unruly lines bypassing the virtual contour of his head and capturing the intensive movement and energy imbuing the medium of comics as well as many of its characters.[17] Using Baudelaire's writings to guide these analyses captures the extent to which romanticism flows into modern and eventually contemporary concerns. Indeed and in spite of Baudelaire's own tendency to deromanticize, he, like Isaiah Berlin, also underscored romanticism's lasting influence on culture by likening it to the stigmata.[18]

Instead of celebrating nature, Baudelaire celebrated the city in the vein of a counterpastoral,[19] which is echoed by the dystopia portrayed in *Monstre*. The play with contrasting notions, emphasizing the beauty in the appalling, as in *Les Fleurs du mal*, is a distinctive tool used by Baudelaire.[20] As we will see in the section that follows, Baudelaire's monsters also indulge in such coupling of the negative with the positive. This is linked to the romantic tendency to merge the beautiful with the terrible, most notably in the sublime.[21] A comparable aestheticization of the terrible and the destructive, albeit from a mocking angle, is present in *Monstre* through Holeraw's orchestration of violent happenings with androids to protest against the violence of war.[22]

The extent of violence prevalent in the comic reflects a particularly Baudelairian and sadistic pleasure in demolition that also recalls Joseph de Maistre's notion of the universality of evil and violence.[23] As in *Les Fleurs du mal*, transience and death prevail over the tetralogy.[24] The centrality of death, especially in "Spleen," is echoed in *Monstre*, the first pages of which evoke the Bosnian war. Similarly, the modern itself was ephemeral for Baudelaire.[25] Although marked by the related, arguably modern elements of fragmentation, disjunction, and artificiality,[26] the Baudelairian atmosphere, especially the theme of the spectacle—watching it, being a part of it—is also a remnant of romanticism.[27] Moreover, in spite of all the bitterness and despair, beauty persists in the worlds of both Baudelaire and Bilal.

The main theme of *Les Fleurs du mal* is ennui, the innate, delicate monster, a companion of modern life, plaguing the solitary man. Northrop Frye has compared it to Blake's concept of negative evil, or the belief that vice is generated by not acting or preventing others from acting.[28] According to literary scholar Frank Kermode, Baudelaire's "mythology is of the perversion, the *ennui*, the metaphysical despair of men and women" experiencing the abjection of the modern city.[29] For Kermode, sordidness also imbues the creative dimension through Baudelaire's awareness, and that of the other romantics, of the unattainable image and the inadequacy of language.[30] Despair is thus also engendered at the level of the artist's struggle with manipulating the medium, trying to stretch its limits by using new techniques of expression.

Another key theme in Baudelaire's *Les Fleurs du mal* is the *correspondances* or interactions between material and spiritual spheres as well as between internal and external worlds.[31] Bridging the gap between the interior and the exterior, the world suggested by these *correspondances* is synesthetic, a place where sensorial perceptions are interchangeable.[32] The dismal atmosphere of the anthology is thus mirrored by the bitter, melancholic mood of the protagonist, a pathetic fallacy. Baudelaire's modern hero was thus romantic through his assertion of individuality, sensitivity, and above all emotionality.[33] Like most of Baudelaire's protagonists or personas, the protagonists of *Monstre*, including the monster himself but also Nike, suffer both psychologically and physically (Baudelaire himself contracted syphilis at an early age). And notably, all of the characters are out of place, much like the alienated, numbed, and haunted *I* of Baudelaire's poems.[34]

Baudelaire's Monster

As noted by Jacques Dupont, Baudelaire transmits a distinct version of the *homo duplex* or divided man by combining agitation and the dramatic play with oppositions.[35] Describing the sensory saturation and satiation in Baudelaire's verses, writer Julien Gracq sees them as relying on "une stricte économie de l'ambiguïté" (a strict economy of ambiguity).[36] This is generated by, among other features, oxymorons, which also lie at the heart of Baudelaire's monster, described already in the opening poem of *Les Fleurs du mal* as a delicate monster.[37] The repulsive is consequently combined with the attractive—a quality that is also discernible in *Monstre* and introduces not only ambiguity but also a rebellious element by rejecting the normative notions of good and bad. The rainy country described in "Spleen" is ruled by a king paralyzed by ennui, an ennui that is the product of (both) Satan and sullen disinterest.[38] Sickness, as described by Isaiah Berlin, is one of the many romantic inclinations that pervade *Monstre*, and it is often provoked by Warhole's flies.[39] To add to the atmosphere of despair and torment, the monster, or Warhole, is himself awoken by the Bosnian war.[40] As will be shown, the effects of illness are openly physical—since they provoke mutations—in *Monstre*, even expressing the far-reaching reverberations of psychological damage. This is the case for the traumatized Nike and the brainwashed Sacha, both of whom undergo various transformations, from changed skin colors and broken noses to partial mutations into a fly or, in the case of Nike, a mutation with Warhole, first as an appendage on his torso[41] and eventually regenerating Warhole's body (fig. 8).[42] This latter image of Nike waking up next to an unrecognizable Warhole (soon to be Rawhloe) on an impersonal white-sheeted hotel bed (which could have easily been a hospital bed) splattered with bloodstains and almost glued to Warhole, visualizes their changing, mutating, but closely connected relationship, even though one has a human body and the other has adopted an anthropomorphic shape but remains inhumanly white. The other and the self, the monstrous and the normal, are juxtaposed and shown to be intimately, inextricably connected. Moreover, Warhole's infiltration shatters the boundaries between Nike's body and the outside world, making Nike himself spill over into the realm of monstrosity. Through the clones and the many ways in which Warhole invades Nike's body and mind, Nike is ultimately as monstrously fluid as Warhole himself. Together they enact the process of transmogrification theorized by Nikki Sullivan, combining and then separating both bodies and mentalities.

Commenting on the monstrosity of Baudelaire's ennui, literary scholar Jean Burgos describes "une réalité profonde, quotidiennement vécue, où le monstre, bien loin de nous déplaire, bien loin surtout de nous paraître effrayant en tout, se révèle au contraire le plus propre à manifester en silence, pour notre plus grand plaisir, ce que nous avons de plus vrai, de plus singulier aussi" (a deep reality, experienced daily, where the monster, far from displeasing us, far from seeming frightening to us, reveals itself, in contrast, as the most appropriate means of silently showing, to our greatest delight, that which is the most truthful and the most singular about us.)[43] This move toward a more human monster that also highlights its positive aspects is one of the few similarities between Baudelaire and Victor Hugo.[44] As literary scholar Léon Cellier points out, Hugo, having been a macrocephalic fetus and susceptible to rickets as a child, described his own body as a horrible monster.[45] Whereas Hugo's monsters incorporate physical defects and the subsequent fear and stigma of not fitting in, the monsters in Bilal's future ensconce the fears of biotechnological manipulation.

Monstrosity more openly personifies a facet of humanity in "Le Masque" (The Mask), in which Baudelaire describes a sensual statue of an allegory by his contemporary, Ernest Christophe.[46] In contrast to its perfect body, the statue has two heads, a corporeal one and a mask. While the latter has a satisfied but hollow expression, the former grimaces because, according to Baudelaire, it is plagued by the problem of living.[47] The monstrous statue has thus absorbed Baudelaire's own fears of the modern world. Indeed, the poet is described as a monster very early in *Les Fleurs du mal*, as someone very different, a disgrace to his family and a pariah, who nonetheless is guarded by an angel and thrives on the overlooked beauty of the natural world.[48] This positive aspect of the monstrous is preserved, in keeping with the anthology's homage to decay, as in "Le Monstre" (The Monster), in which he mentions the "macabre nymphe's" luster of "[d]es choses qui sont très-usées / Mais qui séduisent cependant" (of things that have been often used / But which seduce us none the less).[49] Although this is accompanied by a body that is described as a carcass, irrespective of whether the monster is a poet or an abstraction ("Bénédiction," "Au Lecteur"), the possibility of loving the deformed is recurrent and is even verbalized in "L'Irrémédiable," in which the poet speaks of "l'amour du difforme."[50] *Monstre*'s Warhole and, by the end, the other three protagonists all seem to share this love of the deformed, tacitly accepting their affinity with such creatures.

What *Les Fleurs du mal* does as a whole, and condenses through the perennial figure of ennui, is to bring out the monstrosities swallowing up modern humanity as well as the monstrosity *of* modern humanity. This is literalized in Bilal's worlds through the modified humans populating it. As we will see, Warhole is not the only monster in the comics.

Flawed Worlds and Patchworked Protagonists

Kai Mikkonen's observation of the romantic *quiproquo* trope in the *Nikopol* trilogy, which unfolds both within and beyond the story, is also applicable to *Monstre*. This is most evident in the identity confusion generated by the clones, especially those of Leyla and Nike, but it also persists on an extradiegetic level by transferring the confusion to the reader, who experiences the story through the three main characters.[51]

As Warhole, in the form of his artist-clone Holeraw, takes great pleasure in informing Nike, he can never be too sure about being the real Nike Hatzfield, as a result of which Nike is tormented by doubt.[52] Later, when confined to a bed in Warhole's captivity, he gives in to the "organized nightmare" of paranoia.[53] This perennial uncertainty echoes the fluid space and transforming bodies of the world of *Monstre*, even though the real Warhole, reduced to a head presenting "an obscene spectacle,"⁵⁴ eventually gives the real Nike access to the minds of the other clones, who continue to believe and lead others into believing that they are the real Nikes.

Literary scholar Natascha Ueckmann takes up Hannah Arendt's philosophy to highlight that cloning takes away a sense of connection to fellow beings that is generated by the very act of being born, being able to trace one's origins to another human body.⁵⁵ Planetary exploration likewise contributes toward *Weltentfremdung*. This view, as Ueckmann points out, is echoed by the philosopher Paul Virilio, who regards space exploration and virtual spaces as leading to a loss of the world. Such exploration of outer space and virtual spaces is already advanced in *Monstre* and can be seen as a destabilizing factor for the dystopian world portrayed. The compromising of physical and mental individuality is in itself monstrous, owing to the uncertainty and destabilization it provokes. Such desacralization of the body and manipulation of the mind manifests itself in *Monstre* through the clones as well as through the metamorphoses and psychological manipulation practiced by Warhole. Warhole not only has insight into, and controls, the minds of his clones; he also merges with Nike, taking the form of a mutation, an organic growth firmly attached to Nike's torso in the tetralogy's last book, *Quatre?* In the form of this appendage, Warhole controls Nike's senses, infiltrates his thoughts, and forces him to perform certain actions. Warhole reveals that he himself is not limited to the growth on Nike's torso but is divided across other bodies, including a bloody fly watching Nike and the artist Holeraw, who becomes a megalomaniac and decides to liberate himself from Warhole.⁵⁶ This monster, breathing under his skin, is the monster Nike cannot get rid of, because trying to extract it only results in greater pain.⁵⁷

Rendered as liminal, malleable entities in *Monstre*, the psychological and the physical are not only compromised but also closely interlinked. This is already evident in the tetralogy's first book, *Le Sommeil du monstre*, in which, in the aftermath of Warhole's operation on Nike's nose, when he plants an alien device that provokes intense migraines as well as painful memories of the Yugoslav wars, physical and psychological pain is visualized by red strokes whirling around Nike's head. A little later, this pain is figured as a thick, red block crushing his head when another, unlicensed, surgeon, Koetsu, gives him a red headband to soothe the pain.⁵⁸ Like Warhole, Koetsu is also an artist, managing his own art gallery and manufacturing highly fashionable minianimals, reducing animals from their original size by using a new technique that he himself invented. That these animals also include a brachiosaurus reflects the mélange of temporalities that also occur within Warhole's being, since he has experienced millions of years on earth. It also shows how the fantasy world relies on both futuristic possibilities and memories of a violent past.[59] In *32 Décembre*, as Holeraw takes Nike to meet Warhole, a black spike cuts horizontally through his head as black fish swim around it.[60] The visualization of these intrusions into Nike's head capture the physical pain and psychological manipulation suffered by the protagonist while also highlighting the corporeal and emotional fragility of humans.

As captured by the title of a recent exhibition by Bilal, *Mécanhumanimal*,[61] most of his characters are manipulated psychologically (whereby the possibilities of scientific advances reach supernatural levels) and technologically in *Monstre*. Human-mutants in the tetralogy—including clones as well as other kinds of mutants, such as Sacha with her changing skin color after being brainwashed by the Obscurantis Order—are made by intrusion (Warhole's flies; other chips in Nike) and extension (through alternative suits and appendages such as the helmets enabling their wearers to tap into the consciousness of Warhole's clones). Another example of blatant mechanization and deindividualization are the "Keihilin" suits worn by the militants of the Obscurantis Order as well as the agents of the FBII.[62] Completely black and combining weapons with a jetpack, these thick suits cover every inch of their wearers, leaving them indistinguishable from others wearing similar suits. Here, the suits transform people into android weapons.

Such modification and manufacturing of humans also plays a—more limited—role in *Swamp Thing*. Arcane experiments with the injured of the First World War to create Un-Men, men who are stitched together by harnessing scientific and magical powers. Another kind of mutation occurs in dreams, notably in Amir's erotic dream in which he is gradually transformed into a fish and Sacha into a fly, with both acquiring black skin in the process.[63] This is interpreted by the researcher working on their cases as being an almost expected result of the trauma suffered when they realize that the Obscurantis Order brainwashed all its recruits (who were tricked into joining the Order, made to think that they were taking up security jobs instead of being forcibly enlisted into a fundamentalist sect) in order to make them conform to its extremist doctrines.

In *Monstre*, physical intrusion and manipulation of the body are accomplished by scientists and doctors, mental intrusion and manipulation by fundamentalists and psychologists. Incorporating contemporary concerns, media technology participates in surveillance and distorts reality. This also corresponds to the romantic distrust of technological advancement and the increasing awareness of the evil nesting within humans, the damage they wreak on their world. On the other hand, a mechanized conceptualization of a human had already appeared in the sixteenth and seventeenth centuries, as is evident in the philosophies of René Descartes, Gottfried Wilhelm Leibniz, and John Locke.[64] While Descartes's writings introduced the paradigmatic mind-body division, Leibniz emphasized the mechanical aspect of the human system, almost as if people were automatons. Similarly, Locke, focusing on the interaction between the mind and the body, arrived at the proposition that "our Souls [...] may be nothing but the contexture of several parts of our Bodies to perform those feats of Motion, which for an honourable kind of Distinction we call Thoughts, tho really they are only the Operations of Matter."[65] Bodies become comparably malleable in the hands of Warhole. This is evident when Nike meets a clone of his, who has wires coming out of his body and patchworked body parts.[66]

That another clone of Nike is amputated on Mars, losing both his legs,[67] points toward a key feature of the psychological brokenness manifested by all of the main characters and especially marked in Nike and Warhole. As with Nike's clone, Warhole's legs were also amputated, in World War I, as a result of gangrene, and it is the flesh of these legs that he gives to his clones as a matter of "personal ethic."[68] That Warhole's nose is partially synthetic from the beginning of *Le Sommeil du monstre* foreshadows the original Nike's problems with his nose, including the pain caused by Warhole's surgery as well as his heightened olfactory sense in *Rendez-vous à Paris* and *Quatre?*, which eventually leads him to Leyla and enables him to likewise trace the places in Sarajevo where Amir had recently been.

As one of the main contributors to the Banque Centrale de la Mémoire du Monde (BCMM) (Central Bank of the Memory of the World), Nike is haunted by his exceptional memory, echoing Baudelaire's opening line of "Spleen (II)": "J'ai plus de souvenirs que si j'avais mille ans" (More memories than if I'd lived a thousand years).[69] While these memories are personal for both Nike and Baudelaire, they are also openly interlinked with the evils of their cultural and sociopolitical contexts, concretized by ennui in "Spleen (II)" and war trauma in *Monstre*. It is this trauma that cements the connection between Nike and Warhole, who fought in the trenches of the First World War.[70] Forced to perpetually mutate ever since the interdimensional accident, Warhole found himself in the war, "the antechamber of the human species," directly after having witnessed the evolution of the planet.[71] Introduced to the inhuman, he decided to learn more about the species by choosing extreme specimens of humans, starting with supreme evil (the original Dr. Warhole), turning to art (as Holeraw), and eventually moving toward supreme good (Sutpo Rawhloe), remedying the damage done to Nike, Leyla, Amir, and Sacha by uniting the orphans and giving Amir the fly through which Sacha was being controlled.[72]

Warhole himself is not merely transformed and reworked but also replicated. In the tetralogy's second comic, *32 Décembre*, Warhole—at this point reduced to a head kept in a container filled with the water of the Aral Sea—starts decomposing. This process of "placodermization," the inverse of fossilization, is triggered by contact with "un poisson issu du gouffre des temps" (a fish from the abyss of time) or a placoderm, a prehistoric fish that had a thick, armor-like skin.[73] As discussed below, this can be linked to the skull sitting in the mysterious, incomprehensible "Site de l'Aigle" (Eagle's site), the place where Warhole first came to earth, which is consequently also a site of trauma.

The coexistence of opposites plays a central role in Warhole's characterization. Traumatized by the war, Warhole initially commits monstrous acts of violence, eventually transforming them into a form of artistic protest. Corporealizing the link between the artist and his creation (while also alluding to Christian symbolism), he gives all of his clones a little part of his original flesh. As an artist detached from his rebellious clone, Holeraw, in *Rendez-vous à Paris*, Warhole describes himself as an "Artiste Monstre" who mistrusts the scientific advancements of humans, which enable the perpetuation and normalization of clones.[74] That Warhole keeps on changing his stances is grounded by his claim: "Le parcours d'un artiste se doit d'être zigzagant et imprévu" (An artist's path must be zigzagging and improvised), emphasizing the unpredictability and uncertainty incarnated by the monster.[75] These aspects are visualized in Sutpo Rawhloe's amorphousness.

Amorphousness lies at the core of Warhole's last most important work, *Compression de mort éructée* (Compression of regurgitated death), which is "une œuvre universelle. Contre les guerres et l'aveu-glement des hommes. Mais elle va faire dégâts. L'effet boomerang en quelque sorte" (a universal work. Against wars and the blindness of men. But it will do damage. A boomerang effect of sorts).[76] Writing about this work, an art critic describes Warhole as "une composante à part entière, une composante 'gangrene'" (an integral component, a "gangrenous" component) (fig. 9).[77] The image accompanying this comment on an online newspaper (where only a part of the article is available for free) visualizes the in-betweenness that accompanies the amorphousness of Warhole's artwork and also Warhole himself: first there is the cloud itself, illustrated by frenzied, swirling lines in black; and second is the very nature of the image itself, which is a grim cityscape that Bilal has lightly touched up with crayons (as he is fond of doing for portraits and works such as his Louvre-Futuropolis book, *Les Fantômes du Louvre*). These swirls of color function as a technique of transmogrification that crumbles the boundaries between bodies and the spaces they inhabit. In such cases, the image oscillates between different levels of reality while highlighting the fragility of the photographed buildings (and, by implication, realities) facing impending destruction by the mass of squibbles that is Warhole's piece: the mockery of overly conceptualized art aside, the piece also, paradoxically (and thus appropriately for *Monstre*), affirms the far-reaching, often unquantifiable affects of art. Tying up with the tetralogy's central theme of trauma, Warhole's piece resurrects the memory of previous wars by generating rain made of the "tears" issued from the decomposition of two million soldiers and civilians, victims of war, on the "champ de la connerie" (field of bullshit).[78] Correspondingly, the flying structure emitting this cloud of tears has the shape of a large, plain tomb topped by a cross.[79]

When Nike views Sarajevo for the first time since his birth, he lets out a cry that is described as both inexplicable and Munchian, encapsulating the trauma and frustration of war.[80] Correspondingly, Bilal describes *Monstre* by quoting a comics artist known for his work on the Great War, Jacques Tardi: "un cri de douleur" (a cry of pain).[81] A strong affect, that of pain and frustration, accompanies the various forms of monstrosity—of bodies, beings, and spaces—prevalent in the book.

Nike describes the sound of bombs by juxtaposing the mechanical with the organic, concluding that "les deux conjugués sont synonymes de mort" (the combination of the two is the synonym for death).[82] Like Nike and Warhole, the other characters, Leyla, Amir, and Sacha, also go through traumatic experiences. Leyla loses her companion Finch, then her father and the cloned Nike. Likewise, both Amir and Sacha are traumatized by the Obscurantis Order, with Sacha being more profoundly affected through the mind control enabled by the Warholian fly, which also makes her system increasingly synthetic.[83] This is evident in her physical appearance: her color changes, darkening at first, then becoming patchy, while her head remains shaven, marking the day her hair was forcibly removed by another fly, "a worker of God."[84] Although Sacha is also shown patched up at the beginning of the tetralogy while she was recovering from a contagious disease,[85] it is only through Warhole that she turns into what Amir affectionately calls a "mutant."[86] When Warhole gives Sacha's fly to Amir, who instinctively kills it before waiting for Warhole's instructions, Sacha recovers and escapes from Dr. Irène Laroche's hospital, trailing the doctor's label tied to her ankle, losing her entire memory and reverting to a bestial state.[87]

Nike's enhanced sense of smell likewise brings out his bestial side. With Warhole's growth on him and his voice in his mind in *Rendez-vous à Paris*, Nike ends up moving on all fours in certain quarters of Sarajevo, sniffing out traces of Amir and Leyla. Leyla had gone to Belgrade but was staying at the same hotel as Nike, who had been told he was in Sarajevo, a Sarajevo that was merging with two other post-Yugoslav capitals, Belgrade and Zagreb. At the beginning of the comic, when Nike was still unaware of Warhole's mutation on him, the instances of such spasmodic animalistic behavior added to the doubts already induced by Warhole and the clones regarding his identity and its constituents, creating a split between himself and his conceptualization of Nike Hatzfield, as evinced by one of his remarks that appears upside down as he climbs the walls of his Sarajevo hotel room: "ce comportement animal, dont j'ai conscience, de renifler par moments, air, objets, murs, sols et plafonds, est-ce le mien aussi?" (this animal behavior, which I'm aware of, sniffing from time to time the air, objects, walls, floors, and ceilings, is it mine too?).[88]

That Blake's God-Man or Albion, the "universal Man who is also God [...] is full of noses" as well as eyes,[89] embodies the significance accorded by the romantics to sensory experience. This is also echoed by the "saturation sensuelle du vers baudelairian" (sensual saturation of the Baudelairian verse).[90] *Monstre* is likewise sensual, and in emphasizing the senses and bodily desires, it once again highlights the fragility of the human body and its susceptibility on corporeal and psychological levels. Accompanying the heightened senses, a romantic fascination with the primitive is also present; Nike's heightened olfactory sense, for instance, often results in animalistic behavior.

Nike's refusal to identify with any of the three warring Yugoslav groups—Bosnian, Serbian, Croatian—is evident in *Le Sommeil du monstre*.[91] Amir and Leyla are likewise "mixed." Amir had a Muslim mother. Leyla, whose first name is Muslim and whose last name, Mirkovic-Zohary, is both Serbian and Croatian, has an adopted father of Arab Jewish origin. That Amir's father was the sniper responsible for the death of Nike's father extends the sociopolitical relevance of the friendship that is eventually established between the three: they bring together the mixed prewar state that was Yugoslavia.[92] Ueckmann sees Bilal's images as "a cynical discourse on *métissage* and *créolisation*," whereby *créolisation* takes place on a cultural level.[93] While Bilal's cynicism is unmistakable in other aspects, especially when it comes to scientific and technological developments (and probably ambiguous rather than cynical when it comes to *métissage*), his Sarajevo trio brings in an element of nostalgia for a united Yugoslavia, even incorporating the idealistic possibility of peaceful coexistence. Since Yugoslavia remains broken in *Monstre*'s dystopia, all three remain perpetually displaced, as confirmed by Leyla's remark that she does not have a homeland.[94]

Referring to Baudelairian ennui, Mathias observes: "Le lieu du monstre est bien l'espace sans orientation, un lieu de nulle part et de rien [...] un domaine sur lequel le Démon exerce sa suzeraineté" (The monster's habitat is a place without orientation, a place that is nowhere and of nothing [...] a domain over which the Demon rules).[95] While this is embodied by the Site de l'Aigle, as elaborated below, it also holds for the dystopian world of *Monstre*, where buildings, people, and words float in the air. Moreover, Koetsu's office in New York is situated at the top of incomplete skyscrapers, which recall the ruins that fascinated romantic authors.[96] Already the first few pages of the comic reveal a crowded New York with flying taxis.[97] Red streaks run across its roads and buildings. This sketchy drawing style gives the city the appearance of being incomplete, even spectral. Moreover, because the very first panel of the book shows the hole in the bombed roof of the Sarajevo hospital to which the three orphans were brought, cities' susceptibility to destruction is underscored.[98] This is confirmed a few minutes later when the Obscurantis Order attack a restaurant in the Manhattan Watershop Building in hopes of eliminating Nike, and with him one of the most important reserves of the world's memory. Hence, like their inhabitants, cities are also patched up and in fluid situations, not only because of the flying objects but also because of the uncertainty prevailing over them due to the presence of powerful elements like the Obscurantis Order and Warhole. This is also confirmed in *Rendez-vous à Paris*, when Sacha's exploding head appears in the sky where Leyla, Nike, and Amir are dining with Warhole, streaking the sky with red the instant Amir crushes her fly.[99] Already in the first volume, Nike and his surroundings are engulfed by an emerging cloud of red as his interviewer shouts after him to ask whether he is Serbian, Croatian, or Muslim.

Such anthropomorphization of the surroundings is present in Blake's poem "London" (*Songs of Experience*, 1794), in which the bleak atmosphere of the city reflects the condition of its dwellers:

> I wander thro' each charter'd street,
> Near where the charter'd Thames does flow.
> And mark in every face I meet
> Marks of weakness, marks of woe.
>
> [...]
> In every voice: in every ban,
> The mind-forg'd manacles I hear
>
> How the Chimney-sweepers cry
> Every blackning Church appalls,
> And the hapless Soldiers sigh
> Runs in blood down Palace walls.[100]

The "blackning Church" and blood are visualized in *Monstre*'s New York, but the images also hold for other cities, such as Paris, portrayed in the last comic of the tetralogy as tainted by slogans in the air marking out religious buildings and limiting them to specific Christian and Islamic sects. Playing with references to reality, Bilal uses photographs as backdrops, crudely outlining buildings with crayon and splashing the entire scene with vibrant colors. However, the photographs of the rooftops across Paris are often dismal, revealing an overcrowded city in shadows.[101] In contrast, the Nefud Desert is marked by serene blue skies and a vast sandy terrain.

Not only do Bilal's cities comprise floating structures echoing the uncertainty that haunts Bilal's characters, but they are likewise prone to mutations. When the real Nike finally visits Sarajevo in *Rendez-vous à Paris*, he is told that the city is merging with Belgrade and Zagreb, something that is not only physically but also politically impossible.[102] This information is provided in a dream-like scene in which Nike, unaware of Warhole's control over his ability to perceive, cannot see any other people, and all the places he passes through in Sarajevo appear empty. The first person who gradually appears before his eyes tells him about the "twinning" of the three cities, making Nike unsure whether he is mad or dead.

Fred Botting notes that "[m]onstrosity—as political radicals, like Wollstonecraft and Goodwin argued—was a mark of callous or corrupt political and social structures: the monsters made by those systems reflect back on wider, more monstrous formations."[103] In *Monstre*, similar criticism is channeled through Warhole himself, since he defies both logic and any kind of physical authority. Warhole kidnaps the FBII officer Cobbéa, eliminates the main members of the CSPREA (the equivalent of the UN Security Council), and destroys the Siberian base of the Obscurantis Order.[104] That one of his clones also perishes in each of the actions renders these acts of destruction similar to suicide bombings. Warhole's acts of destruction not only hint toward the inefficacy of international organizations to maintain peace but also uses a tool of fundamentalist organizations—turning people into weapons—against them.

Birthplace of the Monster: The Site de l'Aigle

Spaces of the monster, as described by Mathias, flourish in *Monstre*, encompassing the desert, outer space, and cities, which, reflecting their dwellers, are malleable. Correspondingly, the desert is recurrent in the Baudelairian world, a desert of ennui in which everything is devalorized.[105] Describing the landscape and climate of Baudelairian ennui as a negation of space, a space that is both destroyed and hopeless, much like most of the spaces that unfold in *Monstre*, Mathias sees it as "le monde de la non-valeur, une sorte de degré zéro de la sensibilité figée, malgré ses tentatives de fuite, dans l'immobilité torpide du fumeur de houka" (the world of no value, a sort of degree zero of frozen sensibility, despite its attempts to escape, in the sluggish immobility of the hookah smoker).[106]

The Site de l'Aigle, which marks the place where Warhole entered earth because of an interdimensional accident, is located in Arabia's Nefud Desert. This desert is an erg, meaning that it is characterized by shifting sands; such deserts are also found on other planets such as Mars and Venus. In *32 Décembre*, when Nike's clone visits the site on Leyla's request and as part of a delegation including the president of the New United Nations, the Dalai Lama, the chief rabbi, and the pope, all of the visitors end up being teleported to Mars, reinforcing the link to the essence of the erg.[107] Only a limited number of visitors are allowed to the site, and communication possibilities are rationed because the site is fragile, harmed by each visit, prone to disintegration, and impossible to preserve.[108] Lying underground, the site is preceded by a gallery, also wasting away, containing images of earlier visitors seated in the center of the cave facing the "Skull," the locus of the site's incomprehensible energy.[109] Situated thirty meters under the earth, this Skull transmits information to visitors in a mysterious manner that baffles specialists.[110]

That the visit of Nike's clone to the cave alternates with the real Nike meeting the real Warhole isolated in a glass jar with fish floating in and out of him as part of the impending placodermization mirrors the process of fossilization that the skull at the Site de l'Aigle is likely to undergo. Once again, the dynamics of transmogrification are visualized through mutating bodies and swirling, violently colored lines. At this point, it is worthwhile recalling Foucault's distinction between fossils and monsters, which underscores the monster's incarnation of difference:

> The fossil, with its mixed animal and mineral nature, is the privileged locus of a resemblance required by the historian of the continuum, whereas the space of the taxinomia decomposed it with rigour. The monster and the fossil both play a very precise role in this configuration. On the basis of the power of the continuum held by nature, the monster ensures the emergence of difference. This difference is still without law and without any well-defined structure. [...] The fossil is what permits

resemblances to subsist throughout all the deviations traversed by nature; it functions as a distant and approximative form of identity; it marks a quasi-character in the shift of time.[111]

Yet the skeleton at the Site de l'Aigle, which, due to its size and form, seems to be that of a dinosaur, also resists definition, much like the main monster of the tetralogy, Warhole. Moreover, as suggested by Botting's quotation above, this skeleton, which is in danger of disappearing and possibly leaving only a fossilized trace behind, points toward a sociopolitical issue: all of the visitors to the cave return with the same stick-figure drawing, suggesting that the site is one of trauma.[112] Resembling a cave drawing, this image shows a dinosaur and a stick figure being shot by a sniper. By insisting on the word *sniper*, Warhole establishes a link with the Yugoslav wars and the infamous Sniper Alley in Sarajevo,[113] which is mentioned early in *Le Sommeil du monstre* by Nike, who, suffering from migraines after Warhole's operation on his nose, can still hear the shots that rang out there.

For Burgos, the monster's refuge is in the improbable.[114] That the Site de l'Aigle is beyond comprehension, incorporating pain and loss and placing reality in question, is also reflected in Warhole himself.[115] As concretized by the Site de l'Aigle, Warhole himself comes from another, different dimension but is unable to go home—he missed his chance on 32 December, at the end of the tetralogy's second book, which resulted in the sudden disappearance of all of the visitors to the Site de l'Aigle and their reappearance on Mars, with only Nike's clone surviving the mass teleportation.[116] The other three protagonists of *Monstre* also live through a comparable, irresolvable displacement, a loss of origin and home; as Nike remarks to the journalist interviewing him at the beginning of the tetralogy: "Il n'y a plus aucune trace de notre naissance, là-bas" (There is no longer any trace of our birth there).[117] Even though the city survives, the hospital called Kosevo, to which the three orphans were brought, was destroyed.[118]

While Quasimodo is both attached to Notre Dame and reflects the grotesque sculptures adorning it, and Gwynplaine is essentially at home only in Ursus's traveling hut, which also serves as a stage and is always parked on the outskirts of the city, Warhole's relationship to, and similarities with, space and setting are not limited to the Site de l'Aigle but extend to the entire dystopian future of *Monstre*. This future harbors, and in certain instances even premediates, concerns regarding the postmodern world. Thus, for instance, Virilio's interpretation of nanotechnology as a fatal draining, appropriation, and desecration of the body[119] is reflected by the amorphousness of the bodies and the main monster in *Monstre*.

Fatality is evoked at the beginning of *Notre-Dame de Paris* by a graffito of the Greek word 'ΑΝΆΓΚΗ that Hugo had seen on the cathedral's walls.[120] That the word can be extended to mean destiny, death, and even calamity or signify an intimate relationship (among other things) is another connection between *Monstre* and *Notre-Dame de Paris*. Significantly, however, while Quasimodo is subjected to this law of fatality, Warhole subverts it despite being a victim of it at the beginning through the interdimensional accident. He also incarnates the other meanings of 'ΑΝΆΓΚΗ, by first being a source of calamity and death and later bringing out the relationships between past and present wars, as well as the three protagonists displaced by war. Hence, while Hugo's medieval monster was subject to the whims of fate, Warhole's monster reacts against those whims and molds his destiny much like the rebellious, Promethean model of the romantic artist and protagonist.

Amorphousness as Monstrosity and as Postmodern Aesthetic

On his first night in Sarajevo since the Yugoslav wars, Nike muses: "Le sommeil dans son cinquième stade, le rapide, le paradoxal, est un monstre insaisissable" (Sleep in its fifth, rapid, paradoxical state is an elusive monster).[121] Warhole is also such a monster who is paradoxical, unpredictable, and incomprehensible.

The very transformations of Warhole incorporate the notion of amorphousness, which in itself is seen as monstrosity,[122] starting with the physically revolting Optus Warhole to the androgynous, hyperaestheticized Holeraw, and finally settling for the faceless Sutpo Rawhloe, who comes into being through a bloody detachment of his shapeless growth on Nike's torso. This act captures his rebirth while confirming his close link to Nike.[123] Warhole also induces amorphousness by his interventions on other people's bodies, including his abduction of Nike in *Le Sommeil du monstre* as well as his possession of Leyla's body in *Rendez-vous à Paris*, when she has a brief out-of-body experience and finds her body frozen on a bed, before both disappear in a swirl of white lines.[124]

In saying, as Holeraw does, that "[j]e serai [. . .] aussi insaisissable qu'un placoderme larvé en mutation, ou mieux, une sarcophaga magnifica recyclée" (I will be as incomprehensible as a mutating placoderm larva or better, a recycled sarcophaga magnifica [a flesh fly subspecies]),[125] Warhole establishes a bond with his flies—specified as Sarcophaga or flies that feed on meat—which are the main cause of manipulation and destruction in the tetralogy. This bond highlights Warhole's break away from the material, which is later visualized by his appearance as Sutpo Rawhloe. The amorphous face of Sutpo Rawhloe is the original one of Warhole's youth.[126] For Nike, "il avait une tête qui allait avec son nom re-re-anagrammé... Un peu comme si au moment de sa conception la Nature en avait perdu son latin" (he had a head that matched his repeatedly anagrammed name... a bit as if at the moment of his conception nature had become confused).[127] Similarly, Warhole's above-described *Compression de mort écrutée* also takes the form of an amorphous black cloud traveling across the world.[128] This work illustrates what Ueckmann sees as "an aesthetic of hopelessness, decay and degeneration prevailing" over Bilal's worlds.[129]

In *Monstre*, degradation as well as amorphousness is largely caused by technology: the technological colonization of the world led to a conceptual reduction of the world and resulted in the colonization of the body through technology.[130] This, in turn, echoes Virilio's view of space exploration and the manipulation of the body through genetics and implantation as a sign of universal departure from concrete reality, which creates a *homme-planète*.[131] The notion of the *homme-planète* is echoed in Nike's observation when Warhole kidnaps him and attaches his organic-looking mechanical devices to him: "[D]outer que l'on fait de véritable chair et de véritable sang donne un sentiment de vertige, même en position allongée" (Doubting whether one is made of real flesh and blood makes one dizzy, even when lying down).[132] On another level, this is the aim of every monster, not only Warhole.

Literary scholar David Williams mentions philosopher Edgar Morin's view that the rational, scientific conception of reality is moving toward a more "random world" with its dialogic presence of order and disorder, in which knowledge has to grapple with uncertainty.[133] Uncertainty of events and identities is reflected in the amorphousness of Sutpo, incarnating the uncertainty that Baudin considers to be at the linguistic root of a German word for monster, *Ungeheuer*.[134] As mentioned in the introduction, the notion of strange new bodies emerging in a changing world, as highlighted by the theories of Donna Haraway and Katherine Hayles, is repeatedly taken up by Bilal.[135] Warhole's amorphousness captures what Williams describes as one of the figurations of the monster: through his changing forms and extraordinary capabilities, the monster Warhole illustrates the paradox between the desire for people to understand, and their limited ability to attain understanding.[136]

Premediation in *Monstre* is not only limited to the technologies enabling the production of clones, the psychological manipulation of people, and their surveillance. The tetralogy also premediates specific tendencies that have snowballed in the twenty-first century: the Obscurantis Order refers to international networks of religious fundamentalists, the FBII is indicative of US involvement in international affairs, and the creolization of people can be seen as another face of globalization and increasingly multicultural metropolises.

The monster's presence is characterized by the simultaneous paradox of diffusion (through the clones) and self-effacement (through placodermization) in the course of the tetralogy. This is appropriate, because the monster is defined essentially by its negation of normative, positive values. Testifying to the eruption of the human imagination and its persistence, monsters like Warhole function as vast *lieux de l'imaginaire*, places where the imagination unfolds without bounds and thus also teases ordinary, normativized reality. Tellingly, the last panel in which Warhole appears in the tetralogy shows him floating away with a red question mark over his head.[137]

This volatile presence of the monster, who in turn points toward the volatile presence of humanity, is concretized by the comic's inhabitants and spaces. Consequently, presence, in the sense of Jean-Luc Nancy's and Hans Ulrich Gumbrecht's notion of the word, becomes both fluid and ubiquitous, permeating the entire dystopia of *Monstre*. This presence is not only limited to the monster Warhole (who is omnipresent) but is also concretized by images, which are recurrent in the dystopia, especially with reference to their creation and control. Such images include the 3-D image of Leyla's adoptive father saved in her phone[138] and the "Warhole Mars Live universal channel," broadcasting in "holo-direct-report" form.[139]

In a similar vein, instability is one of the many possible characteristics of the monster mentioned by Baudin when he discusses the two lions or leopards seen by Lancelot in Chrétien de Troyes's *chanson de geste* that disappear when the knight reaches the other end of the bridge.[140] The monster is always prone to change and can also, in the process, reduce its monstrosity by becoming more acceptable. Such instability is exemplified by what is now Bilal's trademark drawing style: the wild, allusive, emotive strokes and colors overflowing outlines. This style imbues the landscape with amorphousness, capturing the excessive mutation and destruction unfolding in the four *Monstre* books. Bilal described this direct-color or mixed-media technique as "hybridising the material of paint and the framing of film," imbuing the panels with a tactile quality through the material presence of paint and combining it with the immediacy and vitality of film shots.[141] His drawing process is both layered and technologically mediated: quick sketches are enlarged on a photocopier and painted over with acrylics, and pastels are used for highlights. Combining the horror of unpredictability and uncertainty with their beauty, the application of this technique, especially in the fragmented medium of comics, complements the fragmentation and monstrosities populating *Monstre*.

The sketchiness and vagueness of Bilal's style allows forms to emerge from washes and strokes without his clearly outlining them, making the images throb with life and imbibe romantic characteristics in a way comparable to Eugène Delacroix's brushstrokes and dynamic forms. Baudelaire's notion of romanticism was exemplified by the melancholia, spirituality, and aspiration toward infinity that he saw in Delacroix's paintings and sketches.[142] Delacroix's strokes were "palipitations éternelles" (eternal throbbings); "les lignes ne sont jamais, comme dans l'arc-en-ciel, que la fusion intimes des couleurs" (the lines are always, as in a rainbow, an intimate fusion of colors).[143] On a metaphorical plane, Bilal's style, with its liberal use of strokes and splashes, also alludes to the human nervous system, which is at stake throughout the series, threatened and subjected to physiological, psychological, technological, and sociopolitical conflicts. This allusion is particularly evident in the event organized by Holeraw in *32 Décembre*. Preceded by an invitation in a miniature atomic bomb that injures Nike's nose again,[144] Holeraw's event consists of people dressed in white and gathered in a white room. Buckets of paint are thrown on the invitees in order to even out any possible variations in color and to emphasize their incorporation in the artwork. The event is triggered by Nike's killing a provocative guest by pushing him over the skyscraper's balcony, after which Holeraw makes his first appearance and describes the act as "[u]ne sublime pointe de rouge sur le blanc!" (a sublime spot of red on the white!).[145] This triggers a series of killings that splash the entire space with streaks and globs of red (fig. 10).[146]

On such occasions when Nike's narrative voice takes over, the panels adopt a certain distance from typical comics through their square captions, splashes of paint, and somewhat experimental drawing style. Hovering between comic, art book, and even scrapbook, the *Monstre* tetralogy is thus monstrous as a book-object. The other comics considered in this book are similarly monstrous in that they also inscribe themselves in networks of intertextuality and often rely on collages from diverse sources (which is most obvious in *The Crow*). Figure 6 reveals another central concern for *Monstre* (and for this book): it is not only the whitened space that serves as a canvas but the bodies of the participants themselves, who were painted on before they entered the room. And it is the body that, when not monstrous itself, commits monstrous acts and consequently continues to be at the center of the spectacle, creating it but also being affected by it. Hence, even though the figures in these panels do not look monstrous, their bodies are caught up in a stream of endless action and even mutation.[147]

Blood, like the bodies, flows in and out of the panels throughout the tetralogy, as with Pamela (in fact an android) making Nike taste her blood and his own in order to confirm her authenticity in *32 Décembre*, or with Sacha's exploding head tainting the Parisian sky in *Rendez-vous à Paris*.[148] Blood is likewise omnipresent in *Les Fleurs du mal*: "Les Phares" (The Beacons) sums up Delacroix's paintings as a "lac de sang hanté des mauvais anges" (lake of blood, the evil angels' haunts); "La Muse malade" (The Sick muse) also bleeds; and blood erupts in "La Fontaine de sang" (The Fountain of blood).[149] As Théophile Gautier declared at Baudelaire's funeral: "He had [...] been able to give beauty to sights that did not possess beauty in themselves."[150] Bilal likewise reconciles the sordid and the beautiful, which can be seen as a continuation of romantic inclinations.

For Charles Hatfield, the Burkean sublime, with its mélange of delight and horror, is manifest in Jack Kirby's comics, such as *The Fantastic Four*, through the energy and grandeur of the images as well as an engagement with science fiction that explores technological possibilities while providing a human perspective in the face of the incomprehensible.[151] In *Monstre*, the incomprehensible is not limited to speculative technological advancements; it also evokes the trauma of war and violence affecting the main characters, especially Warhole, Nike, and Sacha. The sublime, according to Botting, is "[o]ne of the key modes through which romance engages questions of mastery [...] and a sense of the proximity of otherness."[152] That Warhole himself is a source of the sublime, seeking it through his art but also incorporating it at the very end, reinforces this observation; ultimately, it is not so much terror and repulsion but awe that he evokes from the other protagonists. The romantic ambivalence between polarities, especially of good and evil, persists as a guiding principle.

As already shown in the discussion of Ambroise Paré, the incomprehensibility of the monster is linked to the notion of the sacred.[153] Warhole himself has the power of a god, orchestrating the events of the book, omnisciently aware of what the three protagonists are going through and charting out the paths they choose.

Spectacularity and Rebelliousness in *Monstre*

Warhole, in both his good and evil forms, incarnates the figure of the dandy, beginning with the first, odious incarnation and continuing in the androgynously attractive and self-conscious Holeraw as well as in Sutpo Rawhloe. In "Mon cœur mis à nu," Baudelaire describes the dandy as someone who is stylized, contributing to the spectacle of modern life: "Le Dandy doit aspirer à être sublime sans interruption; il doit vivre et dormir devant un miroir" (The dandy must ceaselessly aspire to be sublime; he must live and sleep in front of a mirror).[154]

Warhole is not merely a part of the spectacle but the ringmaster behind it. Warhole, Holeraw, and later Rawhloe take pleasure in spectacles, in arranging destructive events and happenings but also reunions.[155] Most such spectacles as well as the transformation of the clones' lives into spectacles are dependent on futuristic technologies that involve both psychic and bodily intrusions and can also take the form of an all-encompassing virtual reality, as when Warhole attaches himself to Nike's body and controls what he sees in Sarajevo. However, as Holeraw, and later as himself, Warhole creates many art happenings that are also spectacles that tease reality by closely mimicking and sometimes even manipulating it. These spectacles include the holographic invitations from Holeraw for his first happening,[156] as well as *Compression de mort écrutée*, which Amir finds monstrous.[157] Another spectacle is created by Warhole's broadcasting the lives of Leyla's and Nike's clones on Mars through his live channel.[158] In addition, the visualization of Leyla's dream after Nike's clone's disappearance to Mars, like Amir's dream of him and Sacha mutating into other creatures, is cinematic;[159] it turns out that Leyla's dream was unfolding in real time, whereby images were recorded and transmitted to her unconscious by Warhole's devices.[160]

Rebelliousness, one of the driving forces behind Warhole's spectacles and later accompanied by redemption, is also incorporated by the other three protagonists, all of whom have their own goals and a determination to reach them against all odds. Bloom's description of Prometheus as a model romantic hero places revolution on multiple planes and shows how the quest is eventually internalized to become a means of understanding the self.[161] While the most obvious quests involve finding Amir's and Nike's lovers (Sacha and Leyla), more psychological concerns are also discernible: Nike's aim to reunite the three orphans from Sarajevo, for instance, springs from his need to come to terms with his haunting memories.

Notably, the quests of the human characters are orchestrated by Warhole. To a considerable extent, Warhole also takes the form of bygone, unspeakable memories that Nike tries to court, thus resurrecting the ghost of traumatic memories who questions the past and does not let it go, much like Hamlet's father's ghost, who signifies what philosopher Richard Kearney calls "'traumatic' or 'impossible' memory."[162] Warhole's amorphous form concretizes the fleeting remains of a fading collective memory haunted by a war-torn past.

Like memory and spectacularity, images play a central role in the *Monstre* stories. Their presence, which can often be misleading without losing affective hold, as well as their ephemerality is brought out. Soon after emancipating himself from Warhole and assuming that Warhole has completely disintegrated in the process of placodermization, Holeraw resuscitates a hologram of his maker through a shard.[163] In the newspaper article "La Mémoire du miroir," Holeraw explains that this shard was in fact a piece of the original mirror of Warhole's adolescence that had been shattered in the trenches of Verdun in 1916. This brings us back to the trauma of war that persists in *Monstre*. Warhole can be seen as engaged in an internal, romantic quest to overcome the trauma of the Great War as well as the trauma of being displaced from his dimension. This element of dark playfulness and the penchant for spectacles suggests that Warhole incorporates features of not only ennui but also the trickster.

Warhole's manipulation of media as well as the narrative through his orchestration of spectacles illustrates Burgos's comment that the monster is at the head of the game—the game of imagination and desires, but also childlike play itself.[164] This element of play is not only evident in the frivolity glazing the chain of impossible events running through *Monstre* and primarily caused by Warhole, but it is also a feature of the medium of comics itself. Both Thierry Smolderen and Scott Bukatman show how this playfulness is accompanied by an element of rebelliousness. As shown above, Warhole uses his art to rebel, to create instability, and to protest against the main psychologically and physically destructive force in the tetralogy: war. In this use of art, which persists even after his rebellious clone, Holeraw, breaks away from him, Warhole reinforces Friedrich Schiller's concept of the *Spieltrieb* or play-drive, adopting the attitude of play in art, among other fields, as the only means for humans to liberate themselves through unrestrained imagination and invention.[165]

According to Mathias, it is particularly in "Spleen" that "le domaine de l'ennui stagne dans l'indifférenciation des valeurs" (the domain of ennui stagnates in the lack of differentiation of values).[166] Warhole's comparable leveling of values is also rebellious. Highlighting the sociopolitical criticism offered by the monster, Botting specifies that monstrosity is an incarnation of the psychological effects of modernization: "[I]nstinctual, repressed, monsters disclose the other side of the psyche; oppressed and excluded, they reveal the monstrosity of the systems of power and normalization to which all are subjected."[167] In "Lesbos," Baudelaire describes the mythical inhabitants of the Greek island as "chercheuses d'infini" (seekers of the infinite), "des rebelles dressés contre les limites de la nature ou les limitations de la morale" (rebels against the limits of nature and the limitations of morality).[168] Warhole already incarnates a comparable infinitude of possibilities and brings them into *Monstre*'s dystopian world, unsettling it, and even incrementing its nightmarish nature in the beginning. This can be seen as a further extension and liberation from the subaltern status of monstrous protagonists such as Quasimodo. Besides Warhole himself, Leyla's clone, building up on Leyla's original stubbornness, disrupts the mission to Mars, transforming the spaceship into a carnivalesque zone where everything, especially what is usually labeled obscene, is allowed.[169] Besides affecting the characters, rebelliousness also manifests itself in *Monstre*'s indulgence in ludicrousness and the rejection of logic. As mentioned in the previous chapter, this kind of rebelliousness imbues comics and its development at the hands of Rodolphe Töpffer.[170]

Monstre and the Monster Today

That the Taipei Biennial 2012 was consecrated to modern monsters[171] reflects the extent to which monstrosity is becoming an increasing part of contemporary life, by seeping not merely into bodies but also into events and eras, much like Baudelaire's ennui. The biennial's title, "Modern Monsters: Death and Life of Fiction," is based on historian David Der-Wei Wang's observation that in the course of recent history, Chinese historians have started seeing the monster Taowu as a symbol of history itself.[172] The menacing-looking Taowu is able to see both the past and the future but is also violent and misleading, like the trickster. It therefore alludes to different histories that are created, to the pasts that are rewritten and the futures that are subsequently affected. For the curators of the Taipei Biennial, James T. Hong and Anselm Franke, the monster also incarnates the conflicts that have increased with the passage of time and the weapons of mass destruction that have continued to appear since the Second World War.

Throughout the first two volumes of Bilal's tetralogy, his monster Warhole embodies the monster's potential for violence. Warhole also captures, using Franke's words, "the mechanism of monster-making: imposing our own evil as an objectified symptom of others," for it is the impact of the First World War that makes him turn to evil in the first place. Warhole also incarnates Franke's conclusion that "[a]s a symptomatic mirror, the modern *Taowu* is a figure just for that purpose, the purpose of de-monstering."[173] Warhole acts in a similar way by revealing the flaws of the technology-dependent, conflict-ridden dystopia. Franke continues: "If there was a particular experience of modernity represented by the modern *Taowu*, it is the experience of structural violence and the double binds that tie victims to perpetrators, slaves to masters, the minor to the major."[174] Bilal's world, damaged, prone to monstrosities, and run by an alien monster is likewise closely interlinked through the global range of Warhole's spectacles. It thus captures the fluidity of postmodern spaces and bodies. Such monsters, which externalize internal worlds and individualize the implications of otherwise invisible traumas, also function in a romantic manner through their involvement of senses and emotions. Fluidity between the human and the monstrous, already present in *Swamp Thing* and mapped all over the characters populating *Monstre*, persists in *Hellboy*, where porous worlds merge the human with the demonic and reality with fantasy, as we will now see.

CHAPTER 4

HELLBOY

Nostalgia and the Doomed Quest

> There are more things in heaven and earth, Horatio, than are dreamt of in your philosophy.
> —WILLIAM SHAKESPEARE, HAMLET *(ACT 1, SCENE 5)*[1]

> Les diables troublent l'entendement aux sorciers par diverses et estranges illusions, de sorte qu'ils cuident avoir veu, ouy, dict, et faict ce que le diable leur represente en leur fantaisie [. . .] choses qui sont du tout impossibles.
> (Devils trouble the understanding of magicians through diverse and strange illusions because of which they believe having seen, heard, said, and done whatever the devil shows them in their imagination [. . .] things that are completely impossible.)
> —AMBROISE PARÉ[2]

Jeffrey Jerome Cohen's observation that "[m]onsters [. . .] still serve as the ultimate incorporation of our anxieties—about history, about identity, about our very humanity" is perhaps best captured by the *Hellboy* series, since it incorporates tropes and stories from religions and folklore from all over the world. To a certain extent, it also runs parallel to the course of the twentieth century's turbulent historical events; the two world wars and even, by inference, the Cold War are infused in the series with fantastic, supernatural, pulp and other popular cultural elements.[3] The series taps into a rich network of myths, legends, and fairy tales from diverse, essentially Western (including Slavic), cultures. As Claude Lévi-Strauss famously elaborates, myth, while incorporating supernatural elements, is a means of making sense of the world.[4] Although legends include supernatural elements, they also have some element of historical truth. Likewise including fantastic elements, fairy tales have more entertaining attributes and are often told to children. These three offshoots of folklore along with, to a lesser extent, more canonical literary works (such as *Hamlet* and Lord Byron's *Manfred*, which are, unsurprisingly, also concerned with ghosts) are intertwined in *Hellboy*. Such intertextuality, which is gothic in its intensity,[5] evokes a longing for the past, symbolized by the disembodied ghosts and the increasingly entropic dimension of fantasy in Hellboy's world.

As pointed out by Alan Moore in his introduction to the series' second volume, *Hellboy* is one of those comics that offer "new ways for us to interact with History," whereby the capital H emphasizes the series' undermining of conventional, one-dimensional narratives.[6] This chapter focuses on the nostalgia imbuing the *Hellboy* stories through references to a transcultural gamut of fictional worlds coexisting with a familiar reality. Additional romantic elements such as Hellboy's solitude and his struggling quest to subvert destiny persist to the very end of the series; indeed, Hellboy dies trying to prevent an apocalypse that he was supposed to lead.

"The twentieth century began with utopia and ended with nostalgia," writes Svetlana Boym.[7] Boym distinguishes between two kinds of nostalgia: restorative nostalgia, which serves official discourse, and reflective nostalgia, which "dwells on the ambivalences of human longing and belonging and does not shy away from the contradictions of modernity. Restorative nostalgia protects the absolute truth, while reflective nostalgia calls it into doubt."[8] As will become evident in this chapter, *Hellboy* is marked by reflective nostalgia, which is also the more creative kind of nostalgia, the node where individual and cultural memory meet.[9]

Published by Dark Horse Comics, a relatively small but highly successful American comic book publisher, the *Hellboy* miniseries began in 1994 and ended in 2012. It was followed by two volumes of a new, far briefer series, *Hellboy in Hell*. This chapter limits itself to the twelve volumes of the first miniseries. These volumes were written and often also drawn by Mike Mignola. Before *Hellboy*, Mignola had worked at Marvel, doing covers, inking, and penciling for series such as *The Hulk*, *X-Men*, and *Captain America*. He thus hails from a milieu populated by traditional superheroes, such as Captain America, as well as some of the earliest superheroes who openly embraced monstrosity, such as the X-Men.

Hellboy makes his first appearance on earth on December 23, 1944, emerging from a fire in the ruins of a nameless church in the fictional town of East Bromwich, much to the astonishment of the US Army, a superhero called the Torch of Liberty, and members of the British Paranormal Society, all of whom had been warned of Nazi activity in the area and were expecting the worst. Quite different from traditional warfare, the activity of these characters is paranormal. It turns out that Hellboy was the miracle promised to Hitler by Rasputin, a monk turned wizard who, with the aid of a "Ragna Rok" engine made by Nazi scientists, and by chanting pseudo-biblical verses from an isolated Scottish island, intended to summon the beast destined to start the apocalypse, which has the Lovecraftian name of Ogdru Jahad. In its stead, a small, monkey-like demon emerges unscathed from the fire. Despite having a right hand of stone and being red in color, he is very much a child, as one of the members of the British Paranormal Society, Trevor Bruttenholm, is quick to remark. The abnormally large right hand of stone is metonymic for the physical deformity that Hellboy's demonic form is comparable to.

Already, the black-and-white photograph with the American army unit (fig. 11), the paranormal experts, the Torch of Liberty, and the baby Hellboy with the impossibly large hand captures the kind of nostalgia that imbues the series, conjuring a historical past with fantastic elements. The series partakes of all kinds of stories, particularly fantastic ones, without distinguishing between fact and fiction. In this way, it visualizes, both through the visual style and the visual motifs, reflective nostalgia. Reflective nostalgia "can be ironic and humorous" and "cherishes shattered fragments of memory and space."[10] It contrasts with restorative nostalgia, which "evokes national past and future." Reflective nostalgia "is more oriented toward an individual narrative that savors details and memorial signs, perpetually deferring homecoming itself."[11] As it becomes clear in the course of the series, Hellboy himself is on an increasingly difficult quest to defer what the supernatural world assumed is his legitimate homecoming: accepting his throne as the ruler of Hell. The fragments of reflective nostalgia permeating *Hellboy* make up the black-and-white photograph centered in, and highlighted by, the black void that constitutes the lower half of the page. The victorious World War II soldiers stand next to a superhero from the Golden Age of Comics (which was also the golden age of "justifiable" wars and war propaganda). US history and the history of comics smile at the camera with a monster and three paranormal experts.[12]

In addition to the romantic overtones of this nostalgic gaze,[13] the birth of Hellboy also takes place against the backdrop of two romantic motifs: the ruins of a church with relief statues in the background and the blazing fire from which Hellboy emerges. The only words spoken are those of Rasputin: "And I have *made* one,"[14] which theatricalize in many ways the creative myth of the romantic genius as well as the motif of animation, which, as exemplified by *Frankenstein*, bridges romantic and gothic concerns.

Bruttenholm ends up adopting Hellboy and incorporating him in the US government's Bureau of Paranormal Research and Defense (BPRD), established by Bruttenholm soon after Hellboy's appearance. Confirming his human, and American, acculturation, Hellboy is granted "honorary human status" by the United Nations in 1952.[15] In the middle of the series, we are told that Hellboy has another father, a demon prince of Sheol (the land of the dead[16]) and a witch who, it is later revealed, was a descendent of King Arthur (through a bastard daughter of Mordred).[17] However, Rasputin, who has a mechanized hand comparable to Hellboy's, tells him, "I am your *master*. Your *true* father upon this plane," since his was the first voice Hellboy heard on earth.[18] This diverse set of fathers is only one component of the identity crisis that plagues Hellboy and eventually gets the better of him. Destined to lead an army of demons to destroy humans and fulfill the prophecy of the apocalypse, Hellboy decides to do the complete opposite by fighting against the supernatural forces bent on harming humankind. Hence, as foreshadowed by the very first photograph taken with the US Army, the Torch of Liberty, and Bruttenholm soon after his birth, Hellboy's affiliations remain with the United States and humankind.

After narrating Hellboy's birth, the first volume moves to the present (the year 1994), in which Trevor Bruttenholm is killed by frog monsters who, Hellboy is told later in the series, belong to the final, degraded race of humans that will help summon the beast of the apocalypse.[19] Having recently returned after a two-year-long disappearance during an expedition to a sacred site in the Arctic, Bruttenholm had already become "only a *shadow* of the man" who had raised Hellboy.[20] After Bruttenholm's death, the pressure on Hellboy to assume his original role continues to increase, first through Rasputin and later through other dark forces insisting that Hellboy's evil destiny is inevitable. These forces include the witches who try to appoint Hellboy as their king. After leaving the BPRD in the fifth volume, Hellboy distances himself from America and human company, sinking deeper and deeper into the realm of demons, witches, and other evil supernatural beings, most of whom are determined that he must become the prince of darkness.

As exemplified by the Nazis' courting of the paranormal for evil ends, inexplicable threats dominate the human world in the series. Bruttenholm's sudden death by frog monsters, along with the confusion and listlessness that preceded it, is followed by a sequence of deaths or attempted murders at the hands of the monsters controlled by Rasputin, who himself came under the influence of the Ogdru Jahad while drowning in the Neva River. When another BPRD agent, the "pyrotechnic" Liz Sherman, resurrects a fifteenth-century homunculus—who is given the tellingly ordinary name of Roger by Hellboy—she ends up losing the spark of life and the fire that made her an outcast of human society. Her deteriorating condition baffles the doctors and scientists helplessly examining her. It is Roger who ends up transmitting the spark of life back to her and draining himself to death in the process. Roger embodies the uncomfortable combination of monster and human, especially the accompanying tendency of distrusting the former and equating it with evil, as well as issues of animation and control that are the source of the conflict within Hellboy himself. Indeed, both animation or the coming to life as well as the "defiance of programming" are key themes in *Hellboy*, which are also discernible in other works by Mignola.[21] Already a central concern of *Frankenstein*, animation and control are a recurrent issue for the comics monsters examined here.

Supernatural and paranormal elements are not only beyond human understanding, they are also beyond human control. Precisely this element makes Hellboy and his fellow nonhuman agents indispensable, but it also occasionally casts clouds of suspicion about the paranormal detectives' loyalties. This suspicion is internalized by Hellboy and further heightened by knowledge of the prophecies concerning him. In the fifth volume, Hellboy is given a detonator for Roger because the homunculus is not considered human in the eyes of the authorities and is therefore unreliable and expendable.[22] When Hellboy hands in this detonator upon leaving the BPRD at the end of the same volume, he admits to BPRD consultant (and professor of history and folklore) Kate Corrigan that it is the burden of the supernatural elements—his right hand, the invisible crown floating over his head—that made him quit the BPRD.

"I never deal with what I am. I don't think about it," Hellboy confesses to Kate in an earlier volume; "I just do my job, which usually involves me beating the crap out of things a lot like me. But I don't think about that."[23] Although Hellboy tries not to think about his identity, he is, in the course of the series, forced to struggle with the discrepancy between his adopted and destined roles, between his demonic appearance and his humanity. And it is while fighting against the paranormal elements insisting on his demonic essence that Hellboy gradually slips further and further away from human reality, especially in the volumes following his resignation from the BPRD, after which he faces more witches and demons instead of resurrected Nazis. In spite of the increasing supernatural elements in later volumes, *Hellboy*'s paranormal world remains one that overlaps with our tangible reality; the battles unfolding in the supernatural realm have implications that reverberate in the real world (within the stories) because, "even in [...] worlds that are presented as worlds apart, there remain, implicitly or explicitly, relations to the lived world."[24]

The dominance of the supernatural is accompanied by the omnipresence of death in the series. This is also reflected by the static, even statuesque, nature of Mignola's art for *Hellboy*. Both the art and the range of intertextual references concretize Hans Belting's observation that "a medium is but an archive of dead images until we animate the images with our gaze," as well Jared Gardner's claim that "[a]rchives are everywhere in the loosest, messiest sense of the word—archives of the forgotten artifacts and ephemera of American popular culture."[25] In *Hellboy*'s case, these archives include a broad range of stories and romantic art. Death itself, as pointed out by Bukatman, persists through the static quality of Mignola's art as well as the stories themselves. It is further personified by depictions of figures such as death holding an hourglass in the first volume, *The Seed of Destruction*.[26] Bukatman links the contemplative atmosphere and abstracted images of the short story "The Island" (in volume 6, *Strange Places*) to the death drive pervading the entire series, with Hellboy himself being "steeped in death."[27] This is complemented by *The Seed of Destruction*'s opening scene, which shows Hellboy watching the sun rising over a desolate seascape of shipwrecks. This scene echoes the atmosphere of solitude and vista of hazy possibilities in Caspar David Friedrich's *Der Wanderer über dem Nebelmeer* (*Wanderer above the Sea of Fog*) as well as the destruction in *Die gescheiterte Hoffnung* (*The Wreck of Hope*) (fig. 12).[28] For comics writer and artist Walter Simonson, Mignola's abstraction points toward unseen, vast possibilities that are at the same time disturbingly real and acquire mythological proportions "evok[ing] a sense of almost religious iconography, traces of that hidden world where meaning is too powerful or overwhelming to be completely understood."[29] This abstraction, as examined in the final section of this chapter, also visually highlights Hellboy's solitude, as in another panel where he follows the African witch doctor Mohlomi, supposedly dead for two hundred years, to listen to the ocean calling for him (fig. 13).[30] The faces of both figures are free of any markers, and the bird's-eye perspective of the scene and their diminutive size forebode their imminent confrontation with a much higher natural power.

These abstracted images recall silhouette animation, which, as will be shown in the last section of this chapter, ties in with the theme of the spectacle starring Hellboy that the series often alludes to. However, before turning to the relevance of the spectacle itself—the theatrical nature of which is emphasized by the supernatural creatures who watch and comment on Hellboy's struggles from another world—this chapter focuses on the two key components contributing toward the spectacle's construction: first, the series' mélange of storyworlds that overwhelm human reality and reflect a nostalgia for forgotten and fantastic worlds; and second, Hellboy's doomed quest. Another element related to the spectacle that recurs throughout the *Hellboy* comics is the tense relationship between animation and control.

Nostalgia: *Sehnsucht* for Other (Story)Worlds

Figures from comics, myths, legends, and fairy tales populate Hellboy's universe, reflecting a nostalgia for times and realms that are largely forgotten in the contemporary world. According to Bart Beaty, "nostalgia is among the primary drivers of value in the comics world."[31] While Beaty is referring to the practice of collecting and reading comics, the world of *Hellboy* imbibes a similar inclination, more specifically a nostalgia for fantastic stories, both contemporary (superheroes) and old (myths, legends, fairy tales).[32] The series' intertwining of the fantastic and the real is comparable to the medieval imagination, frequently referenced in the *Hellboy* books, which did not distinguish between imaginary figures and real ones.[33] Its constant looking back is also in the vein of the nostalgic inclinations of the graphic novel described by Jan Baetens and Hugo Frey,[34] even though the series remains in between the one-shot graphic novel with literary, autobiographical, and artistic ambitions and the more mainstream superhero comic book.

Inspired by a wealth of stories, these worlds are, in Bukatman's words, "bookish," and weave an intricate, intermedial web: "As Hellboy engages with paranormal activities that stem from numerous folkloric traditions and weird fictions, the book—the *Hellboy* comic—becomes an extension and manifestation of those imaginary, those bookish, worlds: a place where they are reanimated through the acts of writing, drawing, and reading and a meeting ground in which these worlds—literary, authorial, readerly—entwine and ensnare."[35] The "bookishness," which is both a remediation of fictional figures while also being a romantic feature because of its nostalgic drive, is reinforced by the dedications preceding the volumes (most of which are to writers of a broad range of fantasy stories, hinting toward each volume's source of inspiration). The first *Hellboy* volume is dedicated to, among others, Jack Kirby and H. P. Lovecraft. The second is dedicated to "Dracula and all those other vampires I have loved."[36] The sixth, *Strange Places*, is dedicated to Hans Christian Andersen, "King of Mermaids," and William Hope Hodgson, who is known for his horror and fantasy stories, particularly the collection *Sargasso Sea Stories*.[37] Hovering, like the *Sargasso Sea Stories*, on the brink of reality, Hellboy turns to alcohol and the company of other supernatural creatures, especially ghosts, in this sixth volume.[38] Such an escape into an imaginative world, as already suggested by the imagery in "The Island," is in itself romantic. Signaling the overpoweringly horrific fantasy that dominates the series as it nears its end, the penultimate *Hellboy* volume is dedicated to the writers M. R. James and J. Sheridan Le Fanu, both of whom wrote fantastic and gothic fiction.

Myth, especially Christian mythology, has a strong presence in the *Hellboy* world. Already Rasputin's chanting, "Chained in heaven are they. Seven is their number,"[39] in the earlier *Hellboy* volumes evokes John's Book of Revelation. Similarly, when predicting what would happen with the rise of the new queen of the witches, Nimue, under the influence of the beast of the apocalypse, the Ogdru Jahad, directly quotes from Revelation: "I saw another beast which rose out of the earth. It had two horns like a lamb and it spoke like a dragon" (13:11).[40] This beast is Hellboy, and the growing of his usually carefully filed-down horns indicates that he has succumbed to his destiny as a warrior of hell. Hellboy's decision to fight for humans against demons is jestingly portrayed as a reversal of the biblical tale of the fall of man in the short story "Pancakes," one of the several flashbacks to the young Hellboy's life at a US military airbase in New Mexico:[41] here, the apple is replaced by pancakes and heaven by hell. The humor of the reversal is further highlighted by demons exclaiming in pain as Hellboy is fed pancakes by a US Army officer with a fork bearing a "USA" stamp and decides that he likes them.[42] In keeping with the intertwining of different mythologies in the series, this short story also recalls the tale of Persephone in which, after eating the fruit of the underworld, she is forced to become Hades's queen. Here, reflective nostalgia refigures a Greek myth in an idiom that is in between superhero comics and fantasy fiction.

The series' opening scene shows a ruined church haphazardly bordered by graves in the fictional village of East Bromwich. This constellation of a former church and the historical background of World War II is also an expression of reflective memory, interweaving history and religion. Although most likely the result of bombing rather than erosion caused by time and neglect, the church resembles ruins, which have often been the preferred spaces of romantic art and literature, as exemplified by Friedrich's *Klosterfriedhof im Schnee* (*Cloister Cemetery in Snow*) (1817–1818), where, as in the *Seed of Destruction* panels, only the grills of the high windows and rudiments of the building's skeleton remain.[43] Similarly, the short story from the third *Hellboy* volume, "The Wolves of Saint August," is set in 1994 and unfolds in yet another abandoned chapel in Griart, a fictional Alpine town.[44] Even the final *Hellboy* volume, *The Storm and the Fury*, opens in a church in England, where Henry V's knights have left their tombs.[45] Hellboy visits the church to talk to one of his closest friends, the priest Edward Kelly.[46] Hellboy often works with priests and is blessed by the priest Adrian Frost, whose father, Malcolm Frost, was the only BPRD member who insisted that Hellboy should be killed.[47] In the title story of *The Chained Coffin*, Hellboy revisits the place of his birth, the ruined church in East Bromwich.[48] While dreaming there, he learns that he was the favorite child of an important demon in hell who had conceived him with a witch. The witch also had two other human children—one of whom became a priest and the other a nun—who eventually persuaded their mother to turn to Christianity; following her wishes, they kept her coffin chained in a vain attempt to keep her demon lover from coming to claim her and their unborn child.

This exemplifies the prominence of the church as a situating element, which complements the recurrent Christian symbols and references to Christian thought in the series. In contrast, the legend of Saint Leonard the Hermit, who was injured while fighting a dragon and from whose blood lilies sprouted, is only partially modified in the story "The Nature of the Beast," with Hellboy eventually playing a role in the dragon's death and unknowingly leaving a wake of lilies growing from his blood (fig. 14).[49] This image establishes the lily motif, which is another religious motif (usually associated with Mary in Christian mythology) linked to Hellboy. In typical Mignolesque fashion, this reinforcement unfolds silently through a repeated, concentrated focus on the lilies and exemplifies the moment of silence preceding intense action that involves Hellboy struggling against yet another one of the forces hindering his quest toward individuality and humanity. Another short story takes up the "Hand of Glory" folktale (which confers magical powers on a disembodied hand) while also referencing Saint Dunstan.[50] Here, the scheming occultist Igor Bromhead succeeds in releasing a demon imprisoned in a box that had been hidden in the wall of a former convent covered with a fresco of Saint Dunstan. Igor in turn wears a talisman of the same saint to protect him from the evil powers he summons to take revenge on Hellboy and rob him of the invisible crown designating him as a prince of hell.

Images of angels and reproductions of Christian art are recurrent.[51] Panels often focus on specific scenes from the Christian mythos, such as the Descent from the Cross on a wooden altar during a scene situated in the church under which Nimue was imprisoned.[52] The earlier volumes of the *Hellboy* series also include mythologized historical figures, most notably Rasputin, who, after being destroyed by Hellboy and Liz in 1994, reappears, this time aided by three Nazi officers from his Ragna Rok project: Ilsa Haupstein, Leopold Kurtz, and Karl Ruprecht Kroenen. As he explains to Ilsa, he is no longer human, having moved so far beyond it that his previous existence "seems almost like a dream."[53] His return was made possible by Baba Yaga, the one-legged witch of Slavic fairy tales, who had hidden half of Rasputin's soul in the roots of Yggdrasil, the tree growing through the nine worlds of Nordic mythology.

Baba Yaga is one of the many beings seeking revenge against Hellboy after he shot one of her eyes out during a BPRD mission in 1964.[54] Although

Hellboy assumed that he had killed her, Baba Yaga is, in the Mignolaverse at least, Russia's mother and hence immortal—as the animals talking among themselves at the end of the story explain—despite the fact that her body had already been modified with iron for teeth and wood for legs.[55] The bear's little speech about Baba Yaga underscores the immortality of fairy tales and, by extension, stories. It also emphasizes their role in the formation of cultural memory. Such indiscriminate and eclectic combinations of different kinds of worlds are very familiar to comics, especially in the realm of superheroes. Hellboy's coexistence with fairy tales and historical figures, myths, and legends often takes on an allusive dimension, commenting on both the original works and the *Hellboy* series as well as the media—and sometimes, on a vaguer level, the sociopolitical—context in which the comics were created.[56]

The third *Hellboy* volume, *The Chained Coffin*, introduces creatures from Irish and English folklore, the Daoine Sídhe or fairy folk, who reappear throughout the series. Correspondingly, the first of the volume's stories, "The Corpse" opens with a verse from William Allingham's poem "The Fairies," which, like the *Hellboy* story, is about the "wee folk" and their aging leader who stole a human baby and raised her.[57] Set in Ireland in 1959, this is Hellboy's first encounter with the Daoine Sídhe, including the changeling Gruagach, who had been left with the kidnapped baby Alice Monaghan's parents. Trapped in the body of a boar after having tried to kill Hellboy, Gruagach becomes one of the many vengeful enemies resurfacing throughout the series. Having come into contact with the fairies' magic, Alice ends up keeping company with them and other "little people." As revealed in the ninth *Hellboy* volume, *The Wild Hunt*, she is also Hellboy's main love interest.

Already during Hellboy's first encounter with the fairies, it is clear that the supernatural creatures are on the verge of extinction.[58] After Hellboy's refusal to become king of the witches, Gruagach convinces them to appoint Nimue, a powerful but mad witch from Arthurian times, in order to prevent their fading away like the other "children of the earth," as foreshadowed by the elf king Dagda's death at the beginning of the volume that follows.[59] From a distance, and in a scene with faded gold light and bleak colors, Hellboy attends Dagda's funeral in a dreamspace (fig. 15). This indicates both the increasing distance between the world of folklore and the "real" world and the gradual dissolution of the former. Also losing their powers, the desperate witches end up summoning the very witch they had unanimously decided to kill and dismember. Nimue, on becoming the Queen of Blood and having absorbed some of the Ogdru Jahad's power, kills Queen Mab (one of Hellboy's few allies), who had been withering away since the series' beginning. Although dead, Queen Mab reappears as an innkeeper in the final *Hellboy* volume, enacting her description of Ragna Rok as an end that is followed by a beginning. Similarly, Hellboy's life continues in hell after his death from combating Nimue, who had turned into the beast of the apocalypse.[60] Hence, while echoing the superhero comics custom of multiple apocalypses, the *Hellboy* stories stick to the main story arc of the protagonist's despairing struggle against his destiny, which is also an individualistic but eventually unsuccessful struggle to assert free will. This can be seen as a nostalgic nod to superhero stories and a reworking of the mechanics of seriality. Hellboy himself displays more conventionally nostalgic inclinations and attachments to the impossible, including the collection of charms and talismans from all over the world in his coat.[61]

Figures from a wide, transcultural range of storyworlds continue to play important roles in both the main *Hellboy* storyline and the short stories accompanying it. Thus, in the tenth *Hellboy* volume, Blackbeard's legend is accorded a short story,[62] and the volume that follows resurrects the Mayan bat god, Camazotz, who ends up possessing a Mexican wrestler with whom Hellboy had teamed up to fight local paranormal threats.[63] A short story from the eleventh volume, "The Sleeping and the Dead,"[64] lies at the intersection of familiar folklore through its employment of nursery rhymes and vampires.[65] Within the main story arc of the series, this intense intertextual interaction with storyworlds symbolizes Hellboy's growing immersion in the world of ghosts and the paranormal. Hence, in "The Island," a sailor singing the popular maritime song "The Mermaid" is actually a skeleton like the rest of the people in the bar. Popular songs punctuate the narrative as Hellboy willfully sinks into the realm of ghosts. Playing in the background as Hellboy leaves the house of a dead friend, the American folk hero Captain Alfred Bulltop Stormalong's song continues as Hellboy enters a forest, where he is accosted by a trio of pets disguised as humans who assume that he is Stormalong, thus confirming the allusion already made in a panel juxtaposing Hellboy's face with the line "O Stormy, he is dead and gone."[66]

After refusing to become king of the witches, Hellboy is thrust into Baba Yaga's world, a dream world to which Baba Yaga has been confined since her first encounter with Hellboy. As Baba Yaga tells Hellboy, "The world is done with me . . . I live in a dream of a Russia long gone, and there I'll remain."[67] It is also from this dream space that other magical creatures such as the elves, Queen Mab, and the ghost of the nineteenth-century paranormal detective Edward Grey (one of the few beings who holds onto the belief that Hellboy will make his own destiny[68]) watch over earth and comment on Hellboy's actions. In Baba Yaga's dream world, Hellboy encounters several figures from Slavic mythology including the Slavic forest god Leshii, and Koshchei, a Slavic villain, who agrees to help Baba Yaga in return for death. Pointing toward the increasing despair taking over Hellboy's world, where evil forces outweigh the good ones, Baba Yaga kills the Slavic god Perun, the king of the world and god of thunder and lightning. Exemplifying the rewriting and intertwining of stories in *Hellboy*, Mignola's Baba Yaga had once been Koshchei's lover. In the face of the powerful forces Baba Yaga pits against Hellboy, only Vasilisa, the Russian Cinderella, "Vasilisa the Beautiful," offers to help him.[69] While Vasilisa succeeds in opening an exit door so that Hellboy can get out of Baba Yaga's realm and away from Koshchei's unrelenting attacks, she herself is killed by Koshchei.[70]

Coming after stories about Hellboy's wanderings in areas little frequented by humans and favored by ghosts and supernatural creatures, Hellboy's struggles in Baba Yaga's space are indicative of how things continue to spiral out of his control, resulting in increasingly violent and destructive clashes with supernatural forces: nightmare takes over.

The nostalgia in *Hellboy* extends to the images, which either remediate or reproduce. The art in the series alludes to fairy-tale illustrations, as in the case of artwork for the seventh volume's short story, "The Troll Witch," which evokes Ivan Bilibin's art while incorporating Christian themes and motifs. The link to the apocalypse is similarly confirmed by the inclusion of Albrecht Dürer's prints as markers for the second and fourth chapters, the former showing *The Four Horsemen of the Apocalypse* and the latter showing *Saint Michael Fighting the Dragon*.[71] The fourth chapter shows Hellboy fighting a skeleton, which is a key image for the entire series, given that Hellboy is constantly rebelling against the exigencies of his past, echoing the rebelliousness and the assertion of individualism that, according to Bukatman, is part of the "spirit" of the comics medium.[72]

Later volumes also reveal the influence of Francisco Goya, beginning with the incident when Hellboy is carried away by the resurrected corpse of a witch for a witches' Sabbath in Leeds, where they ask him to be king of the witches of England,[73] and culminating in the short story "In the Chapel of Moloch."[74] Set in an abandoned chapel transformed into an artist's studio in southern Portugal, this story remediates the figure of Moloch, visually filtering it through the figure of the goat-like devil looming over a witch torturing a man in Goya's print *Ensayos* (Trials) from *Los Caprichos*.[75] This figure also presides over Goya's Sabbath paintings, including the earlier *Witches' Sabbath* (1798) and a later one in his *Black Paintings* (1821–1823). Similar to other *Hellboy* demons, the Moloch of the legends was also after human blood, requiring his worshippers to sacrifice children at his altar. Possessed by Moloch's spirit, all of the artist Jerry's latest paintings, as Hellboy points out, were inspired by—"ripped off" in Hellboy's words—Goya's *Los Caprichos*. Jerry's agent defends this appropriation by declaring: "[T]hat would have been Jerry's statement—using the old to define the modern, to illustrate the relentless and unchangeable nightmare of human existence" (fig. 16).[76] The agent's claim is to be taken with a grain of salt. What happens in Mignola's remediation of Goya's works in comics is, I think, more radical: in each panel (and especially in the top four ones), the Goyesque monsters writhe with an energy and a vitality that is related to Mignola's own "sculptural" style, which emphasizes the body, and the comics idiom, which has its own intense energy—both contained and yet bursting out of the panel frames. The "braiding" of the comics page further reinforces the meaning and presence of the panels.[77] Jerry never manages to finish these works, because, coming under the influence of Moloch's spirit, he works in the old chapel at night, sleeping feverishly during the day in order to create his first sculpture, a massive Moloch idol. These monstrous corporealities aside, the remediations also preserve the trauma lingering behind Goya's works, including the related trope of a troubled romantic artist. As Hillary Chute has suggested, the line itself is a carrier of memory and even countermemory.[78] The latter performs work similar to Boym's reflective nostalgia, reconfiguring an older memory into a new idiom while arguably retaining its original affective power.

A specific popular image that is referenced more than once when Hellboy is made to participate in a wild hunt against giants is George Cruikshank's "Herne with his steed, hounds and owl, observed by the Duke of Richmond and the Earl of Surrey" (1843).[79] It is during this wild hunt that the possibility that Hellboy is Arthur's successor to the throne of England is raised.[80] This becomes another role that others, including Morgan Le Fay and Alice, insist he should take up. During the wild hunt, his fellow huntsmen, calling him a devil and a monster, try to kill him in order to prevent him from ascending to the throne. It is only toward the end of the series that Arthur's successor is revealed to be someone else.[81]

Ultimately, the theme of "[o]ld stories made new"[82] in *Hellboy* holds not only for the resurrection and reconfiguration of folklore (including mythologies and fairy tales) and iconic images, but also the accompanying transposition of very human concerns to the paranormal realm. The paranormal itself evokes issues of both animation and control that concern all of the monsters examined here. This chapter will now turn toward the two most prominent concerns discernible in the stories: the individualistic assertion of will over prescribed roles, and solitude.

Solitude of Otherness and the Doomed Quest

Hellboy's solitude is visualized by a panel in the "Baba Yaga" story from the third volume showing his tiny, abstracted figure in the snowy Russian countryside, capturing his vulnerability in the face of the unknown, omnipresent forces that have other plans for him.[83] For the main story of the tenth *Hellboy* volume, *The Crooked Man*, Mignola takes up the weird fiction writer Manly Wade Wellman's preferred setting of the woods in the Appalachian Mountains. Due to their relative isolation from human activity, these woods have been a traditional setting for unusual happenings and beings, where nature is free to show its wild, extraordinary facets. As Mignola goes on to elaborate, however, Wellman's influence is not limited to the Appalachian Mountains: the Wellmanian hero, John the Balladeer, a Korean War veteran, living a solitary life in the Appalachian Mountains, was Hellboy's forerunner. While Hellboy's solitude is already established by his demonic appearance, it is paradoxically also part of his human side. A visual pendant to these two sides of Hellboy is provided in a panel from the very first *Hellboy* volume showing Hellboy comforting his adoptive father in the wake of an attack by frog monsters, since it highlights the contrast between his human reaction and his demonic appearance: in one of Mignola's trademark abstracted moments, Hellboy's red form stands out, with his back to the reader, his sawed-down horns, curving tail, massive right hand of stone, and cloven hooves for feet. A genealogical study of Hellboy's general appearance could lead one back to Ambroise Paré's treatise, in particular his twenty-fifth chapter, in which, resorting to religious texts,[84] he mentions that the demons, synonymous with devils, are the bad spirits and the angels are the good ones. In keeping with the biblical concept of the devil, he also describes demons as "malins Anges" or cunning angels, always scheming to ruin humankind through tricks, lies, and false illusions.[85] Paré's phrase captures the conflict propelling the *Hellboy* series: despite looking like a demon and being constantly urged by the darker forces to assume his role as the leader of demons, Hellboy fights against evil.[86]

Describing Hellboy as an existential hero, science fiction writer Jane Yolen sees his story as "a deeply human story for all its monsters," since "[h]ere in Hellboy, we have the unwanted child who overcompensates [. . .] the man who values the world more than himself."[87] Mike Chadbourn likewise underscores how Hellboy struggles against fears that are universal and human.[88] For Bukatman, it is "the very real emotionalism of Hellboy [that] is one continuing point of contact."[89] Indeed, although Hellboy is largely accepted by the humans he works for and protects, his monstrous appearance does not remain unnoticed, as with Earl Reeds, a historian briefly subcontracted by the BPRD to help with Bluebeard's monster. Cowering, terrified at the far end of the boat, Reeds cannot stop himself from staring at Hellboy's feet, and Hellboy understandingly acknowledges: "It's the feet, right? I know, but they get the job done."[90]

Alluding to the limited control Hellboy can assert over his own identity, Ilsa's scathing description of Hellboy as "[t]he American ghost hunter, 'Hellboy.' Some sort of trained circus monkey" is not far off the mark.[91] However, the Nazis themselves manufacture *Kriegaffe* (warrior monkeys),[92] an activity alluding to the notion of the *Übermensch* that fed into the concept of the superhero, who in turn is part of the comics legacy inherited by Hellboy. The reference to the circus also strengthens the link between comics with monstrous protagonists and the circus, both of which thrive on the curiosity and the dialectic of attraction and repulsion incited by monsters. The circus is occasionally mentioned directly, as in a BRPD agent's comment upon seeing the mix of human and nonhuman agents that "it's like working for the goddam circus."[93]

Hellboy's identity is not only conflicted but, as is the case to varying extents with monsters, also obscure. As Trevor Bruttenholm points out, even after fifty years Hellboy remains a mystery for Bruttenholm and the scientists studying his powerful and indestructible right hand, which is immune to pain: "[O]ur best efforts to uncover his secret ultimately left us knowing little more than we did that first day."[94] It is only after encountering Rasputin that Hellboy learns his real name, Anung un Rama, and is forced to face his original identity as denizen of hell and harbinger of the apocalypse. However, already the very first encounter with Rasputin is repulsive for Hellboy: "It feels *bad* down here. All over my body coarse, black little hairs rise and bristle at the touch of *evil*."[95] In contrast, Rasputin has been treated to "*visions* of a world transformed by *holocaust* and *fire*" over which he would preside with Hellboy as his commander. Although Rasputin insists that Hellboy does not have a choice, Hellboy refuses to accept him as his master, adding that he "didn't ask to come" as he kills Rasputin for the first time.[96] Like Rasputin, Hecate addresses Hellboy using his "real" or demonic name, Anung un Rama, and insists that "[t]oo long lost among humans, you have nearly lost *yourself*... You have made war against members of your own family... and mine."[97] For Hecate, Hellboy's kith and kin are the "[a]ncient spirits of the air, the mountains, streams, and pools; old gods of graves and shadows and demons of hell... witches, striges, vampire[s]... ghosts come forth from their tombs."[98] "You cannot escape your *destiny*!," Hecate insists, like Rasputin before her and many others afterward.[99] Yet, when Hellboy's horns start growing, signaling the suppression of his human side in favor of his demonic roots, he breaks them off, insisting: "It's *my* goddamn life, I'll do what I want with it!"[100] This act surprises his spectators, Baba Yaga, Dagda, and the witch finder, Sir Edward Grey, who watch the events unfold from another world. Grey welcomes Hellboy's assertion of his being: "Born of human woman in hell, reborn of human design on earth, and now, finally ... he gives birth to himself."[101]

Hellboy's will, however, is not always enough to withstand his supposed destiny, because parts of his body—his horns and his right hand—compel him to assume his role. As pointed out by the priest Adrian Frost in the fourth volume, *The Right Hand of Doom*, Hellboy's right hand is a burden, prone to fulfilling the prophecies tied to the "hand of doom."[102] As the demon Ualac informs Bromhead in "Box Full of Evil": Hellboy's right hand has the power to order the dragon of the apocalypse and revive the denizens of hell to start a war against heaven.[103] While struggling against the urge to take up the role predicted for him—which increases as his horns grow out in imitation of his demon father—Hellboy ends up in a spiritual space, a forest with the little people he had encountered in Ireland, one of whom, Dagda, points out that Hellboy does not even know what the name Anung un Rama, on which Bromhead's disempowering spell was based, means. Dagda tells him that it means "world destroyer" and that he can easily fight against words. Hellboy consequently breaks the spell and defeats Ualac but refuses to take his crown back, saying: "It's not what I am and it's not what I'm ever gonna be, and that's the end of it!"[104]

In the volume that follows, *Conqueror Worm*, we learn that the alien assassin posing as an American World War II soldier, who planned to kill Hellboy the day he was born, did not do so because he recognized his free will and his ability to change his fate. "Hellboy, to be *other* than human does not necessarily mean to be *less*," the dying alien assures him.[105] In contrast to the alien's encouraging words, the grandmother of mermaids, Bog Roosh, tells Hellboy: "For the world to go on living you have to die. That is the simple truth of it. Nothing less. You are the sentence of ruin passed on from the beginning."[106] Although Hellboy points out that, despite not being (physically) human, he has been fighting evil and consequently striving to do good, he starts losing hope of winning the battle in the next volume, *Strange Places*, even though he does not stop fighting. "The Island" in particular can be read as a tale of being lost but continuing even after losing all hope of redemption. At the story's beginning, Hecate makes an appearance, assuming that the now changed Hellboy is willing to take up his role in bringing about the end of the world with her because, instead of choosing a death at the hands of a mermaid-witch that would have neutralized his destructive powers, he has decided to continue living.[107]

After Hecate fades away, Hellboy enters a ruined church where he watches a group of knights kill an old man, a supposed heretic, whose blood is yellow. A monster—one of the Ogdru Jahad's offspring—emerges from the blood, whom Hellboy struggles to fight off. Finding himself on the brink of death again, Hellboy ends up in an abstract space with the African doctor Mohlomi. He tells Mohlomi that, although he is sure he is dead, he is not ready for it to be over, as a result of which he finds himself again in the ruined church with the old man. "What are you?" the old man asks Hellboy, who replies: "That's a damn good question."[108] Having ancient knowledge, being "the living record of the true origin of all things," the old man tells Hellboy about the origin of the Ogdru Jahad and about himself and his death at the hands of the Spanish Inquisition, which Hellboy had witnessed. Another monster bursts forth from the heretic whom Hellboy is unable to defeat (in spite of Mohlomi's bell, which was supposed to protect him). "Your phantom allies have failed you. You're alone," the monster declares triumphantly.[109] Hellboy only succeeds in defeating the monster with difficulty and with a lot of luck. Even though Hellboy is repeatedly told that he is dead after this incident, he struggles to remain as alive as possible. As Queen Mab tells the vengeful Gruagach: "all these years he has *tried* to live a man's life. But he is *not* a man. And now, with his death, he finally knows it. He feels the weight of his burden."[110] While Mab speaks, Hellboy is shown against a backdrop of the statues of the apostles accompanied by a figuration of death, thus reestablishing how darkly romantic and gothic his situation is.

From his death, Hellboy later only remembers the pain but cannot tell Alice what it was like being dead or why he was resurrected.[111] This augments the lack of direction and purpose that seeps into him as the weight of his prophesied destiny increases, particularly after leaving the BPRD. An increasingly weary Hellboy is shown after *Strange Places*: he is injured far more easily, looks battered, and is also visibly troubled. His doubts regarding his capacity to do good likewise increase as his world whirls out of control with enemies gaining power and attacking unpredictably. He has to face a growing number of unexpected attacks in the second half of the series, especially after Nimue is resurrected in *The Wild Hunt* and gathers an army to destroy the human world, making Hellboy's quest to ensure the victory of good even more difficult.

However, for the demon Ualac, Hellboy is weak precisely because he has "become almost human."[112] Hellboy is indeed very human in his desire to help people and to do good, as in the case of old Mrs. Hatch, whose house has been cursed since her youngest daughter, Annie, was tricked into marrying a demon living with the dead.[113] While Annie Hatch's story combines *Alice in Wonderland* and the myth of Persephone, the dying Mrs. Hatch mistakes Hellboy for Santa Claus, thus exemplifying the wild tangle of supernatural beings from different cultures and beliefs populating the series.

Hence, the tragedy of Hellboy's story is that even though he tries to avoid joining the demons and witches and to stop the apocalypse, the apocalypse remains inevitable (his refusal to lead the witches, for instance, leads to Nimue's resurrection). As Queen Mab tells Hellboy, "that must be the curse of your life—that the ruin of things will come from your good works."[114] Reminding Hellboy how his blood transformed the old man denounced as a heretic into a demon set on destroying the world, she asks:

> I know you destroyed that creature. But all those months in that little boat—wasn't he with you there, every day? Just as he has been with you every day since. Drink, hide with ghosts in their houses, but you cannot escape him—any more than you can escape your own shadow. This thing is part of you, maybe the biggest part, and continue as you have been and it will consume you. The truth is that it's already begun—hasn't it?[115]

Hellboy's clashing identities, the uncomfortable mix of the human and the monstrous, had begun to torment him at an early age—as revealed in the brief story from his childhood in New Mexico[116]—due to his glaring difference from humans and his proximity to the demons he ended up fighting against. This uncertainty regarding his crumbling self-identity persists to the very end of the series. In *The Storm and the Fury*, Queen Mab tells Alice the story of George Washbrook, who, in order to atone for his great aunts' use of witchcraft in an attempt to kill Queen Victoria and for the evil deeds committed by all of his relatives, went off to fight in France during the First World War.[117] Like Hellboy, George wanted "to prove that he could be otherwise."[118] Mysteriously brought back to life as he lay bleeding in the trenches, it turns out that he was Arthur's descendent and the long-awaited king of England.

The inability to acquire a convincing self-identity results in Hellboy's increasing solitude in the course of the series, as he moves away from the real world and starts keeping company with ghosts in *Strange Places*. This in turn is comparable to the behavior of one of his adversaries, the vampire of Prague, who, after the plague had destroyed all of the city's inhabitants, was forced to curb his addiction to gambling by playing with ghosts.[119] The eighth volume, *Darkness Calls*, reveals that Hellboy had started living with the ghosts of people he once knew, imagining that they were still living. The first of such ghosts is Henry Middleton, a close friend of Bruttenholm and Hellboy, who had died in 1984.[120] Ghosts consequently overshadow humans in the later *Hellboy* stories, both the longer ones that are more openly woven into the series' central narrative as well as the shorter, more peripheral stories. For instance, in a short story titled "The Mole," Hellboy plays cards with dead acquaintances.[121] He then notices a mole on his hand that grows to the extent of releasing a demon and pulling off his skin, all of which turns out to be "[j]ust a dream."[122]

Like many romantic protagonists, Hellboy ends up fleeing into an alternative world, a world that is heavily molded by imagination and emotions, populated with skeletons and ghosts that Hellboy seems to animate himself. This shift into a world of dreams is already foreshadowed by Hellboy's ability to communicate with supernatural and dead beings: during his last mission with the BPRD (*Conqueror Worm*), skeletons of dead American soldiers warn him about the trap set by the resurrected Nazis in the castle. The mission's location foreshadows the ruined, haunted spaces Hellboy will seek refuge in after leaving the BPRD, since the castle is also haunted, its ghosts being the offspring of extreme violence, as the old man in the German World War II uniform warns the BPRD team: "All those men in the fiction of war . . . suddenly burned into each other . . . those not burned, crushed by falling walls, enemies ground together . . . bleeding into the other. [. . .] That is how *those* ghosts were made."[123] Bukatman concludes his *Poetics of Slumberland* by suggesting that Winsor McCay's *Little Nemo in Slumberland*'s tropes such as the play with worlds and bodies, especially the sliding into dream worlds, are continued in superhero comics, which often reveal a self-awareness of being products of the imagination, of being fiction and even celebrating it.[124] In addition, the "*queasiness* [. . .] about the modern world" noted by Bukatman in early comics (such as McCay's *Dream of the Rarebit Fiend*) echoes the romantic distrust of progress and Enlightenment ideals.[125] This distrust is magnified to horrific proportions in both *Swamp Thing* and *Hellboy*, where the supernatural and individual psyches unleash chaos in the two comics series' worlds.

In *Hellboy*, the powerful, unfathomable otherworldly forces are fueled by the interpenetration of diverse myths, fairy tales, and legends. They struggle against their disappearance and combat against humans, often rendering modern technology useless. Already in the second *Hellboy* volume, *Wake the Devil*, in which the BPRD tries to recover the vampire Vladimir Giurescu's body, machines and devices are constantly breaking down, sowing the seeds for a distrust of technology. Moreover, it turns out that the multimillionaire owner of the corporation supplying the BPRD with its gadgets and weapons has become one of Rasputin's followers. The supposedly improved jetpack malfunctions and sends Hellboy crashing into the midst of the Nazis, his walkie-talkie does not work, and even the BPRD's rescue plane is faulty, signaling the increasing powerlessness of humans and their technology against supernatural forces. Similarly, when facing the witches of Thessaly who are guarding Giurescu's coffin, Hellboy's gun explodes. Crying, "No more *god damn machines!*," Hellboy resorts to a nearby sword.[126] This disdain for technology is echoed by the vampire Giurescu's skeletal father, who had warned his son not to fall for Ilsa and "her new, *modern* world."[127] Notably, in the earlier volumes, especially while working for the BPRD, Hellboy deals with his enemies using modern but basic weapons such as guns and bombs, and it is usually the Nazis who resort to complex technologies (for manufacturing limbs and soldiers, or for summoning supernatural forces).

Soon after leaving the BPRD, Hellboy turns to alcohol to drown his troubles and trades human company for the company of ghosts. It is only in the last volume, *The Storm and the Fury*, shortly before his death that Hellboy reveals that he has stopped drinking and intends to return to the BPRD in order to help with the increasingly volatile paranormal situation.[128] He mentions this while watching a news report on television in an inn where he has sought refuge with Alice, from whom he is eventually separated in the same story: the tiny television images show a barely contained, raging monster surrounded by barbed wire and soldiers as Kate speaks to the crowd of journalists at the site, as well as a –somewhat ironic and humorous—closeup shot of a doomsday prophet with his "The End is Nigh" sign (fig. 17). This confirms the monstrous, demonic world's entry into human reality. *The Storm and the Fury* consequently concretizes both Hellboy's failing quest to defeat the demons taking over the world and his own persistent solitude, which, as suggested by the image, goes back to his unusual childhood and coming of age as a monster-human shuttling between US Army bases and the Bureau of Paranormal Research and Defense. The childhood memory is in color—in contrast to the black-and-white television images—thus highlighting the affective hold of those memories on Hellboy. The page is divided by Hellboy's saddened eyes, as Alice's small figure sitting at the pub table recedes into the background: his pain is both evident and accessible.

Later in the same volume, as Hellboy and the apocalyptic beast (Nimue merged with the Ogdru Jahad) fight in the skies and Arthur's army struggles against the demons, the consequences of these battles are felt on earth, causing considerable destruction: cathedrals and castles are destroyed and cities uprooted. Antony Gormley's colossal sculpture *Angel of the North* (1998) at

Gateshead, England, loses a wing. In order to help Hellboy, a crying Vasilisa gives him a dagger, which kills the dragon but releases Nimue's spirit, who still wants revenge. The dagger, it is revealed in the epilogue by the occult Osiris Club's clairvoyant, "was that part of Nimue that was still human, that hated and feared what she had become."[129] Thus, in a characteristic nuancing of good and evil recurrent in the comics discussed here, even the evil monster bent on world annihilation is ultimately not completely evil.

However, before dying from Vasilisa's dagger, Nimue takes out Hellboy's heart, as a result of which he turns into stone; loses his human, left hand and gun holster; and falls, eventually crumbling with the impact. Nimue's decisive, final blow thus destroys the material symbols of Hellboy's humanity: heart, hand, and the gun gifted by a superhero. It is eventually revealed that only a small part of the Ogdru Jahad had entered Nimue and died with her; the threat of the Ogdru Jahad consequently persists, as such threats do in many comics storyworlds. While the army of the apocalypse has already been unleashed—beginning with war and followed by pestilence, famine, and death—it is halted and the prophecy overturned, thanks to Hellboy, even though this entails his ultimate death.

Superheroes, Manufactured Beings, and Spectacles

According to Simonson, "[a]lmost blisteringly prosaic in the face of miracles, Hellboy is a proud member of that pulp tradition in which the hero solves problems with a fight that serves up both entertainment and catharsis."[130] This link is further reinforced by reflective nostalgic references to early superheroes and pulp fiction protagonists, most prominently through the vigilante and comics hero Lobster Johnson, who, in keeping with the real-unreal dynamics of the *Hellboy* worlds, appears in person in *Conqueror Worm*. "Hellboy's actions and attitude would be recognizable to anyone familiar with the heroes of the pulp tradition—the tall, laconic, unflappable, immensely courageous protagonist of its honorable tradition," Simonson continues, "[b]ut Hellboy exists and walks through a dream world of nightmare. His is a syncretic world fashioned with bits of obscure lore and strange untapped corners of mythology and legend. There is the occasional whiff, however faint, that is reminiscent of Baudelaire and fever dreams."[131] The dark, romantic atmosphere evoked by Simonson is echoed by the owner of a former convent where the BPRD is sent to investigate in *The Right Hand of Doom*. Soon paralyzed by Bromhead, the owner quotes the following sentence from Edgar Allan Poe's "The Fall of the House of Usher": "about the whole mansion and domain there hung an atmosphere which had no affinity with the air of heaven, but which had reeked up from the decayed trees, and the grey wall, and the silent tarn."[132]

In the fifth volume, named after Poe's poem "The Conqueror Worm," the poem is the sole voice heard during the volume's opening sequence, which narrates Lobster Johnson and the Allied army's attack on a Nazi establishment in 1939.[133] As can be seen in figure 18, Poe's poem is not only the sole text but also the only "sound" in the volume's opening scene: the attack unfolds in silence, in the darkness of the night, while the last stanzas of the poem affirm the ubiquity of death, the inevitable human tragedy. Such melancholia is an emotion that is shared by romantic and gothic works. The homage to pulp fiction is at its most ardent in this fifth *Hellboy* volume, which is dedicated to the 1930s pulp fiction hero Doc Savage and the vigilantes the Shadow and the Spider.[134]

Lobster Johnson and the other costumed hero in the *Hellboy* series, the Torch of Liberty, who, unlike Lobster Johnson, openly collaborated with the US military, not only contribute toward the nostalgic atmosphere in *Hellboy* but also embody the nostalgia imbuing contemporary comics.[135] This is also captured by *Hellboy*'s visual style, which mimics, and idealizes, the comics of yore:

> Images, ideas, and thinly disguised icons from the rich four-color treasure house of comics history are given a fresh lick of paint and are suddenly revealed as every bit as powerful and evocative upon some primal ten-year-old-child level as when we last saw them. [...] *Hellboy*'s greatest and least-obvious accomplishment: the trick, the skill entailed in this delightful necromantic conjuring of things gone by is . . . in the more demanding task of crafting work as good as everyone *remembers* the original as being.[136]

In keeping with the series' anti-authoritarian inclinations, which are embodied by Hellboy, it is not the Torch of Liberty (whose existence is officially recognized) but the supposedly fictional Lobster Johnson who is the more successful, and more prominent, superhero. Yet even the Torch was at first only familiar to the sergeant of his army unit through newsreels. This highlights the remediation of superheroes, which in Lobster Johnson's case unfolds through news reports of his vigilante activities and later through comic books. This remediation in turn contributes toward the building up of a spectacle that these heroes, Hellboy and other monstrous protagonists, find themselves at the center of.

The first image of the Torch, which shows him covered with mud, recalls *Swamp Thing*'s tempering of the indefatigable, omnipotent image of the superhero. Both series juxtapose familiarly conventional superheroes with more powerful monstrous protagonists, underscoring their affiliations as well as their differences. The Torch of Liberty, for instance, trained Hellboy and gifted him the pistol used in many of his early adventures.[137] Exemplifying the overlap between the fantastic and the real, the mythical and scientific, Hellboy combats the supernatural with military weapons. However, technology starts backfiring already in the second volume, when a newly improved jetpack malfunctions and sends Hellboy falling into a Nazi stronghold.[138] In the course of the series, Hellboy seems to give up on modern technology and uses a sword more frequently than a gun, just as the Nazis themselves fade out in favor of more mythical beings.

Although the official position of the BPRD, as reiterated by the bureau's new director, Thomas Manning (who replaced Bruttenholm), is that Lobster Johnson is fictional, Hellboy, who grew up on Lobster Johnson comics and films and who had adopted him as a role model, argues that he is real.[139] In the final volume, *The Storm and the Fury*, Hellboy has a painful flashback of his time as a child at the base in New Mexico in 1947 when he asked his adoptive father, "I'm not a monster, am I?"[140] When told that he was special, Hellboy tried to situate his identity with reference to other abnormal fictional characters: "But not special like Superman. And not like . . . Frankenstein" (mentioning the latter in a hushed voice). Trevor Bruttenholm then promised him that if he behaved himself, he would turn out well, and Hellboy exclaimed: "Like *the Lobster*."[141] Against a panel from a *Lobster Johnson* comic showing the vigilante fighting zombie-like German soldiers, Hellboy gushed: "He doesn't have any powers or anything. He's just a guy, but he fights the bad guys and sometimes *they're* monsters."[142] Besides fighting wrongdoers who are often monsters, Hellboy and the Lobster also have a physical similarity: their strength lies in their right hands. And although Lobster Johnson's hand looks normal, it is nicknamed "the Claw," which is also the symbol the Lobster leaves on defeated villains' foreheads as well as on a note that falls from nowhere before Manning with the question, "Fiction?" (fig. 19). In the same scene, a panel also visualizes the blurry lines between self and other: as he grabs the note, Manning's hand acquires a shape that closely resembles that of the Lobster. That the page ends with the Lobster's question "Fiction?" makes it relevant for the entire series but also for the other comics considered here, since games of perception and multiple, subjective realities form part of romanticism's legacy while also being a concern plaguing all of the comics monsters examined here.[143]

Besides Golden Age superheroes and the many fantastic and fictional characters, *Hellboy*'s landscape is also populated by manufactured beings, most of which are created by Rasputin's Nazi followers who were also involved in the Ragna Rok project for accelerating the apocalypse. This can be interpreted as reflecting the Nazi obsession with manufacturing *Übermenschen* or superheroes. As will be shown in this section, such instances, which evoke the animation of organic and inorganic bodies, highlight the fine line between animated beings and monstrous ones. Comparative literature scholar Zakiya Hanafi writes: "[W]hat makes an automaton monstrous is not the arrangement of its parts (although the automaton is often formed to represent a monster, a highly significant convergence). [...] Rather, it is the fact that matter formed by artificial means and moving of its own volition would seem to be endowed with spirit."[144]

Literature scholar Laura O'Connor's comments, referring to the first *Hellboy* film, complement Hanafi's observations of the monstrous and the animated:

> The notion that the defiance of mortality is what makes monsters monstrous is literalized when a gigantic behemoth grows out of the intestines of the dying Rasputin. Karl Kroenen, a member of Hitler's elite corps who aids in the resurrection of "the master" Rasputin and murders Professor Broom, performs multiple self-surgeries, replacing his flesh and blood with clockwork body mechanisms and dust and turning himself into a kind of living corpse. Kroenen's addiction to self-surgery is a graphic exemplification of popular fantasies and fears about cyborg enhancement at a time of accelerating scientific and technological advances. Hellboy's hybridity makes him a test case for the nature versus nurture argument, for as Broom tells Myers "he was born a demon, and [Myers, after Broom's death] will help him to become a man."[145]

The theme of animation, of awkward coming to life, is connected to Hellboy's desperate attempts to become human while also incorporating contemporary anxieties regarding the manufacturing of life.

The second volume, *Wake the Devil*, opens with the discovery of a secret Nazi establishment, a "sanctuary" in Norway, where Rasputin's Nazi collaborators, Karl Ruprecht Kroenen and Leopold Kurtz, have set up a super-soldier manufacturing factory to prepare an apocalyptic army of 666 soldiers. Reflecting the mechanization and dehumanization of combatants in modern warfare, Kroenen always wears a gas mask that covers his entire face. In a similar gesture of cybernetic modification of the human body, Kroenen cuts off one of Kurtz's forearms and replaces it with an artificial one.[146] The story then shifts to present-day New York City, to a wax museum owned by an old man, Hans Ubler. During the Second World War, Ubler's nightclub in Berlin had also been a freak show and a chamber of horrors, popular with Nazi dabblers in the paranormal.[147] Ilsa Haupstein shoots Ubler and takes a crate supposedly containing the body of the vampire Vladimir Giurescu, whose family was persecuted by the Nazis but with whom Ilsa had fallen in love.[148] When the BPRD sets out to track down Giurescu's body to his Romanian castle,[149] Hellboy crashes before Haupstein, who calls him a circus monkey. It is also here that he has to combat the Nazi Unmensch ("nonhuman" or even "monster"), a modified Nazi soldier with a mechanical right arm of steel including a detachable fist that functions as a flail, once again visualizing the proximity between the Nazi ideology of the *Übermensch* and the superheroes created to counter them, but also mirror them.[150] This volume exemplifies how manufacturing coexists with the resurrected, potentially threatening beings, such as the vampires and the ghosts prevailing over *Hellboy*.

The fifth volume, *Conqueror Worm*, is the curtain call for most of the Nazi characters in the series, who are then superseded by supernatural elements. While the worm here is one of the spawns of the seven-headed dragon or beast of the apocalypse that the Ragna Rok project sought to summon from space,[151] the spectacle and the tragic ending referred to in Poe's poem echoes Hellboy's own situation starring in a doomed spectacle, as well as the creation, resurrection, and remediation of stories that are turned into spectacles through popular culture. Exemplifying the overlap between bodily and ghostly animation in the series, in this volume, Herman von Klempt, one of the Nazis involved in the Ragna Rok project who remained alive but lost his entire body except his head, continues his experiments for manufacturing Kriegaffe and humanoid soldiers in a deserted abode that is still haunted by the ghosts of the American soldiers killed by the Nazis.

In addition to the prominence of the spectacle—as suggested by the show in which Hellboy participates and which the recurrent animations and reanimations appear to allude to and expand into self-reflexive commentary on the medium—there are layers of spectatorship in the series: Hellboy is occasionally shown being watched by other beings, including figures such as Baba Yaga and Edward Grey as well as the Osiris Club, a group well versed in supernatural matters, who hire a clairvoyant to track Hellboy's activities. In other stories, however, Hellboy is shown being part of popular culture, starring in spectacles for ordinary people and not just supernatural beings and occultists.

The short story "Hellboy in Mexico; or, A Drunken Blur" evokes the popular attraction of wrestling, which has affiliations with pulp fiction and the vigilante tradition (both of which have contributed to the superhero genre).[152] This story is triggered by a picture found by Hellboy's companion Abe in 1982, showing Hellboy in Mexico in 1956 with masked wrestlers in the cave of a local deity. The wrestlers, who were brothers, turned to fighting monsters after a vision of the Virgin Mary appeared to them, but one of the brothers, the one whom Hellboy was closest to, became possessed by the demon Camaztoz, whom Hellboy had to ultimately defeat and kill in a wrestling match. Once again incorporating the theme of remediation through popular culture and the creation of spectacles, the short story ends by showing the outer walls of a small Mexican theater adorned with pictures of, among others, Hellboy and Lobster Johnson. Inside, children watch a black-and-white recording of a wrestling match with Hellboy, cheering him on. The movie theater is used to frame the three short stories that follow:[153] before the first of these stories, "Kansas," movie posters of horror films are shown, with the last panel showing a black-and-white screening of lightning striking a person eating in an empty theater. This scene shown on the screen also serves as the opening for the short story "Sullivan's Reward," to which the comic then turns. At the end of the story, a page shows the movie theater again, this time containing a scattered audience of dressed-up skeletons watching the opening scene of the next short story, "The House of Sebak," which deals with a delusional museum employee evoking the spirits of Egyptian mummies and gods only to become a victim to one of the gods' wrath. Possibly in appreciation of the unpredictable power of the dead, the skeletal audience is shown clapping at the end of this story.

Other kinds of animations of dead or organic matter are accorded a prominent role early in the series. In *Wake the Devil*, Liz and two other BPRD agents discover a fifteenth-century homunculus, "[a]n artificial person made from blood and herbs, stewed in a jar and incubated in horse manure . . . sort of a medieval test-tube baby."[154] The short story "Almost Colossus" in the volume that follows (*The Chained Coffin*) introduces the older brother of the homunculus introduced earlier, who been given the ordinary, solid name of Roger by Hellboy. Roger's brother's story is similar to that of Frankenstein's monster: made in the image of man, he is only an imperfect, disappointing copy.[155] And, like Frankenstein's monster, Roger's older brother is also animated by lightning. In keeping with the series' preoccupation with dangerous animations and reanimations, he brings himself back to life and tracks down his creator, who had been imprisoned during the Inquisition, and kills him.

He then creates an army of homunculi, small, imperfect green creatures, and transforms himself into a colossus by jumping into a cauldron in which humans have been cooked. Insisting that they are not monsters but represent the future, the triumph of science over nature, he tries in vain to convince Roger to destroy humanity. Although Roger refuses and has to kill his brother while struggling against a Nazi humanoid in a later volume, he also insists: "Whatever I am, I am more than a machine."[156] He subsequently drains the power generator as a result of which all the Nazi machines break down. As Roger destroys the conqueror worm by sucking its energy into himself, the following lines from Poe's poem appear, evoking the manufacture of beings and the creation of spectacles: "Mimes, in the form of God on high, mutter and mumble low, and hither and thither fly—mere puppets they, who come and go, at bidding of vast formless things that shift the scenery to and fro... flapping from out their condor wings... invisible woe!"[157]

Embodying the theme of animation and control, puppets are present in a more tangible form in other *Hellboy* stories, such as "The Ghoul" in the seventh *Hellboy* volume, *The Troll Witch*, and "The Midnight Circus." Inspired by Hamlet's description of decomposition, "how a king may go a progress through the guts of a beggar" (*Hamlet*, act 4, scene 3, lines 31–32), "The Ghoul; or, Reflections on Death and the Poetry of Worms" is underpinned by quotations from *Hamlet*.[158] Set in London in 1992, the story deals with a BPRD case tracking down a certain Mr. Stokes, who is found in a cemetery reciting lines from *Hamlet* interspersed with lines from two eighteenth-century poems, Thomas Warton's "The Pleasures of Melancholy" (1745) and Robert Blair's "The Grave" (1743). It turns out that Mr. Stokes is not human, and Hellboy only gets to witness the creature's final decomposition. These events are accompanied by panels showing Hamlet on the television screen, which is apparently, a puppet theater production of William Shakespeare's *Hamlet*, thus incorporating an additional level of remediation.[159] Marionettes are also animated in the short story about the vampire of Prague, among other tales.[160] This not only reaffirms the themes of automatons, spectacles, and spectatorship but also evokes the concept of remediation, since a play belonging to the very old medium of the theater is transposed to television. Tellingly for *Hellboy* and the kind of monstrosity dealt with in this book, humans are replaced by puppets, closing the gap between the animate and inanimate, the human and the inhuman.

Hence, when the witches declare war against Hellboy after his refusal to be their king, one of their elders crushes the bust of Hellboy that she was holding in her fist, alluding to the symbolic scope of effigies and their animation through faith.[161] Similarly, when Vasilisa is killed by Koshchei, she transforms into a doll, thus evoking (both visually through the detailed, richly colored style but also conceptually) the doll from her fairy tale who had protected her against the machinations of her wicked stepmother.[162] Similar to the discussion of animation in *Swamp Thing* in light of Bukatman's findings, the transition between the animated and the unanimated is once again fluid. Moreover, the link between animation and the spectacle is more prominent in *Hellboy* than *Swamp Thing*.

During his visit to Morgan Le Fay's castle with Alice in *The Wild Hunt*, Hellboy slips into an alternative realm, forced to watch his transformation into a demon and unleashing the apocalypse.[163] Appearing first in a mirror, his darker, horned reflection insists on his demonic fate, grabbing and absorbing Hellboy, making it seem as if he were part of the destruction (fig. 20). Framed by damaged Gothic stained-glass windows in ruined structures, the mirror reenacts Hellboy's destiny. Besides theatricalizing—and indeed rendering spectacular—Hellboy's unwanted fate, this scene is articulated through the mirror, which in this case is more of a void or an abyss. Issues of (monstrous) identity are thus juxtaposed with the impossibility, melancholia, and destruction evoked by the abyss.

This reflected demon that Hellboy was supposed to be is larger than him, and before he realizes it the whole castle has burned down and he himself is in the place of the demon, wearing his darker color and horns. Vasilisa finally convinces Hellboy to listen to Alice and Morgan Le Fay and draw out his sword while fairies and Edward Grey as well as Baba Yaga and other witches watch from their other world. This triggers Hellboy's transportation back to the real world. Morgan, however, is shown arranging chess pieces representing both the good and evil armies of the dead, Arthur's knights, and the demons against each other. When Alice enters the destroyed castle in the final volume hoping to find Hellboy, she sees Morgan's chess pieces scattered and the piece representing Hellboy crushed and replaced by a stream of Hellboy's blood.[164] Tying up with the theme of spectacle and spectatorship, Morgan's chess pieces also parallel Hellboy's prescribed destiny and the difficulty of breaking away from it, which lies at the heart of the *Hellboy* series.

The spectacle, as can be seen from the very first monster discussed in this book and as reinforced by the next monster to be discussed, is an indispensable facet of the monster. While this in itself is hardly surprising, it is noteworthy that the spectacularity of these monsters is accompanied by persistent, haunting traumas that are, in themselves, also sources of entertainment. These two features are captured in *The Midnight Circus*, a supplementary story to the main series. In this story, the young Hellboy slips away from his home, the BPRD's headquarters, to watch a spectacular and specular circus that only takes place at midnight, summoning its ghostly performers and seemingly catering to no other audience save Hellboy.[165] The story of Pinocchio, who is also part of the sideshow accompanying the circus as "the Wooden Boy," is interwoven in more ways than one in the comic. Hellboy's and Pinocchio's stories merge in the end, since the vagabond child murderers who attack Hellboy are portrayed as the fox and cat from Pinocchio. Earlier, Hellboy had been given an illustrated edition of Pinocchio to read instead of comics. Interrupting Hellboy's exuberant description of Lobster Johnson's escapades against Nazi Frankensteins, the BPRD's secretary led him to the library, saying, "Now I just think it's time we found you a *proper* book."[166] Notably, at that time in 1947, Hellboy was not only reading comics but, like many comics fans, also drawing them. Pinocchio's story, which is the main attraction of *The Midnight Circus* and also the book Hellboy is made to read, begins with the line "He wanted to be a real boy," a desire that Hellboy shares and tries in vain to fulfill throughout his life.[167] According to Bukatman, it is not only morality but also "Pinocchio's *mis*behavior that makes him real."[168] Similarly, it is the rebellious side of monsters, their desire to assert their own will in the face of the most adverse of circumstances, that makes them so relatable for humans. The similarities between Hellboy and Pinocchio brought out in *The Midnight Circus* are likewise hinged on the human side of monsters.

As Mignola points out in a footnote, the words spoken by the clown and the giant in *The Midnight Circus* to summon the other performers are taken from Lord Byron's dramatic poem *Manfred*. Not only does *Manfred*'s eponymous protagonist conjure spirits but his entire reality is heavily molded by his imagination, which is propelled by his guilt and internal conflicts, much like the adult Hellboy. Jeffrey Jerome Cohen's declaration that monsters "still serve as the ultimate incorporation of our anxieties—about history, about identity, about our very humanity," and in particular Georges Canguilhem's observation that "[t]he existence of monsters throws doubt on life's ability to teach us order," are perhaps best and most directly captured by the *Hellboy* series,[169] since it (albeit only roughly) follows the course of the historical events of the twentieth century, indiscriminately interweaving them with supernatural and mythical elements.[170]

While Jim O'Barr's *The Crow* also unfolds against a background of death and Christian and gothic imagery, its protagonist, after a violent death, becomes a monster retaining his human form but acquiring supernatural powers that are accentuated by theatrical makeup and actions.[171]

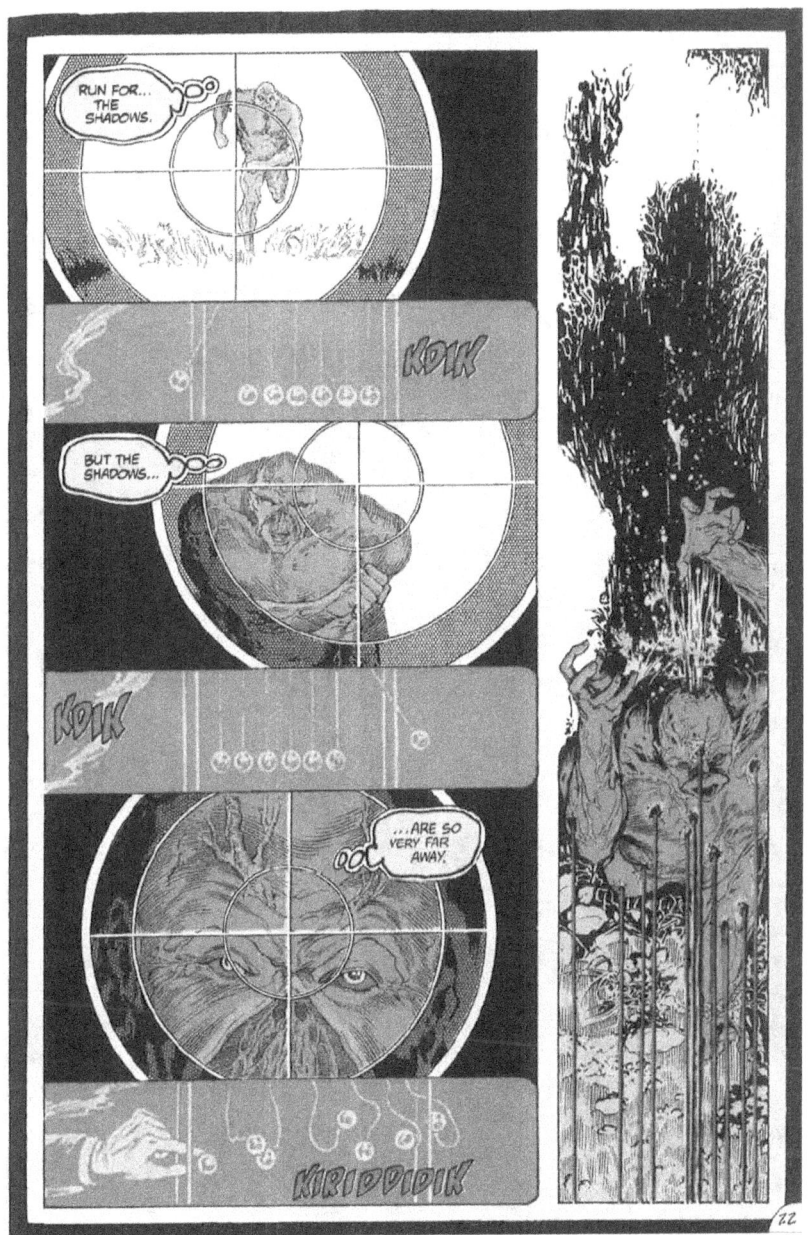

Fig. 1. Targeted. *The Saga of the Swamp Thing*, book 1, 35, © DC Comics.

Fig. 2. The Patchwork Man, the former Gregori Arcane. *The Saga of the Swamp Thing*, book 6, 71, © DC Comics.

Fig. 3. The Swamp Thing regenerating himself, again. *The Saga of the Swamp Thing*, book 3, 71, © DC Comics.

Fig. 4. "Alec isn't in here." *The Saga of the Swamp Thing*, book 1, 69, © DC Comics.

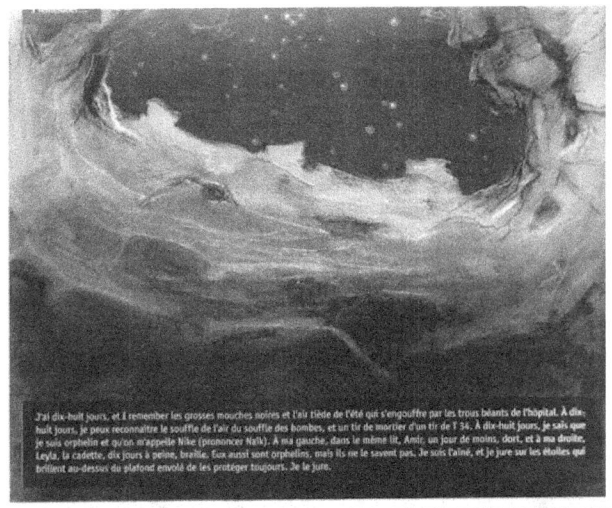

Fig. 5. Opening page: the abyss as a visual motif. *Monstre*, 5, Enki Bilal © Casterman. Reproduced with the kind permission of Enki Bilal and Casterman.

Fig. 6. Warhole at a "Restricted European-American Security Council" meeting promising the destruction of the Obscurantiste Order's site and members. *Monstre*, 39, Enki Bilal © Casterman. Reproduced with the kind permission of Enki Bilal and Casterman.

Fig. 7. "Cosmic mash." *Monstre*, 236, Enki Bilal © Casterman. Reproduced with the kind permission of Enki Bilal and Casterman.

Fig. 8. Warhole and Nike (who does not recognize him). *Monstre*, 220, Enki Bilal © Casterman. Reproduced with the kind permission of Enki Bilal and Casterman.

Fig. 9. Online articles on "Cloud of Death" and "Gangrenous Art." *Monstre*, 125, Enki Bilal © Casterman. Reproduced with the kind permission of Enki Bilal and Casterman.

Fig. 10. The deathly performance. *Monstre*, 197, Enki Bilal © Casterman. Reproduced with the kind permission of Enki Bilal and Casterman.

Fig. 11. The birth of Hellboy. *Hellboy*, vol. 1, *The Seed of Destruction*, n.p., © 1993, 1994, 1997, 1999, and 2003 Mike Mignola.

Fig. 12. Hellboy on the island. *Hellboy*, vol. 6, *Strange Places*, n.p., © 2006, 2005, and 2002 Mike Mignola.

Fig. 13. Hellboy and Mohlomi going to listen to the ocean, their faces abstracted into colored ovals. *Hellboy*, vol. 6, *Strange Places*, n.p., © 2006, 2005, and 2002 Mike Mignola.

Fig. 14. Hellboy's unwilling reenactment of Saint Dunstan's legend. *Hellboy*, vol. 4, *The Right Hand of Doom*, n.p., © 1998, 1999, 2000, and 2003 Mike Mignola.

Fig. 15. Dagda's funeral. *Hellboy*, vol. 9, *The Wild Hunt*, n.p., © 2008, 2009, and 2010 Mike Mignola.

Fig. 16. Jerry, the possessed artist's, Goya-inspired drawings. *Hellboy*, vol. 10, *The Crooked Man*, n.p., © 2008, 2009, and 2010 Mike Mignola.

Fig. 17. TV images suggesting the onset of the apocalypse interspersed with layers of Hellboy's present and his immediate and distant past. *Hellboy*, vol. 12, *The Storm and the Fury*, n.p., © 2010 and 2011 Mike Mignola.

Fig. 18. Lobster Johnson attacking a secret Nazi hideout with Allied soldiers in 1939. *Hellboy*, vol. 5, *Conqueror Worm*, n.p., © 2001, 2002, and 2003 Mike Mignola.

Fig. 19. The Claw raising the question of fiction. *Hellboy*, vol. 5, *Conqueror Worm*, n.p., © 2001, 2002, and 2003 Mike Mignola.

Fig. 20. Hellboy's destructive destiny recounted by his reflection. *Hellboy*, vol. 9, *The Wild Hunt*, n.p., © 2008, 2009, and 2010 Mike Mignola.

Fig. 21. The "*boiling man.*" *The Crow*, n.p., © James O'Barr.

Fig. 22. Five different faces of the Crow.
The Crow, n.p., © James O'Barr.

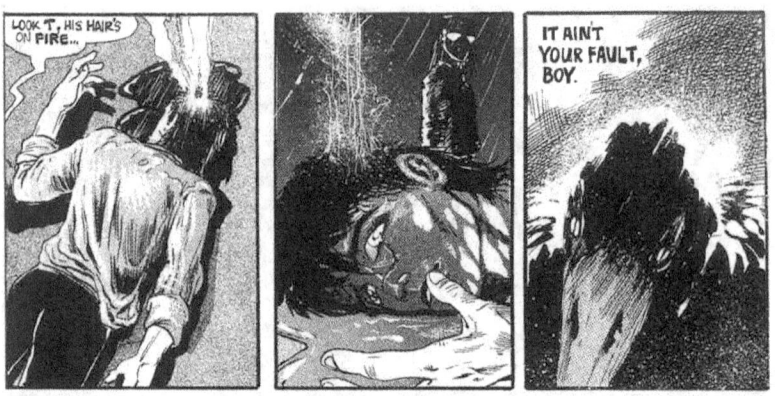

Fig. 23. Eric's death and transition into the Crow. *The Crow*, n.p., © 1981, 1989, 1992, 1993, 1994 James O'Barr.

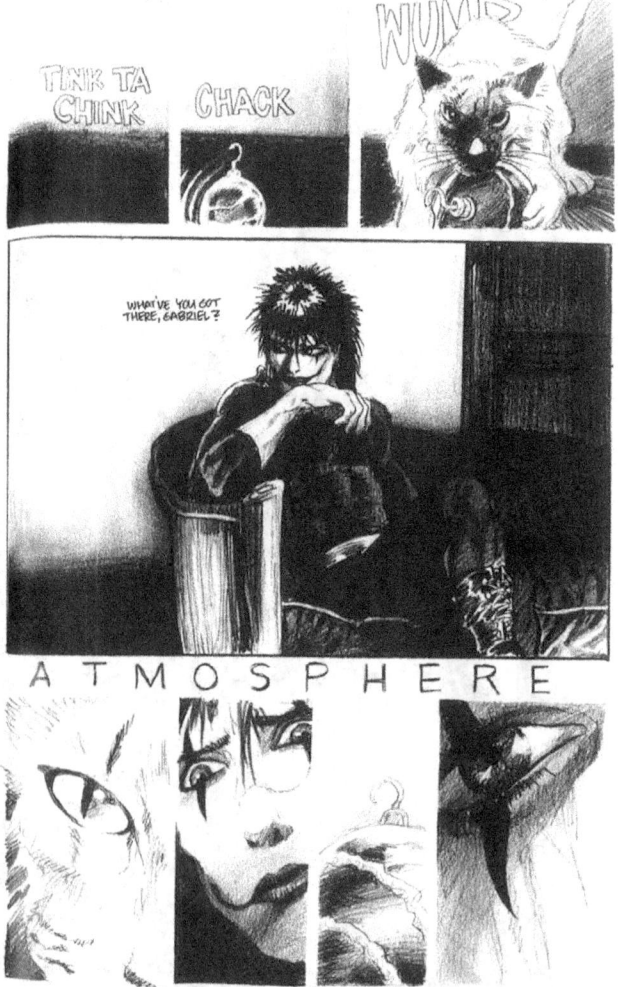

Fig. 24. The Crow's susceptibility to painful memories. *The Crow*, n.p., © James O'Barr.

Fig. 25. Two sides of the Crow and Death. *The Crow*, n.p., © James O'Barr.

Fig. 26. The Crow as an exuberant Saint Sebastian. *The Crow*, n.p., © James O'Barr.

Fig. 27. Collage of church interiors and weapons as the Crow prepares for his revenge. *The Crow*, n.p., © James O'Barr.v

CHAPTER 5

THE CROW

Spectacularity and Emotionality

> Asylums with doors open wide
> Where people had paid to see inside
> For entertainment they watch his body twist
> Behind his eyes he says, "I still exist"
> —JOY DIVISION, "ATROCITY EXHIBITION"[1]

Writer and artist James O'Barr is best known for *The Crow*, which was first published in 1989 as a miniseries and in 1992 collected as a one-shot graphic novel. The comic reflects the contemporaneous goth subculture, which, as Julia Round elaborates, was a subculture of tensions.[2] Attaining a considerable degree of success, the comic was republished in several new editions while also inspiring a television series and several feature films, beginning with the release of *The Crow* in 1994, starring Brandon Lee (who succumbed to an accidental death on set). The film was followed by three sequels with different directors and actors.[3] This chapter relies on the 1994 special edition of *The Crow*, published by Kitchen Sink Press and consisting of five short "books" of around thirty pages each, which are fragmentary to different degrees. Titled "Pain," "Fear," "Irony," "Despair," and "Death," these books are accompanied by additional sections containing brief comics, texts, and images. The images are often portraits of the Crow looking defiantly back at his viewer and thus establishing a link between the reader and the protagonist. The diverse fragments accompanying the narrative complement the main story of the protagonist Eric Draven's revenge for his and his girlfriend Shelly's violent, gratuitous murder at the hands of a drunken gang. Another structure is superimposed on the books through the inclusion of additional episodes that bear titles referring to musical forms of mourning that underscore the intense emotionality underlying the comic: "Pain" and "Fear" are preceded by "Lament"; "Irony" and "Despair" by "Elegy"; and "Death" by "Crescendo."

Draven's revenge in the form of the Crow, which is a means of working through his loss, also unfolds as a quest, with each of his murders being carefully planned, starting with the gang members of the lowest rank and ending with the killing of the gang leader, T-Bird, the most vicious participant in the crime. Although the Crow avenges the crime with the aim of joining Shelly in the grave, he remains as solitary as any typical romantic protagonist (and artist): in the comic's final panel, it is "an androgynous gothic figure" who, having kissed the dead Shelly, "walks off into a dark and barren plane."[4] "He is very much alone," affirms literary scholar Lauren Goodlad.[5] Hence, even though the Crow is the most anthropomorphous and gothic of the monsters examined here, his romantic monstrosity manifests itself in his pain and thirst for revenge as well as in his specular or ghostly, and spectacular or theatrical, inclinations. This is illustrated by the first tier of the book's third page (fig. 21), in which the Crow finds himself stabbed by a thief who remarks: "Man you must be *dusted* not to *feel* that."[6] "Dusted" and "feel" are both crucial components of the Crow. He is dusted not by hallucinogens or angel dust but a mysterious supernatural element. To take up Nikki Sullivan's trope, he embodies transmogrification, combining the normal (or human) with the strange (or supernatural).[7] He is also dusted with makeup powder and black traits that mark him with the unwavering, dark smile of the trickster and suggest that his eyes are open even when they are closed. Staring at the dagger piercing his heart, the Crow seems almost like a puppet and not the *"boiling man"* who feels and suffers too much and who takes a certain pleasure in violent actions, both those he is subjected to and those he carries out. This tension between simply performing and actually feeling persists throughout the comic and also imbues many of its intertextual references, particularly the songs by the band Joy Division.

While insights on the gothic shed considerable light on the workings of *The Crow*, it is also useful to turn to Northrop Frye's chapter, "The Romantic Macabre," in which he focuses on the plays of Thomas Lovell Beddoes, particularly *Death's Jest-Book*, which Frye describes as exemplifying the "tragicomic grotesque," tracing this back to Yorick's skull in the grave-digging scene in *Hamlet*.[8] For Frye, "[t]he root of the conception of the grotesque is the sense of the simultaneous presence of life and death. Ghosts [...] are at once alive and dead, and so inspire the kind of hysteria that is expressed equally by horror and by laughter."[9] This is personified by Death, who also plays the "fool" or the Joker and thus creates space for the absurd to seep in.[10] Finally, as Frye points out, Beddoes's own work was fragmented and can thus be considered a precursor to the (gothic and punk) collage or patchwork aesthetics adopted by O'Barr.[11] As we will now see, the figure of the Crow, harbinger of death for wrongdoers—and thus much like the medieval Death "the leveler [. . .,] the only effective reminder of human equality"[12]—but made up like a clown, embodies the tragicomic grotesque while his story remains one of potentially unending fragments that echo his unending, all-consuming pain.

As is evident in O'Barr's interviews as well as in John Bergin's introduction to the Kitchen Sink Press edition, *The Crow* was triggered not only by a local news report about the murder of a young Detroit couple but, more immediately, by the death of O'Barr's fiancée at the hands of a drunk driver. While O'Barr had hoped that the comic, which took ten years to complete, would have a cathartic, therapeutic effect, the actual outcome was the opposite: the comic's emotional darkness only increased his own torment.[13] Correspondingly, the comic mostly alternates between scenes of emotional pain (when Eric relives his and Shelly's last moments or their idyllic past) and violence (when he carries out his revenge). This dark emotionality that courts anguish and death is only one of several factors contributing toward the comic's status as a goth classic. Other goth features include the dramatic use of chiaroscuro, Eric's self-stylization after his resurrection by wearing theatrical makeup and clothes, and the inclusion of lyrics from several Joy Division songs, whose music is generally regarded as ushering in the darker strains of rock. As literary scholar Michael Bibby points out, the term "gothic" came into use not only because "Joy Division staged an exhibition of melancholia that became a key element of goth style"[14] but also because their music evoked the "looming, imposing spaces of the gothic cathedral," creating a towering sense of space through the use of echo and digital delay.[15] Paul Hodkinson also discerns influences of the gothic on Joy Division's music.[16] The band, similar to other postindustrial Manchester bands that started in the 1970s, particularly the Fall, was influenced by earlier rock bands such as the Doors and the Velvet Underground.[17] The former, Simon Reynolds points out, was one of Joy Division singer Ian Curtis's favorite bands.[18] As literary scholar Wallace Fowlie remembers, the Doors' Jim Morrison himself was fascinated with Arthur Rimbaud and had actually thanked Fowlie for translating Rimbaud's poetry into English.[19] Morrison, known for his dark, poetic music, had also read Antonin Artaud and Friedrich Nietzsche. Such reading probably infused the darkness of Morrison's lyrics as well as the perpetual, romantic drive to fully cater to all senses. "If my poetry aims to achieve anything, it's to deliver people from the limited ways in which they think and feel," he wrote in a "self-interview."[20] Such a drive marks the lyrics of Joy Division, and the poetry of Rimbaud, both of which are incorporated in *The Crow*.

While allusions to gothic and the dark romantic visual styles are recurrent in *The Crow*, melancholia and an excess of painful emotions are the dominant gothic characteristics. In being part of the "moods" pervading the romantic era, these two features are also representative of the overlap between the gothic and the romantic.[21] Discussing Stephen King's work and asserting "the value of reading popular fiction as a form of surrogate public history," Roger Luckhurst concludes that "the gothic might prove appropriate to provide scripts for trauma."[22] While Luckhurst bases this claim primarily on the inclusion of supernatural elements in King's novels, it remains relevant for the use of excess in general, an excess that not only dissolves boundaries between the living and the dead but also loosens control over emotions, especially those of grief. Richard Kearney explains the allure of stories like *The Crow* as follows: "Our contemporary culture in particular exploits our deep ambiguity towards the death instinct, displacing our fearful fascination onto spectacular stories of horror, monstrosity and violence."[23] Joel Faflak and Richard Sha suggest that the focus on emotions is "a romantic response to a modern problem," which continues through the explosion of emotions in works such as *The Crow*.[24]

While emotional excess is both a romantic and a gothic trait, the Crow's self-stylization echoes some of the main stereotypes associated with goths (even though the group itself is widely diversified and merges with other subcultures): wearing tight trousers, large boots, and a trench coat, his face is painted white and contrasts with the heavy, dark eyeliner dripping from his eyes. His lips curve into a broad smile, identical to the nonsmiles worn by the Joker and Gwynplaine (fig. 22).[25] In the Crow's case, this smile expresses the absurdity of his situation: the gang's violence had been uncalled for, and the couple would not have been vulnerable had their car not broken down. The Crow nonetheless reacts to the absurdity and the violence in a manner that is both gothic and romantic: he not only gives in to intense emotions, ceaselessly grieving for his loved one, but also carries out his revenge in a manner so brutal that it throws the difference between good and evil into question. His licking off his own blood in the image shown in figure 22, which is simultaneously playful, suggestive, and disturbing, exemplifies this ambiguity, and the close-up of his face in the same figure reinforces his inhuman, partially animal-like characteristics, which is contradicted by the panel that follows with a side shot of the Crow's anthropomorphic body.

As a subculture built on romantic premises, goth culture also exemplifies the monstrous transformation of romantic inclinations. It is monstrous in its exaggeration as well as its courting and even aestheticization of dark inclinations, among which painful emotions and the spectral are especially relevant for *The Crow*. Here, romanticism can be said to have undergone a double mutation, first through its gothic offshoot and second through that offshoot's resurrection in the form of a subculture. This subculture imports several romantic characteristics often absent from gothic productions of the eighteenth century, such as the glorification of the rebel as well as the spectacularization and celebration of difference. *The Crow* plays out romantic characteristics in a goth idiom that took root in the 1980s music scene and established a distinctive but heterogenous identity. It is a culture that also performs the work of reflective nostalgia, since it culls and reworks elements from the past.[26]

As will be shown in this chapter, both the content and structure of *The Crow* illustrate the notion that the monster is an embodiment of affect and is representative of ruptures with logic and chaos. From the comics discussed in this book, *The Crow* also reflects the disruption that is part of both monstrosity and romanticism. This chapter will first explore the fragmented structure of the comic, which not only takes up a romantic form but also incorporates literary and visual references to romanticism as well as diverse, mostly romantic, poems and postpunk gothic rock lyrics in those fragments, which, being fragments, are also gothic in their intertextual cravings.[27] The role of emotions in the story is then examined, followed by a concluding section on the theatrical aspects of intense emotionality and its central role in the protagonist's quest. Spectacularity is complemented by the Crow's self-stylization as a painted figure with a permanent smile, immortal on one hand but still deeply traumatized; although he quickly heals from the shots directed at him, he does bleed in the beginning. The final section consequently discusses the coexisting ghostliness and spectacularity of the Crow's revenge while also elaborating on the unfulfilled nature of his vengeful quest.

Remediation of Romanticism

Fragmentation

As affirmed by literary scholar D. F. Rauber, "the fragment can be viewed as that form which more completely than any other embodies romantic ideals and aims."[28] He adds that "until recently, the fragment has been an accidental form in the sense that it has just happened rather than being consciously planned."[29] Romantic fragmentation in other words aspired toward a degree of fluidity rather than sharp ruptures. According to literary scholar Alexander Regier, the Lisbon earthquake of 1755 affected, among others,

Kant's and Burke's notions of the sublime as a "taming and domesticating force that ultimately relies on the destructive power of fragmentation."[30] Acknowledging the "supreme importance played by the romantic mind on the creative imagination, as it applies to reader as well as to poet [...] the fragment" for Rauber "is a peculiarly potent means of eliciting an active imaginative response."[31] Distinguishing between fracture and fragmentation, both of which remain relevant to *The Crow*, Regier sees fragmentation as a "process [...] defined by a series of changes."[32] In *The Crow*, these fragmenting changes occur in the form of voices, perspectives, and visual style, all of which reveal different facets of the troubled mind of the protagonist propelling the narrative.

Regier also points out "that many [romantic works] exhibit a meta-critical pattern in connection with fragmentation,"[33] even though "self-examination and criticism" themselves play a rarely acknowledged role in romantic works.[34] In a related vein, literary scholar Lillian Feder mentions how Gérard de Nerval used "fragmentation as a process of self-creation and discovery."[35] Similar to the patchworked Frankenstein's monster, both the Crow and his stories are made up of fragments, merging memories of Eric Draven's past with his plan for revenge, inhabiting an immortal but repeatedly wounded body with a crow as his constant companion. The lyrics, additional drawings, and brief comics stories provide further perspectives on the main narrative.

The Crow's narrative is likewise built on fragments that interweave the Crow's memories with his quest for revenge. The comic is divided into books that, instead of forming a series, are in fact open to different arrangements, especially due to the paratextual art and brief episodes placed in between the books. The narrative is in turn interspersed with visual and literary quotations incorporating Christian symbolism and allusions to the paintings of Caspar David Friedrich, while also citing Arthur Rimbaud's poetry, postpunk lyrics, and children's rhymes and stories, such as *The Cat in the Hat*, or Rose Fyleman's short rhyme "Good Night." The interweaving of material from children's culture with material from adult high and popular culture serves to evoke nostalgia for lost innocence.

The Crow also alludes to Edgar Allan Poe's poem "The Raven," whose solitary narrator, mourning for his dead love, only has an ominous, cryptic raven for company.[36] In contrast to the raven's laconic "nevermore," the crow in the comic does interact more with Eric, chastising him for his reveries and revivification of painful memories. The fourth book, "Despair," which looks back at Shelly and Eric's murder, reveals that the crow first appears as T-Bird takes a second shot at Eric's head. As the crow tries to comfort Eric, telling him that everything will be all right and that Shelly's rape and death are not his fault, Eric's hair lights up, underscoring the intervention of the unreal (fig. 23). The Crow burns visibly, much like the Swamp Thing. Romantic passion and the intensity of emotion are often expressed through the entire body, particularly, in the case of the comics monsters in this book, at the inevitably violent moments when the boundaries between the body and the external world are disrupted. The crow in the last panel in this sequence acquires an almost iconic status by establishing a presence over most of the panel's space and through his words hanging in the air behind him, more like a title than a word balloon.

"Don't look!," the bird urges Eric throughout the comic in vain, beginning with his helpless witnessing of Shelly's final moments. The crow also serves as a kind of angel of death, urging Eric to give up his heartbeat while lying on the hospital bed, assuring him of his future task of avenging the murders. As in Poe's poem, the bird in the comic serves as a supernatural link between the ordinary Eric of the past and the undead, invincible, but ever grieving Eric who has become the Crow.

Already the first book "Pain" contains a section "New Dawn Fades" echoing the title of a Joy Division song. It is in this section that the Crow carries out his first act of revenge by killing Tin-Tin, one of T-Bird's gang members who was involved in Eric and Shelly's murder. The song sums up the Crow's psychological state and the unsatisfied conclusion of his violent quest for revenge: "Directionless so plain to see / A loaded gun won't set you free."[37] Besides alluding to his revenge and unfulfilled quest, the song also captures the extreme of pain that borders on nonfeeling, as exemplified by the Crow's bleeding without dying: "Oh, I've walked on water, run through fire / Can't seem to feel it anymore / It was me, waiting for me / Hoping for something more / Me, seeing me this time, hoping for something else."[38] The same book, "Pain," also has the Crow quoting the opening lines from Joy Division's "Disorder" as he kills his second target, Top Dollar. This song also mentions waiting, this time for someone who could provide a clear direction: "I've been waiting for a guide to take me by the hand."[39] These words express the directionlessness in the face of a difficult, even absurd reality, which both characterizes the band's repertoire and holds for the Crow's situation. Considering absences as a key motif of Joy Division's style,[40] Bibby points out that the band's music as well as its promotional (minimalist, frequently black-and-white) material "seem to emphasize absences in ways that call to mind the Freudian concept of melancholia [. . .] an endless longing for an object that cannot be named" and that nonetheless involves an element of pleasure.[41] This is especially prominent in "New Dawn Fades" and "Disorder." Freudian melancholia, and even more literally the Freudian death drive, can be seen as the main force behind the Crow's evocation of Eric's past life with Shelly. Freud, in turn, as suggested by literary scholar Thomas Pfau, was indebted to romantic ideology.[42]

In addition to the melancholia, and tied to it, is a sense of being lost, of being uncertain of the self and its identity. The Crow himself is a marginal entity, a resurrected being who bleeds without dying, remaining indefinable beyond his painful past and the need for revenge. This ambiguity is increased by his pantomime makeup and the Judeo-Christian references that often equate the protagonist with Christ.

"I've got the spirit, lose the feeling, take the shock away" is the closing line of "Disorder"'s first verse, which is echoed by the song's refrain.[43] Feeling, as will be discussed in the following section, is a vicious cycle for the Crow, who continuously replays scenes from the past in spite of the extreme pain that they provoke. Unlike many other songs by Joy Division, "Disorder" also suggests the possibility of a redemption, but only if one can "lose the feeling," which the Crow never succeeds in doing and which in turn leaves his quest unfulfilled. More directly, "Disorder" echoes the chaos permeating the comic: "Lights are flashing, cars are crashing, getting frequent now."[44]

Exemplifying the scrapbook-like construction of the story, the Crow quotes from Archibald MacLeish's "Mother Goose's Garland" in "Pain" after having killed everyone gambling with Top Dog. This incorporation of songs and rhymes that are so vastly different introduces the form of the fragment, which, when remediated in this comic, reflects the absurdity of the gratuitous violence that triggered the entire story. In addition, it hints toward the intersection of past and present, with the past representing the innocence usually associated with childhood and the present pervaded by the disillusionment expressed by the Joy Division songs.

The Joy Division songs, like the one Cure song cited in the book, "The Hanging Garden," feature percussion that is urgent and follows an almost martial rhythm marked by a dominant bass[45] and generally clear vocals. For Bibby, gothic rock often involves "more overt use of special effects, more emphasis on melody, and an introspective, moody approach."[46] Many of the songs evoke nightmarish scenes that have an abstract significance but are often grounded in an uncanny everydayness, as with "[t]he shadow that stood by the side of the road" in "Komakino"[47] or the setting of "The Hanging Garden."

The first section of the second book, "Fear," bears the title "Dead Souls," a Joy Division song that in turn takes its title from Nikolai Gogol's socially critical novel. This song shows how, from all of the works quoted, the Joy Division lyrics are possibly closest to the mood of the story and its protagonist:

> Someone take these dreams away
> They point me to another day
> A duel of personalities
> That stretch all true realities.[48]

These dreams can be interpreted as those of the future that Eric envisioned with Shelly, which torment him throughout the comic while also alluding to the schism between Eric and the Crow he is resurrected as. And indeed, throughout *The Crow*, "all true realities" are stretched beyond the point of breaking but remain nonetheless grounded in the darker truths of human existence: the shock of random, murderous violence and the subsequent unquenchable thirst for revenge is corporealized by the Crow's incessantly suffering but immortal body. "Where figures from the past stand tall / And mocking voices ring the halls" visualizes the haunting of memories.[49] Moreover, the reference to an "[i]mperialistic house of prayer" in the same song is comparable to the many references to Christianity in *The Crow*, a Christianity that is marked by a certain degree of ambiguity.

"The Hanging Garden" appears before a short section titled "Elegy: Irony and Despair." This section is followed by a piece titled "Atmosphere," which is also a single by Joy Division, originally titled "Licht und Blindheit" (Light and Blindness) and released by the French label Sordide Sentimental (instead of the British label Factory Records, which had released most of the Joy Division albums and was known for its monochrome, minimalist album covers). Here, Eric's memories of Shelly are interspersed with his meeting another one of the gang members, Funboy. "Don't walk away in silence" is the refrain of Joy Division's "Atmosphere,"[50] and it is in the brief comics episode of the same name that the Crow once again slips into an agonizing recollection of his past, this time a Christmas shared with Shelly, triggered by a Christmas tree ornament found by an adopted cat, who is named, in keeping with the Christian references imbuing the entire comic, after the archangel Gabriel (fig. 24). Reinforcing the connection and similarities between the Crow and the animal, the two look each other in the eye in alternating panels as the object triggers a flow of painful memories that begin on the next page. Within the expanse of that one, final row, the Crow's manufactured animality gives in to sentient humanity. In keeping with the section's title, but also with the style used for the memories of Shelly and Eric's life together, the drawings are softer and brighter, with more nuanced shadows created through shades of gray instead of the black-and-white contrasts that dominate the comic. Svetlana Boym writes about an affective romantic geography, which can be a way of understanding the patchwork, intensely emotional structure of *The Crow*: "The romantics looked for 'memorative signs' and correspondences between their inner landscape and the shape of the world. They charted an affective geography of the native land that often mirrored the melancholic landscape of their own psyches. It is the romantic traveler who sees from a distance the wholeness of the vanishing world."[51] The Crow's world is a crumbling city that only knows poverty and crime. In this context, the Crow's outbursts of pain and violence are protests against, as well as mirrors of, a broken city.

The references to postpunk and gothic music are not limited to Joy Division songs alone, for when the Crow visits Funboy, a poster of a Stiff Kittens gig (one of Joy Division's early names) hangs above Funboy's bed. Moreover, a section titled "The Atrocity Exhibition: One Year Ago" appears just before the fourth book, "Despair," which recounts Eric and Shelly's murder. Referring to an eponymous J. G. Ballard novel, which brought together fragments of short stories and which also influenced the Joy Division song of the same name, the title "Atrocity Exhibition" works on several levels. It alludes to Roman coliseum games and their practice of transforming cruel situations into spectacles, such as gladiators fighting for their lives.[52] For Joy Division, the title also refers to lead singer Ian Curtis's epileptic fits, which, triggered during performances, were a source of the band's popularity and were seen as "evidence of his authentic vision of pain and horror."[53] "Disturbing-compelling" is how cultural critic Mark Fisher describes Curtis's performances and words, which also holds for the Crow.[54] Much like Curtis (and Gwynplaine), the Crow ends up inadvertently creating and starring in his own atrocity exhibition, which is, at least for the fictional characters, a source of both pain and transient satisfaction; for its duration at least, the spectacle is comforting. Two of the Joy Division songs referenced in *The Crow*, "Atrocity Exhibition" and "Komakino," also blend the themes of the specular and spectacularization through the presence of ghosts of the past and their exploitation for purposes of entertainment. This is also the case in *The Crow* as well as Hugo's *The Man Who Laughs*, with which the comic shares the theme of a damaged, partially monstrous protagonist whose life unfolds through spectacles and who is destined for tragedy.

In the section titled "Coda" that ends the comic, "Decades," the first of the last two Joy Division songs quoted in their entirety and interspersed with various drawings of the Crow, reverses the stereotype of the carefree young man to describe a generation of weary young men traumatized by the weight of the past and trapped by the helplessness of being unable to alter the past or participate fully in their lives in the present: "[W]e dragged ourselves in / Watched from the wings as the scenes were replaying."[55] A sense of being lost, frozen by the pain of the past, and relegated to the state of remaining a spectator of life also permeates the last Joy Division song cited in the comic: "Komakino" or coma cinema.[56] Appropriately enough for the dark mood of gothic rock and *The Crow*, the song's title connects the sense of being not only lost but almost dead with the modern passive entertainment of watching movies simulating lives. Another commonality in both songs is the unchanging circularity of painful events (the death drive), which reflects the psychological torture the Crow inflicts on himself while also suggesting that revenge will bring him little peace, and he will remain trapped in the vicious patterns of the Komakino or the replayed scenes mentioned in "Decades." This sensation is reinforced by the repetitive, haunting rhythms prevailing over the band's repertoire. The Crow's revenge and melancholic episodes have a similar repetitive pattern.

Suggesting the overlap between romantic and New Wave aesthetics, which is remediated in *The Crow* via its patchwork of references, the package front for Joy Division's free flexi disc for the singles "Komakino" and "Incubation" carries a black-and-white reproduction of William Blake's watercolor print *Newton* (1804–1805), which shows a naked Isaac Newton bending over a piece of paper with a compass. The figure's pose and the compass recall Blake's depiction of Urizen in another watercolor print, often referred to as *The Ancient of Days*,[57] which served as the frontispiece for his illuminated book *Europe a Prophecy* (1794). The compass, as art historian Anthony Blunt points out, can be traced back to medieval manuscripts, where it symbolized the imposition of rational order over chaos.[58] Correspondingly, the name "Urizen" itself is a homophone of "your reason."[59] Urizen in Blake's mythology was the power working against imagination. It was the voice of logic and reason "crush[ing] man's sense of the infinite [...] to shut him up within the narrow wall of his five senses."[60] This ties in with the sense of being caged and the need to break away, which is discernible in many Joy Division songs, two of which in particular, "Decades" and "New Dawn Fades," are included in *The Crow*. These references capture the Crow's state of being, eternally caged by his pain and melancholia.

Hinting toward a major source of symbolism and ideology for *The Crow*, the very last section of the comic, in which the Crow visits Shelly's graveyard, is titled "Passover," the feast celebrating the end of the Israelites' period of slavery in Egypt. Because the ending suggests that, despite having carried out his revenge, the Crow does not really attain the peace he had hoped for in the form of an eternal union with Shelly but instead remains alone, enslaved by his memories, this reference also exemplifies the ambiguity that pervades the many Christian allusions in the comic.

Christian allusions are already suggested on the Crow's first appearance, which is captioned by the robber Jones's expletive "Jesus... Christ!"[61] When the Crow's next victim, Tom Tom, echoes the expletive, the Crow puts out the light in the room, says a brief prayer, and tells a joke about Jesus Christ walking into an inn, giving the innkeeper three nails, and asking him, "Can you put me up for the night?" Since these words are positioned right next to the Crow's face in the panel, they allude to his possible status as a modern, damaged Jesus, reversing his doctrine of eternal forgiveness in the face of unending human evil. His constant taunts to T-Bird's attacking men as he eliminates them also include some—slightly transformed—Christian references: "Oh, you sewer rats are so *faithful*, you cause me to *blush* to my *bones*... you *never stop dying for me!*" and "Come on, kids... this isn't *Calvary Hill*." Similarly, when the Crow quotes Emily Dickinson's "Because I could not stop for Death" as he kills Funboy's lackeys and orders Funboy to tell T-Bird to meet him for a final confrontation, the image of Christ appears twice in the same scene, accompanying references to Christianity and then death.

Before meeting the junkie Funboy to give a place and time for their final showdown, the Crow runs into a little girl, Sherri, whose mother is with Funboy. When Funboy, who had seen Eric Draven die, tries to understand what the Crow is, the panels start bleeding and the Crow cites Revelation (20:12): "And *I* saw the dead, small and great stand before God," which is closely followed by a line echoing Joy Division's "Wilderness": "I saw the *blood* of Christ on their skins."[62] The same song ends with the phrase "Tears in their eyes," referring to the tears of the martyrs seen by the singer and tying in with the many references to the suffering of saints and the passion of Christ in *The Crow*. The comic's third book, "Irony," opens in a cathedral as the Crow loads his guns, and the panels establish parallels between him and an unusually muscular Christ on the cross. A line in the section "Immolation" similarly echoes the image of the suffering Christ: "Death, like virtue has its degrees... and he was clothed in a vesture dipped in blood."[63] And, unsurprisingly, one of the final portraits of the Crow is subtitled "Dies Irae, Dies Illa," the title of a medieval hymn referring to God's wrath on the Day of Judgment.

Another set of references that recur fragmentarily throughout the comic are the visual allusions to the German romantic painter Caspar David Friedrich's work. The first panel of the "Passover" section, in which the Crow, having avenged Eric's and Shelly's deaths, returns to the cemetery to finally unite with his lover, is a monochrome reproduction of Friedrich's *Abtei im Eichwald* (*The Abbey in the Oakwood*; also known as *Mönchsgräbnis im*

Eichenhain, or *Monk's Grave in Oak Grove*, 1809–1810). Somewhat faded and blurred, the painting's reproduction in the comic seems to be a memory of the original. The comic's final panel shares a certain similarity with another Friedrich painting, *Der Mönch am Meer* (*The Monk by the Sea*, 1808–1810), not so much in the disparity of size between figure and space but in the portrayal of the main, solitary figure looking out onto the sea with his back turned to the viewer. Confirming the protagonist's loneliness, these references also strengthen the strong romantic undercurrent coursing through the gothic characteristics of *The Crow*, particularly the prevalence of ruins (the house Eric inhabits is old; he frequents run-down areas of the city) and the protagonist's solitude and emotionality, which are, to a certain extent, accompanied by a sense of pleasure. The comic's fragmentation reflects the brokenness of the protagonist as well his milieu of a downtrodden, strife-ridden city, recalling Detroit, the city of ruins where O'Barr grew up and which was also the crime scene for the news story the comic at least in part is based on.[64]

As already suggested, the intertextual, intermedial references mentioned above—most prominently from Christian ideology, Joy Division's music, and romantic painting—themselves reflect the romantic use of fragments, building a scrapbook of references, roughly defined paths for the imagination to travel on. Comics, however, as Jared Gardner writes, are "always rooted in the narrative structure of shocks, fragments, and discontinuities."[65] In *The Crow*, these fragments are exacerbated by the collage of interspersed sketches, lyrics, and poetry as well as by a narrative that unfolds in an episodic, fragmented structure.

Emotionality

The Crow is full of extreme, often stylized emotion. The many Judeo-Christian references pointed out in the previous section indicate that such references, especially those of suffering (the Passion of Christ, Saint Sebastian), function as a means of universalizing and channeling the pain but also justifying the Crow's unrelenting vengeance. Moreover, in *The Crow*, like "so many gothic narratives, feeling is itself the ultimate object of male desire."[66] For the Crow, indulgence in feeling is also the only means through which he can approach his first object of desire, Shelly, since pain is inextricably bound with the memories of his previous life. Pain, the title of the first book, is also the driving force behind the action: the physical and psychological pain inflicted on Eric and Shelly leads to Eric's resurrection and methodic, violent revenge. The extreme pain captured in *The Crow* gives form to Georges Bataille's claim "that writing is the 'mask' of a cry and non-knowledge."[67] The comic's intense emotionality ushers in the unreasonable.

Introduced as "[g]rey and despairing, strong as steel but collapsed inside," the Crow "laughs under a street light, [with] a voodoo smile of one who lived and died and still yet lives... He makes his way home where he can be shapeless in the dark and paint his face in colors of joy."[68] Early in the comic, when menacing Jones in order to send a message to T-Bird's gang, the Crow shocks the petty criminal with his inability to feel the knife wounds Jones inflicts on him. Calmly drawing out the bloody knife, the Crow says, "Pain? I know *pain* at the molecular *level*... it pulls at my *atoms*... *sings* to me in an alphabet of *fear*." "I am the *boiling man*... come to break the *bones* of your *sins*, meat puppet," he adds, licking the knife and thus confirming the extent to which he relishes his violent revenge.[69]

When, in the next scene, Tin-Tin asks him why he is "all *painted up*," the Crow answers: "A funeral march."[70] These words, appearing without a speech balloon or pointer toward their speaker, seem to function as a caption under the Crow's slightly upward-tilted face whereby his thin, painted smile and the streaks pouring from his eyes that stare into the distance recall portrayals of the suffering Christ. As is frequent throughout the comic, O'Barr uses chiaroscuro for theatrical effect, in this case by inserting alternating streaks of white and black that cut through the Crow's face and thus allude to his suffering. The theatricality already manifest in the Crow's makeup attains vertiginous dimensions, as confirmed by the Crow's brief introductory speech to the terrified police officer trying to arrest him for killing the pawnbroker Gideon, who had Shelly's engagement ring: "I am *pilot error*, I am *fetal distress*, I am the *random chromosome*... I am complete and *total madness*... I am *fear*."[71] This gleeful description of himself also brings out the Crow's monstrosity, since he embodies fear as well as chaos and unpredictability.

Unsurprisingly, pain is the most recurrent sensation evoked in *The Crow*. The extent to which it is described ties in with the gothic and romantic exaggeration of emotions. For instance, alone with his thoughts and memories, the Crow is "a man... playing a violin... and the strings... are the nerves on his own arm," "[a] twisted soul—the mortar... despair—the bricks... to build a temple to sadness" (fig. 25).[72] This page, with its fragmented text reflecting the Crow's brokenness, places the Crow in a strange, unreal place: he finds himself alternately behind barbed wire and behind a window in a blank space looking at a feminine figure who turns out to be Death. There are two Crows, one performing against the barbed wire and the other, who is dressed in black, with his face turned away from the reader. This latter Crow meditatively fixes a "*spent shell*" (which is also slang for a used condom) in his hair, thus sabotaging his pining for Shelly with crass irony.

Goodlad points out that "[a]s in The Cure's lyrics, pain is [...] posited as the antidote to the existential emptiness left in the wake of failed heterosexual coupling."[73] Indulging in it throughout the comic, the Crow establishes pain as the motivating force behind his revenge: "Eric screams and screams and pounds his head against the wall until phantom fire trucks race across his vision. All he wants is *pain*. *Pain* and *hate*. Yes, hate."[74] Writes Goodlad: "[W]hen Eric plunges two hypodermic needles full of morphine into his breast, he reifies—by way of nullifying—the pain upon which his identity depends. Androgyny is both the sign and the effect of this subject-constituting pain."[75] Similar to his androgyny, Eric's ghost-like essence can also be linked to his suffering.

Like Funboy before him, T-Bird calls Eric a ghost man during their final confrontation as Eric bares his body for him and his lackeys to shoot at. And later, as T-Bird tries to run away, he calls the Crow a nightmare due to his ubiquity and immortality. Besides the labels of clown or painted boy, the Crow is also called a vampire or likened to Dracula, thus combining his spectrality with monstrosity and specifying that monstrosity as one thirsting for blood. Allowing them to shoot in vain at first, with his bare wounded torso recalling that of Saint Sebastian and stretched spectacularly across two pages (fig. 26), the Crow then starts attacking T-Bird's men while quoting the last line from Antonin Artaud's "Jardin noir" ("Black Garden"): "Behold the night, offering / The key that opens wide her gates of horn / To the emanations of delivered souls."[76] Continuing to cite and recontextualize Artaud—this time from his essay "Van Gogh ou le suicidé de la société"("Van Gogh, the Man Suicided by Society")—the Crow calls his fight against the gang a sanctification of society, an exorcism of the devil housed in it.[77] Artaud's original words, however, blamed society for Van Gogh's suicide and likened society to the crows in Van Gogh's *Wheatfield with Crows* (1890), which, "[l]ike an inundation of black crows in the fibres of his internal tree, overwhelmed him with one final swell."[78] The Crow replaces "inundation" with "flood" and minimally alters the last phrase into "submerged him in a *last swell*."[79] The Crow's recitation of Artaud's words is especially apt, since Artaud came up with the notion of the "theatre of cruelty," with cruelty referring to the suffering entailed by existence, a notion that reflected Artaud's physical and psychological turmoil. Van Gogh himself, who suffered from depression and cut off his right ear, shares the characteristics of intense emotions and their bodily expression with the Crow. Artaud's description of Van Gogh and modern humanity in general also applies to the Crow: "[H]e has never been able to live, has never thought of living, except as one possessed."[80] More directly, however, several portraits of the Crow evoke the suffering Christ or, as in the case of the image for the title page of the first section, "Lament," Saint Sebastian.

Just as the Crow himself is a being traversing the realms of life and death, his city is a more nightmarish version of Baudelaire's Paris seeped in death and violence,[81] where "black shadows are alive with the dead, twisted poetry in broken English, flesh and blood and staring faces,"[82] a macabre stage where the worst of humankind is revealed. Congruently, the largest part of the narrative unfolds at night. During the day, the Crow remains in the old house he had renovated with Shelly. Located in a deserted, run-down portion of the city, the house with its high windows also echoes the gothic, dark romantic aesthetic imbuing the comic. The exaggerated theatricality of the renditions makes the Crow appear deformed. This, combined with his supernatural powers of a revenant who cannot die and his traumatic "origin" story, also reveals similarities with the superhero, the dominant genre of the medium in which *The Crow* is inscribed. While the indulgence in spectacularity is another commonality between *The Crow* and the superhero genre, the comic's protagonist has a stronger link with the character type of the trickster and the clown. The Crow's proximity to these figures, in turn, enhances the element of the spectacle dominating the comic while functioning self-reflexively, since, as pointed out by Scott Bukatman, the figure of the trickster reflects the medium of comics itself.[83]

Excess and Ambiguity

Spectacle, Spectrality, and Spectacularity

According to Feder, "[t]he Nietzschean Dionysus as a symbol of psychic renewal through the dissolution of the self, is the climactic expression of the instinctual yearnings of European romanticism and the prophet of their social and aesthetic development in the twentieth century."[84] Also relevant for *The Crow* is the background story of Dionysus's resurrection after his brutal death (the Titans tore away and ate all but his heart in one version of the myth).[85] Brought back to life like Dionysus, the Crow is not only a monster but also a ghost, comparable to Hellboy, who becomes a ghost as a result of succumbing to the violence inflicted on him. The Crow's very existence, however, is based on Eric's and Shelly's deaths. Death is therefore a constant presence, not only as a personification, which occasionally interacts with the Crow as described below, but also as triggering factor and goal in the comic. In this way, the Crow also embodies the kind of ghost mentioned by Richard Kearney, who, using Hamlet's father's ghost as prototype, sees ghosts as incarnations of unresolved issues and troubles of memory.[86] Eric Draven's ghost, the Crow, incarnates the troubles of memory in a different sense, since the ghost is tormented by memories of a perfect past and its abrupt end but takes matters into his own hands to avenge the crime. Hence, although the ghost here is as troubled as Hamlet's father's ghost, it has greater agency. As will now be discussed, in *The Crow*, the ghost's spectrality or ghostliness co-exists with the spectacularity of his intense pain and the revenge he carries out, because excessive grief and desire for revenge are the forces that make the protagonist come back as a supernatural being.

For Kearney, the confrontation with death is also a confrontation with the Lacanian Real,[87] existing beyond the realm of possible symbolization and thus causing the breakdown of meaning, as reflected by the absurdity impregnating *The Crow*. As mentioned in the chapter on *Hellboy* above, death has always been part of the image, according to Hans Belting.[88] In the case of *The Crow*, it is the ghostly persistence of death, rather than the threat of death and inaction in *Hellboy*, that is paramount. The depiction of memories in *The Crow*, their fading in and out of reality, plays with the notion that what is captured in an image is already part of the past, a ghost as it were. The notion of the ghost can thus be seen as pervading the comic on several levels, referring to the workings of the ambiguous drawings that leave suggestions lurking in the shadows but also persisting in the story itself, existing at the very core of the protagonist by being both his essence and his source of despair, since he is constantly haunted by memories.

Death itself is personified in the comic. Eric is shown dancing with a feminized death in the "Crescendo" preceding the fifth book, "Death." Other personifications of death as a male figure accompany the Crow from the beginning of the comic, with the first reverie of death opening with Eric sitting peacefully in an empty train and watching a white horse run alongside. The horse runs into a barbed wire fence and bleeds to death as Death, the train conductor, turns up and asks Eric for his tickets. Toward the end of the first book, Death appears again, to shoot (literally, with a gun) through the Crow's reverie of Shelly. Moreover, some of the gang members, particularly the emaciated figures of Top Dollar and the junkie Funboy, already look like skeletons before their deaths, which, along with the images of the ghetto, complement the image of the deteriorating city structure coursing through the story. The Crow's appearance, with his dark, spiked, shoulder-length hair and long coat, is comparable to Dream, the protagonist of Neil Gaiman's *Sandman* series, who, despite being the brother of Death, is likewise a dark, tortured, gothic character. Correspondingly, T-Bird tauntingly calls the Crow "Mister Ghost Man" when he tries to kill him. The Crow himself, through his appearance, words, and actions, builds on this simultaneously theatrical and abstracted (and thus dehumanized) conception of himself. As he tells the thug Patrick in the comic's final book, "Death": "I am he who can dissolve the terror of being a man and going among the dead. I am morphine for a wooden leg."[89]

In warning Funboy that "[w]hoever fights *monsters* should see to it that in the *process* he *does not become a monster*,"[90] the Crow cites the famous Nietzschean aphorism (no. 146) that ends: "And when you stare for a long time into an abyss, the abyss stares back at you."[91] These words hint at the unfulfilled essence of the Crow's quest while also alluding to its moral ambiguity. On an intertextual level, the quotation, much like the smiley face graffitied in a church that the Crow goes to in the first two pages of "Irony" before launching the next phase of his revenge, are possibly references to Alan Moore and Dave Gibbons's *Watchmen*, which highlights the ambiguity of superheroes and the dangers of power (fig. 27). This double-spread functions in many ways like a collage with its abundance of disconnected images including a somewhat jarring juxtaposition of shots of the interior of the church and the Crow's gun. This jarring essence is recognized by the narrative caption on the second page, which suggests that despite being opposites, "absolution and redemption, salvation and a means to an end [...] they have a *common ground*."[92] As suggested in the course of this book, monsters themselves throw differences and opposites into question.

Correspondingly, grotesqueness and monstrosity are regularly associated with the gang members, beginning with the description of Tin-Tin in the first book as having a "*soul so twisted with evil* it could only have drifted off a *Bosch* painting."[93] The italicized and thus emphasized reference to the exuberant monstrosity in the medieval painter Hieronymus Bosch's works is significant in that both the comic and the painting share a fascination for monstrosity and excess, an excess that has been tailored to different contexts. The crow on Eric's shoulder calls another gangster, Patrick, a "chemical monster," once again underscoring the monstrosity of people who, unlike the Crow, appear normal. On the other hand, as his remark to Funboy indicates, the Crow himself is not far from being a monster in his thirst for bloody revenge. Indeed, one of the splashes before the final book bears the title "Angel, all fire," emphasizing the Crow's violent nature. This is comparable to the notion of the monstrous God, such as W. B. Yeats's "rough beast" in "The Second Coming."[94] The Crow, like the Baudelairian monster who combines the demonic and the angelic, also embodies the juxtaposition of opposites.[95]

Although the Crow is not a monster per se (his body, for instance, looks human), he has superhuman abilities and wears a smile drawn in lipstick across his face, emphasizing the absurdity of his situation as well as his status as an outsider and an ambivalent being. His makeup also reflects the element of spectacularity permeating his revenge.

In placing Arthur Rimbaud's poetry at the beginning and at the end of the comic, followed by Joy Division lyrics, similarities between the two are suggested. Rimbaud's "Nocturne vulgaire" ("Ordinary Nocturne") opens the comic, and "Being Beauteous" is one of the last fragments of citations, followed by Joy Division's "Decades" and "Komakino." Unsurprisingly, beauty and death are intertwined in "Being Beauteous," and specters, or the ghosts symbolizing memories, persist in "Komakino": "The shadow that stood by the side of the road / Always reminds me of you."[96] Rimbaud's "Ordinary Nocturne" sums up the progress of *The Crow*, from the destructive opening to the quiet ending insinuating death—"One breath dispels the limits of the hearth."[97] Moreover, the passionate, dizzy fantasy imbuing the poem's atmosphere also echoes *The Crow*'s world, which is driven by emotions and cedes to the unreal as captured by one of the splashes interrupting the main story in which "the crow spirals down through a collapsed dream and the only sound he makes is ... *like a concave scream.*"[98]

In contrast to the extreme emotionality pervading the comic as well as its fragmented structure, which once again confirms the brokenness of the main character, the Crow's quest for vengeance is so carefully planned out that one may speak of it as being staged, as is confirmed by the heavy makeup and stylized, choreographed moves of its director and protagonist. Shadows and dramatization coexist in both the chiaroscuro and the fragmentary dialogues, as for instance during the Crow's narration of Eric's and Shelly's deaths to Tin-Tin: "A *year* ago ... a *cold* October night ... a broken down *car* on a *dirt* road ... a *man* ... a *girl* ... *madness* ... *pain* ... and ... *shadows* ... my God, the *shadows*!!"[99] The theatricality of the Crow, along with his intense emotionality and appearance, renders him comparable to Gwynplaine. Like Eric Draven, Gwynplaine is also a victim of his circumstances. Likened to a monster or a devil, Gwynplaine's monstrosity only comes to the forefront when he becomes infatuated with the Duchess and her aristocratic society, for which he forsakes Ursus, Dea, and the other pariahs. Like the gang members in *The Crow*, the real monster in *The Man Who Laughs*, Barkilphedro, who indulges in acts of evil for the sake of evil, is also human. Hence, while the monstrous-looking protagonists in both works are far from flawless, they are, to a considerable extent, victims of their circumstances. Pain also plays a central role in Gwynplaine's life, being externalized at a young age by the scar in the shape of a smile that could only scare others and culminating in his suicide in the wake of his rejected lover Dea's death. Moreover, both Gwynplaine and the Crow are characters who are to a considerable extent lost. Although this lack of direction is more evident in Gwynplaine's story, it also exists in the Crow, since, in spite of his quest for revenge, he does not attain peace of mind. Hugo's worlds in both *The Hunchback of Notre-Dame* and *The Man Who Laughs* know only tragic ends. The tragedy persists in *The Crow*, where it is only in death that the protagonist is reunited with his lover. Finally, on a visual level, Hugo's own preference for chiaroscuro and romantic landscapes in his art is comparable to both the harsher styles in *The Crow* and the fluid, blurred nature of the panels capturing Eric's memories.

The Trickster's Ambiguity

Through Ian Curtis's attacks, Joy Division concerts were in many ways performances of excess, since they diverged from the givens of "normal" behavior and brought, inadvertently, intense emotional and physical sensations to the stage. The Crow builds the bridge between such excessive emotionality and the figure of the trickster. The trickster is quintessentially a performer who mocks normality and provides entertainment. The Crow, an essentially abnormal figure hovering between human and monster, is caught up in an unending, hectic performance, dressed up as an entertainer who, paradoxically, does not entertain in his actual storyworld but enacts and even renders ironic popular culture's drive to entertain, and consequently attract and maintain, its readership.

Indicating the Crow's link with tricksters—character types who, like Gwynplaine, also thrive on the stage—tricks and surprises are part of the Crow's modus operandi. The little girl Sherri fondly calls the Crow "Mr. Clown." Studying transformations in conceptions of the monster in the seventeenth century, and drawing out the transfer of fascination and awe from monsters to machines, Zakiya Hanafi shows how treatises on natural magic associated "monsters with parlour tricks and optical illusions," a conception adopted by contemporaneous museum collections in which "[m]onsters appear in deforming mirrors, in catoptric machines, and in automatic theaters."[100] The elements of trickery evoked by Hanafi are brought to the surface in the case of the Crow, equating him with the Joker, the supervillain who unleashes chaos in Batman's Gotham City. Although positioned on the opposite ends of the spectrum of good and evil, the Crow and the Joker share a certain commonality that goes beyond their appearance, including the tendency toward anarchy, toward rejecting the law or taking it in their own hands, which, to a considerable extent, is inscribed in the monster's very being through his default outsider status.

The Joker is also someone who gleefully and carefully orchestrates his violent crimes, often with considerable theatricality, as can be seen in the graphic novels *The Killing Joke* (in which he kidnaps Commissioner Gordon and sets up a horror show for him in an abandoned amusement park), *Arkham Asylum* (in which he takes over the asylum and arranges a series of physical and psychological battles between Batman with the asylum inmates), and *The Man Who Laughs* (in which he embarks on another killing rampage using a special gas that makes the victims laugh hysterically and die with distorted, clown-like faces). *The Killing Joke* in particular reveals glaring parallels between the Joker's and the Crow's lives, especially the loss of a loved one at the hands of ruthless local gangsters coupled with their own traumatic deaths, or near-deaths, after which they are transformed into the gleefully mad characters replacing their names with titles referring to types rather than individuals (the Joker, the Crow). However, in contrast to the Crow, who obsessively holds onto the memories of his past, the Joker in *The Killing Joke* claims to not know the exact details of the past that drove him mad enough to plan his elaborate, murderous schemes.[101]

In his study on the trickster in American Indian mythology, the anthropologist Paul Radin paints the trickster as an ambiguous being, combining good qualities with evil ones.[102] Like the Crow, the trickster in American Indian mythology is connected to the raven.[103] When discussing the trickster and his links with the poltergeist and the shaman, Carl Jung also discerns resemblances between the trickster's ambiguity and the "demonic features exhibited by Yahweh in the Old Testament."[104] An echo of a comparably angry god resonates in the Crow's bloody revenge, which was only possible through his supernatural powers.

Radin's description of the trickster as *"the spirit of disorder, the enemy of boundaries"* captures the contradiction that lies at the trickster's core and emphasizes his close link to entropy.[105] Likening the trickster to the poltergeist, Jung notes that he "has on occasion described himself as a soul in hell, the motif of subjectivity suffering."[106] This description applies to both the Joker and the Crow, the Crow tries to overcome what he believes is the source of his suffering, giving into monstrous acts but also becoming increasingly caught up in his own monstrosity and liminality (between humanity and monstrosity, between life and death). Thus, while the Crow reflects Jung's observation that there is something of the medicine man and the shaman in the trickster's character as well as the more general notion of the savior, or "the wounded wounder [who] is the agent of healing," the possibility of redemption is absent in the comic.[107]

The Crow's link to the Joker also raises the connection to madness provoked by trauma, which is in keeping with Feder's claim that "[m]adness as a theme in myth and literature has always dealt with personal responses to environmental influences."[108] In both cases, madness results in violence (although the Crow's violence is propelled by a certain logic) and an excess of emotion, which culminates in laughter in the face of cruelty. The combination of violence and laughter already existed in the circus pantomime figure of the clown, a figure to whom both the Crow and the Joker are connected.[109] As literary scholar Anna-Sophie Jürgens points out, the clown is the symbol of anarchy per se and embodies ambivalence, which is further incremented in the violent clown.[110] Jürgens shows how violence was a part of the modern clown's history, as exemplified by the gore prevalent in the famous circus pantomimes of the Hanlon-Lees, since,[111] following the tradition of mime, "the meaning of the act(ion) is suspended" in such performances, thereby encouraging, or at least facilitating, the recurrence of violent acts.[112] While "literary clowns with their mask-like faces embody a corpo-reality that appears stylized into artificiality," for Jürgens, the clowns in comics enter into daily life.[113] However, this distinction does not hold for the Crow, who incorporates the abovementioned characteristics of both literary and comics clowns. Jürgens adds that the Joker is a nobody,[114] an observation that also applies to the Crow. A comparable universality is discernible in the clown, since "[t]he clown reminds us of our fragmented state by tackling acrobatic or special jobs in the spirit of the whole or integral man."[115] As discussed at the beginning of this chapter, romanticism was likewise based on the painful awareness of the fragmentation of the self.

Like the monsters discussed earlier, the trickster, too, is a solitary hero. According to Feder: "In imaginative writing from the late romantic period to the present, the increasing sense of aloneness in an indifferent universe and amoral society is symbolically transformed into assaults on the very notion of the autonomous self."[116] She adds that such fictions revolve around "conveying instinctual aims converted to social alienation: personal gratification in regressive fantasies, the renunciation of psychic integration for illusions of omnipotence, the expansion of consciousness in dissociation and hallucinations as an avenue to individual and communal rebirth."[117] This mechanism is discernible in *The Crow* but crumbles toward the end because the protagonist's revenge proves to be unsatisfactory.

Unlike the figure of the clown or the trickster, who would rarely embark on a quest (which would involve imbuing their actions with unambiguous meaning), the Crow, like the protagonists of the other comics discussed here, does have a quest, albeit a traumatic one. This involves both the process of trying to come to terms with loss and enacting a revenge that is methodically carried out, often with theatrical glee. The spectacularity that coexists with the protagonist's specularity already hints toward a certain emptiness of his actions, of their inability to provide the Crow with the peace of mind he craves, possibly due to the brutality of his carefully premeditated vengeance and the impossibility of restoring the past. The quest for revenge and retribution for the crime committed is a means of coming to terms with the trauma of his and his lover's violent deaths. Notably, as the Crow's quest nears its unsatisfactory apogee, the references to Christianity increase, as in the third book, "Irony," which opens in a cathedral and where it becomes clear that the Crow's quest will remain unfulfilled.

Goodlad shows how the ambiguity seeping through *The Crow* is embodied by both the androgyny and the ghostliness of its protagonist: "Although the body of the killing machine is recognizably macho, the repeated, self-inflicted, and explicitly Christ-like mortification and penetration of Eric's flesh—the spectacularization of his wounds, his sentience, and his pain—blur the distinction between masculinized blood and feminized tears."[118] The Crow's ambiguity can thus be seen as rooted in his liminal being and feeding into his somewhat ambivalent morality spurred by his need for cathartic closure. Consequently, he hovers on the fence between good and evil when it comes to carrying out his revenge, embodying Christian symbolism (especially that of suffering) on the one hand, while trading its doctrine of forgiveness for the Old Testament tenet of an eye for an eye, a tooth for a tooth, on the other. That his revenge unfolds as a spectacle extends the ambiguity from the protagonist to the world of entertainment, where anything, even violence, can be transformed into a spectacle that is to be consumed uncritically and incessantly. Once again, a certain irony seeps through the comic, for instance through the juxtaposition of church and weapon shown in figure 27.

Cultural theorist Guy Debord famously connected the madness and identity crisis induced by modernity to the power and fascination commanded by the spectacle:

Le spectacle, qui est l'effacement des limites du moi et du monde par l'écrasement du moi qu'assiège la présence-absence du monde, est également l'effacement des limites du vrai et du faux par le refoulement de toute vérité vécue sous la *présence réelle* de la fausseté qu'assure l'organisation de l'apparence. Celui qui subit passivement son sort quotidiennement étranger est donc poussé vers une folie qui réagit illusoirement à ce sort, en recourant à des techniques magiques. La reconnaissance et la consommation des marchandises sont au centre de cette pseudo-réponse à une communication sans réponse.[119]

(The spectacle erases the dividing line between self and world, in that the self, under siege by the presence/absence of the world is eventually overwhelmed; it likewise erases the dividing line between true and false, repressing all directly lived truth beneath the *real presence* of falsehood maintained by the organization of appearance. The individual, though condemned to the passive acceptance of an alien everyday reality, is thus driven into a form of madness in which, by resorting to magical devices, he entertains the illusion that he is reacting to this fate. The recognition and consumption of commodities are at the core of this pseudo-response to a communication to which no response is required.)[120]

I would argue that not just *The Crow* but also *Hellboy*, *Swamp Thing*, and *Monstre* are all intensely involved in negotiating a space for a self that is monstrocized by an increasingly monstrous world of persecution and gratuitous violence, where options for expressing individuality and the possibilities to enact one's desires are constrained and often unfold in the form of a spectacle. The monstrosity of the worlds in the four comics brings to light the constant persecution faced by the protagonists and their inability to break away from their "marked bodies."[121] As is the fate of many othered bodies going back to Frankenstein's monster, Quasimodo, Gwynplaine, and, with less gravity, the trickster, the spectacularization of these figures is inevitable. The struggles of these othered creatures thus shed light on the bodies of knowledge that determine and enforce normalization.

Looking at the interactions between reality and fantasy, as well as the treatment of pariahs in early American comics such as Richard Outcault's *Hogan's Alley* and *Poor Lil' Mose*, literary scholar David Westbrook concludes that "[t]he minority becomes a sideshow attraction, and the marginal becomes an escape."[122] These features of the minority and the marginal are combined in monsters, since they are marginal creatures embodying the escape from the norm. More directly reflected by the figure of the Crow is Jean-François Lyotard's description of trauma as "a bit monstrous, unformed, confusing, confounding."[123] However, as has been shown by the monsters in this book, they are all, like Lyotard's trauma, confounding and ambiguous. Northrop Frye saw Lord Byron as "popularizing a new sense of moral ambiguity: the sense of the curse of genius, the isolation caused by the possession of greater powers than ordinary."[124] Such an isolation and ambiguity (albeit often without the plague of genius) infects all monsters examined here. Their rebelliousness is rooted in their ambiguity, in their ability to actively confound logic. These two central characteristics of the comics monsters in this book are examined further in the conclusion.

CONCLUSION

COMICS MONSTERS

Per Monstra ad Astra

> The proper study of Mankind is Man.
> Plac'd on this isthmus of a middle state,
> A being darkly wise, and rudely great:
> [...]
> He hangs between; in doubt to act, or rest,
> In doubt to deem himself a God, or Beast;
> In doubt his Mind or Body to prefer
> [...]
> Chaos of Thought and Passion, all confus'd;
> Still by himself abused or disabus'd;
> Created half to rise, and half to fall [...]
> —ALEXANDER POPE, *AN ESSAY ON MAN*, BOOK 2

The anthropomorphic monsters encountered in this book confirm that the monster does make a man, to quote Trinculo.[1] His words evoke the freak shows in London in which monsters were in many ways created through the apparatus of display and exclusion from the realm of humans. Trinculo's words acquire further precision in the above quotation from Alexander Pope's *An Essay on Man*, since it is the combination of the animal and the divine in man that is echoed and exaggerated by the monster.[2] In her study on the transfer of monsters from the realm of the sacred or the incomprehensibly marvelous to the machine from the sixteenth into the eighteenth centuries, Zakiya Hanafi suggests that the emotions monsters provoke in their beholders are in themselves "monstrous affects," with the main one being that of wonder, as exemplified, quite literally, in the comics analyzed here by monsters such as Warhole and the Crow, who go to elaborate lengths to create spectacles. The Swamp Thing's regeneration and Hellboy's resilience in the face of increasingly powerful adversaries also provoke wonder.[3] These stories, like their beings, are spectacular. The analyses above have also highlighted how comics monsters, especially Warhole and the Swamp Thing, reflect the spaces they inhabit. They are therefore intimately connected with the spaces of spectacle or entertainment that they generate around themselves. *Wonders* is precisely how Ambroise Paré, one of the earliest theoreticians of the monstrous, qualified the monster. The state of wonderment, as Hanafi elaborates, is both desirable and dangerous, much like monsters themselves.[4] As suggested by all of the monsters analyzed here, rebelliousness and ambiguity are two additional features contributing toward the potential dangerousness of monsters.

This concluding chapter traces the forms of rebelliousness discernible in comics monsters by highlighting the rebellious romantic heritage ensconced in the comics medium itself. It therefore starts by summarizing the shared and distinct romantic features embodied by the monstrous protagonists in the previous chapters. This is followed by a brief, close reading of Emil Ferris's *My Favorite Thing Is Monsters* to show how many of the romantic features brought out through the other comics reappear in this graphic novel. Drawing links between the prominence of the spectacular and the spectacle in the analyzed stories as well as the medium, I then elaborate on the embedding of romantic features and monstrous inclinations in comics, especially on spectacularity as an inevitable accompaniment to rebelliousness. I end with a brief coda on the presence of romanticism in contemporary culture.

Besides the shared tempering of good and evil, several romantic features are discernible in the comics monsters analyzed above. The most prominent features include: Warhole's fluidity and similarities with the abstract Baudelairian monster, ennui; the Swamp Thing's bond with nature, specifically the untamable monstrosity and expressive pantheism of his vegetal world; the nostalgia of Hellboy's world; and, finally, the theatrical emotionality exuded by the Crow. However, a degree of spectacularity, of creating and enjoying spectacles, perseveres in most of the comics here, as does the related motif of automatons or mechanized figures set in motion for entertainment. Closely tied to animation, automation or the imitation of life is already personified by Frankenstein's monster. The comics monsters examined in this book are often accompanied by automatons or some form of ventriloquism or puppeteering. Automatons themselves seem monstrous because of "the fact that matter formed by artificial means and moving of its own volition would seem to be endowed with spirit."[5] More often than not, as Hanafi goes on to elaborate, automatons, through their transformational potential, were often seen as expressions of the diabolical spirit associated with mutations.[6] In a similar vein, critic Norman Klein highlights the anarchic energy of cartoons by describing cartoon characters as "automata that struggle."[7] Just like the predilection for mutation and organic energy, this spirit of celebrating difference, of defying norms and encouraging outright revolution that was also the zeitgeist of the late eighteenth and nineteenth centuries (witnesses to the French Revolution and the revolutions of 1848, among others), is common to romanticism, monsters, and comics.

According to Northrop Frye, "[i]n *The Marriage of Heaven and Hell*, Blake presents the revolutionary vision of man as self-centered anxious ego sitting on top of a rebellious desire, and he associates the emancipating of desire with the end of the world as we know it."[8] In Blake's later works, this emancipation of desire was "the effect of the purging of reality."[9] The monster has inherited this desire and its destructive potential; Warhole, the Swamp Thing, and Hellboy are involved to different extents in the purging of the reality and tapping into a transsubjective, supernatural consciousness. The Crow's revenge is also an attempt, albeit an unsuccessful one, to purge his memories. Blake's *The Marriage of Heaven and Hell* "gives us both aspects of the romantic movement: the reaction to political revolution and the manifesto of feeling and desire as opposed to the domination of reason."[10] As Isaiah Berlin, among others, writes, the romantic hero is a rebel.[11] Berlin adds that "the free untrammelled will and the denial of the fact that there is a nature of things, the attempt to blow up and explode the very notion of a stable structure of anything—are the deepest and in a sense the most insane elements in this extremely valuable and important movement."[12] This is comparable to the traits of the monster listed by Jeffrey Cohen: "the monster threatens to destroy not just individual members of society, but the very cultural apparatus through which individuality is constituted and allowed."[13] By being "an assertion of self, an assertion of free will in more or less playful terms," rebelliousness is also a relatable human quality and a possible source of cathartic energy, which is expressed by the very human struggles of the monsters analyzed here.[14] For Thierry Smolderen, rebelliousness manifests itself in, among other aspects, the graffiti in the caricaturist George Cruikshank's prints on Jack Sheppard, along with the act of making Sheppard, the infamous eighteenth-century English thief who was also known for his prison breaks, the star of the series.[15] In a similar vein, Jared Gardner reads the graffiti "Ghost World" that anonymously appears in Daniel Clowes's graphic novel of the same name "as a potent symbol of the graphic writing we call 'comics': simultaneously image and text (not to mention vandalism and art)."[16]

In addition to this element of rebellion and the penchant for alternative, often denigrated forms of expression, both comics and romanticism have shared roots in the struggle to come to terms with the modern experience. The medium of comics "was dedicated to diagramming the serial complexities of modern life and fixing the fragments of modernity on the page."[17] Ennui is a reaction to the drastic changes in modern life and experience. The body of Frankenstein's monster is made up of fragments. The struggle with modern experience and existence continues in the comics discussed above, with their imperfect, troubled, and frequently traumatized protagonists, such as Nike and Warhole, the Swamp Thing and the Crow, and their impassioned but not completely successful quests, especially in the case of Hellboy and the Crow. Following a trajectory started by the spectacle-generating ability of monsters discernible in romanticism, monsters in the modern era, as indicated by Trinculo's words, became freaks,[18] which was accompanied by "a movement from a narrative of the marvelous to a narrative of the deviant."[19] Disability studies specialist Rosemarie Garland-Thomson adds that "freak discourse is both imbricated in and reflective of our collective cultural transformation into modernity."[20] In contrast, however, the deviant in comics and its ancestors from the romantic era, has often been allocated a more central role. This is particularly evident in Ferris's *My Favorite Thing Is Monsters*. We first encounter the young protagonist, Karen Reyes, in her nightmare, in which she changes into a were-girl with a Frankenstein's monster–like face and a hunchback. The townsfolk soon become aware of her transformation. With chants such as "Let's smoke that Freak!" and "Kill the Monster!," a horde soon gathers outside her apartment and a frightened but determined gunman ends up shooting her, at which point Karen wakes up, searching in vain for injuries. The graphic novel thus opens with a scene of persecution targeting the freak, the monster. In doing so, the mob ignores the suggestion of a homeless Native American to leave the monster alone because "it can't help being different."[21] The graphic novel is, among many other things, a plea for accepting difference. It highlights the innocuity of monsters. In doing so, Ferris cleverly intertwines one of the most persecuted genres in comics history: horror comics.

For Gardner, who emphasizes the anarchic tendencies of comics, "[b]y only sporadically being profitable and almost never being respectful, comics has been left to develop its own language and its own unique relationship with readers, often for long periods, with few or no attempts to make the form respectable."[22] As Scott Bukatman fondly puts it, "[c]omics are little monsters."[23] The disregard for respectability is already discernible in what Smolderen describes as the inimitable flair and liveliness of Rodolphe Töpffer's anti-academic style of drawing, which also persists in the graffiti adorning the walls in Cruikshank's *Jack Sheppard*.[24] For Berlin, it was the philosopher Johann Georg Hamann who carried out one of the earliest attacks against the ideals of the Enlightenment by, among other aspects, emphasizing the importance of caprice and fancy in art[25]—features that are also part of the playful nature of comics.

Romantic predilections for the "primitive," including, for instance, children's drawings, graffiti, and caricature, can already be traced in Töpffer's works.[26] Töpffer was influenced by German romanticism as well as the latest developments in caricature across the English Channel.[27] The link between romanticism and caricature, which unfolds through the grotesque as mentioned in the beginning of this book, can be discerned in one of Berlin's description of romanticism as "the primitive, the untutored[;] it is youth, the exuberant sense of life of the natural man."[28] Describing comics' vitality and "primitivity," Bukatman suggests that comics "offer up little utopias of disorder, provisional sites of temporary resistance."[29] Such rebellious utopias as well as the romantic features brought up by the comics discussed here can already be discerned in early comics, including, for instance, the solitude of characters such as Lyonel Feininger's Wee Willie Winkie and Winsor McCay's Little Nemo, and the playful freedom of their worlds, which harbor the almost perennial possibility of chaos that characterizes many comics.[30] Indeed, with brief moments of respite, chaos permeates the structure of the comics' stories examined here, often triggered by the persecution of monsters (*Swamp Thing*, *Hellboy*) or the monster's own violence (*Monstre*, *The Crow*). It is also visually prominent in all of the comics examined, albeit in different ways, ranging from the chaotic whirlwind that is Warhole's head and that also reflects the elusiveness of ennui (fig. 7) and Gregori Arcane's delusions as the Patchwork Man (fig. 2) to the Swamp Thing's nightmares, Hellboy's struggle against an ever-increasing list of demonic forces including himself (fig. 20), and the episodes of violence in *The Crow*, which often burst through panel frames (fig. 26).

The romantic aspects explored in this book can be said to undergo their own transformation through the presence of monstrosity. The perpetual ambiguity and rebelliousness of these monsters in turn has strong roots in, or at least affiliations with, both romanticism and comics; deviancy, while being part of the rebellious ideology of romanticism, is also a characteristic of marginal, antinormative works, such as comics, which "pose a threat to established order and orderliness."[31]

My Favorite Thing Is Monsters: Monstrosity and Comics History

Emil Ferris's graphic novel debut *My Favorite Thing Is Monsters* (2017) captures the different strands of interactions between monstrosity, comics, and the romantic strains underlying them. Partly autobiographical, partly fantastic, the graphic novel unfolds as a diary of the young Karen Reyes growing up in a working-class neighborhood in Chicago during the turbulent late 1960s. An outcast with few friends at school, the mixed-race, gay Karen depicts herself as a were-girl who eventually puts on the garb of a noir detective (aka Kare) to solve the murder of her upstairs neighbor and friend, Anka Silverberg, who died under strange, unexplained circumstances. The richly illustrated diary, which conserves the lines and holes of a spiralbound notebook, records Kare's attempts to piece together the traumatized Anka's past in Nazi Germany and to find potential suspects. This crime story is interwoven with Karen's difficult childhood as the school "freak," and her joy and escape in horror comics and the paintings at the Art Institute of Chicago. Karen's own troubled family story, with her single mother who eventually passes away from cancer and her loving but wayward brother, is closely interwoven with other storylines, including those imagined by Kare/Karen.

The work is heavily permeated by the imaginaries of both horror comics and the fine arts. This includes Henry Fuseli's *The Nightmare*. Like many of the artworks and monsters Karen sees and imagines, the painting's creature comes alive and interacts with her. Karen also has a potentially imagined schoolmate, Franklin, a "tall, scary kid" who resembles Frankenstein's monster and who "has a whole bunch of bad scars [...] and he *never* speaks at all."[32] He even figures on a reproduced cover of *Gory Stories*, an underground comic reviving the horror genre, as Frankenstein's monster: "Franklin looks like he was assembled in the laboratory of a mad (but artistic) scientist."[33] In keeping with her affinity for monsters and all things monstrous, Karen muses that "if all the pieces fell away, I got the idea that what was inside of him was a big ball of bright light."[34] Here, Franklin-Frankenstein's monster not only captures the irreparable brokenness of an othered human (Franklin is African American) but also evokes the issue of animation, of giving life, which occupies a central role with the death of Karen's mother and the impossibility of bringing her back to life. Echoing the recurrence of the trope of animation in the comics discussed earlier, one of Karen's solitary neighbors is a ventriloquist who is strongly attached to his puppets.

Each segment of the graphic novel is marked by covers Karen copies from publications that often avoided the Comics Code Authority's approval by adopting a different, magazine-style format (like *Mad* magazine): *Ghastly, Dread, Spectral, Creepy*, and others. These covers are not only penciled copies, but they also reflect on the direction in which Karen's story unfolds, suggesting that the horrors experienced by Karen and her family and friends are not too distant from the flagrant horrors represented in the comics magazines. The monsters, despite their horrific appearances, are rarely harmful; it's the people themselves who are, as one of the monsters suggests to Karen. He adds: "It's perfectly normal to bury a thing that you'd rather not admit. . . . We—in my profession—definitely encourage humans to keep secrets from themselves."[35] The monster once again reveals himself as a creature who is closely connected to humans and even understands humans better than they do themselves.

Almost at the very end of the book, after her mother's funeral, Karen dreams of Anka and then searches for the "green island," the name she gave to the fleck of green in her mother's gray eyes. Paintings in large panels and splashes capture the expanse of the landscapes they portray. Even though not all of the paintings openly belong to the movement, they are romantic in essence. Once again, Karen dives into these paintings, effectively experiencing them as three-dimensional worlds, as panoramic experiences. This in turn brings to light the intense presence and sensuality of the paintings. She shouts for her mother on top of a rock in George Inness's *A Marine* and runs through Claude Monet's *Rocks at Port-Goulphar, Belle-Île*. She visits the secluded cottage in Harald Sohlberg's *Fisherman's Cottage*. Recalling Frankenstein's monster, she hides in the woods in Gustave Doré's *Alpine Scene*.

As exemplified by these last pages, *My Favorite Thing Is Monsters* bridges horror, comics, and the romantic. In interweaving the entertaining, escapist qualities of horror, it highlights its persistence in lived realities. By extension, it points to the monsters that all of us have to face, within ourselves and around us, that are often not monstrous in appearance. A plaidoyer against the unfair monstrocization of others, the graphic novel embraces the denigrated genre of horror and its frequent denizens, monsters, as well as the popular medium of comics and its fraught history.

Remediation of Romanticism in Comics: Spectacularity and Rebelliousness

In describing the blind Dea's perception of Gwynplaine, Victor Hugo captures the ambiguous essence and prominence of monsters: "Pour Dea Gwynplaine était la présence. La présence, profond mystère qui divinise l'invisible et d'où résulte cet autre mystère, la confiance. Il n'y a dans les religions que cela d'irréductible. Mais cet irréductible suffit. On ne voit pas l'immense être nécessaire; on le sent" (For Dea, Gwynplaine was a presence. The mysterious, profound presence that deified the invisible and that produced that other mystery, faith. This does not occur in religions other than those of the irreducible. But this irreducible is sufficient. One does not see the necessary, great being, one senses him).[36] This presence can be linked to monsters' potential for spectacularity but also to the energy that Bukatman discerns in comics, which in turn generates spectacles. While examining the spectacle in comics and referring to the similarities between Laura Mulvey's and Tom Gunning's essays on cinema, Bukatman proposes the spectacle "as narrative's other [...] that [...] has broken with the linearity, causality, and closure of classical narrative models."[37] Although not all comics are humorous, they do humor very well[38] and can get away with inserting humor in the most impossible of situations. In addition, the advantage of the lack of reality limits allows comics to immerse readers in very unusual worlds, as evinced by monsters and mutations, which seem to come almost naturally to the sequential art of comics, in which the sequence itself is not always synonymous with linearity (of time, space, or even narrative progression).

Although she examines "wax fictions," or stories in which wax figures come to life,[39] art historian Michelle Bloom suggests that metamorphosis is "appropriate for the simulation of human beings."[40] Described by Benoît Peeters as a governing principle of comics, metamorphosis has been a recurrent feature of the medium due to, at least in part, the medium's sequential nature.[41] However in remediating other media and simulators of movement such as film and automatons, the rebellious or at least caricaturing energy of comics gravitates more easily toward producing monstrous effects. Anthropomorphic or positively rendered monsters in comics distort simulations of humans and perfection, consequently throwing into question categories of the human and the nonhuman.

Writing about how early comics construe a narrative of marketplace culture, David Westbrook draws a link between Ishmael Reed's novel *Mumbo Jumbo* (about a reckless America in the Jazz Age) and George Herriman's *Krazy Kat*: "Like Reed's fantasy, the unreality of Krazy Kat and the comic strip in general can be read as a measure of its liveliness rather than a measure of its bad faith. It shows us the utopian side of a popular culture born in the marketplace, a fantasy that grows out of commercial culture but promises to transform it and acquire a life of its own. It offers the hope that the diminutive will have its revenge."[42] Hence, once again, the spectacle, in this case a seemingly harmless, humorous one, is interwoven with rebellious strains.

Spectacularity is not only linked to the nature of good monsters who defy the nonhuman implications of their extraordinary appearances, but it is also one of the commonalities between comics and other visual media, building on the presence effects of images. Referring to cinema, Michelle Bloom declares that "[t]he very medium embodies the longstanding human desire for the animation of the inanimate."[43] This echoes the observations made by Hans Belting on the nature of images and our desire to make them come to life, "even though we know very well that it is we who are lending them a life."[44] It is especially in the current media-saturated environment that "the ontological difference between the shadow [or image] and body" is frequently overlooked, adds Belting, thereby underscoring the psychosomatic power of the image, which enhances the affective qualities of the monster, the affects it incarnates and enacts, potentially vicariously, for the reader: the Crow's revenge, Hellboy's struggle with his destiny, the Swamp Thing's drive for existence and an expanded consciousness, and even Warhole's alternately cruel and redemptive games.[45] All of these motifs contribute to the spectacularity of the monster and his stories as well as his lasting presence, emphasized by the humanity and consequent reliability of his actions but also visually, through his very comic-ness, which implies both an intense presence but also constant action and mutability. Comics images such as the Swamp Thing and Abby's lovemaking scene or the opening page of the *Hellboy* story "The Island" (fig. 12) also remediate in many ways the fascination of the panorama through the comics page by immersing the reader in an interactive experience of the double-page spread, where events overflow and dissolve the familiar limits of the panel frame and engender a dialectic of movement and simultaneity.[46]

Westbrook links the rebelliousness of comics and their protagonists to the medium's entertainment value:

> Rowdiness defined both the Kid and the Yellow press, and a defiance of disciplined spectatorship constituted a crucial element of that rowdiness. [...] The image of rowdy spectatorship thus served many functions in the early comic strip: it helped newspaper publishers cultivate a working-class image, it helped comic strip artists portray themselves in similar terms (sometimes in opposition to their publisher bosses), and it played into a culture of participatory mass spectatorship that helped make a community out of a city of strangers. The large single panel format that dominated both versions of the Yellow Kid lent itself especially well to representing scenes of rowdy spectatorship, letting the reader's eye wander free from the tight focus of disciplined spectatorship and letting the characters' eyes wander within a spacious cartoon world.[47]

This rowdiness is one of the many expressive outcomes of what Bukatman calls *plasmatic*: the extreme transformational tendencies of comics and animations owing to which "comics (and cartoons) themselves are the trickster."[48] For Bukatman, the plasmatic and animistic energies of both comics and cartoons allow "fantasies of metamorphosis and expanded possibility" to unfold, unhindered by the sense of logic and reason.[49] This occurs in all of the monsters and the worlds encountered in this book, starting with *Monstre* and including *Swamp Thing*, *Hellboy*, and *The Crow*. Notably, this plasmatism and animism is not only embodied by the monsters, as in the case of Warhole and the Swamp Thing; it also extends to the worlds and book forms they inhabit, which is made up of intertwining stories (of the characters but also the storyworlds and texts, in the broadest sense of the word, that are tapped into).

In addition, what Bukatman calls "play as an animating force" is the same vital energy that was accorded a central role in cultural historian Johan Huizinga's concept of *homo ludens* (the playing man).[50] For Friedrich Schiller, the *Spieltrieb* (play-drive), which is in many ways personified by the trickster, was an important activity contributing toward aesthetic development and ideally resulting in spiritual emancipation.[51] Monsters, to a considerable extent, embody the concept of play by toying with the notions of norms and humanness, much like the medium of comics plays with the image of the body[52] and the givens of reality. Like Bukatman, comics scholar Saige Walton also underscores the centrality of the superhero's (and other comics protagonists') energy, which she likens to the "energy of the musical [...] at the same time as it is matched with the energy of the westerns."[53] In being focused on the energy of individual bodies, musicals and Westerns often serve to "resolve narrative conflict in the larger community."[54] While it is not possible to generalize that monstrous bodies resolve any kind of conflict, they do make conflicts and uneasiness visible. The "*queasiness* [...] about the modern world" noted by Bukatman[55] and Gardner[56] in early comics such as *Dream of the Rarebit Fiend* is comparable to the romantic distrust of rapid industrialization and the concept of progress, which in turn is magnified to horrific proportions in both *Swamp Thing* and *Hellboy*, where the world gives in to supernatural and individual psyches.[57] *The Crow* and *Monstre* with their trickster-like protagonists add another twist to this horror. This twist is in many ways typical for comics, because it combines humor and irony with horror. Another romantic feature that is strongly present in the comics monsters discussed here is that of the protagonists succumbing to their emotions; what was bestial in their lack of control and mutations for Alexander Pope was glorified by the romantics. According to Pope, people, by giving in to such passions, "'[t]ransform themselves' like 'Proteus,' they become monsters, a 'many-headed Beast,' because they have abandoned to the body their prerogative of mastery, and the body transmogrifies the self into its own incoherent energies."[58] In other words, the monsters' passions and emotionality are reflected in (or foreshadowed by) their abnormal bodies.

While the romantic imaginary is in itself monstrous due to its emotional and rebellious inclinations, it is distorted in the comics analyzed here and filtered through monstrous protagonists. "A dark mirror, monstrosity turns into a screen for transcendent fantasies and the site for the potential reversal of myth and sacred, infusing the lower 'night world' of romance with its questing ideal and ascendant trajectory" writes Fred Botting.[59] Part of this "night world" involves the combination of fear and fascination that makes monsters.[60] The monster incarnates the impossible, embodies it, and hence makes it possible and, to a certain extent, containable, even if its identity is based on negation or not-being, wherein lies its rebelliousness against the modern world. The comics monster also tests its range of possibilities. Recalling the philosopher Gaston Bachelard's understanding of the reverie as an escape from time, Bukatman suggests that "this escape can be understood as a form of resistance, liberation."[61] In *My Favorite Thing Is Monsters*, Karen (day)dreams constantly, while sleeping or through artworks and her role-playing as detective. The comics monsters in this book are also active dreamers. Both comics' and monsters' resistance to authority can therefore also be seen in their dismissal of reality, their refusal to abide by its rules.

The combination of fear and fascination, like the rebelliousness and hybridity of monsters, extends to the medium of comics itself. Fearful events and characters abound on comics pages, and yet this fear is superseded by a fascination and hankering for finding out what happens next as well as a reconfiguring of binaries, especially by encouraging identification with the monstrous protagonist. As a result, that which is fearsome is not necessarily evil, and vice versa. The English-language comics interact with the legacy of the notoriously violent horror and crime comics that prompted a backlash against comics and the establishment of the Comics Code of 1954: *Swamp Thing* pays homage to the rich legacy of horror comics; *Hellboy*, too, recuperates this legacy in a nostalgic mode;[62] and *The Crow* remediates it through a contemporary gothic mode. *Monstre* manifests a more traditionally science-fictional horror and like *Swamp Thing*, and to a lesser degree *Hellboy*, has political undertones.

Referring to the verses opening this chapter, Dennis Todd points out that "Pope implicitly defines man as a monster here," based on the liminality of the self.[63] The emphasis on doubt is significant in that it echoes the monster's effect. According to Henri Baudin, as already mentioned in the chapter on *Monstre*, we have developed a certain affinity for the monster, and the monster can even reflect certain human truths.[64] He not only channels emotions, as shown in the preceding chapters, but also reveals the more ambiguous, rebellious side of humankind. "Man is the greatest of the monsters because he is the creature most completely composed of contrariety."[65] Monsters, for Todd, also mirrored the perplexing, not fully comprehensible relationship between mind and body during the Enlightenment.[66] Hailing from the contemporary period, the anthropomorphic monsters analyzed here perpetuate those uncertainties from the Enlightenment, incorporating them in their very being and embodying the vast gray area where the human and the inhuman, the psychological and the corporeal, become indistinguishable. Such ambiguities are often highlighted through the merging of physical and psychological planes; by not being contained physically, the very limits of monstrosity are rendered ambiguous.[67] According to David Williams, the monster transcends dualities, violating logic but also generating ambiguity, since "there has always been in the world in the recesses of the mind the sense of a divided self, an ambiguous identity that in the world of reason is labeled monstrous or even pathological."[68] Hence monsters that are not openly monstrous, who have an internal monster for instance, are the most frightening, because of their ambivalence, particularly their ontological blurring of the difference between human and monster.[69] However, as Bachelard writes, "les images les plus belles sont souvent les foyers d'ambivalence" (the most beautiful images often harbor ambivalence).[70] Ambivalence also contributes to the fascination wielded by the monster.

As mentioned in chapter 2, the ambiguity of form and the reactions provoked—as, for instance, by Eugène Thivier's *Cauchemar* or Baudelaire's "Revolt" section in *Les Fleurs du mal*, which rebelled against the binary opposition of good and evil—are shared by all monsters and are part of their inherent rebelliousness. The monsters' ambivalence and ambiguity also have the tendency to infect the notion of the norm itself. According to Georges Canguilhem, the monster reinvented the notion of norms.[71] Referring to Foucault's *Les Anormaux*, Barroux describes the notion of the monster as a juridico-biological concept because it defines what breaks the laws (of society, nature, and so on). In other words, intellectuals used the monster "pour briser l'esprit du système" (for destroying the system's spirit).[72] Williams makes a similar observation: "It is often said that the monster functions to negate, to contradict, even vitiate, social structures, philosophical concepts and human vanities of all kinds."[73] He goes on to elaborate on the complexity of this negation, which questions the boundaries of being and highlights the arbitrariness of human intellectual structures in a manner that is comparable to the mockery of academic style and rationality in Töpffer's proto-comics.[74] The good comics monsters analyzed here incarnate these concerns of confounding and questioning categories and identities by virtue of being good monsters. Although they often have greater agency and are at times luckier than their romantic counterparts, they still incorporate romantic concerns. These concerns include:

- Ambiguity, which is rooted in the comics monsters' ambivalent relationship with humanity;
- Solitude, which stems from the monster's difference and outsider status;
- Spectacularity, or fascination with spectacles and immersive experiences;
- Fascination with alternative and subjective realities and changing perceptions, which is tied to the romantics' worship of the imagination as a supreme force. Many comics, especially comics with monstrous protagonists, are likewise eager worshippers of the imagination;
- Nostalgia for an idealized past, which is primordial for the Swamp Thing and dominated by folklore in *Hellboy*. The main characters in *Monstre* and *The Crow* also long for a past before the violence they suffered;
- Collapse of the human-animal-machine divide, which concretizes the questioning self's boundaries while also inciting empathy for other living organisms as well as manifesting the (once again romantic) fascination with new mechanical technologies, especially automatons. This is closely linked to the persistence of animation and reanimation in the comics, which function self-reflexively in a medium that thrives on generating movement and hence (animated and reanimated) life. This in turn harks back to the much older obsession of giving life through art (as concretized by the myth of Pygmalion and Galatea), which acquires additional relevance in romanticism owing to the degree of importance accorded to the creative power of the imagination; and
- Strong emotionality, which ties back to the ambivalent but quintessential humanity of monsters and involves mapping out the anthropomorphic monster's subjectivity through comics.

Coda

A conclusion for a book on monsters is something of a paradox, if not an impossibility, since "[l]a figure du monstre [...] interroge l'idée d'une finalité" (the figure of the monster [...] questions the idea of finality).[75] The aim of this book has been to interrogate the anthropomorphic comics monster by considering the extent to which it resurrects the vestiges of romanticism.

For Beate Ochsner, the very variety and recurrence of monsters in various contemporary media is an act of liberation, especially since they also encourage the apprehension of one's own monsters.[76] Comics reading, which itself brings in elements of guilt and shame, is also a site of apprehending or indulging in the monsters within and around the reader.[77] Comics monsters can thus be seen as interacting with the monstrosity of comics, which is linked in many ways to the degeneracy and marginalized status historically accorded to the medium.[78] As exemplified by *My Favorite Thing Is Monsters*, the rise of the graphic novel and the absorption of candid, confessional autobiographical and autofictional accounts by the mainstream have also created space for expressing anormality and deviancy that transcends the binaries of good and evil to remain essentially human.

Fredric Jameson considers postmodernism as a possible stage of romanticism.[79] This is tied to the possibility of tracing "the emergence (and creation) of fundamental categories of thinking (such as aesthetics, literature, or the subject)" to the romantic era from the mid-eighteenth century to the nineteenth century, which in itself was a period of turbulence and rebellion.[80] Having pointed out that the romantic ideal of the authenticity of individual expression plays a central role in rock music,[81] Christoph Reinfandt describes romanticism as the formation of a discourse, "deren Funktion darin liegt, das für die Kultur der Moderne zentrale Problem der kulturellen Relevanz subjektiver Erfahrung in einer sich zunehmend ausdifferenzierenden sozialen Wirklichkeit zu bearbeiten" (the function of which lies in processing the, for modern culture, central problem of the cultural relevance of subjective experience in an increasingly differentiating social reality).[82] Subjectivities and in particular strange, abnormal, but empathic subjectivities reign over the comics presented in this book, garnering sympathy for their monstrous protagonists and by extension all outcasts, while also protesting against norms and hierarchies.

For Alexander Regier, romanticism contains "the broken origins of our own interests. It provides a bridge that connects eighteenth-century sources with their twenty-first-century counterparts."[83] The relevance of romanticism for the current era, particularly the emotional experience of this era, can also be discerned in Joel Faflak and Richard C. Sha's observation that "in a world too much with and upon us, the romantic desire to distill essence from accumulation calls for us to respond with measured urgency to the shock and awe of a history in flux. Romanticism confronts historical experience as flux, a traumatic and traumatizing sense of history that locates affect beyond the pleasure principle."⁸⁴ Using the works of Coleridge, David Vallins makes the case for how feeling and thought, the rational and the irrational, blur into one another: such "contrasted feelings of alienation and transcendence" are also incorporated by the monster, who transcends boundaries and, in doing so, remains a perpetual other.⁸⁵ The monster serves, ironically, as a recipient of the residue of the human—both "good" and "bad"—that is not allowed to inhabit other forms.

For Aby Warburg, cultural history unfolded as a major *psychomachia* or conflict between *monstra* (monsters, chaos) and *astra* (stars, clarity), moving from the former to the latter as suggested by the subtitle of this conclusion.⁸⁶ What art historian Georges Didi-Huberman describes as "l'inquiétante dualité de tous les faits de la culture" (the unsettling duality of all the facts of culture) plays out between the monsters and the stars.⁸⁷ Building on Warburg's claim, Richard Kearney holds that "[m]onsters show us that if our aims are celestial, our origins are terrestrial."⁸⁸ The comics monsters discussed above, while harboring and inciting considerable chaos, also contain more than a little of the stars' light, not through their contrast with the concept of humanity but because of their proximity to it, particularly through their Promethean desire to struggle and survive in the face of all adversity. In *My Favorite Thing Is Monsters*, for instance, Karen as a were-girl facing and bearing witness to everyday hostilities ends up embracing her monstrous otherness and finding her own sources of wonder and respite.

The Promethean drive manifested by most of these monsters to go beyond what is destined for them is their first instance of rebellion because of the very humanity and consequent relatability of this drive. This rebellion is also manifested through their monstrous bodies, which are simultaneously dissected—and joined together—by the comics panels. Constantly struggling, often mutating, these monsters test the limits of the frames that try to bind them, especially within the categories of monstrosity and humanity themselves. They are, moreover, like most comics bodies, extremely resilient.

Monsters imbue the destructive with elements of entertainment and fascination. They are outcomes of the romantic notion of the imagination as a generative activity, which was appropriated from the realm of the female and brought into the realm of the male and thus legitimized during romanticism.⁸⁹ Comics monsters are the outcomes of popular culture's remediation of the legitimized romantic imagination. However, all of the monsters examined here are closely allied with, and contribute toward, comics' own process of legitimization through their unconventional narratives and evocative styles, their embedding in an intermedial and intertextual world that extends from popular culture to the "higher" arts.

The hybridity and rebelliousness of comics monsters is thus accentuated by the medium itself, while harking back to older traces of romanticism, with its distrust of modernity, its feverish struggle for individual liberation, and the sublimation (albeit limited) of binaries, especially regarding the difference between the human and the animal or even the machine as highlighted by Heinrich von Kleist's famous essay on the marionette. This rebelliousness and hybridity is manifest in the mutating, frame-bursting, category-defying, ambiguous monstrous bodies of the comics protagonists examined here. Their bodies likewise reject the laws of the universe and their prescribed destiny. Their stories and the book forms that contain them also question the limits of categories by incorporating images and stories from other (literary and popular) sources, but also direct fragments of poetry and lyrics. These comics stories consequently inscribe themselves in a rich intermedial web of popular and literary memories. They break the barriers between the arts through, for instance, intertextuality in *Hellboy* and *The Crow*, painterliness in *Monstre*, and poetic language in *Swamp Thing*. The most prominent literary and visual memory is that of Frankenstein's monster, closely followed by the more abstract ennui and the transmedial, atemporal trickster.

In the words of John Updike: "Cartoon characters have soul as Carl Jung defined it in his *Archetypes and the Collective Unconscious*: 'soul is life-giving demon who plays his elfin game above and below human existence.'"[90] The monsters discussed in this book incarnate Updike's observation through their perpetual, playful confounding of the good and the bad, appearances and essences; and further, the human, the bestial, and the divine. For Theodor Adorno, the "distinctly postmodern preoccupation with *alterity* and the *sublime*"[91] also permeates the very notion of culture: "What has become alien to men is the human component of culture, its closest part, which upholds them against the world."[92] The ambivalent, anthropomorphic comics monsters, with their rebellious propensities and unpredictable dynamism, can be seen as working (even if only to a limited extent) against such alienation by embracing the very embodiment of alienation in an increasingly isolating world. That they do so by maintaining the characteristics and inclinations of othered romantic protagonists attests to the continuity of romanticism in popular culture and its ability to resonate with readers more than a century later. That they thrive in comics attests to the medium's embracement of otherness, which even imbues the presence of seemingly normative stereotypes, the most blatant example being that of superheroes, who remain outsiders in the world they struggle for and who are also subjected to an endless stream of comic-strip parodies that exaggerate their weirdness. Exemplifying the intertwining of form and content, weirdness is also what colors the energy of comics and is closely tied to the medium's romantic inclinations, including the romantic understanding for othered beings, the romantic adoration of originality and idiosyncrasy, and the romantic penchant for performativity and excess. Although this book has focused on the medium's proclivities and the storyworlds unfolding in it, the influence of romanticism extends even further to mold our very perception of comics and comics creators.[93] This, it is hoped, will be taken up in future studies examining the many connections between the romantic consciousness and popular culture.

NOTES

INTRODUCTION. CHARTING MONSTROUS TERRITORY

1. Harold Bloom, "The Internalization of Quest-Romance," in *Romanticism and Consciousness: Essays in Criticism*, ed. Harold Bloom (New York: W. W. Norton, 1970), 12.

2. Vampires, for instance, are "no longer absolutely Other," as Julia Round points out, citing Fred Botting; Julia Round, "Mutilation and Monsters: Transcending the Human in Garth Ennis/Steve Dillon's *Preacher*," in *The Human Body in Contemporary Literatures in English*, ed. Sabine Coelsch-Foisner and Marta Fernández Morales (Frankfurt: Peter Lang, 2009), 117. Brandy Ball Blake and L. Andrew Cooper likewise declare in the introduction to their textbook that "[o]ver time, the humanoid monster has become the norm"; Brandy Ball Blake and L. Andrew Cooper, *Monsters* (Southlake, TX: Fountain Head Press, 2012), 5.

3. Pierre Boaistuau's *Histoires prodigieuses et mémorables* (with Claude de Tesserant's additions) was also one of Paré's sources, the others being Jean Wier's *Cinq livres de l'imposture et tromperie des diables* and Ludwig Lavater's *Trois livres des apparitions des esprits*. See Jean Céard's introduction to Ambroise Paré's *Des monstres et prodiges* (Geneva: Droz, 1971), xii.

4. This etymological connection of monsters, traceable to Jacques Derrida's "La main de Heidegger: Geschlecht II," in *Heidegger et la question: De l'esprit et autres essais* (Paris: Flammarion, 2010), 182, features in the opening pages of several publications on monsters, including Edward J. Ingebretsen, *At Stake: Monsters and the Rhetoric of Fear in Public Culture* (Chicago: University of Chicago Press, 2001); and Beate Ochsner, *DeMONSRAtion: Zur Repräsentation des Monsters und des Monströsen in Literatur, Fotografie und Film* (Heidelberg: Synchron, 2010). Jeffrey Jerome Cohen begins with the root of *monstrum* meaning "that which reveals" or "that which warns"; see "Monster Culture: Seven Theses," *Monster Theory: Reading Culture*, ed. Jeffrey Jerome Cohen (Minneapolis: University of Minnesota Press, 1996), 4.

5. Jean Burgos, "Le monstre, même et autre," in *Circé* 4, "Le monstre 1: Présence du monstre, mythe et réalité," ed. Jean Burgos (Paris: Éditions Lettres Modernes, 1975), 13.

6. Underscored, as elaborated below, by Cohen in "Monster Culture," 16–19. See also Ingebretsen's first chapter in *At Stake*, 19–41.

7. Stephen T. Asma, *On Monsters: An Unnatural History of Our Worst Fears* (New York: Oxford University Press, 2009), 13.

8. Two notable exceptions include a chapter by Christopher Murray on romantic ideology in Grant Morrison's comics and allusions to romantic influences, particularly the romantic sublime, in Charles Hatfield's monograph on Jack Kirby. See Christopher Murray, "Subverting the Sublime: Romantic Ideology in the Comics of Grant Morrison," in *Sub/versions: Cultural*

Status, Genre and Critique, ed. Pauline MacPherson, Christopher Murray, Gordon Spark, and Kevin Corstorphine (Newcastle upon Tyne: Cambridge Scholars Publishing, 2008), 34–51; and Charles Hatfield, *Hand of Fire: The Comics Art of Jack Kirby* (Jackson: University Press of Mississippi, 2012), 147, 149, 150. There are of course other instances of highlighting generic romantic traits in comics (e.g., Thierry Groensteen on Hugo Pratt in *La bande dessinée: Une art en expansion* and Thierry Smolderen on Rodolphe Töpffer in *Naissances de la bande dessinée*), but the legacy of romanticism has not been excavated in more detail.

9. Julia Round, *Gothic in Comics and Graphic Novels: A Critical Approach* (Jefferson, NC: McFarland, 2014); Scott Bukatman, *Hellboy's World: Comics and Monsters on the Margins* (Berkeley: University of California Press, 2016); Katherine Shaeffer and Spencer Chalifour, eds., "Forum: Monsters in the Margins," *ImageText* 8, no. 1 (2015); and Aidan Diamond and Lauranne Poharec's introduction to *Journal of Graphic Novels and Comics* 8, no. 5, "Freaked and Othered Bodies" (2017): 402–16.

10. Scholarly work on *The Crow* and *Monstre* is mostly limited to chapters such as Natascha Ueckmann, "Hybride Kreaturen im modernen französischen Comic: Enki Bilal," in *Der automatisierte Körper: Literarische Visionen des künstlichen Menschen vom Mittelalter bis zum 21. Jahrhundert*, ed. Cerstin Bauer-Funke and Gisela Febel (Berlin: Weidler, 2005), 291–320; and Lauren M. E. Goodlad, "Men in Black: Androgyny and Ethics in *The Crow* and *Fight Club*," in *Goth: Undead Culture*, ed. Michael Bibby and Lauren M. E. Goodlad (Durham, NC: Duke University Press, 2007), 89–118.

11. A representative but inevitably aleatory overview of recent publications could include Beate Ochsner's extensive analysis of the discursive rendition of teratology, *DeMONSTRAtion*; Pierre Ancet's study on the broader implications of human abnormalities, *Phénoménologie des corps monstrueux* (Paris: Presses Universitaires de France, 2006); Aurélie Martinez's monograph *Images du corps monstrueux* (Paris: Éditions L'Harmattan, 2011) on the mise-en-scène of monsters in artworks and the exploitation of their unavoidable role as spectacle makers; Johanna Drucker's chapter "Visual Un-Pleasure or Monsters in Flesh" in her book *Sweet Dreams: Contemporary Art and Complicity* (Chicago: University of Chicago Press, 2005); and Paul Ardenne's chapter on the contemporary era of monsters in *L'image corps: Figures de l'humaine dans l'art du XXe siècle* (Paris: Éditions du Regard, 2001), which focuses on monsters in art from the twentieth century onward. Also writing about the contemporary era, visual artist and scholar Alexa Wright explores the presence of the human monster in art and public discourse in *Monstrosity: The Human Monster in Visual Culture* (London: I. B. Tauris, 2013). Simone Guidi and Antonio Lucci edited an issue of *Lo Sguardo* on "Spazi del mostruoso: Luoghi filosofici della mostruosità / Spaces of the Monstrous: Philosophical Topics about Monstrosity," no. 9 (2012). Other essay collections on monsters and their historical and social significance include Anna Caiozzo and Anne-Emmanuelle Demartini, eds., *Monstre et imaginaire social: Approches historiques* (Paris: Créaphis, 2008); Didier Manuel, ed., *La figure du monstre: Phénoménologie de la monstruosité dans l'imaginaire contemporain* (Nancy, France: Presses Universitaires de Nancy, 2009); and Régis Bertrand and Anne Carol, eds., *Le "monstre" humain, imaginaire et société* (Aix-en-Provence, France: Presses Universitaires de Provence, 2005).

12. Barbara Creed's *The Monstrous-Feminine: Film, Feminism and Psychoanalysis* (London: Routledge, 1993) and Margrit Shildrick's *Embodying the Monster: Encounters with the Vulnerable Self* (London: Sage, 2002) have used feminist theories to interpret monstrosity. Similarly, in "The

Promises of Monsters: A Regenerative Politics for Inappropriate/d Others," Donna Haraway considers the lessons taught by racial and sexual acts of othering and even monstrocizing (in *Cultural Studies*, ed. Lawrence Grossberg, Cary Nelson, and Paula A. Treichler [London: Routledge, 1992], 295–337).

13. Asa Simon Mittman, "Introduction: The Impact of Monsters and Monster Studies," in *The Ashgate Research Companion to Monsters and the Monstrous*, ed. Asa Simon Mittman with Peter J. Dendle (Farnham, Surrey, England: Ashgate, 2013), 1.

14. Judith Halberstam, *Skin Shows: Gothic Horror and the Technology of Monsters* (Durham, NC: Duke University Press, 1995), 2.

15. Cohen, "Monster Culture," 3.

16. "We live in a time of monsters" is the first line of Cohen's preface, "In a Time of Monsters" (Cohen, "Monster Culture," vii). See also Ingebretsen, *At Stake*, 21.

17. Ingebretsen, *At Stake*, 210n14.

18. Annie Le Brun, "La révolution, la nuit," in *L'ange du bizarre: Le romantisme noir de Goya à Max Ernst*, ed. Côme Fabre and Felix Krämer (Paris: Musée d'Orsay; Ostfildern, Germany: Hatje Cantz, 2013), 20: "alors que la présence de Dieu s'efface [...] la figure humaine devient de plus en plus incertaine" (as God's presence is effaced [...] the human figure becomes increasingly uncertain).

19. Cohen, "Monster Culture," 4–20. My insertions are in square brackets.

20. Allen S. Weiss, "Ten Theses on Monsters and Monstrosity," *Drama Review* 48, no. 1 (2004): 124–25.

21. Bukatman, *Hellboy's World*, 9.

22. Cohen, "Monster Culture," 11.

23. Nerina Santorius, "Les fils du Satan: L'héritage de la déraison dans le romantisme français," in *L'Ange du bizarre: Le romantisme noir de Goya à Max Ernst*, ed. Côme Fabre and Felix Krämer (Paris: Musée d'Orsay; Ostfildern, Germany: Hatje Cantz, 2013), 102.

24. Cohen, "Monster Culture," xii.

25. Susan Stryker, "My Words to Victor Frankenstein above the Village of Chamounix: Performing Transgender Rage," in *The Transgender Studies Reader*, ed. Susan Stryker and Stephen Whittle (London: Routledge, 2006).

26. Nikki Sullivan, "Transmogrification: (Un)Becoming Other(s)," in *The Transgender Studies Reader*, ed. Susan Stryker and Stephen Whittle (London: Routledge, 2006), 562.

27. Sullivan, "Transmogrification," 561.

28. See also Catherine Spooner's studies on gothic continuities in contemporary culture: *Contemporary Gothic* (London: Reaktion, 2006); and *Post-Millennial Gothic: Comedy, Romance and the Rise of Happy Gothic* (London: Bloomsbury, 2017).

29. Spooner, *Contemporary Gothic*, 7.

30. Fred Botting, *Gothic Romanced: Consumption, Gender and Technologies in Contemporary Fictions* (Milton Park, Abingdon, England: Routledge, 2008), 8. That the publication of Mary Shelley's *Frankenstein* coincided with Caspar David Friedrich's iconic painting *Wanderer above the Sea of Fog* (1818) indicates the confluence of traditionally romantic and dark romantic strains.

31. Jean Burgos, for instance, begins his article by underscoring the monster's presence and permanence (Burgos, "Le monstre, même et autre," 11–12).

32. Ochsner, *DeMONSTRation*, 11.

33. John Tresch, *The Romantic Machine: Utopian Science and Technology after Napoleon* (Chicago: University of Chicago Press, 2014), 131.

34. Tresch, *The Romantic Machine*, 131.

35. See Jann Matlock, "Optique-Monde," *Romantisme* 2, no. 136 (2007): 39–53.

36. Cohen, "Monster Culture," 5.

37. Frederick Whiting, "Monstrosity on Trial: The Case of *Naked Lunch*," *Twentieth-Century Literature* 52 (2006): 146–47.

38. See Mary Favret, "The Study of Affect and Romanticism," *Literature Compass* 6, no. 6 (2009): 1159.

39. Silvan Tomkins, "Modifications in the Theory: 1978," in *Exploring Affect: The Selected Writings of Silvan S. Tomkins*, ed. E. Virginia Devos (Cambridge: Cambridge University Press, 1995), 86.

40. For the link between affect and romanticism, see Favret, "The Study of Affect and Romanticism," 1161. See also Joel Faflak and Richard C. Sha, "Introduction: Feeling Romantic," in *Romanticism and the Emotions*, ed. Joel Faflak and Richard C. Sha (Cambridge: Cambridge University Press, 2014), 3. For other romantic characteristics featured in this book, see Isaiah Berlin's *The Roots of Romanticism* (Princeton, NJ: Princeton University Press, 1999).

41. Round, *Gothic in Comics and Graphic Novels*, 156.

42. Emma McEvoy, "Gothic and the Romantics," in *The Routledge Companion to Gothic*, ed. Catherine Spooner and Emma McEvoy (London: Routledge, 2007), 19–28, 19.

43. Such an approach was adopted by a much older collection of essays, taking up three volumes of *Circé* (*Cahiers du Centre de Recherche sur l'Imaginaire*) brought out during 1975–1976: Jean Burgos, ed., *Circé* 4, "Le monstre 1: Présence du monstre, mythe et réalité"; Jean Burgos, ed., *Circé* 5, "Le monstre 2: Les monstres dans la Divine Comédie"; and Henri Baudin, ed., *Circé* 6, "Le monstre 3: Les monstres dans la science-fiction."

44. For more on the at times closely intertwined relationship between the gothic and romanticism, see McEvoy, "Gothic and the Romantics."

45. Gilbert Durand, *Les Structures anthropologiques de l'imaginaire: Introduction à l'archétypologie générale* (Paris: Dunod, 1992).

46. Cornelius Castoriadis, *Imaginary Institution of Society*, trans. Kathleen Blamey (Cambridge: Polity Press, 1987), 3.

47. Arjun Appadurai, *Modernity at Large: Cultural Dimensions of Globalization* (Minneapolis: University of Minnesota Press, 1996), 38.

48. Wolfgang Iser, *The Fictive and the Imaginary: Charting Literary Anthropology* (Baltimore: Johns Hopkins University Press, 1993).

49. Consider, for instance, Áron Kibédi Varga's table mapping different word-image relations, "Criteria for Describing Word-and-Image Relations," *Poetics Today* 10, no. 1 (1989): 34; as well as W. J. T. Mitchell's use of image/text, imagetext, and image-text in his *Picture Theory* for highlighting the symbioses and the tensions involved in different kinds of word-image relationships, *Picture Theory: Essays on Verbal and Visual Representation* (Chicago: University of Chicago Press, 1994), 89.

50. Jan Baetens, "L'animal et l'humain dans le 'roman graphique' contemporain," in *Corps et technologies: Penser l'hybridité*, ed. Nathalie Grandjean and Claire Lobet-Maris (Brussels: Peter Lang, 2013), 179.

51. Jay David Bolter and Richard Grusin, *Remediation: Understanding New Media* (Cambridge, MA: MIT Press, 2000), 45.

52. Karin Kukkonen, "Comics as a Test Case for Transmedial Narratology," *SubStance* 40, no. 1 (2011): 41.

53. The third and last part of Bolter and Grusin's *Remediation* is on the "Self" (230–65). See also Hans Belting, *An Anthropology of Images: Picture, Medium, Body*, trans. Thomas Dunlap (Princeton, NJ: Princeton University Press, 2011).

54. See Philippe Despoix and Yvonne Spielmann, "Présentation," *Intermédialités* 6, "Remédier/Remediation" (2006): 9.

55. Richard A. Grusin, "Premediation," *Criticism* 46, no. 1 (2004): 21n1.

56. Grusin, "Premediation," 18.

57. Bolter and Grusin, *Remediation*, 21.

58. Tom Lubbock, "De Ribera, Jusepe: The Boy with the Club Foot (1642)," *Independent*, March 14, 2008.

59. Jeffrey Jerome Cohen, ed, *Monster Theory: Reading Culture* (Minneapolis: University of Minnesota Press, 1996), viii.

60. Hans Ulrich Gumbrecht, *Production of Presence: What Meaning Cannot Convey* (Stanford, CA: Stanford University Press, 2003).

61. Anne Hollander, *Moving Pictures* (New York: Alfred A. Knopf, 1989), 6.

62. Gumbrecht, *Production of Presence*, 58.

63. Gumbrecht, *Production of Presence*, 45–46.

64. Gumbrecht, *Production of Presence*, 109.

65. Gumbrecht, *Production of Presence*, 110.

66. Gumbrecht, *Production of Presence*, 111.

67. Thierry Groensteen, *Un objet culturel non identifié: La bande dessinée* (Angoulême, France: Éditions de l'An 2, 2006), 30.

68. Belting, *An Anthropology of Images*, 15.

69. Belting, *An Anthropology of Images*, 15.

70. Belting, *An Anthropology of Images*, 21.

71. As already suggested, this word, which combines the spectacle, the spectacular, and the specular while alluding to the wild entertainment promised by many mainstream comics, seems better suited than "theatricality" for a discussion of monsters remediating romanticism in comics.

72. Christoph Reinfandt, *Romantische Kommunikation: Zur Kontinuität der Romantik in der Kultur der Moderne* (Heidelberg: Winter Verlag, 2003).

73. Jerome J. McGann, *The Romantic Ideology: A Critical Investigation* (Chicago: University of Chicago Press, 1983).

74. Cohen, *Monster Theory*, ix–x.

75. See Mario Praz, *La chair, la mort et le diable: Le romantisme noir* (Paris: Gallimard, 2013).

76. As emphasized by Isaiah Berlin. Also consider the example of Edmund Burke, whose theory of the sublime is central to romantic consciousness but who was, politically at least, a conservative (Bloom, *Romanticism and Consciousness*, 3). As Bloom points out in the brief texts introducing each section of *Romanticism and Consciousness*, contradictions are likewise discernible in scholarship on romanticism.

77. Northrop Frye, *A Study of English Romanticism* (New York: Random House, 1968), 4.

78. Frye, *A Study of English Romanticism*, 48. For more on comics and anarchy, see Frederik Byrn Køhlert and Ole Birk Laursen, eds., "Rebel Lines: Comics and the Anarchist Imagination," special issue, *SubStance* 46, no. 3 (2017).

79. See Praz, *La chair, la mort et le diable*.

80. Isaiah Berlin, "In Search of a Definition," in *The Roots of Romanticism*, 1–25.

81. Berlin, "Unbridled Romanticism," in *The Roots of Romanticism*, 107–36.

82. Berlin, "Unbridled Romanticism," in *The Roots of Romanticism*, 125.

83. Berlin, "Unbridled Romanticism," in *The Roots of Romanticism*, 120.

84. Berlin, "Unbridled Romanticism," in *The Roots of Romanticism*, 120–21.

85. Berlin, "Unbridled Romanticism," in *The Roots of Romanticism*, 16. See also Joel Faflak and Richard C. Sha, eds., *Romanticism and the Emotions* (Cambridge: Cambridge University Press, 2014).

86. Cited in Richard C. Sha, "Imagination," in *A Handbook of Romanticism Studies*, ed. Joel Faflak and Julia M. Wright (Malden, MA: Wiley-Blackwell, 2012), 20. See also Julie Ellison's contribution in the same volume, which highlights the centrality of sensibility for romanticism as well as the movement's lasting impact on the concept: "Sensibility," 37–53.

87. Frye, *A Study of English Romanticism*, 62.

88. Frye, *A Study of English Romanticism*, 125–65, 87–124.

89. Notably, two recently published monographs discuss the connections between Goya's prints and comics: Hillary L. Chute, *Disaster Drawn: Visual Witness, Comics, and Documentary Form* (Cambridge, MA: Belknap Press, 2016); and Bukatman, *Hellboy's World*, 200–208. For the influence of Blake in comics, see Roger Whitson and Donald Ault, eds., "William Blake and Visual Culture," special issue, *ImageText* 3, no. 2 (2006).

CHAPTER 1. ROMANTIC MONSTERS: A BRIEF HISTORY

1. Charles Baudelaire, "Les Phares," in *Les Fleurs du mal* (Paris: Flammarion, 2010), 4.

2. Dennis Todd, *Imagining Monsters: Miscreations of the Self in Eighteenth-Century England* (Chicago: University of Chicago Press, 1995), 5.

3. William Shakespeare, *The Tempest*, in *The Arden Shakespeare Complete Works*, ed. Ann Thompson, David Scott Kastan, and Richard Proudfoot (London: Bloomsbury, 2002), 1083.

4. Asma, *On Monsters*, 134.

5. Ochsner, *DeMONSTRAtion*, 16.

6. Asma, *On Monsters*, 140.

7. Cited in Todd, *Imagining Monsters*, 262.

8. Michel Foucault, *The Order of Things: An Archaeology of Human Sciences* (New York: Vintage, 1994), 156.

9. Todd, *Imagining Monsters*, 97. This quotation is taken from Todd's discussion of Enthusiasm's almost exclusive reliance on imagination and its mockery by William Hogarth, Jonathan Swift, and Alexander Pope, among others.

10. Todd, *Imagining Monsters*, 98.

11. See Durand's *Les Structures anthropologiques de l'imaginaire*.

12. Arnold I. Davidson, introduction to *Abnormal: Lectures at the Collège de France, 1974–1975*, by Michel Foucault (London: Verso, 2003), xvii.

13. Mario Praz, *Romantic Agony*, trans. Angus Davidson (Oxford: Oxford University Press, 1951), 27.

14. James Peller Malcolm, *An Historical Sketch of the Art of Caricaturing* (London: Longman, Hurst, Rees, Orme and Brown, 1813), 3.

15. Malcolm, *An Historical Sketch*, 6–7.

16. Malcolm, *An Historical Sketch*, 11.

17. Hollander, *Moving Pictures*, 255.

18. Hollander, *Moving Pictures*, 254.

19. Bukatman, *Hellboy's World*, 208.

20. Chute, *Disaster Drawn*, 40.

21. Chute, *Disaster Drawn*, 53.

22. Hollander, *Moving Pictures*, 6.

23. See Scott Bukatman, "Sculpture, Stasis, the Comics, and Hellboy," *Critical Inquiry* 40, no. 3 (2014): 104–7.

24. David Kunzle, *History of the Comic Strip*, vol. 2, *The Nineteenth Century* (Berkeley: University of California Press, 1973), 359.

25. Hollander, *Moving Pictures*, 245.

26. Malcolm, *An Historical Sketch*, 12.

27. Malcolm, *An Historical Sketch*, 12.

28. Kunzle, *History of the Comic Strip*, vol. 2, 357.

29. Malcolm, *An Historical Sketch*, 34.

30. Malcolm, *An Historical Sketch*, 55.

31. Hollander, *Moving Pictures*, 247.

32. Gilles Barroux, "Quels éléments d'anthropologie et de pensée médicale s'expriment dans la figure du 'monstre' au XVIIIe siècle?" *Lo Sguardo*, no. 9 (2012): 119.

33. Barroux, "Quels éléments d'anthropologie," 122.

34. Victor Hugo, *Notre-Dame de Paris*, trans. John Sturrock (Harmondsworth, England: Penguin, 1978), 71.

35. Todd, *Imagining Monsters*, 48. The Mary Toft incident, in which a woman allegedly gave birth to rabbits, provoked teratological debates and insights that proved to be foundational in their insistence that monstrous deformities were not a product of the imagination but an inevitable part of natural processes (Todd, *Imagining Monsters*, 112).

36. See, for instance, David Williams, "Monsters, Then and Now," *Lo Sguardo*, no. 9 (2012): 239–58.

37. Todd, *Imagining Monsters*, 52–53.

38. Ancet, *Phénoménologie des corps monstrueux*, 394.

39. Williams, "Monsters, Then and Now," 246.

40. Todd, *Imagining Monsters*, 95.

41. Edmund Burke, *A Philosophical Enquiry into the Origin of Our Ideas of the Sublime and Beautiful*, ed. James T. Boulton (London: Routledge and Kegan Paul; New York: Columbia University Press, 1958), part 1, sec. 7, "On the Sublime," 39.

42. Burke, *A Philosophical Enquiry*, part 1, sec. 11, 43.

43. Hollander, *Moving Pictures*, 4.

44. Goya's *Los Desastres de la guerra* series was also titled *Fatales consequencias de la sangrienta guerra en España con Buonaparte, y otros caprichos enfáticos* (Fatal consequences of Spain's bloody war with Bonaparte, and other emphatic caprices).

45. Hollander, *Moving Pictures*, 49.

46. Mike Mignola, with Jason Shawn Alexander, Richard Corben, Joshua Dysart, and Duncan Fegredo, *Hellboy*, vol. 10: *The Crooked Man and Others* (Milwaukie, OR: Dark Horse, 2010), n.p.

47. Burke, *A Philosophical Enquiry*, part 2, sec. 4, 60.

48. See Baudelaire's *Journaux intimes*, cited in Praz, *La chair, la mort et le diable*, 47. Isaiah Berlin also positions romanticism as a reaction to the ideals of the Enlightenment (*The Roots of Romanticism*). See also Morse Peckham, "Toward a Theory of Romanticism: II. Reconsiderations," *Studies in Romanticism* 1, no. 1 (1961): 1.

49. See Chute, *Disaster Drawn*, 40–41.

50. Felix Krämer, "Le romanticisme noir: Une approche," in *L'ange du bizarre: Le romantisme noir de Goya à Max Ernst*, ed. Côme Fabre and Felix Krämer (Paris: Musée d'Orsay; Ostfildern, Germany: Hatje Cantz, 2013), 35.

51. Hollander, *Moving Pictures*, 253.

52. Hollander, *Moving Pictures*, 255.

53. Hollander, *Moving Pictures*, 260.

54. Juan Bordes, "Goya, chroniquer de toutes les guerres: *Les Désastres* et la photographie de guerre," in *Goya cronista de todas las guerras:* Los Desastres *y la fotografía de guerra*, ed. Juan Bordes and Enrique Bordes (Madrid: Instituto Cervantes, 2012), 81.

55. Durand, *Les Structures anthropologiques de l'imaginaire*, 96. My insertions are in square brackets.

56. Ian Haywood and John Halliwell, "Romantic Spectacle: An Introduction," *Romanticism on the Net*, no. 46, "Romantic Spectacle" (2007).

57. Hollander, *Moving Pictures*, 255.

58. Bukatman, "Sculpture, Stasis, the Comics, and Hellboy," 104–17.

59. Northrop Frye, "The Keys to the Gates," in *Romanticism and Consciousness: Essays in Criticism*, ed. Harold Bloom (New York: W. W. Norton, 1970), 36.

60. Martin Price, "The Standard of Energy," in *Romanticism and Consciousness: Essays in Criticism*, ed. Harold Bloom (New York: W. W. Norton, 1970), 272. See Todd, *Imagining Monsters*, for the difficulties faced in comprehending the mind-body interaction during the Enlightenment.

61. Frye, "The Keys to the Gates," 254.

62. Price, "The Standard of Energy," 257.

63. Frye, "The Keys to the Gates," 244.

64. William Blake, *America a Prophecy* (copy O, 1821, Fitzwilliam Museum), at *The William Blake Archive*, available at http://www.blakearchive.org/exist/blake/archive/transcription.xq?objectid=america.o.illbk.04, retrieved May 6, 2016.

65. Bloom, *Romanticism and Consciousness*, back flap.

66. Frye, *A Study of English Romanticism*, 13.

67. Price, "The Standard of Energy," 269.

68. Price, "The Standard of Energy," 269.

69. Price, "The Standard of Energy," 272.

70. Frye, "The Keys to the Gates," 237.

71. Illustrations to the Book of Job, object 15 (Butlin 550.15), "Behemoth and Leviathan," at *The William Blake Archive*, available at http://www.blakearchive.org/exist/blake/archive/object .xq?objectid=but550.1.wc.15, retrieved July 27, 2016.

72. Mitchell, *Picture Theory*, 91.

73. Charles Baudelaire, *Écrits sur l'art* (Paris: Le Livre de Poche, 1992), 142–43.

74. Baudin, *Circé* 6, "Les monstres dans la science-fiction," 8.

75. Baudin, *Circé* 6, "Les monstres dans la science-fiction," 9.

76. Alan Moore, with Alfredo Alcala, John Totleben, and Rick Veitch, *The Saga of the Swamp Thing*, book 5 (New York: Vertigo, 2013), 29.

77. Chute, *Disaster Drawn*, 27.

78. Victor Hugo, *Notre-Dame de Paris* (Paris: Le Livre de Poche, 2012), 143, 244.

79. Hugo, *Notre-Dame de Paris* (Le Livre de Poche), 525.

80. Hugo, *Notre-Dame de Paris* (Le Livre de Poche), 677–78.

81. Moore et al., *The Saga of the Swamp Thing*, book 5, 164.

82. Moore et al., *The Saga of the Swamp Thing*, book 5, 164.

83. Hugo, *Notre-Dame de Paris* (Le Livre de Poche), 19.

84. Hugo, *Notre-Dame de Paris* (Le Livre de Poche), 19.

85. Hugo, *Notre-Dame de Paris* (Le Livre de Poche), 19.

86. Quoted in Gorka López de Munain Iturrospe, "Los Caprichos de Goya: Estampas y textos contra el sueño de la razón," *Revista Sans Soleil: Estudios de la Imagen* 2 (2011): 79.

87. Asma, *On Monsters*, 12.

88. Brigitte Munier, "La monstruosité du Golem, figure tutélaire de la modernité occidentale," *Lo Sguardo*, no. 9 (2012): 230.

89. Asma, *On Monsters*, 69.

90. See Thierry Groensteen, "The Art of Braiding: A Clarification," *European Comic Art* 9, no. 1 (2016): 88–98.

91. This concept of patchworking has been mentioned by Pierre Fresnault-Deruelle in his essay "Entre l'ersatz et le simulacre: La bande dessinée," *Cahiers du 20e siècle*, no. 6 (1976): 139–53. See also my article on the collage in Dave McKean's work: "Collages in Comics: The Case of Dave McKean," in *The Cultural Standing of Comics / Le statut culturel de la BD*, ed. Maaheen Ahmed, Stéphanie Delneste, and Jean-Louis Tilleuil (Louvain-la-Neuve, Belgium: Academia/ Éditions L'Harmattan, 2017), 53–74.

92. Mary Shelley, *Frankenstein; or, The Modern Prometheus* (Boston: Sever, Francis and Company, 1869), 101–3.

93. Shelley, *Frankenstein*, 175.

94. Shelley, *Frankenstein*, 11–12.

95. Munier, "La monstruosité du Golem," 222.

96. Munier, "La monstruosité du Golem," 221.

97. See, for instance, Shelley, *Frankenstein*, p. 176.

98. Williams, "Monsters, Then and Now," 245.

99. Munier, "La monstruosité du Golem," 231.

100. Munier, "La monstruosité du Golem," 232.

101. Shelley, *Frankenstein*, 107.

102. Shelley, *Frankenstein*, 45–46.

103. Frye, *A Study of English Romanticism*, 44–45.

104. Ancet, *Phénoménologie des corps monstrueux*, 425.

105. Shelley, *Frankenstein*, 11.

106. Shelley, *Frankenstein*, 40.

107. See Ochsner, *DeMONSTRAtion*, 119.

108. Ochsner, *DeMONSTRAtion*, 121.

109. Victor Hugo, *L'Homme qui rit* (Paris: Pocket, 2012), 358–60.

110. Hugo, *L'Homme qui rit*, 447–48.

111. Baudelaire, *Écrits sur l'art*, 144.

112. Hugo, *L'Homme qui rit*, 79.

113. Hugo, *L'Homme qui rit*, 365.

114. Abigail Lee Six and Hannah Thompson, "From Hideous to Hedonist: The Changing Face of the Nineteenth-Century Monster," in *The Ashgate Research Companion to Monsters and the Monstrous*, ed. Asa Simon Mittman with Peter J. Dendle (Farnham, Surrey, England: Ashgate, 2013), 236–55.

115. Asma, *On Monsters*, 251–52.

116. Hugo, *L'Homme qui rit*, 42.

117. Harold Bloom, "Nature and Consciousness," in *Romanticism and Consciousness: Essays in Criticism*, ed. Harold Bloom (New York: W. W. Norton, 1970), 2. Bloom here refers to Owen Barfield's *Saving the Appearances: A Study in Idolatry* (Middletown, CT: Wesleyan University Press, 1957).

118. Bloom, "Nature and Consciousness," 2.

119. Tom Gunning, "Fantasmagorie et fabrication de l'illusion: Pour une culture optique du dispositif cinématographique," *Cinémas: Revue d'Études Cinématographiques* 14, no. 1 (2003): 72.

120. Todd, *Imagining Monsters*, 157.

121. Todd, *Imagining Monsters*, 164–72.

122. Thierry Smolderen, *Naissances de la bande dessinée: De William Hogarth à Winsor McCay* (Brussels: Les Impressions Nouvelles, 2009), 10.

123. Smolderen, *Naissances de la bande dessinée*, 11.

124. Umberto Eco, "Le mythe de Superman," *Communications* 24, no. 1 (1976): 39.

125. Sarah Sepulchre, "Super-corps, super-technologie, super-monstre: Hulk ou l'inquiétante mise en garde," in *Corps et technologies: Penser l'hybridité*, ed. Nathalie Grandjean and Claire Lobet-Maris (Brussels: Peter Lang, 2013), 163.

126. Haywood and Halliwell, "Romantic Spectacle: An Introduction."

127. See Botting, *Gothic Romanced*.

128. Bloom, "The Internalization of Quest-Romance," 5.

129. Bloom, "The Internalization of Quest-Romance," 9.

130. Bloom, "The Internalization of Quest-Romance," 9.

131. Peckham, "Toward a Theory of Romanticism: II," 1.

132. Bloom, "The Internalization of Quest-Romance," 9.

133. Bloom, "The Internalization of Quest-Romance," 9.

134. James D. Wilson, "Tirso, Molière and Byron: The Emergence of Don Juan as Romantic Hero," *South Central Bulletin* 32, no. 4 (1972): 246.

135. Hollander, *Moving Pictures*, 7.

136. Hollander, *Moving Pictures*, 7.
137. Hollander, *Moving Pictures*, 7.
138. Grant Morrison, *Supergods: Our World in the Age of the Superhero* (London: Vintage, 2012), 125; and Hatfield, *Hand of Fire*, 146.
139. Smolderen, *Naissances de la bande dessinée*, 10, 30.
140. Smolderen, *Naissances de la bande dessinée*, 5.
141. Smolderen, *Naissances de la bande dessinée*, 6.
142. Smolderen, *Naissances de la bande dessinée*, 6.
143. Smolderen, *Naissances de la bande dessinée*, 6.
144. Smolderen, *Naissances de la bande dessinée*, 6.
145. Scott Bukatman, *The Poetics of Slumberland: Animated Spirits and the Animating Spirit* (Berkeley: University of California Press, 2012), 2.
146. Smolderen, *Naissances de la bande dessinée*, 6.
147. Philippe Willems, "Rodolphe Töpffer and Romanticism," *Nineteenth-Century French Studies* 37, nos. 3–4 (2009): 228.
148. Foucault, *The Order of Things*, 155.
149. Smolderen, *Naissances de la bande dessinée*, 37.
150. Haywood and Halliwell, "Romantic Spectacle: An Introduction." For a detailed, media archeological study on the panorama, see Erkki Huhtamo, *Illusions in Motion: Media Archaeology of the Moving Panorama and Related Spectacles* (Cambridge, MA: MIT Press, 2013).
151. Haywood and Halliwell, "Romantic Spectacle: An Introduction."
152. Todd, *Imagining Monsters*, 148.
153. Todd, *Imagining Monsters*, 149–50.
154. Tresch, *The Romantic Machine*, 136.
155. Haywood and Halliwell, "Romantic Spectacle: An Introduction."
156. Bukatman, *The Poetics of Slumberland*, 29.
157. Tresch, *The Romantic Machine*, 126.

CHAPTER 2. *SWAMP THING*: PATCHWORKS AND PANORAMAS IN MONSTER COMICS

1. Baudelaire, "Correspondances," in *Les Fleurs du mal*, 19.
2. From "Muck Monster," in Bernie Wrightson, *Creepy Presents Bernie Wrightson: The Definitive Collection of the Artist's Work from Creepy and Eerie!* (Milwaukie, OR: Dark Horse, 2011), 100.
3. Wrightson, *Creepy Presents Bernie Wrightson*, 103.
4. Round, *Gothic in Comics and Graphic Novels*, 43; and Qiana J. Whitted, "Of Slaves and Other Swamp Things: Black Southern History as Comic Book Horror," in *Comics and the U.S. South*, ed. Brannon Costello and Qiana J. Whitted (Jackson: University Press of Mississippi, 2012), 187.
5. Whitted, "Of Slaves and Other Swamp Things," 188.
6. Whitted, "Of Slaves and Other Swamp Things," 188.
7. Whitted, "Of Slaves and Other Swamp Things," 188.
8. Alan Moore, with Stephen Bissette and John Totleben, *The Saga of the Swamp Thing*, book 2 (New York: Vertigo, 2012), 86. The CCA's seal of approval does, however, reappear on the thirty-fifth issue from April 1985, Alan Moore, with Stephen Bissette and John Totleben, *The Saga of the Swamp Thing*, book 3 (New York: Vertigo, 2013), 11; and the fiftieth anniversary

issue from July 1986, Alan Moore, with Stephen Bissette, John Totleben, and Stan Woch, *The Saga of the Swamp Thing*, book 4 (New York: Vertigo, 2013), 181.

9. Jean-Paul Gabilliet, *Of Comics and Men: A Cultural History of American Comic Books* (Jackson: University Press of Mississippi, 2010), 90.

10. Gabilliet, *Of Comics and Men*, 91–92.

11. See Gary Groth, "The Alan Moore Interview," *Comics Journal*, no. 118 (2012).

12. Gabilliet, *Of Comics and Men*, 168.

13. Unless specified otherwise, *Swamp Thing* refers to Moore's *The Saga of the Swamp Thing* as collected in the Vertigo volumes.

14. John Block Friedman, foreword to *The Ashgate Research Companion to Monsters and the Monstrous*, ed. Asa Simon Mittman with Peter J. Dendle (Farnham, Surrey, England: Ashgate, 2013), xxvi. One of the many swamp things discovered by Moore's *Swamp Thing* was a German World War II pilot, just like the Heap. A similar swamp monster, Man-Thing, was created and then resurrected for Marvel: based on an idea by Stan Lee and Roy Thomas and drawn by Gray Morrow, the first *Man-Thing* story appeared in *Savage Tales*, no. 1 (1971). The character was taken up and dropped over the years with runs by writers such as Steve Gerber and Chris Claremont.

15. Gabilliet, *Of Comics and Men*, 90; and Whitted, "Of Slaves and Other Swamp Things," 188.

16. Alan Moore, with Stephen Bissette and John Totleben, *The Saga of the Swamp Thing*, book 1 (New York: Vertigo, 2012), 48.

17. The passions and solitude of the Swamp Thing have also been mentioned by Alvise Mattozzi in his study of innovations taking place in superhero characters; "Innovating Superheroes," *Reconstruction* 3, no. 2 (2003).

18. For Northrop Frye, for instance, "expanded consciousness" was a "central theme of Romanticism," even though he made a distinction between "the genuine or creative consciousness and the introverted or subjective one" (Frye, *A Study of English Romanticism*, 42).

19. Colin Beineke, "'Her Guardiner': Alan Moore's Swamp Thing as the Green Man," *ImageText* 5, no. 4 (2010).

20. Moore et al., *The Saga of the Swamp Thing*, book 1, 21.

21. Moore et al., *The Saga of the Swamp Thing*, book 1, 21.

22. Moore et al., *The Saga of the Swamp Thing*, book 1, 22.

23. Moore et al., *The Saga of the Swamp Thing*, book 2, 63.

24. Moore, Alan, with Alfredo Alcala, John Totleben, and Rick Veitch, *The Saga of the Swamp Thing*, book 6 (New York: Vertigo, 2011), 80.

25. Moore et al., *The Saga of the Swamp Thing*, book 6, 80.

26. Moore et al., *The Saga of the Swamp Thing*, book 6, 79.

27. McEvoy, "Gothic and the Romantics," 23.

28. Moore et al., *The Saga of the Swamp Thing*, book 6, 176.

29. Moore et al., *The Saga of the Swamp Thing*, book 5, 29.

30. Moore et al., *The Saga of the Swamp Thing*, book 1, 137–57.

31. Moore et al., *The Saga of the Swamp Thing*, book 1, 11.

32. McEvoy, "Gothic and the Romantics," 23.

33. Moore et al., *The Saga of the Swamp Thing*, book 1, 15.

34. Moore et al., *The Saga of the Swamp Thing*, book 3, 121.

35. Moore et al., *The Saga of the Swamp Thing*, book 1, 77.

36. Moore et al., *The Saga of the Swamp Thing*, book 1, 4–5.
37. Moore et al., *The Saga of the Swamp Thing*, book 1, 137–57.
38. Moore et al., *The Saga of the Swamp Thing*, book 1, 20.
39. Moore et al., *The Saga of the Swamp Thing*, book 1, 87.
40. Moore et al., *The Saga of the Swamp Thing*, book 1, 89.
41. Moore et al., *The Saga of the Swamp Thing*, book 1, 93.
42. Moore et al., *The Saga of the Swamp Thing*, book 1, 93.
43. Moore et al., *The Saga of the Swamp Thing*, book 1, 10.
44. Moore et al., *The Saga of the Swamp Thing*, book 1, 45.
45. Moore et al., *The Saga of the Swamp Thing*, book 4, 32.
46. Moore et al., *The Saga of the Swamp Thing*, book 1, 109, 45.
47. Moore et al., *The Saga of the Swamp Thing*, book 1, 126–31.
48. Moore et al., *The Saga of the Swamp Thing*, book 1, 123.
49. Moore et al., *The Saga of the Swamp Thing*, book 3, 12–58.
50. Baudin, *Circé* 6, "Les monstres dans la science-fiction," 41–43.
51. Aude Campmas, "La monstruosité cachée: Huysmans et les hybrides artificiels," *Fabula: La Recherche en Littérature*, Séminaire "Signe, déchiffrement, et interprétation," January 11, 2008.
52. Campmas, "La monstruosité cachée."
53. Moore et al., *The Saga of the Swamp Thing*, book 1, 160–81.
54. Moore et al., *The Saga of the Swamp Thing*, book 1, 201.
55. Moore et al., *The Saga of the Swamp Thing*, book 2, 16.
56. Moore et al., *The Saga of the Swamp Thing*, book 2, 19.
57. Moore et al., *The Saga of the Swamp Thing*, book 1, 48–49.
58. Moore et al., *The Saga of the Swamp Thing*, book 1, 113.
59. Moore et al., *The Saga of the Swamp Thing*, book 5, 38.
60. Moore et al., *The Saga of the Swamp Thing*, book 4, 44.
61. Moore et al., *The Saga of the Swamp Thing*, book 4, 94.
62. Moore et al., *The Saga of the Swamp Thing*, book 3, 12.
63. Moore et al., *The Saga of the Swamp Thing*, book 2, 98.
64. Moore et al., *The Saga of the Swamp Thing*, book 2, 99.
65. Moore et al., *The Saga of the Swamp Thing*, book 2, 131; and Moore et al., *The Saga of the Swamp Thing*, book 3, 74.
66. Moore et al., *The Saga of the Swamp Thing*, book 4, 115.
67. Moore et al., *The Saga of the Swamp Thing*, book 4, 118.
68. Moore et al., *The Saga of the Swamp Thing*, book 4, 121.
69. Moore et al., *The Saga of the Swamp Thing*, book 4, 121. Although the tree claims that the pilot was shot down in 1942, the plane is a German triplane—most likely a Fokker—used during the First World War. This is confirmed by a later *Swamp Thing* issue, "Brothers in Arms" (no. 83, February 1989).
70. Paul Mathias, "Un monstre délicat," in *Circé* 4, "Le monstre 1: Présence du monstre, mythe et réalité," ed. Jean Burgos (Paris: Éditions Lettres Modernes, 1975), 76. See also chapter 3 of this volume.
71. Moore et al., *The Saga of the Swamp Thing*, book 2, 111.
72. Moore et al., *The Saga of the Swamp Thing*, book 5, 27.

73. Moore et al., *The Saga of the Swamp Thing*, book 5, 38.
74. Moore et al., *The Saga of the Swamp Thing*, book 5, 54.
75. Moore et al., *The Saga of the Swamp Thing*, book 5, 147, 161.
76. Moore et al., *The Saga of the Swamp Thing*, book 5, 148.
77. Steven Brower, "Jack Kirby's Collages in Context," *Print*, April 17, 2012.
78. Bukatman, *The Poetics of Slumberland*, 23.
79. Moore et al., *The Saga of the Swamp Thing*, book 6, 148.
80. Moore et al., *The Saga of the Swamp Thing*, book 4, 85.
81. Moore et al., *The Saga of the Swamp Thing*, book 4, 91.
82. Moore et al., *The Saga of the Swamp Thing*, book 4, 59.
83. Moore et al., *The Saga of the Swamp Thing*, book 2, 176–77.
84. Moore et al., *The Saga of the Swamp Thing*, book 4, 184.
85. Moore et al., *The Saga of the Swamp Thing*, book 2, 181.
86. Moore et al., *The Saga of the Swamp Thing*, book 2, 190.
87. Moore et al., *The Saga of the Swamp Thing*, book 3, 165–97.
88. Moore et al., *The Saga of the Swamp Thing*, book 4, 201.
89. Moore et al., *The Saga of the Swamp Thing*, book 4, 197.
90. Moore et al., *The Saga of the Swamp Thing*, book 4, 198.
91. Moore et al., *The Saga of the Swamp Thing*, book 4, 198.
92. Moore et al., *The Saga of the Swamp Thing*, book 4, 213–14.
93. Moore et al., *The Saga of the Swamp Thing*, book 4, 217.
94. Moore et al., *The Saga of the Swamp Thing*, book 4, 220.
95. Moore et al., *The Saga of the Swamp Thing*, book 1, 18.
96. Moore et al., *The Saga of the Swamp Thing*, book 5, 115.
97. Moore et al., *The Saga of the Swamp Thing*, book 5, 114.
98. Moore et al., *The Saga of the Swamp Thing*, book 5, 115.
99. Moore et al., *The Saga of the Swamp Thing*, book 1, 152, 157.
100. Moore et al., *The Saga of the Swamp Thing*, book 2, 141.
101. Moore et al., *The Saga of the Swamp Thing*, book 2, 41–42, 49.
102. Moore et al., *The Saga of the Swamp Thing*, book 1, 195.
103. Moore et al., *The Saga of the Swamp Thing*, book 2, 96.
104. Moore et al., *The Saga of the Swamp Thing*, book 3, 22.
105. Moore et al., *The Saga of the Swamp Thing*, book 2, 69–70, 145.
106. Moore et al., *The Saga of the Swamp Thing*, book 1, 12, 71.
107. Moore et al., *The Saga of the Swamp Thing*, book 1, 95.
108. Moore et al., *The Saga of the Swamp Thing*, book 6, 60.
109. Moore et al., *The Saga of the Swamp Thing*, book 1, 210–17.
110. Moore et al., *The Saga of the Swamp Thing*, book 4, 22, 26.
111. Moore et al., *The Saga of the Swamp Thing*, book 4, 28.
112. Bukatman, *The Poetics of Slumberland*, 73.
113. Moore et al., *The Saga of the Swamp Thing*, book 2, 212–13.
114. Moore et al., *The Saga of the Swamp Thing*, book 6, 193.
115. Berlin, *The Roots of Romanticism*, 140–41.
116. Moore et al., *The Saga of the Swamp Thing*, book 1, 100.

117. Moore et al., *The Saga of the Swamp Thing*, book 3, 53.
118. Moore et al., *The Saga of the Swamp Thing*, book 4, 95.
119. Moore et al., *The Saga of the Swamp Thing*, book 2, 214–15, 218–19.
120. Moore et al., *The Saga of the Swamp Thing*, book 3, 71.
121. Moore et al., *The Saga of the Swamp Thing*, book 2, 113, 115.
122. Moore et al., *The Saga of the Swamp Thing*, book 2, 118, 121.
123. Moore et al., *The Saga of the Swamp Thing*, book 2, 130.
124. Moore et al., *The Saga of the Swamp Thing*, book 2, 147.
125. Moore et al., *The Saga of the Swamp Thing*, book 3, 71.
126. Moore et al., *The Saga of the Swamp Thing*, book 3, 74.
127. Moore et al., *The Saga of the Swamp Thing*, book 3, 121.
128. Moore et al., *The Saga of the Swamp Thing*, book 4, 111.
129. Moore et al., *The Saga of the Swamp Thing*, book 4, 123.
130. Moore et al., *The Saga of the Swamp Thing*, book 4, 124.
131. Moore et al., *The Saga of the Swamp Thing*, book 4, 125.
132. Berlin, *The Roots of Romanticism*, 12.
133. Berlin, *The Roots of Romanticism*, 13.
134. Moore et al., *The Saga of the Swamp Thing*, book 3, 200.
135. Moore et al., *The Saga of the Swamp Thing*, book 2, 19.
136. Moore et al., *The Saga of the Swamp Thing*, book 2, 25.
137. Richard Kearney, *Strangers, Gods and Monsters: Interpreting Otherness* (London: Routledge, 2003), 142.
138. Moore et al., *The Saga of the Swamp Thing*, book 3, 199–200.
139. Bloom, "The Internalization of Quest-Romance," 8.
140. Moore et al., *The Saga of the Swamp Thing*, book 2, 30–33.
141. Moore et al., *The Saga of the Swamp Thing*, book 1, 58.
142. Moore et al., *The Saga of the Swamp Thing*, book 3, 201.
143. Moore et al., *The Saga of the Swamp Thing*, book 4, 128.
144. Moore et al., *The Saga of the Swamp Thing*, book 5, 95.
145. Moore et al., *The Saga of the Swamp Thing*, book 5, 23.
146. Moore et al., *The Saga of the Swamp Thing*, book 5, 35, 49.
147. Moore et al., *The Saga of the Swamp Thing*, book 1, 135.
148. Moore et al., *The Saga of the Swamp Thing*, book 2, 135.
149. Moore et al., *The Saga of the Swamp Thing*, book 5, 145.
150. Moore et al., *The Saga of the Swamp Thing*, book 5, 149.
151. Moore et al., *The Saga of the Swamp Thing*, book 5, 164.
152. Moore et al., *The Saga of the Swamp Thing*, book 5, 151.
153. Moore et al., *The Saga of the Swamp Thing*, book 5, 194–95.
154. Tresch, *The Romantic Machine*, 136.
155. Bloom, "The Internalization of Quest-Romance," 11.
156. Moore et al., *The Saga of the Swamp Thing*, book 6, 196.
157. Moore et al., *The Saga of the Swamp Thing*, book 6, 195.
158. Moore et al., *The Saga of the Swamp Thing*, book 4, 96.
159. Moore et al., *The Saga of the Swamp Thing*, book 6, 149.

160. Todd, *Imagining Monsters*, 227–28.
161. Moore et al., *The Saga of the Swamp Thing*, book 1, 8–9.
162. Moore et al., *The Saga of the Swamp Thing*, book 2, 137.
163. Moore et al., *The Saga of the Swamp Thing*, book 2, 138.
164. Moore et al., *The Saga of the Swamp Thing*, book 6, 32.
165. Moore et al., *The Saga of the Swamp Thing*, book 1, 194.
166. Moore et al., *The Saga of the Swamp Thing*, book 4, 56.
167. See Ingebretsen, *At Stake*.
168. Moore et al., *The Saga of the Swamp Thing*, book 4, 53.
169. Moore et al., *The Saga of the Swamp Thing*, book 5, 82–83.
170. Moore et al., *The Saga of the Swamp Thing*, book 4, 122.
171. Moore et al., *The Saga of the Swamp Thing*, book 1, 7.
172. Len Wein, Bernie Wrightson, and Nestor Redondo, *Roots of the Swamp Thing* (New York: DC Comics, 2011), 31.
173. Moore et al., *The Saga of the Swamp Thing*, book 1, 127.
174. Moore et al., *The Saga of the Swamp Thing*, book 1, 43–44.
175. Moore et al., *The Saga of the Swamp Thing*, book 1, 49.
176. Moore et al., *The Saga of the Swamp Thing*, book 1, 66.
177. Moore et al., *The Saga of the Swamp Thing*, book 1, 58.
178. Moore et al., *The Saga of the Swamp Thing*, book 1, 66.
179. Moore et al., *The Saga of the Swamp Thing*, book 1, 68–69.
180. Moore et al., *The Saga of the Swamp Thing*, book 1, 74, 77–78, 81.
181. Moore et al., *The Saga of the Swamp Thing*, book 2, 35.
182. Moore et al., *The Saga of the Swamp Thing*, book 1, 69.
183. Moore et al., *The Saga of the Swamp Thing*, book 1, 69.
184. Moore et al., *The Saga of the Swamp Thing*, book 1, 77.
185. Moore et al., *The Saga of the Swamp Thing*, book 2, 19.
186. Moore et al., *The Saga of the Swamp Thing*, book 1, 49.
187. Moore et al., *The Saga of the Swamp Thing*, book 3, 125.
188. Moore et al., *The Saga of the Swamp Thing*, book 5, 124.
189. Foucault, *The Order of Things*, 164–71.
190. Moore et al., *The Saga of the Swamp Thing*, book 6, 156.
191. Bukatman, *The Poetics of Slumberland*, 3.
192. Moore et al., *The Saga of the Swamp Thing*, book 5, 129.
193. Bukatman, *The Poetics of Slumberland*, 19–20.
194. Moore et al., *The Saga of the Swamp Thing*, book 6, 60.
195. Moore et al., *The Saga of the Swamp Thing*, book 6, 61, 71.
196. Moore et al., *The Saga of the Swamp Thing*, book 6, 68, 71.
197. Moore et al., *The Saga of the Swamp Thing*, book 6, 68, 78.
198. Moore et al., *The Saga of the Swamp Thing*, book 6, 65.
199. Ancet, *Phénoménologie des corps monstrueux*, 385, 392.
200. Moore et al., *The Saga of the Swamp Thing*, book 5, 152.
201. Moore et al., *The Saga of the Swamp Thing*, book 5, 155.
202. Moore et al., *The Saga of the Swamp Thing*, book 5, 156.

203. Moore et al., *The Saga of the Swamp Thing*, book 5, 157.
204. Moore et al., *The Saga of the Swamp Thing*, book 5, 158.
205. Moore et al., *The Saga of the Swamp Thing*, book 5, 159.
206. Moore et al., *The Saga of the Swamp Thing*, book 5, 160.
207. Moore et al., *The Saga of the Swamp Thing*, book 5, 163.
208. Moore et al., *The Saga of the Swamp Thing*, book 5, 165.
209. Bukatman, *The Poetics of Slumberland*, 22.
210. Bukatman, *The Poetics of Slumberland*, 21.
211. Bukatman, *The Poetics of Slumberland*, 21.
212. Moore et al., *The Saga of the Swamp Thing*, book 2, 6.
213. Bukatman, *The Poetics of Slumberland*, 18.

CHAPTER 3. *MONSTRE*: MONSTROUS FLUIDITY

1. Enki Bilal, *Monstre: L'intégrale* (Brussels: Casterman, 2007), 57.
2. See Mathias, "Un monstre délicat," 69–82.
3. Bilal, *Monstre*, 5.
4. Baudelaire, *Les Fleurs du mal*, 162.
5. Bilal, *Monstre*, 35.
6. Bilal, *Monstre*, 5.
7. Baudelaire, *Les Fleurs du mal*, 292–93.
8. See Enki Bilal, *La Trilogie Nikopol: La Foire aux immortels, La Femme piège, Froid Équateur* (Brussels: Casterman, 2009).
9. Baudin, *Circé* 6, "Les monstres dans la science-fiction," 31.
10. Baudin, *Circé* 6, "Les monstres dans la science-fiction," 31.
11. Bilal, *Monstre*, 40.
12. Bilal, *Monstre*, 102.
13. Bilal, *Monstre*, 39.
14. Bilal, *Monstre*, 260.
15. Bilal, *Monstre*, 260.
16. Baudelaire, *Écrits sur l'art*, 145.
17. Bilal, *Monstre*, 236. Leyla: "C'est de la pure bouillie cosmique, gazeuse, et de surcroît spiralée … Je ne sais pas d'où il peut bien venir." The visual amorphousness is consequently an ink screen camouflaging or mixing up the amorphous being's origin and identity.
18. Jacques Dupont, introduction to *Les Fleurs du mal*, by Charles Baudelaire (Paris: Flammarion, 1991), 33.
19. Marshall Berman, *All That Is Solid Melts into Air: The Experience of Modernity* (New York: Penguin, 1982), 72.
20. For Dupont, the organization of *Les Fleurs du mal* is in the vein of the romantic album that brings together different pieces. Dupont, introduction to *Les Fleurs du mal*, 24.
21. As Scott Bukatman suggests, comics can convey the sublime, despite—and even because of—being contained by the page. While Mike Mignola's works do so only rarely, "[Jack] Kirby evoked the sublime through more than the content and energy of the imagery; he exploited the fundamental tension between the panel and the page to evoke awe or transcendence." Bukatman, *Hellboy's World*, 65–69.

22. See Bilal, *Monstre*, 114.
23. Dupont, introduction to *Les Fleurs du mal*, 18, 21–22.
24. See, for instance, "Une Charogne."
25. Berman, *All That Is Solid Melts into Air*, 133.
26. Dupont, introduction to *Les Fleurs du mal*, 13.
27. Haywood and Halliwell, "Romantic Spectacle: An Introduction."
28. Northrop Frye, *Fearful Symmetry: A Study of William Blake* (Princeton, NJ: Princeton University Press, 1990), 55–56.
29. Frank Kermode, *Romantic Image* (London: Routledge and Kegan Paul, 1966), 5.
30. Kermode, *Romantic Image*.
31. Dupont, introduction to *Les Fleurs du mal*, 11.
32. Dupont, introduction to *Les Fleurs du mal*, 35.
33. Berman, *All That Is Solid Melts into Air*, 132.
34. Dupont, introduction to *Les Fleurs du mal*, 20.
35. Dupont, introduction to *Les Fleurs du mal*, 27.
36. Dupont, introduction to *Les Fleurs du mal*, 36 (quoting Julien Gracq).
37. Charles Baudelaire, *The Flowers of Evil*, trans. James McGowan (Oxford: Oxford University Press, 2008), 6–7. See also Baudin, *Circé* 6, "Les monstres dans la science-fiction," 9.
38. Mathias, "Un monstre délicat," 73–74.
39. Berlin, *The Roots of Romanticism*, 20.
40. Bilal, *Monstre*, 64.
41. Bilal, *Monstre*, 171.
42. Bilal, *Monstre*, 97.
43. Burgos, "Le monstre, même et autre," 14.
44. Léon Cellier, "Les rêves de Dieu," in *Circé* 4, "Le monstre 1: Présence du monstre, mythe et réalité," ed. Jean Burgos (Paris: Éditions Lettres Modernes, 1975), 86. Cf., for instance, Baudelaire's "Les Métamorphoses du vampire" (The Metamorphoses of the vampire), which portrays the vampire in a more human light by likening a wanton woman to a vampire and emphasizing her mortality. Baudelaire, *Les Fleurs du mal*, 252–55.
45. Cellier, "Les rêves de Dieu," 85.
46. Burgos, "Le monstre, même et autre," 13–14. See also Mathias, "Un monstre délicat."
47. Baudelaire, *Les Fleurs du mal*, 42–43.
48. Baudelaire, *Les Fleurs du mal*, 10–11.
49. Baudelaire, *Les Fleurs du mal*, 304–5.
50. Baudelaire, *Les Fleurs du mal*, 158.
51. Kai Mikkonen, "The Paradox of Intersemiotic Translation and the Comic Book: Examples from Enki Bilal's *Nikopol* Trilogy," *Word and Image* 22, no. 2 (2006): 103, 115.
52. Bilal, *Monstre*, 98.
53. Bilal, *Monstre*, 101.
54. Bilal, *Monstre*, 108.
55. Ueckmann, "Hybride Kreaturen im modernen französischen Comic," 303.
56. Bilal, *Monstre*, 174.
57. Bilal, *Monstre*, 187.
58. Bilal, *Monstre*, 21, 35.

59. Bilal, *Monstre*, 21, 35.
60. Bilal, *Monstre*, 109.
61. Bilal's *Mécanhumanimal* exhibition was held at the Musée des Arts et Métiers, Paris, June 4, 2013–March 2, 2014.
62. Bilal, *Monstre*, 14, 18.
63. Bilal, *Monstre*, 75.
64. Todd, *Imagining Monsters*, 120.
65. Quoted by Todd, *Imagining Monsters*, 120.
66. Bilal, *Monstre*, 59.
67. Bilal, *Monstre*, 256.
68. Bilal, *Monstre*, 49.
69. Baudelaire, *Les Fleurs du mal*, 146, 147.
70. Bilal, *Monstre*, 260.
71. Bilal, *Monstre*, 260.
72. Bilal, *Monstre*, 242.
73. Bilal, *Monstre*, 152.
74. Bilal, *Monstre*, 232.
75. Bilal, *Monstre*, 238.
76. Bilal, *Monstre*, 114.
77. Bilal, *Monstre*, 125.
78. Bilal, *Monstre*, 114.
79. Bilal, *Monstre*, 112.
80. Bilal, *Monstre*, p. 56.
81. See Etienne Sorin, "Exposition 'La Ville Dessinée' à La Cité d'Architecture et du Patrimoine: Planches de Cité," *Le Figaro*, June 8, 2010.
82. Bilal, *Monstre*, 69.
83. Bilal, *Monstre*, 209.
84. Bilal, *Monstre*, 43.
85. Bilal, *Monstre*, 16.
86. Bilal, *Monstre*, 153.
87. Bilal, *Monstre*, 244.
88. Bilal, *Monstre*, 159.
89. Frye, "The Keys to the Gates," 244.
90. Dupont, introduction to *Les Fleurs du mal*, 35.
91. Bilal, *Monstre*, 8, 15.
92. Bilal, *Monstre*, 120.
93. Ueckmann, "Hybride Kreaturen im modernen französischen Comic," 309.
94. Bilal, *Monstre*, 161.
95. Mathias, "Un monstre délicat," 76.
96. Bilal, *Monstre*, 33.
97. Bilal, *Monstre*, 6–8.
98. Bilal, *Monstre*, 5.
99. Bilal, *Monstre*, 243.

100. William Blake, "London," at *The William Blake Archive*, available at http://www.blakearchive.org/exist/blake/archive/object.xq?objectid=songsie.b.illbk.36&java=, retrieved August 16, 2014.
101. Bilal, *Monstre*, 246, 248.
102. Bilal, *Monstre*, 163.
103. Botting, *Gothic Romanced*, 15.
104. Bilal, *Monstre*, 41, 67.
105. Bilal, *Monstre*, 41, 67.
106. Bilal, *Monstre*, 78.
107. Bilal, *Monstre*, 104.
108. Bilal, *Monstre*, 104.
109. Bilal, *Monstre*, 106–7.
110. Bilal, *Monstre*, 122.
111. Foucault, *The Order of Things*, 155–56.
112. Bilal, *Monstre*, 124.
113. Bilal, *Monstre*, 124, 127.
114. Burgos, "Le monstre, même et autre," 12.
115. Bilal, *Monstre*, 132.
116. Bilal, *Monstre*, 131, 260.
117. Bilal, *Monstre*, 7.
118. Bilal, *Monstre*, 7.
119. Ueckmann, "Hybride Kreaturen im modernen französischen Comic," 305.
120. Hugo, *Notre-Dame de Paris* (Le Livre de Poche), 53–54.
121. Bilal, *Monstre*, 57.
122. Todd, *Imagining Monsters*, 260–64.
123. Bilal, *Monstre*, 220–21.
124. Bilal, *Monstre*, 101, 203.
125. Bilal, *Monstre*, 151.
126. Bilal, *Monstre*, 222.
127. Bilal, *Monstre*, 236.
128. Bilal, *Monstre*, p. 125.
129. Ueckmann, "Hybride Kreaturen im modernen französischen Comic," 325.
130. Bilal, *Monstre*, p. 304.
131. Bilal, *Monstre*, 304. See also Paul Virilio, "Du surhomme à l'homme surexcité (1)," *Alliage*, nos. 20–21 (1994).
132. Bilal, *Monstre*, 101.
133. Williams, "Monsters, Then and Now," 242.
134. Baudin, *Circé* 6, "Les monstres dans la science-fiction," 7.
135. Nathalie Grandjean, introduction to *Corps et technologies: Penser l'hybridité*, ed. Nathalie Grandjean and Claire Lobet-Maris (Brussels: Peter Lang, 2013), 9.
136. Williams, "Monsters, Then and Now," 242.
137. Bilal, *Monstre*, 249.
138. Bilal, *Monstre*, 198.
139. Bilal, *Monstre*, 227, 231.

140. Baudin, *Circé* 6, "Les monstres dans la science-fiction," 65.
141. Paul Gravett, "Enki Bilal: Haunted by the Future."
142. Dupont, introduction to *Les Fleurs du mal*, 16–19.
143. Baudelaire, *Écrits sur l'art*, 161–62.
144. Bilal, *Monstre*, 83.
145. Bilal, *Monstre*, 95.
146. Bilal, *Monstre*, 97.
147. As elaborated in the course of this book, these reflections are greatly indebted to analyses by both Jared Gardner in *Projections: Comics and the History of Twenty-First-Century Storytelling* (Stanford, CA: Stanford University Press, 2012); as well by Scott Bukatman in *The Poetics of Slumberland*.
148. Bilal, *Monstre*, 84, 243.
149. Baudelaire, *Les Fleurs du mal*, 20–23, 24–25, 248–49.
150. Berman, *All That Is Solid Melts into Air*, 132.
151. Hatfield, *Hand of Fire*, 149.
152. Botting, *Gothic Romanced*, 12.
153. Baudin, *Circé* 6, "Les monstres dans la science-fiction," 29.
154. Charles Baudelaire, *Mon cœur mis à nu* (Geneva: Droz, 2001), 16.
155. Bilal, *Monstre*, 110.
156. Bilal, *Monstre*, 83.
157. Bilal, *Monstre*, 110.
158. Bilal, *Monstre*, 227.
159. Bilal, *Monstre*, 142.
160. Bilal, *Monstre*, 169.
161. Bloom, "The Internalization of Quest-Romance," 11.
162. Kearney, *Strangers, Gods and Monsters*, 142.
163. Bilal, *Monstre*, 205.
164. Burgos, "Le monstre, même et autre," 13.
165. Berlin, *The Roots of Romanticism*, 99.
166. Mathias, "Un monstre délicat," 79.
167. Botting, *Gothic Romanced*, 15.
168. Dupont, introduction to *Les Fleurs du mal*, 16.
169. Bilal, *Monstre*, 214–15, 227.
170. See Smolderen, *Naissances de la bande dessinée*.
171. James T. Hong and Anselm Franke, "The Museum of the Monster That Is History," Taipei Biennial 2012.
172. Anselm Franke, "Death and Life of Fiction or the Modern Taowu," Taipei Biennial 2012, 1.
173. Franke, "Death and Life of Fiction," 6.
174. Franke, "Death and Life of Fiction," 2.

CHAPTER 4. *HELLBOY*: NOSTALGIA AND THE DOOMED QUEST

1. Shakespeare, *Hamlet*, in *The Arden Shakespeare*, 301.
2. Paré, *Des monstres et prodiges*, 81.

3. Cohen, *Monster Theory*, xii. For a detailed discussion of the workings of the *Hellboy* series through an examination of the complex range of sources feeding into the comics, see Bukatman, *Hellboy's World*.

4. Claude Lévi-Strauss, *The Savage Mind* (London: Weidenfeld and Nicolson, 1966), 16.

5. Round, *Gothic in Comics and Graphic Novels*, 53.

6. Mike Mignola, *Hellboy*, vol. 2, *Wake the Devil* (Milwaukie, OR: Dark Horse, 2003), n.p.

7. Svetlana Boym, "Nostalgia and Its Discontents," *Hedgehog Review* 9, no. 2 (Summer 2007): 7.

8. Svetlana Boym, *The Future of Nostalgia* (New York: Basic Books, 2002), 49.

9. Boym, *The Future of Nostalgia*, 49.

10. Boym, *The Future of Nostalgia*, 49.

11. Boym, *The Future of Nostalgia*, 49.

12. See also Maaheen Ahmed, "State Protection and Identification in *Hellboy*: Of Reformed Devils and Other Others in the Pentagon," *European Journal of American Studies* 10, no. 2 (2015).

13. See Boym, *The Future of Nostalgia*.

14. Mignola, *Hellboy*, vol. 2, *Wake the Devil*.

15. Mike Mignola, *Hellboy*, vol. 4, *The Right Hand of Doom* (Milwaukie, OR: Dark Horse, 2003), n.p.

16. Mike Mignola, *Hellboy*, vol. 6, *Strange Places* (Milwaukie, OR: Dark Horse, 2006), n.p.

17. Mike Mignola with Duncan Fegredo, *Hellboy*, vol. 9, *The Wild Hunt* (Milwaukie, OR: Dark Horse, 2010), n.p.

18. Mike Mignola with John Byrne, *Hellboy*, vol. 1, *The Seed of Destruction* (Milwaukie, OR: Dark Horse, 2003), n.p.

19. Mignola, *Hellboy*, vol. 6, *Strange Places*.

20. Mignola and Byrne, *Hellboy*, vol. 1, *The Seed of Destruction*.

21. Bukatman, *Hellboy's World*, 79.

22. Mike Mignola, *Hellboy*, vol. 5, *Conqueror Worm* (Milwaukie, OR: Dark Horse, 2003), n.p.

23. Mignola, *Hellboy*, vol. 4, *The Right Hand of Doom*.

24. Bukatman, *Hellboy's World*, 26. Here, Bukatman references Eric Hayot's essay on literary worlds and their connections to real worlds, irrespective of the degree of reality present in the works; see Eric Hayot, *On Literary Worlds* (Oxford: Oxford University Press, 2012).

25. Belting, *An Anthropology of Images*, 145; and Gardner, *Projections*, 150.

26. Bukatman, "Sculpture, Stasis, the Comics, and Hellboy," 110.

27. Bukatman, "Sculpture, Stasis, the Comics, and Hellboy," 110; and Mignola, *Hellboy*, vol. 6, *Strange Places*.

28. Mignola, *Hellboy*, vol. 6, *Strange Places*.

29. Mike Mignola with Richard Corben and P. Craig Russell, *Hellboy*, vol. 7, *The Troll Witch and Other Stories* (Milwaukie, OR: Dark Horse, 2007), n.p.

30. Mignola, *Hellboy*, vol. 6, *Strange Places*.

31. Bart Beaty, *Comics versus Art* (Toronto: University of Toronto Press, 2012), 193.

32. For more insight on superheroes as myth, see, for instance, Richards Reynolds, *Super Heroes: A Modern Mythology* (Jackson: University Press of Mississippi, 1992); and Will Brooker, *Batman Unmasked: Analyzing a Cultural Icon* (London: Bloomsbury, 2001).

33. Wright, *Monstrosity*, 24. As Wright points out, the absence of such distinctions made monstrous creatures serve purposes similar to those of the more human monsters of today, namely to distinguish "the acceptably human from what is unacceptably 'other.'"

34. See Jan Baetens and Hugo Frey, *The Graphic Novel: An Introduction* (New York: Cambridge University Press, 2014), 217–45.

35. Bukatman, "Sculpture, Stasis, the Comics, and Hellboy," 117.

36. Mignola, *Hellboy*, vol. 2, *Wake the Devil*.

37. Mignola, *Hellboy*, vol. 5, *Strange Places*.

38. Mignola, *Hellboy*, vol. 5, *Strange Places*.

39. Mignola and Byrne, *Hellboy*, vol. 1, *The Seed of Destruction*.

40. Mignola and Fegredo, *Hellboy*, vol. 9, *The Wild Hunt*.

41. Mike Mignola with Duncan Fegredo, *Hellboy*, vol. 12, *The Storm and the Fury* (Milwaukie, OR: Dark Horse, 2010), n.p.

42. Mignola, *Hellboy*, vol. 4, *The Right Hand of Doom*.

43. Mignola and Byrne, *Hellboy*, vol. 1, *The Seed of Destruction*.

44. Mike Mignola, *Hellboy*, vol. 3, *The Chained Coffin and Other Stories* (Milwaukie, OR: Dark Horse, 2004), n.p.

45. Mignola and Fegredo, *Hellboy*, vol. 12, *The Storm and the Fury*.

46. Mignola, *Hellboy*, vol. 3, *The Chained Coffin*.

47. Mignola, *Hellboy*, vol. 4, *The Right Hand of Doom*.

48. Mignola, *Hellboy*, vol. 3, *The Chained Coffin*.

49. Mignola, *Hellboy*, vol. 4, *The Right Hand of Doom*.

50. Mignola, *Hellboy*, vol. 4, *The Right Hand of Doom*.

51. Mike Mignola with Duncan Fegredo, *Hellboy*, vol. 8, *Darkness Calls* (Milwaukie, OR: Dark Horse, 2007), n.p.

52. Mignola and Fegredo, *Hellboy*, vol. 8, *Darkness Calls*.

53. Mignola, *Hellboy*, vol. 2, *Wake the Devil*.

54. Mignola, *Hellboy*, vol. 3, *The Chained Coffin*.

55. Mignola, *Hellboy*, vol. 3, *The Chained Coffin*.

56. For instance, Mignola acknowledges the context's nebulous influence in the forward to the short story "The Third Wish" in *Strange Places*. The story not only combines Hans Christian Andersen's fairy tales with African stories but is also affected by the events of 9/11, in the wake of which "it seemed like a good time to do a cute little fairytale about mermaids." "The Third Wish" ended up being darker than originally planned, possibly, as Mignola muses, because of 9/11, but also because of the approaching battle between Hellboy and the Beast of Apocalypse. Mignola, *Hellboy*, vol. 6, *Strange Places*.

57. Mignola, *Hellboy*, vol. 3, *The Chained Coffin*.

58. Mignola, *Hellboy*, vol. 3, *The Chained Coffin*.

59. Mignola and Fegredo, *Hellboy*, vol. 8, *Darkness Calls*.

60. For the moment limited to two volumes of the *Hellboy in Hell* series.

61. Mignola and Byrne, *Hellboy*, vol. 1, *The Seed of Destruction*. Similarly, to resolve an earlier case, he had used the plant arbutus (which, according to superstition, wards off evil) to defeat the ectoplasm emanating from Todd, a drugged medium. Mignola, *Hellboy*, vol. 4, *The Right Hand of Doom*.

62. Mignola et al., *Hellboy*, vol. 10, *The Crooked Man*.

63. Mike Mignola, with Richard Corben, Kevin Nowlan, and Scott Hampton, *Hellboy*, vol. 11, *The Bride of Hell and Others* (Milwaukie, OR: Dark Horse, 2011).

64. Mignola et al., *Hellboy*, vol. 11, *The Bride of Hell*.
65. A cat's ghost assures Hellboy that he did nothing wrong in inadvertently paving the way for the cat's mistress Mary's revenge against the vampire who had made her into a monster; turned into a monster at a young age, Mary had been confined to the cellars of her family's house, speaking only in nursery rhymes.
66. Mignola and Fegredo, *Hellboy*, vol. 8, *Darkness Calls*.
67. Mignola and Fegredo, *Hellboy*, vol. 12, *The Storm and the Fury*.
68. See Mignola, *Hellboy*, vol. 2, *Wake the Devil*.
69. Mignola and Fegredo, *Hellboy*, vol. 8, *Darkness Calls*.
70. Mignola and Fegredo, *Hellboy*, vol. 8, *Darkness Calls*.
71. Mignola and Byrne, *Hellboy*, vol. 1, *The Seed of Destruction*.
72. See Bukatman, *The Poetics of Slumberland*.
73. Mignola et al., *Hellboy*, vol. 7, *The Troll Witch*.
74. Mignola et al., *Hellboy*, vol. 10, *The Crooked Man*.
75. Mignola et al., *Hellboy*, vol. 10, *The Crooked Man*.
76. Mignola et al., *Hellboy*, vol. 10, *The Crooked Man*.
77. See Groensteen, "The Art of Braiding."
78. Chute, *Disaster Drawn*, 8.
79. Mignola and Fegredo, *Hellboy*, vol. 9, *The Wild Hunt*.
80. Mignola and Fegredo, *Hellboy*, vol. 9, *The Wild Hunt*.
81. Mignola and Fegredo, *Hellboy*, vol. 12, *The Storm and the Fury*.
82. Mignola and Fegredo, *Hellboy*, vol. 9, *The Wild Hunt*.
83. Mignola, *Hellboy*, vol. 3, *The Chained Coffin*.
84. Paré, *Des monstres et prodiges*, 80–82.
85. Paré, *Des monstres et prodiges*, 81.
86. Moreover, the frog monsters in *The Seed of Destruction*, who resemble Hellboy's companion Abe; the "icthyo sapien"; and Blake's *The Ghost of a Flea* also echo Paré's renditions of amphibious monsters, particularly that of a child with the face of a frog (*Des monstres et prodiges*, 38).
87. Mignola and Fegredo, *Hellboy*, vol. 8, *Darkness Calls*.
88. Mignola and Fegredo, *Hellboy*, vol. 9, *The Wild Hunt*.
89. Bukatman, *Hellboy's World*, 198.
90. Mignola et al., *Hellboy*, vol. 10, *The Crooked Man*.
91. Mignola, *Hellboy*, vol. 2, *Wake the Devil*.
92. The grammatically correct spelling in German would be *Kriegsaffe*.
93. Mignola, *Hellboy*, vol. 5, *Conqueror Worm*.
94. Mignola and Byrne, *Hellboy*, vol. 1, *The Seed of Destruction*.
95. Mignola and Byrne, *Hellboy*, vol. 1, *The Seed of Destruction*.
96. Mignola and Byrne, *Hellboy*, vol. 1, *The Seed of Destruction*.
97. Mignola, *Hellboy*, vol. 2, *Wake the Devil*.
98. Mignola, *Hellboy*, vol. 2, *Wake the Devil*.
99. Mignola, *Hellboy*, vol. 2, *Wake the Devil*.
100. Mignola, *Hellboy*, vol. 2, *Wake the Devil*.
101. Mignola, *Hellboy*, vol. 2, *Wake the Devil*.

102. Mignola, *Hellboy*, vol. 4, *The Right Hand of Doom*.
103. Mignola, *Hellboy*, vol. 4, *The Right Hand of Doom*.
104. Mignola, *Hellboy*, vol. 4, *The Right Hand of Doom*.
105. Mignola, *Hellboy*, vol. 5, *Conqueror Worm*.
106. Mignola, *Hellboy*, vol. 6, *Strange Places*.
107. Mignola, *Hellboy*, vol. 6, *Strange Places*.
108. Mignola, *Hellboy*, vol. 6, *Strange Places*.
109. Mignola, *Hellboy*, vol. 6, *Strange Places*.
110. Mignola, *Hellboy*, vol. 6, *Strange Places*.
111. Mignola and Fegredo, *Hellboy*, vol. 9, *The Wild Hunt*.
112. Mignola and Fegredo, *Hellboy*, vol. 9, *The Wild Hunt*.
113. Mignola, *Hellboy*, vol. 3, *The Chained Coffin*.
114. Mignola and Fegredo, *Hellboy*, vol. 9, *The Wild Hunt*.
115. Mignola and Fegredo, *Hellboy*, vol. 9, *The Wild Hunt*.
116. Mignola and Fegredo, *Hellboy*, vol. 12, *The Storm and the Fury*.
117. Mignola and Fegredo, *Hellboy*, vol. 12, *The Storm and the Fury*.
118. Mignola and Fegredo, *Hellboy*, vol. 12, *The Storm and the Fury*.
119. Mignola et al., *Hellboy*, vol. 7, *The Troll Witch*.
120. Mignola and Fegredo, *Hellboy*, vol. 8, *Darkness Calls*.
121. Mignola et al., *Hellboy*, vol. 10, *The Crooked Man*.
122. Mignola et al., *Hellboy*, vol. 10, *The Crooked Man*.
123. Mignola, *Hellboy*, vol. 5, *Conqueror Worm*.
124. Bukatman, *The Poetics of Slumberland*, 204.
125. Bukatman, *The Poetics of Slumberland*, 51.
126. Mignola, *Hellboy*, vol. 2, *Wake the Devil*.
127. Mignola, *Hellboy*, vol. 2, *Wake the Devil*.
128. Mignola, *Hellboy*, vol. 2, *Wake the Devil*.
129. Mignola, *Hellboy*, vol. 2, *Wake the Devil*.
130. Mignola et al., *Hellboy*, vol. 7, *The Troll Witch*.
131. Mignola et al., *Hellboy*, vol. 7, *The Troll Witch*.
132. Mignola, *Hellboy*, vol. 4, *The Right Hand of Doom*.
133. Mignola, *Hellboy*, vol. 5, *Conqueror Worm*.
134. Mignola, *Hellboy*, vol. 5, *Conqueror Worm*.
135. See Baetens and Frey, *The Graphic Novel*, especially the chapter on nostalgia in graphic novels; see also Christophe Dony on the nostalgic tendencies of DC Comics' Vertigo imprint: "The Rewriting Ethos of the Vertigo Imprint: Critical Perspectives on Memory-Making and Canon Formation in the American Comics Field," *Comicalités*, 2014.
136. Alan Moore, introduction to *Hellboy*, vol. 2, *Wake the Devil*, by Mike Mignola (Milwaukie, OR: Dark Horse, 2003).
137. Mignola and Byrne, *Hellboy*, vol. 1, *The Seed of Destruction*.
138. Mignola, *Hellboy*, vol. 2, *Wake the Devil*.
139. Mignola, *Hellboy*, vol. 5, *Conqueror Worm*.
140. Mignola and Fegredo, *Hellboy*, vol. 12, *The Storm and the Fury*.
141. Mignola and Fegredo, *Hellboy*, vol. 12, *The Storm and the Fury*.

142. Mignola and Fegredo, *Hellboy*, vol. 12, *The Storm and the Fury*.
143. McEvoy, "Gothic and the Romantics," 23.
144. Zakiya Hanafi, *The Monster in the Machine: Magic, Medicine, and the Marvelous in the Time of the Scientific Revolution* (Durham, NC: Duke University Press, 2000), 54.
145. Laura O'Connor, "The Corpse on Hellboy's Back: Translating a Graphic Image," *Journal of Popular Culture* 43, no. 3 (2010): 558–59.
146. Mignola, *Hellboy*, vol. 2, *Wake the Devil*.
147. Mignola, *Hellboy*, vol. 2, *Wake the Devil*.
148. Mignola, *Hellboy*, vol. 2, *Wake the Devil*.
149. Indicative of the persistence of romantic thought, Ilsa, after returning the corpse to its ancestral castle in Romania, recites Blake's "The Tyger."
150. Mignola, *Hellboy*, vol. 2, *Wake the Devil*.
151. Mignola, *Hellboy*, vol. 5, *Conqueror Worm*.
152. Mignola et al., *Hellboy*, vol. 11, *The Bride of Hell*.
153. Mignola et al., *Hellboy*, vol. 11, *The Bride of Hell*.
154. Mignola, *Hellboy*, vol. 2, *Wake the Devil*.
155. Mignola, *Hellboy*, vol. 3, *The Chained Coffin*.
156. Mignola, *Hellboy*, vol. 5, *Conqueror Worm*.
157. Mignola, *Hellboy*, vol. 5, *Conqueror Worm*.
158. Mignola et al., *Hellboy*, vol. 7, *The Troll Witch*.
159. Mignola et al., *Hellboy*, vol. 7, *The Troll Witch*.
160. Mignola et al., *Hellboy*, vol. 7, *The Troll Witch*.
161. Mignola and Fegredo, *Hellboy*, vol. 8, *Darkness Calls*.
162. Mignola and Fegredo, *Hellboy*, vol. 8, *Darkness Calls*.
163. Mignola and Fegredo, *Hellboy*, vol. 9, *The Wild Hunt*.
164. Mignola and Fegredo, *Hellboy*, vol. 12, *The Storm and the Fury*.
165. Mike Mignola, with Duncan Fegredo and Dave Stewart, *Hellboy: The Midnight Circus* (Milwaukie, OR: Dark Horse, 2013), n.p.
166. Mignola et al., *Hellboy: The Midnight Circus*.
167. Mignola et al., *Hellboy: The Midnight Circus*.
168. Bukatman, *The Poetics of Slumberland*, 145.
169. Georges Canguilhem, "Monstrosity and the Monstrous," *Diogenes* 10, no. 40 (1962): 27.
170. Cohen, *Monster Theory*, xii.
171. See Ingebretsen, *At Stake*.

CHAPTER 5. *THE CROW*: SPECTACULARITY AND EMOTIONALITY

1. Ian Curtis, *So This Is Permanence: Joy Division Lyrics and Notebooks*, ed. Deborah Curtis and Jon Savage (London: Faber and Faber, 2014), 81.
2. For the characteristics and implications of goth subculture, see Round, *Gothic in Comics and Graphic Novels*, 142. For Round, "the practice of Goth and its subculture can be more effectively summarized as enacting a series of tensions, including: A much-vaunted individuality versus a strongly coded individual style. Isolation and introversion versus a tightly knit (and often cliquey and hierarchical) social scene and community. DIY tropes (torn clothes and holes) versus expensive costuming. A reciprocal relationship with its own media and artefacts."

3. Jared Gardner sees *The Crow* films as the precursors to the current superhero blockbuster boom (Gardner, *Projections*, 180).

4. Goodlad, "Men in Black," 102.

5. Goodlad, "Men in Black," 102.

6. James O'Barr, *The Crow* (Northampton, MA: Kitchen Sink Press, 1994).

7. Sullivan, "Transmogrification," 561.

8. Frye, *A Study of English Romanticism*, 60.

9. Frye, *A Study of English Romanticism*, 60.

10. Frye, *A Study of English Romanticism*, 66, 85.

11. Frye, *A Study of English Romanticism*, 66–67. For more on the significance of the collage, see Dick Hebdige, *Subculture: The Meaning of Style* (London: Routledge, 2002).

12. Frye, *A Study of English Romanticism*, 65.

13. James O'Barr, "Interview with James O'Barr," *KAOS2000 Magazine*, July 20, 2000.

14. Michael Bibby, "Atrocity Exhibitions: Joy Division, Factory Records, and Goth Style," in *Goth: Undead Subculture*, ed. Michael Bibby and Lauren M. E. Goodlad (Durham, NC: Duke University Press, 2007), 234.

15. Bibby, "Atrocity Exhibitions," 240, 243.

16. Paul Hodkinson, "Gothic Music and Subculture," in *The Routledge Companion to Gothic*, ed. Catherine Spooner and Emma McEvoy (London: Routledge, 2007), 262.

17. Simon Reynolds, *Rip It Up and Start Again: Postpunk, 1978–1984* (London: Faber and Faber, 2006), 173.

18. Reynolds, *Rip It Up*, 183.

19. Wallace Fowlie, *Rimbaud and Jim Morrison: The Rebel as Poet* (Durham, NC: Duke University Press, 1994).

20. Jim Morrison, "Prologue: Self-Interview," in *The Lost Writings of Jim Morrison*, vol. 1, *Wilderness* (London: Vintage, 1989), 3.

21. See Thomas Pfau, *Romantic Moods: Paranoia, Trauma, and Melancholy, 1790–1840* (Baltimore: John Hopkins University Press, 2005).

22. Roger Luckhurst, *The Trauma Question* (New York: Routledge, 2008), 98.

23. Kearney, *Strangers, Gods and Monsters*, 8.

24. Faflak and Sha, "Introduction: Feeling Romantic," 4.

25. See Anna-Sophie Jürgens, "Batman's Joker, a Neo-Modern Clown of Violence," *Journal of Graphic Novels and Comics* 5, no. 1 (2014): 441–54, for the link between the Joker and Gwynplaine as well as the circus pantomimes of the Hanlon-Lees, whose popularity reached its zenith during the same period as that of Hugo's *L'Homme qui rit* and the Comte de Lautréamont's *Les Chants de Maldoror*, whose protagonist also disfigured his own mouth into a permanent smile (Jürgens, "Batman's Joker," 445–46).

26. Boym, *The Future of Nostalgia*.

27. Although not literary metafiction, the loosely connected intertextuality in *The Crow* in itself resembles Frankenstein's monster of cultural fragments stemming from both its "higher" and its "lower" echelons. Julia Round makes a comparable analogy to Frankenstein's monster with reference to the comics series *The Unwritten* (Round, *Gothic in Comics and Graphic Novels*, 161).

28. D. F. Rauber, "The Fragment as Romantic Form," *Modern Language Quarterly* 30, no. 2 (1969), 212.

29. Rauber, "The Fragment as Romantic Form," 219.
30. Alexander Regier, *Fracture and Fragmentation in British Romanticism* (Cambridge: Cambridge University Press, 2010), 77.
31. Rauber, "The Fragment as Romantic Form," 221.
32. Regier, *Romanticism and Fragmentation*, 7.
33. Regier, *Romanticism and Fragmentation*, 13.
34. Regier, *Romanticism and Fragmentation*, 14.
35. Lillian Feder, *Madness in Literature* (Princeton, NJ: Princeton University Press, 1980), 249.
36. Goodlad, "Men in Black," 95.
37. Curtis, *So This Is Permanence*, 43.
38. Curtis, *So This Is Permanence*, 43.
39. Curtis, *So This Is Permanence*, 35.
40. Bibby, "Atrocity Exhibitions," 235.
41. Bibby, "Atrocity Exhibitions," 234.
42. Pfau, *Romantic Moods*, 19.
43. Pfau, *Romantic Moods*, 35.
44. Curtis, *So This Is Permanence*, 35.
45. Bibby, "Atrocity Exhibitions," 240.
46. Bibby, "Atrocity Exhibitions," 239.
47. Curtis, *So This Is Permanence*, 101.
48. Curtis, *So This Is Permanence*, 69.
49. Curtis, *So This Is Permanence*, 69.
50. Curtis, *So This Is Permanence*, 67.
51. Boym, *The Future of Nostalgia*, 12.
52. Bibby, "Atrocity Exhibitions," 237.
53. Bibby, "Atrocity Exhibitions," 38.
54. Mark Fisher, "No Longer the Pleasures: Joy Division," in *Ghosts of My Life: Writings on Depression, Hauntology and Lost Futures* (London: Zero Books, 2004), n.p.
55. Deborah Curtis, *Touching from a Distance: Ian Curtis and Joy Division* (London: Faber and Faber, 2007), 181.
56. Curtis, *So This Is Permanence*, 101.
57. Anthony Blunt, "Blake's 'Ancient of Days': The Symbolism of the Compasses," *Journal of the Warburg Institute* 2, no. 1 (1938): 53.
58. Blunt, "Blake's 'Ancient of Days,'" 53–54.
59. Blunt, "Blake's 'Ancient of Days,'" 53–54.
60. Blunt, "Blake's 'Ancient of Days,'" 57.
61. O'Barr, *The Crow*.
62. See Curtis, *Touching from a Distance*, 163.
63. O'Barr, *The Crow*.
64. O'Barr, "Interview with James O'Barr."
65. Gardner, *Projections*, 5.
66. Goodlad, "Men in Black," 97.
67. Jean-Luc Nancy, "Exscription," *Yale French Studies*, no. 78 (1990): 61.
68. O'Barr, *The Crow*.

69. O'Barr, *The Crow*.
70. O'Barr, *The Crow*.
71. O'Barr, *The Crow*.
72. O'Barr, *The Crow*.
73. Goodlad, "Men in Black," 97.
74. O'Barr, *The Crow*. The quotation is from the title page of the second book, "Fear."
75. Goodlad, "Men in Black," 97.
76. Antonin Artaud, *Selected Writings*, ed. Susan Sontag (Berkeley: University of California Press, 1992), 4.
77. Artaud, *Selected Writings*, 487.
78. Artaud, *Selected Writings*, 487.
79. O'Barr, *The Crow*.
80. Artaud, *Selected Writings*, 487.
81. Even though *The Crow* bears a stronger influence of the Cure's earlier albums, the song "How Beautiful You Are" from the album *Kiss Me, Kiss Me, Kiss Me* (1987) incorporates phrases from Baudelaire's essay "The Eyes of the Poor," highlighting the poet's impact on Robert Smith, the Cure's principal singer and songwriter. I would like to warmly thank Brian Cremins for pointing this out.
82. O'Barr, *The Crow*.
83. Bukatman, *The Poetics of Slumberland*, 12.
84. Feder, *Madness in Literature*, 204.
85. Feder, *Madness in Literature*, 244.
86. Kearney, *Strangers, Gods and Monsters*, 141–46.
87. Kearney, *Strangers, Gods and Monsters*, 155.
88. See Belting, *An Anthropology of Images*.
89. Belting, *An Anthropology of Images*.
90. Belting, *An Anthropology of Images*.
91. Friedrich Nietzsche, *Beyond Good and Evil: Prelude to a Philosophy of the Future*, ed. Rolf-Peter Horstmann, trans. Judith Norman (Cambridge: Cambridge University Press, 2003), 69.
92. O'Barr, *The Crow*.
93. O'Barr, *The Crow*.
94. Kearney, *Strangers, Gods and Monsters*, 6.
95. Shun-Liang Chao, *Rethinking the Concept of the Grotesque: Crashaw, Baudelaire, Magritte* (London: Legenda, 2000), 99.
96. Curtis, *So This Is Permanence*, 101.
97. O'Barr, *The Crow*.
98. O'Barr, *The Crow*.
99. O'Barr, *The Crow*.
100. Hanafi, *The Monster in the Machine*, 67.
101. Alan Moore and Brian Bolland, *Batman: The Killing Joke* (New York: DC Comics, 2008); Grant Morrison and Dave McKean, *Arkham Asylum: A Serious House on Serious Earth* (New York: DC Comics, 1989); and Ed Brubaker, Doug Mahnke, Patrick Zircher, and Aaron Sowd, *Batman: The Man Who Laughs* (New York: DC Comics, 2008).

102. Paul Radin, *The Trickster: A Study in American Indian Mythology* (New York: Schocken Books, 1972), xxiii.
103. Radin, *The Trickster*, xxiv.
104. Carl Jung, "On the Psychology of the Trickster Figure," in *The Trickster: A Study in American Indian Mythology*, by Paul Radin (New York: Schocken Books, 1972), 196.
105. Radin, *The Trickster*, 185 (italics in original).
106. Jung, "On the Psychology of the Trickster Figure," 196.
107. Jung, "On the Psychology of the Trickster Figure," 196.
108. Feder, *Madness in Literature*, xi.
109. Jürgens, "Batman's Joker," 441–42.
110. Jürgens, "Batman's Joker," 442.
111. Jürgens, "Batman's Joker," 444.
112. Jürgens, "Batman's Joker," 448.
113. Jürgens, "Batman's Joker," 448.
114. Jürgens, "Batman's Joker," 449.
115. Marshall McLuhan, cited in Bukatman, *The Poetics of Slumberland*, 160.
116. Feder, *Madness in Literature*, 279.
117. Feder, *Madness in Literature*, 279.
118. Goodlad, "Men in Black," 97–101.
119. Guy Debord, *La société du spectacle* (Paris: Gallimard, 1992), 131n219.
120. Guy Debord, *Society of the Spectacle*, trans. Donald Nicholson-Smith (New York: Zone Books, 1995), 153.
121. See Sullivan, "Transmogrification."
122. David Westbrook, "From Hogan's Alley to Coconino County: Four Narratives of the Early Comic Strip, *American Quarterly*, 1999.
123. Luckhurst, *The Trauma Question*, 81.
124. Frye, *A Study of English Romanticism*, 74.

CONCLUSION. COMICS MONSTERS: *PER MONSTRA AD ASTRA*

On the chapter title, see Georges Didi-Huberman, "Échantillonner le chaos: Aby Warburg et l'atlas photographique de la Grande Guerre," *Études photographiques*, no. 27 (2011).
1. Shakespeare, *The Tempest*, in *The Arden Shakespeare*, 1083.
2. Hanafi, *The Monster in the Machine*, 3.
3. Hanafi, *The Monster in the Machine*, 187.
4. Hanafi, *The Monster in the Machine*, 190–91.
5. Hanafi, *The Monster in the Machine*, 54.
6. Hanafi, *The Monster in the Machine*, 74.
7. Bukatman, *The Poetics of Slumberland*, 135–36.
8. Frye, *A Study of English Romanticism*, 250.
9. Frye, *A Study of English Romanticism*, 250.
10. Frye, *A Study of English Romanticism*, 237–38.
11. Berlin, *The Roots of Romanticism*, 21
12. Berlin, *The Roots of Romanticism*, 136.

13. Cohen, "Monster Culture," 12.

14. Bukatman, *The Poetics of Slumberland*, 146.

15. Smolderen, *Naissances de la bande dessinée*, 30.

16. Jared Gardner, "Archives, Collectors, and the New Media Work of Comics," *Modern Fiction Studies* 52, no. 4 (2006):787–806.

17. Gardner, *Projections*, 7.

18. Rosemarie Garland Thomson, "Introduction: From Wonder to Error; A Genealogy of Freak Discourse in Modernity," in *Freakery: Cultural Spectacles of the Extraordinary Body*, ed. Rosemarie Garland Thomson (New York: New York University Press, 1996), 1.

19. Garland Thomson, "Introduction: From Wonder to Error," 3.

20. Garland Thomson, "Introduction: From Wonder to Error," 3.

21. Emil Ferris, *My Favorite Thing Is Monsters* (Seattle: Fantagraphics, 2017).

22. Gardner, *Projections*, ix.

23. Bukatman, *Hellboy's World*, 19.

24. Smolderen, *Naissances de la bande dessinée*, 34.

25. Berlin, *The Roots of Romanticism*, 53.

26. Smolderen, *Naissances de la bande dessinée*, 31–40.

27. Smolderen, *Naissances de la bande dessinée*, 31.

28. Berlin, *The Roots of Romanticism*, 20.

29. Bukatman, *The Poetics of Slumberland*, 2.

30. Smolderen, *Naissances de la bande dessinée*, 133.

31. Bukatman, *Hellboy's World*, 208.

32. Ferris, *My Favorite Thing*.

33. This issue of *Gory Stories* was published by Shroud in 1972. See Michael Walton, *The Horror Comic Never Dies: A Grisly History* (Jefferson, NC: McFarland, 2019), 85.

34. Ferris, *My Favorite Thing*.

35. Ferris, *My Favorite Thing*.

36. Hugo, *L'Homme qui rit*, 162.

37. Bukatman, "Sculpture, Stasis, the Comics, and Hellboy," 203.

38. See Smolderen, *Naisssances de la bande dessinée*, 50.

39. Michelle E. Bloom, "Pygmalionesque Delusions and Illusions of Movement: Animation from Hoffmann to Truffaut," *Comparative Literature* 52, no. 4 (2000): 293.

40. Bloom, "Pygmalionesque Delusions," 294.

41. Benoît Peeters, *Case, planche, récit: Lire la bande dessinée* (Brussels: Casterman, 1998), 24–30.

42. Westbrook, "From Hogan's Alley to Coconino County."

43. Bloom, "Pygmalionesque Delusions," 292.

44. Belting, *An Anthropology of Images*, 130.

45. Belting, *An Anthropology of Images*, 131.

46. For Erkki Huhtamo, panoramas, while often focusing on nonfictional narratives, are the precursors to contemporary media culture or a "shared state of mind, internalized in different degrees by each individual living under its spell" (Huhtamo, *Illusions in Motion*, 364), which has resulted in "personal interactive media" (368). Even though comics are not exactly new media, they do incorporate the characteristics of interaction and ephemerality that characterize contemporary media.

47. Westbrook, "From Hogan's Alley to Coconino County."
48. Bukatman, *The Poetics of Slumberland*, 12.
49. Bukatman, *The Poetics of Slumberland*, 13.
50. Bukatman, *The Poetics of Slumberland*, 62.
51. Leonhard Herrmann, "Friedrich Schiller (1759–1805), *Über die ästhetische Erziehung des Menschen in einer Reihe von Briefen* (1795)," *KulturPoetik* 10, no. 1 (2010): 103.
52. See, for instance, Bukatman's comment regarding the superhero film's "fascination [...] with the transforming body" (*The Poetics of Slumberland*, 203).
53. Saige Walton, "Baroque Mutants in the 21st Century? Re-thinking Genre through the Superhero," in *The Contemporary Comic Book Superhero*, ed. Angela Ndalianis (New York: Routledge, 2009), 93.
54. Walton, "Baroque Mutants in the 21st Century?"
55. Bukatman, *The Poetics of Slumberland*, 51.
56. Gardner, *Projections*, 11.
57. Bukatman, *The Poetics of Slumberland*, 51.
58. Todd, *Imagining Monsters*, 264.
59. Botting, *Gothic Romanced*, 15–16.
60. Baudin, *Circé* 6, "Les monstres dans la science-fiction," 8.
61. Bukatman, *The Poetics of Slumberland*, 59.
62. See Ahmed, "State Protection and Identification."
63. Todd, *Imagining Monsters*, 177.
64. Baudin, *Circé* 6, "Les monstres dans la science-fiction," 14.
65. Williams, "Monsters, Then and Now," 258.
66. Todd, *Imagining Monsters*, 267.
67. See Todd, *Imagining Monsters*, 92.
68. Williams, "Monsters, Then and Now," 253.
69. Sepulchre, "Super-corps, super-technologie, super-monstre," 165.
70. Durand, *Les structures anthropologiques de l'imaginaire*, 32.
71. Quoted in Barroux, "Quels éléments d'anthropologie," 132.
72. Barroux, "Quels éléments d'anthropologie," 131.
73. Williams, "Monsters, Then and Now," 248.
74. Williams, "Monsters, Then and Now," 250.
75. Barroux, "Quels éléments d'anthropologie," 120.
76. Ochsner, *DeMONSTRAtion*, 13.
77. See, for instance, Daniel Worden, "The Shameful Art: *McSweeney's Quarterly Concern*, Comics, and the Politics of Affect," *Modern Fiction Studies* 52, no. 4 (2006): 891–917; and Christopher Pizzino, *Arresting Development: Comics at the Boundaries of Literature* (Austin: University of Texas Press, 2016).
78. See Pizzino, *Arresting Development*, for a detailed examination of the American context.
79. Fredric Jameson, "The Cultural Logic of Late Capitalism," in *Postmodernism; or, The Cultural Logic of Late Capitalism* (Durham, NC: Duke University Press, 1991), 4. Morse Peckham had already declared that "modern culture, in its vital areas, is a romantic culture"; Peckham, "Toward a Theory of Romanticism: II," 8.
80. Regier, *Romanticism and Fragmentation*, 10.

81. Reinfandt, *Romantische Kommunikation*, 10.

82. Reinfandt, *Romantische Kommunikation*, 11.

83. Reinfandt, *Romantische Kommunikation*, 11.

84. Faflak and Sha, "Introduction: Feeling Romantic," 5.

85. David Vallins, *Coleridge and the Psychology of Romanticism: Feeling and Thought* (New York: St. Martin's Press, 2000), 4.

86. Didi-Huberman, "Échantillonner le chaos."

87. Didi-Huberman, "Échantillonner le chaos."

88. Kearney, *Strangers, Gods and Monsters*, 4.

89. Marie-Hélène Huet, *Monstrous Imagination* (Cambridge, MA: Harvard University Press, 1993), 8.

90. John Updike, "The Mystery of Mickey Mouse," in *The Best American Essays*, ed. Robert Atwan (Boston: Houghton Mifflin, 1995), 389.

91. Kearney, *Strangers, Gods and Monsters*, 9.

92. Theodor Adorno, *Minima Moralia: Reflections on a Damaged Life*, trans. E. F. N. Jephcott (London: Verso, 2005), 146.

93. Maaheen Ahmed, "Comics and Authorship: An Introduction," *Authorship* 6, no. 2 (2017): 3–8.

BIBLIOGRAPHY

PRIMARY SOURCES

Baudelaire, Charles. *Les Fleurs du mal*. Introduced by Jacques Dupont. Paris: Flammarion, 1991.
Baudelaire, Charles. *The Flowers of Evil*. Translated by James McGowan. Oxford: Oxford University Press, 2008.
Bilal, Enki. *Monstre: L'intégrale*. Brussels: Casterman, 2007.
Bilal, Enki. *La Trilogie Nikopol: La Foire aux immortels, La Femme piège, Froid Équateur*. Brussels: Casterman, 2009.
Blake, William. *The William Blake Archive*. Available at http://www.blakearchive.org/blake/. Retrieved July 27, 2016.
Brubaker, Ed, Doug Mahnke, Patrick Zircher, and Aaron Sowd. *Batman: The Man Who Laughs*. New York: DC Comics, 2008.
Ferris, Emil. *My Favorite Thing Is Monsters*. Seattle: Fantagraphics, 2017.
Hugo, Victor. *L'Homme qui rit*. Paris: Pocket, 2012.
Hugo, Victor. *Notre-Dame de Paris*. Paris: Le Livre de Poche, 2012.
Hugo, Victor. *Notre-Dame de Paris*. Translated by John Sturrock. Harmondsworth, England: Penguin, 1978.
Mignola, Mike, with John Byrne. *Hellboy*. Vol. 1, *The Seed of Destruction*. Milwaukie, OR: Dark Horse, 2003.
Mignola, Mike. *Hellboy*. Vol. 2, *Wake the Devil*. Milwaukie, OR: Dark Horse, 2003.
Mignola, Mike. *Hellboy*. Vol. 3, *The Chained Coffin and Other Stories*. Milwaukie, OR: Dark Horse, 2004.
Mignola, Mike. *Hellboy*. Vol. 4, *The Right Hand of Doom*. Milwaukie, OR: Dark Horse, 2003.
Mignola, Mike. *Hellboy*. Vol. 5, *Conqueror Worm*. Milwaukie, OR: Dark Horse, 2003.
Mignola, Mike. *Hellboy*. Vol. 6, *Strange Places*. Milwaukie, OR: Dark Horse, 2006.
Mignola, Mike, with Richard Corben and P. Craig Russell. *Hellboy*. Vol. 7, *The Troll Witch and Other Stories*. Milwaukie, OR: Dark Horse, 2007.
Mignola, Mike, with Duncan Fegredo. *Hellboy*. Vol. 8, *Darkness Calls*. Milwaukie, OR: Dark Horse, 2007.
Mignola, Mike, with Duncan Fegredo. *Hellboy*. Vol. 9, *The Wild Hunt*. Milwaukie, OR: Dark Horse, 2010.
Mignola, Mike, with Jason Shawn Alexander, Richard Corben, Joshua Dysart, and Duncan Fegredo. *Hellboy*. Vol. 10, *The Crooked Man and Others*. Milwaukie, OR: Dark Horse, 2010.
Mignola, Mike, with Richard Corben, Kevin Nowlan, and Scott Hampton. *Hellboy*. Vol. 11, *The Bride of Hell and Others*. Milwaukie, OR: Dark Horse, 2011.

Mignola, Mike, with Duncan Fegredo. *Hellboy*. Vol. 12, *The Storm and the Fury*. Milwaukie, OR: Dark Horse, 2010.
Mignola, Mike, with Duncan Fegredo and Dave Stewart. *Hellboy: The Midnight Circus*. Milwaukie, OR: Dark Horse, 2013.
Moore, Alan, with Stephen Bissette and John Totleben. *The Saga of the Swamp Thing*, book 1. New York: Vertigo, 2012.
Moore, Alan, with Stephen Bissette and John Totleben. *The Saga of the Swamp Thing*, book 2. New York: Vertigo, 2012.
Moore, Alan, with Stephen Bissette and John Totleben. *The Saga of the Swamp Thing*, book 3. New York: Vertigo, 2013.
Moore, Alan, with Stephen Bissette, John Totleben, and Stan Woch. *The Saga of the Swamp Thing*, book 4. New York: Vertigo, 2013.
Moore, Alan, with Alfredo Alcala, John Totleben, and Rick Veitch. *The Saga of the Swamp Thing*, book 5. New York: Vertigo, 2013.
Moore, Alan, with Alfredo Alcala, John Totleben, and Rick Veitch. *The Saga of the Swamp Thing*, book 6. New York: Vertigo, 2011.
Moore, Allen, and Brian Bolland. *Batman: The Killing Joke*. New York: DC Comics, 2008.
Morrison, Grant, and Dave McKean. *Arkham Asylum: A Serious House on Serious Earth*. New York: DC Comics, 1989.
O'Barr, James. *The Crow*. Northampton, MA: Kitchen Sink Press, 1994.
Shakespeare, William. *The Arden Shakespeare Complete Works*. Edited by Ann Thompson, David Scott Kastan, and Richard Proudfoot. London: Bloomsbury, 2002.
Shelley, Mary. *Frankenstein; or, The Modern Prometheus*. Boston: Sever, Francis and Company, 1869.
Wein, Len, Bernie Wrightson, and Nestor Redondo. *Roots of the Swamp Thing*. New York: DC Comics, 2011.
Wrightson, Bernie. *Creepy Presents Bernie Wrightson: The Definitive Collection of the Artist's Work from* Creepy *and* Eerie! Milwaukie, OR: Dark Horse, 2011.

SECONDARY SOURCES

Adorno, Theodor. *Minima Moralia: Reflections on a Damaged Life*. Translated by E. F. N. Jephcott. London: Verso, 2005.
Ahmed, Maaheen. "Collages in Comics: The Case of Dave McKean." In *The Cultural Standing of Comics / Le statut culturel de la BD*, edited by Maaheen Ahmed, Stéphanie Delneste, and Jean-Louis Tilleuil, 53–74. Louvain-la-Neuve, Belgium: Academia/Éditions L'Harmattan, 2017.
Ahmed, Maaheen. "Comics and Authorship: An Introduction." *Authorship* 6, no. 2 (2017): 1–13. Available at http://www.authorship.ugent.be/article/view/7702/7658. Retrieved January 1, 2018.
Ahmed, Maaheen. "State Protection and Identification in *Hellboy*: Of Reformed Devils and Other Others in the Pentagon." *European Journal of American Studies* 10, no. 2 (2015). Available at https://ejas.revues.org/10938. Retrieved October 16, 2017.
Ancet, Pierre. *Phénoménologie des corps monstrueux*. Paris: Presses Universitaires de France, 2006.

Appadurai, Arjun. *Modernity at Large: Cultural Dimensions of Globalization*. Minneapolis: University of Minnesota Press, 1996.

Ardenne, Paul. *L'image corps: Figures de l'humaine dans l'art du XXe siècle*. Paris: Éditions du Regard, 2001.

Artaud, Antonin. *Selected Writings*. Edited by Susan Sontag. Berkeley: University of California Press, 1992.

Asma, Stephen T. *On Monsters: An Unnatural History of Our Worst Fears*. New York: Oxford University Press, 2009.

Baetens, Jan. "L'animal et l'humain dans le 'roman graphique' contemporain." In *Corps et technologies: Penser l'hybridité*, edited by Nathalie Grandjean and Claire Lobet-Maris, 177–92. Brussels: Peter Lang, 2013.

Baetens, Jan, and Hugo Frey. *The Graphic Novel: An Introduction*. New York: Cambridge University Press, 2014.

Barfield, Owen. *Saving the Appearances: A Study in Idolatry*. Middletown, CT: Wesleyan University Press, 1957.

Barroux, Gilles. "Quels éléments d'anthropologie et de pensée médicale s'expriment dans la figure du 'monstre' au XVIIIe siècle?" *Lo Sguardo*, no. 9 (2012): 119–35.

Baudelaire, Charles. *Écrits sur l'art*. Paris: Le Livre de Poche, 1992.

Baudelaire, Charles. *Mon cœur mis à nu*. Geneva: Droz, 2001.

Baudin, Henri, ed. *Circé 6, "Le monstre 3: Les monstres dans la science-fiction."* Paris: Éditions Lettres Modernes, 1976.

Beaty, Bart. *Comics versus Art*. Toronto: University of Toronto Press, 2012.

Beineke, Colin. "'Her Guardiner': Alan Moore's Swamp Thing as the Green Man." *ImageText* 5, no. 4 (2010). Available at http://www.english.ufl.edu/imagetext/archives/v5_4/beineke/. Retrieved March 2, 2015.

Belting, Hans. *An Anthropology of Images: Picture, Medium, Body*. Translated by Thomas Dunlap. Princeton, NJ: Princeton University Press, 2011.

Berlin, Isaiah. *The Roots of Romanticism*. Princeton, NJ: Princeton University Press, 1999.

Berman, Marshall. *All That Is Solid Melts into Air: The Experience of Modernity*. New York: Penguin, 1982.

Bertrand, Régis, and Anne Carol, eds. *Le "monstre" humain, imaginaire et société*. Aix-en-Provence, France: Presses Universitaires de Provence, 2005.

Bibby, Michael. "Atrocity Exhibitions: Joy Division, Factory Records, and Goth Style." In *Goth: Undead Culture*, edited by Michael Bibby and Lauren M. E. Goodlad, 233–56. Durham, NC: Duke University Press, 2007.

Bibby, Michael, and Lauren M. E. Goodlad, eds. *Goth: Undead Culture*. Durham, NC: Duke University Press, 2007.

Blake, Brandy Ball, and L. Andrew Cooper. *Monsters*. Southlake, TX: Fountain Head Press, 2012.

Bloom, Harold. "The Internalization of Quest-Romance." In *Romanticism and Consciousness: Essays in Criticism*, edited by Harold Bloom, 3–24. New York: W. W. Norton, 1970.

Bloom, Harold. "Nature and Consciousness." In *Romanticism and Consciousness: Essays in Criticism*, edited by Harold Bloom, 1–2. New York: W. W. Norton, 1970.

Bloom, Harold, ed. *Romanticism and Consciousness: Essays in Criticism*. New York: W. W. Norton, 1970.

Bloom, Michelle E. "Pygmalionesque Delusions and Illusions of Movement: Animation from Hoffmann to Truffaut." *Comparative Literature* 52, no. 4 (2000), 291–320.
Blunt, Anthony. "Blake's 'Ancient of Days': The Symbolism of the Compasses." *Journal of the Warburg Institute* 2, no. 1 (1938): 53–63.
Bolter, Jay David, and Richard Grusin. *Remediation: Understanding New Media*. Cambridge, MA: MIT Press, 2000.
Bordes, Juan. "Goya, chroniquer de toutes les guerres: *Les Désastres* et la photographie de guerre." In *Goya cronista de todas las guerras: Los Desastres y la fotografía de guerra*, edited by Juan Bordes and Enrique Bordes, 80–90. Madrid: Instituto Cervantes, 2012.
Botting, Fred. *Gothic Romanced: Consumption, Gender and Technologies in Contemporary Fictions*. Milton Park, Abingdon, England: Routledge, 2008.
Botting, Fred, and Catherine Spooner, eds. *Monstrous Media/Spectral Subjects: Imaging Gothic from the Nineteenth Century to the Present*. Manchester: Manchester University Press, 2017.
Boym, Svetlana. *The Future of Nostalgia*. New York: Basic Books, 2002.
Boym, Svetlana. "Nostalgia and Its Discontents." *Hedgehog Review* 9, no. 2 (Summer 2007): 7–18.
Brooker, Will. *Batman Unmasked: Analyzing a Cultural Icon*. London: Bloomsbury, 2001.
Brower, Steven. "Jack Kirby's Collages in Context." *Print*, April 17, 2012. Available at http://www.printmag.com/illustration/jack-kirbys-collages-in-context/. Retrieved October 18, 2017.
Bukatman, Scott. *Hellboy's World: Comics and Monsters on the Margins*. Berkeley: University of California Press, 2016.
Bukatman, Scott. *The Poetics of Slumberland: Animated Spirits and the Animating Spirit*. Berkeley: University of California Press, 2012.
Bukatman, Scott. "Sculpture, Stasis, the Comics, and Hellboy." *Critical Inquiry* 40, no. 3 (2014): 104–17.
Burgos, Jean, ed. *Circé* 4, "Le monstre 1: Présence du monstre, mythe et réalité." Paris: Éditions Lettres Modernes, 1975.
Burgos, Jean, ed. *Circé* 5, "Le monstre 2: Les monstres dans la Divine Comédie." Paris: Éditions Lettres Modernes, 1975.
Burgos, Jean. "Le monstre, même et autre." In *Circé* 4, "Le monstre 1: Présence du monstre, mythe et réalité," edited by Jean Burgos, 11–24. Paris: Éditions Lettres Modernes, 1975.
Burke, Edmund. *A Philosophical Enquiry into the Origin of Our Ideas of the Sublime and Beautiful*. Edited by James T. Boulton. London: Routledge and Kegan Paul; New York: Columbia University Press, 1958.
Caiozzo, Anna, and Anne-Emmanuelle Demartini, eds. *Monstre et imaginaire social: Approches historiques*. Paris: Créaphis, 2008.
Campmas, Aude. "La monstruosité cachée: Huysmans et les hybrides artificiels." *Fabula: La Recherche en Littérature*, Séminaire "Signe, déchiffrement, et interprétation," January 11, 2008. Available at http://www.fabula.org/colloques/document869.php. Retrieved August 20, 2014.
Canguilhem, Georges. "Monstrosity and the Monstrous." *Diogenes* 10, no. 40 (1962): 27–42.
Castoriadis, Cornelius. *The Imaginary Institution of Society*. Translated by Kathleen Blamey. Cambridge: Polity Press, 1987.
Cellier, Léon. "Les rêves de Dieu." In *Circé* 4, "Le monstre 1: Présence du monstre, mythe et réalité," edited by Jean Burgos, 83–86. Paris: Éditions Lettres Modernes, 1975.
Chao, Shun-Liang. *Rethinking the Concept of the Grotesque: Crashaw, Baudelaire, Magritte*. London: Legenda, 2000.

Chute, Hillary L. *Disaster Drawn: Visual Witness, Comics, and Documentary Form.* Cambridge, MA: Belknap Press, 2016.
Cohen, Jeffrey Jerome. "Monster Culture: Seven Theses." In *Monster Theory: Reading Culture,* edited by Jeffrey Jerome Cohen, 3–25. Minneapolis: University of Minnesota Press, 1996.
Cohen, Jeffrey Jerome, ed. *Monster Theory: Reading Culture.* Minneapolis: University of Minnesota Press, 1996.
Creed, Barbara. *The Monstrous-Feminine: Film, Feminism and Psychoanalysis.* London: Routledge, 1993.
Curtis, Deborah. *Touching from a Distance: Ian Curtis and Joy Division.* London: Faber and Faber, 2007.
Curtis, Ian. *So This Is Permanence: Joy Division Lyrics and Notebooks.* Edited by Deborah Curtis and Jon Savage. London: Faber and Faber, 2014.
Davidson, Arnold I. Introduction to *Abnormal: Lectures at the Collège de France, 1974–1975,* by Michel Foucault, xvii–xxvi. London: Verso, 2003.
Debord, Guy. *La société du spectacle.* Paris: Gallimard, 1992.
Debord, Guy. *Society of the Spectacle.* Translated by Donald Nicholson-Smith. New York: Zone Books, 1995.
De Bruyn, Ben. "The Anthropological Criticism of Wolfgang Iser and Hans Belting." *Image [&] Narrative,* no. 15 (2006). Available at http://www.imageandnarrative.be/inarchive/iconoclasm/debruyn.htm. Retrieved September 5, 2014.
Derrida, Jacques. "La main de Heidegger: Geschlecht II." In *Heidegger et la question: De l'esprit et autres essais,* 175–222. Paris: Flammarion, 2010.
Despoix, Philippe, and Yvonne Spielmann. "Présentation." *Intermédialités* 6, "Remédier/Remediation" (2006): 9–11.
Devos, E. Virginia, ed. *Exploring Affect: The Selected Writings of Silvan S. Tomkins.* Cambridge: Cambridge University Press, 1995.
Diamond, Aidan, and Lauranne Poharec. "Introduction." *Journal of Graphic Novels and Comics* 8, no. 5, "Freaked and Othered Bodies" (2017): 402–16.
Didi-Huberman, Georges. "Échantillonner le chaos: Aby Warburg et l'atlas photographique de la Grande Guerre." *Études photographiques,* no. 27 (2011). Available at https://etudesphotographiques.revues.org/3173. Retrieved January 9, 2016.
Dony, Christophe. "The Rewriting Ethos of the Vertigo Imprint: Critical Perspectives on Memory-Making and Canon Formation in the American Comics Field." *Comicalités,* 2014. Available at http://comicalites.revues.org/1918. Retrieved August 11, 2015.
Drucker, Johanna. *Sweet Dreams: Contemporary Art and Complicity.* Chicago: University of Chicago Press, 2005.
Dupont, Jacques. Introduction to *Les Fleurs du mal,* by Charles Baudelaire, 7–49. Paris: Flammarion, 1991.
Durand, Gilbert. *Les Structures anthropologiques de l'imaginaire: Introduction à l'archétypologie générale.* Paris: Dunod, 1992.
Eco, Umberto. "Le mythe de Superman." *Communications* 24, no. 1 (1976): 24–40.
Ellison, Julie. "Imagination." In *A Handbook of Romanticism Studies,* edited by Joel Faflak and Julia M. Wright, 37–53. Malden, MA: Wiley-Blackwell, 2012.

Fabre, Côme, and Felix Krämer, eds. *L'ange du bizarre: Le romantisme noir de Goya à Max Ernst*. Paris: Musée d'Orsay; Ostfilern, Germany: Hatje Cantz, 2013.

Faflak, Joel, and Richard C. Sha. "Introduction: Feeling Romantic." In *Romanticism and the Emotions*, edited by Joel Faflak and Richard C. Sha, 1–18. Cambridge: Cambridge University Press, 2014.

Faflak, Joel, and Richard C. Sha, eds. *Romanticism and the Emotions*. Cambridge: Cambridge University Press, 2014.

Faflak, Joel, and Julia M. Wright, eds. *A Handbook of Romanticism Studies*. Malden, MA: Wiley-Blackwell, 2012.

Favret, Mary. "The Study of Affect and Romanticism." *Literature Compass* 6, no. 6 (2009): 1159–66.

Feder, Lillian. *Madness in Literature*. Princeton, NJ: Princeton University Press, 1980.

Fisher, Mark. "No Longer the Pleasures: Joy Division." In *Ghosts of My Life: Writings on Depression, Hauntology and Lost Futures*, 32–39. London: Zero Books, 2004.

Foucault, Michel. *Abnormal: Lectures at the Collège de France, 1974–1975*. Translated by Graham Burchell. London: Verso, 2003.

Foucault, Michel. *The Order of Things: An Archaeology of Human Sciences*. New York: Vintage, 1994.

Fowlie, Wallace. *Rimbaud and Jim Morrison: The Rebel as Poet*. Durham, NC: Duke University Press, 1994.

Franke, Anselm. "Death and Life of Fiction or the Modern Taowu." Taipei Biennial 2012. Available at http://www.taipeibiennial.org/2012/en/death_and_life_anselm_franke.pdf. Retrieved August 18, 2014.

Fresnault-Deruelle, Pierre. "Entre l'ersatz et le simulacre: La bande dessinée." *Cahiers du 20e siècle*, no. 6 (1976): 139–53.

Friedman, John Block. Foreword to *The Ashgate Research Companion to Monsters and the Monstrous*, edited by Asa Simon Mittman with Peter J. Dendle, xxv–xxxix. Farnham, Surrey, England: Ashgate, 2013.

Frye, Northrop. *Fearful Symmetry: A Study of William Blake*. Princeton, NJ: Princeton University Press, 1990.

Frye, Northrop. "The Keys to the Gates." In *Romanticism and Consciousness: Essays in Criticism*, edited by Harold Bloom, 233–54. New York: W. W. Norton, 1970.

Frye, Northrop. *A Study of English Romanticism*. New York: Random House, 1968.

Gabilliet, Jean-Paul. *Of Comics and Men: A Cultural History of American Comic Books*. Jackson: University Press of Mississippi, 2010.

Gardner, Jared. "Archives, Collectors, and the New Media Work of Comics." *Modern Fiction Studies* 52, no. 4 (2006): 787–806.

Gardner, Jared. *Projections: Comics and the History of Twenty-First-Century Storytelling*. Stanford, CA: Stanford University Press, 2012.

Garland Thomson, Rosemarie. "Introduction: From Wonder to Error; A Genealogy of Freak Discourse in Modernity." In *Freakery: Cultural Spectacles of the Extraordinary Body*, edited by Rosemarie Garland Thomson, 1–19. New York: New York University Press, 1996.

Goodlad, Lauren M. E. "Men in Black: Androgyny and Ethics in The Crow and Fight Club." In *Goth: Undead Culture*, edited by Michael Bibby and Lauren M. E. Goodlad, 89–118. Durham, NC: Duke University Press, 2007.

Grandjean, Nathalie. Introduction to *Corps et technologies: Penser l'hybridité*, edited by Nathalie Grandjean and Claire Lobet-Maris, 9–16. Brussels: Peter Lang, 2013.

Grandjean, Nathalie, and Claire Lobet-Maris, eds. *Corps et technologies: Penser l'hybridité*. Brussels: Peter Lang, 2013.

Gravett, Paul. "Enki Bilal: Haunted by the Future." Available at http://www.paulgravett.com/index.php/articles/article/enki_bilal1. Retrieved August 17, 2014.

Groensteen, Thierry. "The Art of Braiding: A Clarification." *European Comic Art* 9, no. 1 (2016): 88–98.

Groensteen, Thierry. *Un objet culturel non identifié: La bande dessinée*. Angoulême, France: Éditions de l'An 2, 2006.

Groth, Gary. "The Alan Moore Interview." *Comics Journal*, no. 118 (2012). Available at http://www.tcj.com/the-alan-moore-interview-118/. Retrieved October 7, 2018.

Grusin, Richard A. "Premediation." *Criticism* 46, no. 1 (2004): 17–39.

Guidi, Simone, and Antonio Lucci, eds. "Spazi del mostruoso: Luoghi filosofici della mostruosità / Spaces of the Monstrous: Philosophical Topics about Monstrosity." *Lo Sguardo*, no. 9 (2012). Available at http://www.losguardo.net/public/archivio/arch_09.html. Retrieved February 21, 2014.

Gumbrecht, Hans Ulrich. *Production of Presence: What Meaning Cannot Convey*. Stanford, CA: Stanford University Press, 2003.

Gunning, Tom. "Fantasmagorie et fabrication de l'illusion: Pour une culture optique du dispositif cinématographique." *Cinémas: Revue d'Études Cinématographiques* 14, no. 1 (2003): 67–89.

Halberstam, Judith. *Skin Shows: Gothic Horror and the Technology of Monsters*. Durham, NC: Duke University Press, 1995.

Hanafi, Zakiya. *The Monster in the Machine: Magic, Medicine, and the Marvelous in the Time of the Scientific Revolution*. Durham, NC: Duke University Press, 2000.

Haraway, Donna. "The Promises of Monsters: A Regenerative Politics for Inappropriate/d Others." In *Cultural Studies*, edited by Lawrence Grossberg, Cary Nelson, and Paula A. Treichler, 295–337. London: Routledge, 1992.

Hassan, Ihab. "Toward a Concept of Postmodernism." In *The Postmodern Turn: Essays in Postmodern Theory and Culture*, 84–96. Columbus: Ohio State University Press, 1987.

Hatfield, Charles. *Hand of Fire: The Comics Art of Jack Kirby*. Jackson: University Press of Mississippi, 2012.

Hayot, Eric. *On Literary Worlds*. Oxford: Oxford University Press, 2012.

Haywood, Ian, and John Halliwell. "Romantic Spectacle: An Introduction." *Romanticism on the Net*, no. 46, "Romantic Spectacle" (2007). Available at http://www.erudit.org/revue/ron/2007/v/n46/index.html. Retrieved September 5, 2014.

Hebdige, Dick. *Subculture: The Meaning of Style*. London: Routledge, 2002.

Herrmann, Leonhard. "Friedrich Schiller (1759–1805), *Über die ästhetische Erziehung des Menschen in einer Reihe von Briefen* (1795)." *KulturPoetik* 10, no. 1 (2010): 99–107.

Hodkinson, Paul. "Gothic Music and Subculture." In *The Routledge Companion to Gothic*, edited by Catherine Spooner and Emma McEvoy, 260–69. London: Routledge, 2007.

Hollander, Anne. *Moving Pictures*. New York: Alfred A. Knopf, 1989.

Hong, James T., and Anselm Franke. "The Museum of the Monster That Is History." Taipei Biennial 2012. Available at http://www.taipeibiennial.org/2012/en/participants/the_museum_of_the_monster_that_is_history/index.html. Retrieved August 23, 2014.

Huet, Marie-Hélène. *Monstrous Imagination*. Cambridge, MA: Harvard University Press, 1993.

Huhtamo, Erkki. *Illusions in Motion: Media Archaeology of the Moving Panorama and Related Spectacles*. Cambridge, MA: MIT Press, 2013.

Ingebretsen, Edward J. *At Stake: Monsters and the Rhetoric of Fear in Public Culture*. Chicago: University of Chicago Press, 2001.

Iser, Wolfgang. *The Fictive and the Imaginary: Charting Literary Anthropology*. Baltimore: Johns Hopkins University Press, 1993.

Jain, Sarah S. "The Prosthetic Imagination: Enabling and Disabling the Prosthesis Trope." *Science, Technology, and Human Values* 24, no. 1 (1999): 31–54.

Jameson, Fredric. "The Cultural Logic of Late Capitalism." In *Postmodernism; or, The Cultural Logic of Late Capitalism*, 1–54. Durham, NC: Duke University Press, 1991.

Jung, Carl. "On the Psychology of the Trickster Figure." In *The Trickster: A Study in American Indian Mythology*, by Paul Radin, 195–211. New York: Schocken Books, 1972.

Jürgens, Anna-Sophie. "Batman's Joker, a Neo-Modern Clown of Violence." *Journal of Graphic Novels and Comics* 5, no. 1 (2014): 441–54.

Kearney, Richard. *Strangers, Gods and Monsters: Interpreting Otherness*. London: Routledge, 2003.

Kermode, Frank. *Romantic Image*. London: Routledge and Kegan Paul, 1966.

Køhlert, Frederik Byrn, and Ole Birk Laursen, eds. "Rebel Lines: Comics and the Anarchist Imagination." Special issue, *SubStance* 46, no. 3 (2017).

Krämer, Felix. "Le romanticisme noir: Une approche." In *L'ange du bizarre: Le romantisme noir de Goya à Max Ernst*, edited by Côme Fabre and Felix Krämer, 27–38. Paris: Musée d'Orsay; Ostfildern, Germany: Hatje Cantz, 2013.

Kukkonen, Karin. "Comics as a Test Case for Transmedial Narratology." *SubStance* 40, no. 1 (2011): 34–52.

Kukkonen, Karin. "Popular Cultural Memory: Comics, Communities and Context Knowledge." *Nordicom Review* 29, no. 2 (2008): 261–73.

Kunzle, David. *History of the Comic Strip*. Vol. 2, *The Nineteenth Century*. Berkeley: University of California Press, 1973.

Le Brun, Annie. "La révolution, la nuit." In *L'ange du bizarre: Le romantisme noir de Goya à Max Ernst*, edited by Côme Fabre and Felix Krämer, 15–26. Paris: Musée d'Orsay; Ostfildern, Germany: Hatje Cantz, 2013.

Lévi-Strauss, Claude. *The Savage Mind*. London: Weidenfeld and Nicolson, 1966.

López de Munain Iturrospe, Gorka. "Los Caprichos de Goya: Estampas y textos contra el sueño de la razón." *Revista Sans Soleil: Estudios de la Imagen* 2 (2011): 79–101. Available at http://revista-sanssoleil.com/wp-content/uploads/2011/04/caprichos_goya.pdf.

Lubbock, Tom. "De Ribera, Jusepe: The Boy with the Club Foot (1642)." *Independent*, March 14, 2008. Available at http://www.independent.co.uk/arts-entertainment/art/great-works/de-ribera-jusepe-the-boy-with-the-club-foot-1642-795447.html. Retrieved July 5, 2016.

Luckhurst, Roger. *The Trauma Question*. New York: Routledge, 2008.

Malcolm, James Peller. *An Historical Sketch of the Art of Caricaturing*. London: Longman, Hurst, Rees, Orme and Brown, 1813.

Manuel, Didier, ed. *La figure du monstre: Phénoménologie de la monstruosité dans l'imaginaire contemporain*. Nancy, France: Presses Universitaires de Nancy, 2009.

Martinez, Aurélie. *Images du corps monstrueux*. Paris: Éditions L'Harmattan, 2011.

Mathias, Paul. "Un monstre délicat." In *Circé* 4, "Le monstre 1: Présence du monstre, mythe et réalité," edited by Jean Burgos, 69–82. Paris: Éditions Lettres Modernes, 1975.

Matlock, Jann. "Optique-Monde." *Romantisme* 2, no. 136 (2007): 39–53.

Mattozzi, Alvise. "Innovating Superheroes." *Reconstruction* 3, no. 2 (2003). Available at http://reconstruction.eserver.org/Issues/032/mattozzi.htm. Retrieved February 5, 2015.

McEvoy, Emma. "Gothic and the Romantics." In *The Routledge Companion to Gothic*, edited by Catherine Spooner and Emma McEvoy, 19–28. London: Routledge, 2007.

McFarland, Thomas. *Romanticism and the Forms of Ruin: Wordsworth, Coleridge, and the Modalities of Fragmentation*. Princeton, NJ: Princeton University Press, 1981.

McGann, Jerome J. *The Romantic Ideology: A Critical Investigation*. Chicago: University of Chicago Press, 1983.

Mikkonen, Kai. "The Paradox of Intersemiotic Translation and the Comic Book: Examples from Enki Bilal's *Nikopol* Trilogy." *Word and Image* 22, no. 2 (2006): 101–17.

Mitchell, W. J. T. *Picture Theory: Essays on Verbal and Visual Representation*. Chicago: University of Chicago Press, 1994.

Mittman, Asa Simon. "Introduction: The Impact of Monsters and Monster Studies." In *The Ashgate Research Companion to Monsters and the Monstrous*, edited by Asa Simon Mittman with Peter J. Dendle, 1–14. Farnham, Surrey, England: Ashgate, 2013.

Mittman, Asa Simon, with Peter J. Dendle, eds. *The Ashgate Research Companion to Monsters and the Monstrous*. Farnham, Surrey, England: Ashgate, 2013.

Moore, Alan. Introduction to *Hellboy*, vol. 2, *Wake the Devil*, by Mike Mignola. Milwaukie, OR: Dark Horse, 2003.

Morrison, Grant. *Supergods: Our World in the Age of the Superhero*. London: Vintage, 2012.

Morrison, Jim. "Prologue: Self-Interview." In *The Lost Writings of Jim Morrison*. Vol. 1, *Wilderness*, 1–3. London: Vintage, 1989.

Munier, Brigitte. "La monstruosité du Golem, figure tutélaire de la modernité occidentale." *Lo Sguardo*, no. 9 (2012): 219–38.

Murray, Christopher. "Subverting the Sublime: Romantic Ideology in the Comics of Grant Morrison." In *Sub/versions: Cultural Status, Genre and Critique*, edited by Pauline MacPherson, Christopher Murray, Gordon Spark, and Kevin Corstorphine, 34–51. Newcastle upon Tyne: Cambridge Scholars Publishing, 2008.

Nancy, Jean-Luc. "Exscription." *Yale French Studies*, no. 78 (1990): 47–65.

Nietzsche, Friedrich. *Beyond Good and Evil: Prelude to a Philosophy of the Future*. Edited by Rolf-Peter Horstmann. Translated by Judith Norman. Cambridge: Cambridge University Press, 2003.

O'Barr, James. "Interview with James O'Barr." *KAOS2000 Magazine*, July 20, 2000. Available at http://www.kaos2000.net/interviews/jamesobarr/. Retrieved November 28, 2014.

Ochsner, Beate. *DeMONSRAtion: Zur Repräsentation des Monsters und des Monströsen in Literatur, Fotografie und Film*. Heidelberg: Synchron, 2010.

O'Connor, Laura. "The Corpse on Hellboy's Back: Translating a Graphic Image." *Journal of Popular Culture* 43, no. 3 (2010): 540–63.

Paré, Ambroise. *Des monstres et prodiges*. Introduction and commentary by Jean Céard. Geneva: Droz, 1971.

Peckham, Morse. "Toward a Theory of Romanticism: II. Reconsiderations." *Studies in Romanticism* 1, no. 1 (1961): 1–8.

Peeters, Benoît. *Case, planche, récit: Lire la bande dessinée.* Brussels: Casterman, 1998.
Pfau, Thomas. *Romantic Moods: Paranoia, Trauma, and Melancholy, 1790–1840.* Baltimore: John Hopkins University Press, 2005.
Pizzino, Christopher. *Arresting Development: Comics at the Boundaries of Literature.* Austin: University of Texas Press, 2016.
Praz, Mario. *La chair, la mort et le diable: Le romantisme noir.* Translated by Constance Thompson Pasquali. Paris: Gallimard, 2013.
Praz, Mario. *Romantic Agony.* Translated by Angus Davidson. Oxford: Oxford University Press, 1951.
Price, Martin. "The Standard of Energy." In *Romanticism and Consciousness: Essays in Criticism,* edited by Harold Bloom, 255–73. New York: W. W. Norton, 1970.
Radin, Paul. *The Trickster: A Study in American Indian Mythology.* New York: Schocken Books, 1972.
Rauber, D. F. "The Fragment as Romantic Form." *Modern Language Quarterly* 30, no. 2 (1969): 212–21.
Regier, Alexander. *Fracture and Fragmentation in British Romanticism.* Cambridge: Cambridge University Press, 2010.
Reinfandt, Christoph. *Romantische Kommunikation: Zur Kontinuität der Romantik in der Kultur der Moderne.* Heidelberg: Winter Verlag, 2003.
Reynolds, Richards. *Super Heroes: A Modern Mythology.* Jackson: University Press of Mississippi, 1992.
Reynolds, Simon. *Rip It Up and Start Again: Postpunk, 1978–1984.* London: Faber and Faber, 2006.
Round, Julia. *Gothic in Comics and Graphic Novels: A Critical Approach.* Jefferson, NC: McFarland, 2014.
Round, Julia. "Mutilation and Monsters: Transcending the Human in Garth Ennis/Steve Dillon's *Preacher.*" In *The Human Body in Contemporary Literatures in English,* edited by Sabine Coelsch-Foisner and Marta Fernández Morales, 109–28. Frankfurt: Peter Lang, 2009.
Santorius, Nerina. "Les fils du Satan: L'héritage de la déraison dans le romantisme français." In *L'Ange du bizarre: Le romantisme noir de Goya à Max Ernst,* edited by Côme Fabre and Felix Krämer, 101–28. Paris: Musée d'Orsay; Ostfildern, Germany: Hatje Cantz, 2013.
Sepulchre, Sarah. "Super-corps, super-technologie, super-monstre: Hulk ou l'inquiétante mise en garde." In *Corps et technologies: Penser l'hybridité,* edited by Nathalie Grandjean and Claire Lobet-Maris, 155–76. Brussels: Peter Lang, 2013.
Sha, Richard C. "Imagination." In *A Handbook of Romanticism Studies,* edited by Joel Faflak and Julia M. Wright, 19–36. Malden, MA: Wiley-Blackwell, 2012.
Shaeffer, Katherine, and Spencer Chalifour, eds. "Forum: Monsters in the Margins." *ImageText* 8, no. 1 (2015).
Shildrick, Margrit. *Embodying the Monster: Encounters with the Vulnerable Self.* London: Sage, 2002.
Six, Abigail Lee, and Hannah Thompson. "From Hideous to Hedonist: The Changing Face of the Nineteenth-Century Monster." In *The Ashgate Research Companion to Monsters and the Monstrous,* edited by Asa Simon Mittman with Peter J. Dendle, 237–55. Farnham, Surrey, England: Ashgate, 2013.

Smolderen, Thierry. "Histoire de la bande dessinée: questions de la méthodologie." In *La bande dessinée: Une médiaculture*, edited by Éric Maigret and Matteo Stefanelli, 71–90. Paris: Armand Colin, 2012.

Smolderen, Thierry. *Naissances de la bande dessinée: De William Hogarth à Winsor McCay*. Brussels: Les Impressions Nouvelles, 2009.

Sobchack, Vivian. *Carnal Thoughts: Embodiment and Moving Image Culture*. Berkeley: University of California Press, 2004.

Sorin, Etienne. "Exposition 'La Ville Dessinée' à La Cité d'Architecture et du Patrimoine: Planches de Cité." *Le Figaro*, June 8, 2010. Available at http://www.evene.fr/arts/actualite/architecture-bande-dessinee-bd-cite-patrimoine-2760.php. Retrieved August 12, 2014.

Spooner, Catherine. *Contemporary Gothic*. London: Reaktion, 2006.

Spooner, Catherine. *Post-Millennial Gothic: Comedy, Romance and the Rise of Happy Gothic*. London: Bloomsbury, 2017.

Spooner Catherine, and Emma McEvoy, eds. *The Routledge Companion to Gothic*. London: Routledge, 2007.

Stryker, Susan. "My Words to Victor Frankenstein above the Village of Chamounix: Performing Transgender Rage." In *The Transgender Studies Reader*, edited by Susan Stryker and Stephen Whittle, 244–56. London: Routledge, 2006.

Sullivan, Nikki. "Transmogrification: (Un)Becoming Other(s)." In *The Transgender Studies Reader*, edited by Susan Stryker and Stephen Whittle, 552–64. London: Routledge, 2006.

Thurston, Alan J. "Paré and Prosthetics: The Early History of Artificial Limbs." *ANZ Journal of Surgery* 77, no. 12 (2007): 1114–19.

Todd, Dennis. *Imagining Monsters: Miscreations of the Self in Eighteenth-Century England*. Chicago: University of Chicago Press, 1995.

Tomkins, Silvan. "Modifications in the Theory: 1978." In *Exploring Affect: The Selected Writings of Silvan S. Tomkins*, edited by E. Virginia Devos, 86–96. Cambridge: Cambridge University Press, 1995.

Tresch, John. *The Romantic Machine: Utopian Science and Technology after Napoleon*. Chicago: University of Chicago Press, 2014.

Ueckmann, Natascha. "Hybride Kreaturen im modernen französischen Comic: Enki Bilal." In *Der automatisierte Körper: Literarische Visionen des künstlichen Menschen vom Mittelalter bis zum 21. Jahrhundert*, edited by Cerstin Bauer-Funke and Gisela Febel, 291–320. Berlin: Weidler, 2005.

Updike, John. "The Mystery of Mickey Mouse." In *The Best American Essays*, edited by Robert Atwan, 385–92. Boston: Houghton Mifflin, 1995.

Vallins, David. *Coleridge and the Psychology of Romanticism: Feeling and Thought*. New York: St. Martin's Press, 2000.

Varga, Áron Kibédi. "Criteria for Describing Word-and-Image Relations." *Poetics Today* 10, no. 1 (1989): 31–53.

Virilio, Paul. "Du surhomme à l'homme surexcité (1)." *Alliage*, nos. 20–21 (1994). Available at http://www.tribunes.com/tribune/alliage/20-21/viri.htm. Retrieved August 15, 2014.

Viscomi, Joseph. "Blake's Invention of Illuminated Printing, 1788." *BRANCH: Britain, Representation, and Nineteenth-Century History*, edited by Dino Franco Felluga. Available at http://www.branchcollective.org/?ps_articles=joseph-viscomi-blakes-invention-of-illuminated-printing-1788. Retrieved September 5, 2014.

Walton, Michael. *The Horror Comic Never Dies: A Grisly History*. Jefferson, NC: McFarland, 2019.

Walton, Saige. "Baroque Mutants in the 21st Century? Re-thinking Genre through the Superhero." In *The Contemporary Comic Book Superhero*, edited by Angela Ndalianis, 86–106. New York: Routledge, 2009.

Weiss, Allen S. "Ten Theses on Monsters and Monstrosity." *Drama Review* 48, no. 1 (2004): 124–25.

Westbrook, David. "From Hogan's Alley to Coconino County: Four Narratives of the Early Comic Strip." *American Quarterly*, 1999. Available at http://chnm.gmu.edu/aq/comics/softfr_w.html. Retrieved January 20, 2015.

Westphal, Bertrand. *Geocriticism: Real and Fictional Spaces*. Translated by Robert T. Tally Jr. New York: Palgrave Macmillan, 2011.

Whiting, Frederick. "Monstrosity on Trial: The Case of *Naked Lunch*." *Twentieth-Century Literature* 52 (2006): 145–74.

Whitson, Roger, and Donald Ault, eds. "William Blake and Visual Culture." Special issue, *ImageText* 3, no. 2 (2006). Available at http://www.english.ufl.edu/imagetext/archives/v3_2/. Retrieved, October 11, 2017.

Whitted, Qiana J. "Of Slaves and Other Swamp Things: Black Southern History as Comic Book Horror." In *Comics and the U.S. South*, edited by Brannon Costello and Qiana J. Whitted, 187–213. Jackson: University Press of Mississippi, 2012.

Willems, Philippe. "Rodolphe Töpffer and Romanticism." *Nineteenth-Century French Studies* 37, nos. 3–4 (2009): 227–46.

Williams, David. "Monsters, Then and Now." *Lo Sguardo*, no. 9 (2012): 239–58.

Wilson, James D. "Tirso, Molière and Byron: The Emergence of Don Juan as Romantic Hero." *South Central Bulletin* 32, no. 4 (1972): 246–48.

Worden, Daniel. "The Shameful Art: *McSweeney's Quarterly Concern*, Comics, and the Politics of Affect." *Modern Fiction Studies* 52, no. 4 (2006): 891–917.

Wright, Alexa. *Monstrosity: The Human Monster in Visual Culture*. London: I. B. Taurus, 2013.

INDEX

Abrams, M. H., 19–20
Adorno, Theodor, 181
Ainsworth, William Harrison, 49; *Jack Sheppard*, 49
Alcala, Alfredo, 66
Alice in Wonderland, 129
ambiguity: in *The Crow*, 144, 148, 149, 151, 158, 160–65; as romantic theme, 9–10, 15–16, 18, 43–44, 176–77, 181; in *Swamp Thing*, 61, 64, 68, 77–80. *See also* identity confusion
amorphousness, 96–97, 102, 103–5, 199n17
Ampère, Jean-Jacques, 8, 52
Ancet, Pierre, 41, 82
Andersen, Hans Christian, 118, 205n56
androgyny, 103, 107–8, 142, 155, 163
androids, 87
animation: and automatons, 50, 83, 95, 135, 167–68; as concept, 7–8; in *Frankenstein*, 41; in *Hellboy*, 115–16, 135–39; in *Monstre*, 87; in *My Favorite Thing Is Monsters*, 171; puppets and dolls, 8, 81–82, 138–39, 142, 167; in *Swamp Thing*, 58–60, 70, 81–84, 94; and transmogrification, 6, 91, 96–97, 101, 142
anthropomorphism, as concept, 7–8. *See also* ambiguity
Appadurai, Arjun, 10–11
Arendt, Hannah, 93
Arkham Asylum, 161
Artaud, Antonin, 143, 155; "Jardin noir," 155; "Van Gogh ou le suicidé de la société," 155
Asma, Stephen, 22, 38, 43–44

automatons, 50, 83, 95, 135, 167–68. *See also* animation

Bachelard, Gaston, 176, 177
Bacon, Francis, 77
Baker, Robert, 52
Ballard, J. G., 150
Barfield, Owen, 192n117
Barnum, P. T., 42
Bataille, Georges, 153–54
Baudelaire, Charles: aesthetic of, 19, 107, 156; compared to Hugo, 91; *Les Fleurs du mal*, 89–92, 107, 200n44; influence on *Monstre*, 85–86, 88–92; influence on the Cure, 211n81; Poe's influence on, 20, 23; on romanticism, 35, 43, 106
Baudin, Henri, 36, 63, 87, 104, 105, 177
Beaty, Bart, 118
Beddoes, Thomas Lovell, 20, 142–43; *Death's Jest-Book*, 20, 142–43
Beineke, Colin, 58
Belting, Hans, 11, 14, 60, 117, 157, 174
Bergin, John, 143
Berlin, Isaiah, 19, 89, 90, 168, 170, 187n76, 190n48
Bibby, Michael, 143, 147, 148
Bilal, Enki. See *Monstre* (Bilal)
Bilibin, Ivan, 123
Bissette, Steve, 17, 54, 55, 66
Blair, Robert, 138; "The Grave," 138
Blake, Brandy Ball, 183n2
Blake, William, 32–35; *America a Prophecy*, 33; amphibious monsters, 206n86; *The Ancient of Days*, 151; cosmology, 18,

228

32–34, 151; *Europe a Prophecy*, 35, 151; *The Ghost of a Flea*, 34, 35, 206n86; Goya's influence on, 24; "London," 66, 99; *The Marriage of Heaven and Hell*, 168; nature in works of, 34–35, 62; *Newton*, 151; poetry, 66, 99; rebelliousness, 23, 49, 51, 168; sensory experience, 98; *Songs of Innocence and Experience*, 34–35
Bloom, Harold, 33, 46, 47, 108, 187n76, 192n117
Bloom, Michelle, 173, 174
Blunt, Anthony, 151
Boaistuau, Pierre, 3
body. *See* ambiguity; animation
Böhne, Hartmut, 6
Bolter, Jay, 11–12
bookishness, 118
Bosch, Hieronymus, 158
Botting, Fred, 7, 176, 183n2
Boym, Svetlana, 113, 124, 149–50
Brainard, Joe, 85; *I Remember*, 85
Bukatman, Scott, 5, 23–24, 50, 67, 71, 81, 83, 109, 117, 118, 125, 130, 140, 156, 169, 170, 173, 175, 199n21, 204n24
Burgos, Jean, 91, 102, 109, 185n31
Burke, Edmund, 27, 29, 51, 187n76; *Cincinnatus in Retirement*, 51
Byron, Lord, 113, 140, 165; *Manfred*, 113, 140

Caliber Press, 17
Callot, Jacques, 24, 25
Campbell, Ramsey, 63
Campmas, Aude, 63–64
Canguilhem, Georges, 140, 177
Captain America, 113
caricature, 23, 24–25, 49, 50–51, 168, 170
Carlyle, Thomas, 74
Carracci, Agostino, 25
Casterman (publisher), 16
Castoriadis, Cornelius, 10
CCA (Comics Code Authority), 56–57, 67, 171–72, 193n8
Cellier, Léon, 91
Chadbourn, Mike, 125

chiaroscuro, 24, 29, 143, 154, 159
Chrétien de Troyes, 105
Christian symbolism, 119–20, 123, 148, 149, 151–52, 154, 156, 163
Christophe, Ernest, 92
Chute, Hillary, 24, 124
cinema/film, 14, 30, 48, 174
circus, 126, 136, 140, 162
Claremont, Chris, 194n14
Clowes, Daniel, 168
Cohen, Jeffrey Jerome, 5, 6, 15, 112, 168, 183n4
collage, 39, 66, 106, 143, 153, 158. *See also* fragment; patchwork
control and free will, 80–81, 93, 116, 122, 127, 138
Cooper, L. Andrew, 183n2
correspondances, 90
cosmology, 32–34, 151
counterpastorals, 89
Craven, Wes, 54; *Swamp Thing*, 54
Crow, The (film), 141
Crow, The (O'Barr), 141–65; ambiguity in, 144, 148, 149, 151, 158, 160–65; art style in, 24, 29; emotionality in, 143–44, 153–56, 159–60; *Frankenstein* similarities, 209n27; melancholia in, 143–44, 147–48, 151; nostalgia in, 145, 146; publication of, 17, 141; spectacle in, 156–60, 163–64; structure of, 141–42, 145–53
Cruikshank, George, 49, 124, 168, 170; "Herne with his steed, hounds and owl, observed by the Duke of Richmond and the Earl of Surrey," 124; *Jack Sheppard*, 168, 170
Crumb, Robert, 24
Cure, The (band), 148, 155, 211n81
Curtis, Ian, 143, 150, 160. *See also* Joy Division

Dark Horse Comics, 17
DC Comics (publisher), 17, 55, 56
DC Comics universe, 57, 62, 63, 64–65, 67
death, 89, 116–17, 142–43, 156–58
Debord, Guy, 162–63

deformity, 30–31, 36–37, 41–43, 91–92
Delacroix, Eugène, 106, 107
Delano, Jamie, 83–84; *Hellblazer*, 84
Derrida, Jacques, 183n4
Descartes, René, 95
Dickinson, Emily, 152; "Because I could not stop for Death," 152
Didi-Huberman, Georges, 180
dolls and puppets, 8, 81–82, 138–39, 142, 167
Doors, The (band), 143
Doré, Gustave, 172; *Alpine Scene*, 172
dreams, 69–71, 122–23, 130
Dupont, Jacques, 90, 199n20
Durand, Gilbert, 10, 30–31
Dürer, Albrecht, 123; *The Four Horsemen of the Apocalypse*, 123; *Saint Michael Fighting the Dragon*, 123

Ellison, Julie, 188n86
emotionality: in *The Crow*, 143–44, 153–56, 159–60; of Frankenstein's monster, 40; as romantic theme, 9, 19–20, 45–46, 175–76; in *Swamp Thing*, 61, 83
emotions, 9, 17, 26, 31, 35, 40, 42, 57, 60, 77, 111, 130, 144–45, 154, 155, 159, 166, 175, 177. *See also* emotionality
Enlightenment, 26, 77, 83, 177, 190n48
ennui, 89–90, 95, 98–99, 101, 109, 169
Entzauberung, 40
etching, 24, 32
evil, 9, 15, 40, 67–69, 89–90, 95, 132. *See also* ambiguity
evolution theory, 21–22
exile, 44, 66, 76

Faflak, Joel, 144, 179–80
Fantastic Four, 66, 107
Feder, Lillian, 146, 156, 162
Feininger, Lyonel, 170
Ferris, Emil, 171–72, 176, 180; *My Favorite Thing Is Monsters*, 171–72, 176, 180
Fisher, Mark, 150
folklore, 112–13, 116, 121, 122, 124, 178
Foucault, Michel, 22, 50, 80, 101–2, 177

Fowlie, Wallace, 143
fragment, 11, 15, 30, 114, 141, 142–43, 145–46, 148, 150, 153, 154, 159, 169, 181, 209n27; fragmentation, 89, 106, 145–53, 162
Franke, Anselm, 110–11
Frankenstein; or, The Modern Prometheus (Shelley), 38–41; ambiguity in, 9; appearance and characteristics of Frankenstein's monster, 6, 38–41, 43, 44, 47; connection to *Wanderer above the Sea of Fog*, 185n30; *The Crow* similarities, 209n27; *Hellboy* similarities, 114, 116, 134, 137; illustrations in, 24, 39; influences on, 38, 39; *Monstre* similarities, 87; *My Favorite Thing Is Monsters* similarities, 171; *Swamp Thing* similarities, 38–39, 59–60, 81, 83
freak discourse, 169
freak shows, 21–22, 26, 42, 45, 136, 166
free will and control, 80–81, 93, 116, 122, 127, 138
Friedman, John Block, 57
Friedrich, Caspar David, 117, 119, 146, 152–53, 185n30; *Abtei im Eichwald*, 152–53; *Die gescheiterte Hoffnung*, 117; *Klosterfriedhof im Schnee*, 119; *Der Mönch am Meer*, 153; *Der Wanderer über dem Nebelmeer*, 117, 185n30
Frye, Northrop, 19, 20, 32–34, 40, 75, 89–90, 142–43, 165, 168, 194n18
Fuseli, Henry, 23, 29, 35, 171; *The Nightmare*, 29, 35, 171
Fyleman, Rose, 146; "Good Night," 146

Gabilliet, Jean-Paul, 56–57
Gaiman, Neil, 157; *Sandman*, 157
Gardner, Jared, 117, 168, 169, 175
Garland-Thomson, Rosemarie, 169
Gautier, Théophile, 107
Gerber, Steve, 194n14
Gibbons, Dave, 158; *Watchmen*, 158
Gillray, James, 24, 50–51; *The Gout*, 51; *A Great Stream from a Petty Fountain*, 51
Girard, René, 5–6

Goethe, Johann Wolfgang von, 39, 42, 60; *Faust*, 60; *The Sorrows of Young Werther*, 39, 42
Gogh, Vincent van, 155
Gogol, Nikolai, 148
Goodlad, Lauren, 142, 155, 163
goth culture, 143–45, 208n2
gothic, distinction from romanticism, 7, 15, 144
gothic rock, 142, 143, 147–51, 159, 160
Goya, Francisco, 27–32; anthropomorphism in works of, 23, 27–32; *Black Paintings*, 32, 123; *Buen viaje*, 28; *Los Caprichos*, 27, 28–31, 123–24; *Los Chinchillas*, 30; *Contra el bien general*, 28, 30; *Los Desastres de la guerra*, 27, 30–31, 68, 190n44; *Disparate de desordenado*, 31; *Los Disparates*, 27, 32; *Disparate volante*, 28, 32; *Duendecitos*, 28; *Ensayos*, 123; influence on comics, 23–24, 60, 62, 69, 123–24; *Modo de volar*, 28, 32; as monster, 38; *Nadie nos ha visto*, 28; *¡Quien lo creyara!*, 29; *Se repulen*, 28; *Soplones*, 28; *El Sueño de la razón produce monstruos*, 28–29, 60, 62, 69; *Todos caerán*, 28; *Witches' Sabbath*, 123; *Ya van desplumandos*, 28; *Yo lo vi*, 30
graffiti, 49, 168, 170
Greek tragedies, 38
Green Man, 58
Groensteen, Thierry, 14, 39
grotesque, the, 20, 24, 31, 50, 102, 142–43, 170
Grusin, Richard, 11–12
Gumbrecht, Hans Ulrich, 13–14, 105
Gunning, Tom, 45, 173
Gwynplaine (*The Man Who Laughs*), 41–43, 44, 47, 102, 150, 159–60, 172–73

Halberstam, Jack, 4, 6–7
Halliwell, John, 31, 45, 51–52
Hamann, Johann Georg, 170
Hanafi, Zakiya, 135, 160, 166, 167–68
Haraway, Donna, 7, 104
Hatfield, Charles, 48, 107, 183n8
Hayles, Katherine, 104

Hayot, Eric, 204n24
Haywood, Ian, 31, 45, 51–52
Heap, the, 57
Hellboy (Mignola), 112–40; animation in, 115–16, 135–39; art style in, 24, 117, 123–24, 133; Blake's influence on, 33; control and free will in, 116, 122, 127, 138; identity and quest in, 115, 116, 125–32, 139; nostalgia in, 114, 118–24; overview, 113–17; publication of, 17, 113; Quasimodo similarity, 37; sociopolitical contexts, 121, 205n56; solitude in, 125, 129, 131; spectacle in, 136–37, 138–40; superhero tradition in, 132–34
Herriman, George, 173; *Krazy Kat*, 173
Hodgson, William Hope, 118; *Sargasso Sea Stories*, 118
Hodkinson, Paul, 143
Hoffmann, E. T. A., 52
Hogarth, William, 24, 25, 45, 49, 188n9; *The Four Stages of Cruelty*, 49
Hollander, Anne, 24–25, 27–28, 30, 31, 48
homme-planète, 104
Hong, James T., 110
House of Mystery series, 55, 57, 67
House of Secrets series, 54, 57, 67
Hugo, Victor: compared to Baudelaire, 91; *The Hunchback of Notre Dame*, 23, 36–37, 43, 44, 47–48, 102, 103; *The Man Who Laughs*, 41–43, 44, 47, 102, 150, 159–60, 172–73; *Notre-Dame de Paris*, 23, 36–37, 43, 44, 47–48, 102, 103
Huhtamo, Erkki, 213n46
Huizinga, Johan, 175
Hulk, The, 113
Humanoïdes Associés, 16
human *vs.* monster. *See* ambiguity
Huysmans, Joris-Karl, 63–64; *À rebours*, 63–64
hybrids, 26, 27, 28, 32

identity confusion: in *The Crow*, 148; in *Hellboy*, 115, 116, 125–29, 139; in *Monstre*, 92–95, 98; in *Swamp Thing*, 74, 79–80, 81. *See also* ambiguity

Image Comics, 17
Ingebretsen, Edward J., 5
Inness, George, 172; *A Marine*, 172
intaglio print-making technique, 32
intertextuality, 9, 59–60, 106, 113, 117, 122, 142, 153, 158
Iser, Wolfgang, 11

James, M. R., 118
Jameson, Fredric, 179
Joker, the, 160–62
Joy Division, 142, 143, 147–51, 159, 160
Jung, Carl, 161, 181
Jürgens, Anna-Sophie, 162

Kearney, Richard, 144, 157, 180
Keates, Tom, 54
Keats, John, 20
Kermode, Frank, 90
Killing Joke, The, 161
King, Stephen, 144
Kirby, Jack, 48, 66, 118, 183n8, 199n21
Klein, Norman, 83, 168
Kleist, Heinrich von, 8, 77, 181; "Über das Marionettentheater," 8
Krämer, Felix, 30
Krauss, Rosalind, 83
Kukkonen, Karin, 11
Kunzle, David, 24

Lacanian Real, 157
Laster, Arnaud, 37
Leav, Mort, 57
Le Brun, Annie, 5, 185n18
Lee, Brandon, 141
Lee, Stan, 194n14
Le Fanu, J. Sheridan, 118
Leibniz, Gottfried Wilhelm, 95
Lévi-Strauss, Claude, 112
Liber Psalmorum sec. tradit. S. Hieronimi, 25
Locke, John, 20
Lovecraft, H. P., 118
Luckhurst, Roger, 144
Lyotard, Jean-François, 164

MacLeish, Archibald, 148; "Mother Goose's Garland," 148
Malcolm, James Peller, 23, 25; *An Historical Sketch on the Art of Caricaturing*, 23
Man-Thing, 194n14
Man Who Laughs, The (graphic novel), 161
Mary Toft hoax, 21, 26, 189n35
Massumi, Brian, 9
Mattozzi, Alvise, 194n17
McCay, Winsor, 130, 170; *Dream of the Rarebit Fiend*, 130, 175; *Little Nemo in Slumberland*, 130
McEvoy, Emma, 9
McGann, Jerome, 15
melancholia, 66, 133, 143–44, 147–48, 151. See also emotionality
memory: in *The Crow*, 157; in *Hellboy*, 124, 131; in *Monstre*, 86, 92–93, 95, 97, 108–9; in *Swamp Thing*, 74, 80. See also nostalgia
Mignola, Mike, 113, 199n21. See also *Hellboy* (Mignola)
Miller, Frank, 56
Milton, John, 9, 29, 33, 38, 39, 40, 46; *Paradise Lost* (Milton), 9, 29, 33, 38, 39, 40
Mittman, Asa, 4
modernization, 23, 50, 66, 109. See also technology
Monet, Claude, 172; *Rocks at Port-Goulphar, Belle-Île*, 172
monsters and monstrosity: etymology, 3, 183n4; scholarship on, 4–7, 184–85nn11–12; ways of interpreting, overview, 7–15. See also *Crow, The* (O'Barr); *Hellboy* (Mignola); *Monstre* (Bilal); romantic monsters and monstrous imaginary; *Swamp Thing* (Moore)
Monstre (Bilal), 85–111; amorphousness in, 96–97, 102, 103–5, 199n17; art style in, 24, 105–7; Baudelairian similarities, 85–86, 88–92; dystopian setting, 99–100; and ennui, 89–90, 95, 98–99, 101, 109; *Frankenstein* similarity, 38; identity confusion in, 92–95, 98; monstrous spaces in, 100–102; overview, 86–88; publication

of, 16, 86; Quasimodo similarity, 37, 102, 103; rebelliousness in, 103, 108–10; spectacularity in, 107–8; technology and modernization in, 87, 94–95, 104, 110–11; trauma and memory in, 92–93, 95–96, 97, 102, 108–9

Moore, Alan, 54, 113, 158; *Watchmen*, 158. See also *Swamp Thing* (Moore)

Morin, Edgar, 104

Morrison, Grant, 48, 183n8

Morrison, Jim, 143; The Doors, 143

Morrow, Gray, 194n14

Muck Monster, 54, 55

Mulvey, Laura, 173

Munier, Brigitte, 38, 39

Murray, Christopher, 183n8

music, gothic. See gothic rock

mutation, 85, 91–92, 97–98, 101

mutilation, 30–31, 41, 44

myth, 18, 27, 35, 38, 58, 90, 109, 112, 114, 118–24, 129, 130, 156, 161, 162, 178

Nancy, Jean-Luc, 13, 105

nature, 34–35, 38, 62–66

Nerval, Gérard de, 146

Ngai, Sianne, 83

Nietzsche, Friedrich, 143

nostalgia: as concept, 19, 113; in *The Crow*, 145, 146; in *Hellboy*, 114, 118–24; in *Monstre*, 98. See also memory

O'Barr, James, 141, 143. See also *Crow, The* (O'Barr)

Ochsner, Beate, 41, 179

O'Connor, Laura, 135

Oppenheimer, Paul, 5

Ortega y Gasset, José, 38

otherness. See ambiguity; identity confusion; solitude

Otto, Peter, 9, 59

Outcault, Richard, 164; *Hogan's Alley*, 164 (see also Yellow Kid); *Poor Lil' Mose*, 164

pain, 27, 147, 148, 150, 153–55, 160. See also trauma

Palmer, Samuel, 51, 62; *Early Morning*, 51; *The Garden in Shoreham*, 51; *Oak Trees, Lullingstone Park*, 62

panoramas, 174, 213n46

Paré, Ambroise, 3, 125, 167, 206n86

Pasko, Martin, 54

patchwork, 8, 39, 53, 60, 69, 81, 87, 95, 143, 146, 149. See also collage; fragment

Peckham, Morse, 46, 214n79

Peeters, Benoît, 173

Perec, Georges, 85; *Je me souviens*, 85

Perez, George, 67

Persephone, 119, 129

Pfau, Thomas, 148

phantasmagorias, 45, 52

Pliny the Elder, 26; *Natural History*, 26

Poe, Edgar Allan, 20, 23, 132–33, 138, 146; "The Conqueror Worm," 133; "The Fall of the House of Usher," 132–33; "The Raven," 146

Pope, Alexander, 22, 166, 175, 188n9; *An Essay on Man*, 166; "The First Epistle of the First Book of Horace," 22

postmodernism, 179

Praz, Mario, 15

premediation, 12, 104–5

Price, Martin, 33

primitivity, 19, 32, 49–50, 98, 170

prosthetics, 87

psychological manipulation, 92–95. See also identity confusion

pulp fiction, 50, 132–33, 137

puppets and dolls, 8, 81–82, 138–39, 142, 167

Quasimodo (*The Hunchback of Notre Dame*), 23, 36–37, 43, 44, 47–48, 102, 103

quests, 46–47, 71–76, 83, 108–10, 125–32, 163

Radin, Paul, 161

Rauber, D. F., 145

reality: in *Hellboy*, 118, 121–23, 130, 139–40; in *Monstre*, 104; in *Swamp Thing*, 67–68, 69–71, 75, 82–83 rebelliousness: in Blake's works, 33; in *Hellboy*, 140; in *Monstre*, 103, 108–10; as romantic theme, 47–48; in *Swamp Thing*, 83–84; in visual media, 49–51, 168–70, 174–75, 180–81

Reed, Ishmael, 173; *Mumbo Jumbo*, 173

reflective nostalgia, 113, 114, 124, 145

Regier, Alexander, 145–46, 179

Reinfandt, Christoph, 15, 179

religion and spirituality, 5, 34, 117, 119–24. *See also* Christian symbolism

resurrection and regeneration, 58–60, 81–82, 115. *See also* animation

Reynolds, Joshua, 33–34

Reynolds, Simon, 143

Ribera, Jusepe de, 28; *El Pievaro*, 28

Rimbaud, Arthur, 143, 146, 159; "Nocturne vulgaire," 159

romantic monsters and monstrous imaginary: comics adaptation of, overview, 9–10, 48–53, 166–70, 172–78; distinction from gothic, 7, 15, 144; themes, overview, 7–10, 15–19, 43–48; visualizations, overview, 23–27, 48–53, 168, 170. *See also* ambiguity; emotionality; nostalgia; reality; solitude; spectacle and spectacularity

Rosa, Salvator, 12–13; *Pittura*, 12–13

Round, Julia, 7, 9, 10, 141, 183n2, 208n2

Rowlandson, Thomas, 24, 35–36; *The Convent Garden Night Mare*, 35–36

Said, Edward, 5–6

Satan, 9, 29, 33, 38, 39

Schiller, Friedrich, 109, 175

senses, 8, 98, 111, 143

Sepulchre, Sarah, 45

Seuss, Dr., 146; *The Cat in the Hat*, 146

Sha, Richard, 144, 179–80

Shakespeare, William, 21, 38, 74, 113, 138, 142; *Hamlet*, 74, 113, 138, 142; *The Tempest*, 21

Shelley, Mary, 38. *See also Frankenstein; or, The Modern Prometheus* (Shelley)

Shelley, Percy Bysshe, 20, 83. *Prometheus Unbound*, 83

Simonson, Walter, 117, 132

Smith, Robert, 211n81

Smolderen, Thierry, 49, 109, 168, 170

sociopolitical contexts, 95, 98, 102, 104–5, 109–10, 121, 205n56

Sohlberg, Harald, 172; *Fisherman's Cottage*, 172

solitude: in *The Crow*, 162; of Frankenstein's monster, 40; of Gwynplaine, 43; in *Hellboy*, 125, 129, 131; as romantic theme, 17–18, 46; in *Swamp Thing*, 65, 66, 75–76

sordid, the, 24, 31, 90, 107

spaces, monstrous, 100–102

spectacle and spectacularity: in *The Crow*, 156–60, 163–64; in *Hellboy*, 136–37, 138–40; in *Monstre*, 107–8; in romantic era, 45–46; as term, 187n71; in visual media, 173–74

Spiegelman, Art, 24

spirituality and religion, 5, 34, 117, 119–24. *See also* Christian symbolism

Stein, Harry, 57

Steiner, George, 13

Strange Days (film), 12

Stryker, Susan, 6

sublime, the, 27, 66, 89, 107, 187n76, 199n21

Sullivan, Nikki, 6, 91, 142

surrealism, 51, 83

Swamp Thing (Moore), 54–84; ambiguity in, 61, 64, 68, 77–80; art style in, 24, 29–30, 60, 62, 66, 72–73; emotionality in, 61, 83; *Frankenstein* similarity, 38–39, 59–60, 81, 83; good *vs.* evil in, 67–69; nature in, 62–66; publication of, 16–17, 54–57; Quasimodo similarity, 37; quest in, 71–76, 78; reality in, 67–68, 69–71, 75, 82–83; rebelliousness in, 83–84; resurrection and reanimation in, 58–60, 81–82, 94; solitude in, 65, 66, 75–76

Swift, Jonathan, 52, 188n9

Taipei Biennial (2012), 110

Taowu, 110–11

Tardi, Jacques, 97

technology, 7–8, 87, 94–95, 104, 110–11, 131, 134
Tennyson, Alfred, 72; "The Lotos-Eaters," 72
Tétralogie du monstre. See *Monstre*
theatricality. *See* spectacle and spectacularity
Thivier, Eugène, 36, 60; *Cauchemar*, 36, 60
Thomas, Roy, 194n14
Todd, Dennis, 21, 26, 45, 176, 188n9
Tomkins, Silvan, 9
Töpffer, Rodolphe, 44, 49, 50, 110, 170, 178
Totleben, John, 17, 54, 55, 66
transmogrification, 6, 91, 96–97, 101, 142
trauma: in *The Crow*, 143, 162, 164; in Goya's works, 124; in *Monstre*, 95–96, 97, 102, 108–9; in *Swamp Thing*, 79–80
Tresch, John, 8, 52
trickster, 156, 160–63

Ueckmann, Natascha, 93, 104
Updike, John, 181

Vallins, David, 180
van Gogh, Vincent, 155; *Wheatfield with Crows*, 155
Vaucanson, Jacques de, 50; *Le joueur de flûte traversière*, 50
Veitch, Rick, 54, 66
Velázquez, Diego, 28; *Las Meninas*, 28
Vertigo (publisher), 17, 55
Vickars, John, 25
violence, 30–31, 51, 58, 89, 144, 162
Virilio, Paul, 93, 104

Waldeinsamkeit, 19
Walton, Saige, 175
Wang, David Der-Wei, 110
Warburg, Aby, 180
Warton, Thomas, 138; "The Pleasures of Melancholy," 138
Weber, Max, 40
Wein, Len, 54, 78; *Swamp Thing*, 54, 78
Weiss, Allen S., 5
Wellman, Manly Wade, 125
Weltentfremdung, 93
Westbrook, David, 164, 173, 174
Whale, James, 30; *Frankenstein*, 30
Whitted, Qiana, 56
Willems, Philippe, 50
Williams, David, 104, 177–78
Wolfman, Marv, 67
Wood, Tatjana, 55, 66
Wright, Alexa, 204n33
Wrightson, Bernie, 24, 54, 55, 56; *Swamp Thing*, 54, 78

X-Men, 44, 54, 113

Yeats, W. B., 158; "The Second Coming," 158
Yellow Kid, 44, 174. *See also* Outcault, Richard: *Hogan's Alley*
Yolen, Jane, 125

ABOUT THE AUTHOR

Maaheen Ahmed is associate professor of comparative literature at Ghent University. She has held postdoctoral fellowships from the Research Foundation–Flanders and the Marie Curie COFUND at Ghent University and the University of Louvain (Belgium). She is currently principal investigator of a project on children in comics funded by a European Research Council Starting Grant.

With a keen interest in comics and graphic novels in English and French, Ahmed has written and presented on superheroes, autobiographical comics, the representation of war in comics, and, more recently, children in comics. She has written about renowned and diverse authors such as Moebius, Hugo Pratt, David McKean, and Mike Mignola.

Ahmed's first book, *Openness of Comics: Generating Meaning within Flexible Structures*, was published by the University Press of Mississippi in 2016. She has edited and coedited volumes such as *The Cultural Standing of Comics: Ambiguities and Evolutions / Le Statut culturel de la BD: Ambiguïtés et évolutions*, with Stéphanie Delneste and Jean-Louis Tilleuil (Academia/Éditions L'Harmattan, 2017); and, most recently, with Benoît Crucifix, *Comics Memory: Archives and Styles* (Palgrave, 2018). She has edited special issues of journals including "Comics and Authorship," *Authorship* 6, no. 2 (2017); and (with Kees Ribbens and Martin Lund) "The Great War in Comics," *European Comic Art* 11, no. 2 (2015). She has also reviewed comics studies books for *European Comic Art* and *Image [&] Narrative*.

Her articles and chapters include "State Protection and Identification in *Hellboy*: Of Reformed Devils and Other Others in the Pentagon," *European Journal of American Studies* 10, no. 2 (2015); and the chapters "Historicizing in Graphic Novels: The Welcome Subjective G(l)aze," in *Graphic History: Critical Essays on Graphic Novels and/as History*, edited by Richard Iadonisi (2012), and "Children in Comics: Between Education and Entertainment, Conformity and Agency," in the forthcoming *Oxford Handbook of Comics Studies*, edited by Frederick Luis Aldama.

www.ingramcontent.com/pod-product-compliance
Lightning Source LLC
Chambersburg PA
CBHW070314240426
43661CB00057B/2638